CULTURE OF INTOLERANCE

MARK NATHAN COHEN

Culture of Intolerance

Chauvinism, Class, and Racism in the United States

Yale University Press   New Haven and London

Designed by James J. Johnson and set in Stemple Garamond type by Rainsford Type.
Printed in the United States of America by Book Crafters, Inc., Chelsea, Michigan.

Library of Congress Cataloging-in-Publication Data

Cohen, Mark Nathan.
   Culture of intolerance : chauvinism, class, and racism in the
United States / Mark Nathan Cohen.
      p. cm.
   Includes bibliographical references and index.
   ISBN 0-300-07072-1 (cloth : alk. paper)
   ISBN 0-300-08066-2 (pbk. : alk. paper)

   1. United States—Race relations. 2. Racism—United States.
3. United States—Ethnic relations. 4. Culture conflict—United
States. 5. Toleration. I. Title.
E185.615.C642 1998
305.8'00973—dc21   97-17951

A catalogue record for this book is available from the British Library.

The paper in this book meets the guidelines for permanence and durability of the Committee on Production Guidelines for Book Longevity of the Council on Library Resources.

10 9 8 7 6 5 4 3 2

To my parents, Milton H. Cohen and Rowna C. Cohen, who *taught* me to have a high "IQ" and provided my education at home and at school—and who also taught me respect for others.

And to my own teachers in human understanding, including Wendell Carpenter, Ernie Banks, Joseph McCloskey, Bill Veeck, Sam Amoni, Li Hsia Wang, Douglass Roby, Robert Walsh, Big George of Hull House, Kinyanjui of Kenya, Shirley Gorenstein, Geraldyne Pemberton, LaRuth and Norris Gray, Peg Clark, Julius and Anola Archibald, Jan Edwards, Jan Saunders, Luis Godoy and Doña Lupe of Belize, Taher and Jaleh Zandi, Richard Robbins, Yolanda Moses, Suzann Buckley, Patricia Higgins, and many of my students.

Contents

Preface   ix

CHAPTER ONE The Real American Tragedy   1

CHAPTER TWO The Innocent Scapegoat: Human
   Biological Variation and "Race"   11

CHAPTER THREE Understanding the Rules People Live By:
   Cultural Systems and Cultural Variation   60

CHAPTER FOUR The Real Meaning of Cultural Relativism   111

CHAPTER FIVE Some Assumptions of American Culture
   and the Problems They Generate   134

CHAPTER SIX Justifying Inequality: Cultural Assumptions
   About Intelligence and Competence   204

CHAPTER SEVEN Affirmative Action and Curriculum
   Inclusion   252

CHAPTER EIGHT Transforming the Culture of Intolerance   293

Suggested Reading   313

Index   317

Preface

Many Americans seem to be moving toward increasing indifference to others. Intolerance—even outright hatred—of people who are "different" is on the rise. This attitude, in turn, divides people who ought to be united and supports a variety of political agendas that do not address our real needs. If we are to believe the propaganda with which we are bombarded, science itself justifies our disdain for others. According to this propaganda, science affirms the need to shape the political order on the basis of inherent inequality and mutual disdain. This book is intended to counter that propaganda and those perceptions. It summarizes what scientific data really have to say about biological differences among human beings. It explores the depth, power, beauty, and potential value of cultural differences among groups of people (even in the same country). It shows how cultural *differences* (not biological or cultural "inferiority") contribute to Americans' misperceptions of others. It shows how our own cultural blinders cause us to misunderstand others and even ourselves. And it looks at questionable assumptions in our own culture that promote intolerance and generate problems where none need exist.

This is not intended to be a scholarly book in the formal sense, though it grows out of knowledge that scholars have gleaned over the past century or more. My goal is to fashion new insights from this existing knowledge. All that is needed to make the points I want to make is to assemble some well-established pieces of popular and scholarly knowledge and hold them up to the light. The important insights emerge without much further help.

Although the facts presented reflect current knowledge, I have not tried to supply all of the most up-to-date scholarly research or styles of analysis. These recent variations often involve complex nuances and obscure language that are not necessary to make the relatively straightforward points discussed here. More important, those new variations are often fragile and ephemeral. I have tried to present information and ideas near the core of our knowledge that have stood the test of time (the only real test in science) and that have not changed significantly with fashions in scholarship or intellectual styles. The scholarly knowledge presented is fairly basic, and most of it is not very controversial. For this reason I do not provide primary sources for facts and interpretations that are common knowledge; this common knowledge can be verified in textbooks or secondary sources listed in the suggested reading. More controversial or personal interpretations are documented in the text and in the suggested reading. In chapters 5, 6, 7, and 8, which deal with American cultural blinders and their implications, the arguments, unless otherwise noted, are my own. Some will find these interpretations controversial although the underlying facts are not. The arguments may seem obvious to some people, but I hope readers will find them worthy of consideration.

In this volume I use the first-person "us" or "we" to emphasize three points.

First, I wish to underscore the idea that the social and political problems which should concern us reside in people rather than implacable institutions or forces of nature. It is people who generate the problems and who must react to them. Referring to "us" reinforces this sense of responsibility.

Second, I wish to emphasize that the people in question, as often as not, are mainstream Americans (not the "others" we so often blame); to show that American culture is as arbitrary and narrow as any other; and to suggest that given American power in the world, it is this culture that needs to be explored.

Third, I want to make clear that I consider myself a member of the groups I am criticizing—groups that need to reexamine their priorities and behaviors. I am not simply pointing a finger at "others" within mainstream American society.

"We" always has the same core meaning (segments of the American population to which I belong), but the boundaries of the group referred to vary a bit from chapter to chapter in ways that can usually be determined from context. In the second chapter, concerning the biology of human variation, "we" largely refers to those of us who are familiar with the collective knowledge of Western science, knowledge available to anyone willing to learn. In other chapters, particularly where the needs of people outside the borders of the United States are discussed, "we" refers to the people of the United States as a whole, or at least to all Americans who consider themselves to be represented by the U.S. government. When the discussion concerns treatment of minority individuals within our own borders, "we" refers to those, often relatively privileged and mostly but not exclusively whites, who are enjoying the fruits of American society and consider themselves part of the American mainstream distinct from those minority groups. In discussions of affirmative action in chapter 7, "we" refers to the generally privileged population of middle- and upper-class white males. In the final chapter, "we" refers to all Americans in the context of our collective responsibility for change. In using the word "we" it is certainly not my intention to widen divisions in the population or to emphasize the "otherness" of non-Western, non-American, or non-white people or women. It is my hope and goal that "we" can eventually embrace everyone.

Although the book is not written in a scholarly style, it is based on a lifetime devoted to studying and teaching about biological and cultural variations among human beings. As a scholar and professor of anthropology, I have attempted throughout my career to tease out the complex relationships between human biology and human culture. I have focused on relations between culture and the size of populations, the nature of technologies and exchange, the availability of resources, the threats in the natural environment, and the way societies organize themselves. I have also studied patterns of human health, nutrition, reproduction, and death associated with social change. I have read, taught about, and published on these subjects. Because I teach at a small college, I also teach, research, and think about a wide range of additional subjects instead of being a narrow specialist. In addition to the main areas of my scholarly research and publication, I have read and taught about topics ranging from the biology of human variation ("race") to the structure of health care delivery, the nature of colonial societies, and even the IQ debate, all of which figure in this book. I have also had to think continually about how my scholarly knowledge relates to the lives of my students, most of whom will never be scholars or care about scholarly debates. I have had to work hard to make knowledge accessible and meaningful to them.

This book stems, in part, from my dismay at the trivializing of anthropology by people both outside and inside the field. Anthropology has generated many important ideas, understandings, and perceptions about people that I think ought to be part of every individual's education—indeed, must be part of that education if we are to make good choices and interact successfully with other people or even among ourselves. Unfortunately, public perception of anthropology tends to focus on its findings about the bizarre, the exotic, or the "primitive" and on the search for fossil ancestors. None of these are central to what anthropologists do or to the needs of our society. The critical contribution that anthropology makes is to provide a comparative perspective on the actions and beliefs of human beings throughout the world and through the history of our species. It offers the only basis we have for understanding what human nature and human biology really consist of (as distinguished from American stereotypes and preconceptions). It also provides the best basis we have for understanding why people in any culture (including our own) do things the way they do. It teaches us how we might examine ourselves more critically and interact more positively with others. Perhaps the key understanding that anthropology contributes is an awareness that there is more than one way for human beings to behave, more than one paradigm in which to think. The freedom that comes from recognizing that alternative paradigms exist is the central theme of this book.

This book has also developed out a number of experiences I have had outside the academy. As a social worker, teacher, anthropologist, and archaeologist, I have spent many years living with people from different backgrounds. I have lived and worked among a variety of ethnic, "racial," regional, and occupational groups within the United States, and I have lived in several communities in other parts of the world and visited many others, not to see the tourist attractions but to walk the streets, ride the local buses, and haunt the markets, talking to the local people with whatever language we could manage. Sometimes, our "language" consisted mostly of smiles, which along with respectful attention and demeanor and real warmth are amazingly universal. As individuals, people from all over the world have a dignity and value not visible in our stereotypes or even in our educational media. There are aspects of "other" people both within the United States and abroad that most Americans never see and don't consider in their calculations.

Finally, I have been watching the American social and political scene—and have seen the damage we do to one another in ignorance—for some time now in light of those experiences. It is this last aspect of education that prompts me to write about some things we know and about how popular "knowledge," pandered to and twisted by pseudoscience, is being allowed to harm us, our friends and neighbors, and the "others" around us, in the United States and throughout the world.

I am heavily indebted for this and many other things to Patricia J. Higgins, a fellow anthropologist at Plattsburgh and an excellent editor. I would also like to express my gratitude to E. Thomas Moran, who found a way to give me sabbatical support to write in the midst of hard times; and to Peter J. White, Robin Torrence, Judy Birmingham, and Annie Ross, who made a stay in Australia possible, enjoyable, stimulating, and warm and freed me to write this book. Higgins and my colleagues Richard Robbins, Douglas Skopp, Elizabeth Petrick-Steward, Suzann Buckley, Lonnie Fairchild, Bonnie Seidel-Rogol, my editors, Gladys Topkis and Noreen O'Connor, and two anonymous reviewers (one later revealed to be Katherine Dettwyler) have offered valuable suggestions.

CULTURE OF INTOLERANCE

CHAPTER ONE

The Real American Tragedy

RACISM, GREED, AND INDIFFERENCE to the needs of others are back in fashion. Tolerance for others—almost anyone who is a little different from ourselves—is out of style. Compromising with the needs of others no longer seems necessary.

After decades of slowly bringing minorities toward full partnership and gradually starting to protect the poor from the worst ravages of poverty, there has been an upsurge of indifference, fear, or outright hatred of others on the part of the American public and cynical manipulation of our fears by elected leaders, political candidates, media, and political commentators. It is once again fashionable to blame those who are the victims of these pressures for their own problems and for many of society's other problems as well. It is also fashionable to assume that their failures must be rooted in the immutable nature of things—in their own inherent biology—and not in the American political system or the circumstances of their birth and life.

There has been a resurgence of the conviction that the privileges that affluent Americans enjoy (and that most Americans enjoy in comparison to much of the rest of the world) are simply the fruits of natural superiority and are deserved. Disdain for others, injustice, and inequality are somehow considered to be natural and even necessary.

These trends are seen in many sectors of American society. They are evident in voting patterns and the people chosen to represent and lead us. Students seem to have lost their idealism and no longer see a need to contribute to society or even to gain knowledge about the richness of the world. Rather, they want to be prepared as quickly and narrowly as possible for careers in which success is measured only by monetary rewards. In the business world, profit has gone from being one motivation among others (or even the first among many) to being the *only* motive, unbalanced and unfettered by any other human or social consideration or any concern for nature or the future. The public at large, as well as politicians and corporations, seems willing to accept the bizarre and damaging proposition that the only activities worth doing are those that make a monetary profit.

The trends are expressed most powerfully in attitudes toward government, the only institution with the power, wealth, and purpose to concern itself with the public interest, to address the collective needs of people, and to balance individual and corporate selfishness. There is a growing conviction that government is somehow illegitimate and that its powers should be reduced. We seem to have forgotten the important things that a wise government ought to do with our taxes. Rather than urging our elected officials to invest tax money in the desirable or even essential things that only a government can do, it has become fashionable to think that the elimination of government and taxes will solve our problems. And of course leaders in the government itself have repeatedly betrayed the public interest, misinterpreting or abusing their mission and feeding public skepticism. Our politicians promise to save the country, but they seem to want to do it by sacrificing some or even all of the people as well as the beauty, ideals, and other qualities that make the United States great. Or they simply advance their own careers by pandering to private interests or the wealthy while pitting the middle class against the poor or whites against blacks.

In their zeal to manipulate us, politicians who could lead us in building a more just society instead feed us with empty slogans. They twist meanings to the point where words no longer refer to the things they used to represent. We are bombarded by messages from leaders of the Christian right, who might be expected to be voices of tolerance, concern, and moderation because they claim to represent Christian religion and its values. They have instead emerged as voices of very un-Christian intolerance, ignorance, and hatred. We endure and even celebrate profit-motivated shock-mongers in the media, some of whom have gained great fame and wealth by pandering to the ignorance of their audiences and encouraging their pettiest and ugliest thoughts.

There has been an upsurge in bad scholarship and shallow "intellectual" contributions—bad biology, history, psychology, sociology, and anthropology. The result is a distorted view of ourselves, of others, and of history, which reinforces racist assumptions and prejudices by purporting to give them scientific or scholarly legitimacy. In the process, public understanding of the nature of scientific and scholarly argument has fallen drastically, to the point where honest intellectual debate and shallow political propaganda or even mere advertising are constantly confused.

I was prompted to write this book, in the most immediate sense, by the publication and extraordinary popularity of *The Bell Curve: Intelligence and Class Structure in American Life*, by Richard J. Herrnstein and Charles Murray, the most influential of such recent "scholarly" efforts. I disagree profoundly with the conclusions of that book for reasons that I shall amply document. But I am more concerned that so much serious attention has been devoted to a book whose low standards of logic and proof, whose abuse of data and ideas, and whose misleading packaging of arguments belie its scholarly pretensions. Published in 1994, *The Bell Curve* revived the old argument that class divisions in society reflect the natural biological superiority of some people and the inferiority of others, particularly the poor and the black. (This argument, in fact, isn't just old; it is a universal or near-universal set of claims by which ruling classes throughout history and around the world have attempted to justify their privileged position whatever their own biology or that of their subjects. In fact, an amazing array of people, including many that we regard as quite "primitive," have a similar image of their own superiority, which suggests very strongly that such a view resides in the nature of group belief, not objective measurement.)

Herrnstein and Murray use the assembled data of a variety of "intelligence" tests to "prove" the natural superiority of the current elite. In doing so they are following a discredited tradition of racist misuse of intelligence-measuring "data" that began in the United States and Europe more than a century ago—a tradition that the authors acknowledge but attempt to defend. But they are also working out of another tradition, one that is not quite so apparent. It is the tradition of cultural chauvinism that ebbs and flows in American history but has recently been identified with such authors as Allan Bloom (*The Closing of the American Mind*) who essentially assert that the knowledge of the mainstream Euro-American tradition is all we need to know, and all others can be ignored. Working from a similar premise, Herrnstein and Murray assume that anyone in the world can be tested to measure his or her innate, biologically driven "intelligence" simply by comparing their scores on American-designed tests to standards of learned knowledge and cultural patterns of thinking held by white American males. Both books ignore or deny the fact that there are other valid sets of knowledge and styles of thinking.

But the specific data and the way that Herrnstein and Murray use them are almost irrelevant; the real issue is the persistence and dangers of the ideology of innate group superiority. Some people would defend that ideology on any grounds, whether or not IQ test data were available. *The Bell Curve* would not be worth mentioning were it not for the political climate in which the book was published, the political support it received, and the way people have sought to use it for fashionable political purposes. (The book itself certainly isn't important for its scientific merit or intellectual contribution or the strength of its argument.)

All these issues are symptoms of the Real American Tragedy. But they are only the symptoms, not the essence, of the tragedy. In the sense derived from Shakespearean drama, a tragedy is a situation in which inappropriate, incorrect, or flawed assumptions and perceptions on the part of some characters lead inexorably—but quite unnecessarily—to a tragic end. That outcome does not derive from the immutability of natural laws or "human nature"; it comes from the assumptions and misperceptions themselves. America is on the path toward such an end—which will result, if we persist, in the development of extreme racism, intolerance, poverty, and social stratification. We will create a world in which private interests and corporations rule, a world in which the society as a whole, "the public" (and therefore the "have-nots," which by then may include most of us) owns nothing, and no agency provides services or invests in the health, well-being, enjoyment, or quality of life of any but the rich. We will create a future in which incarceration (which has already reached extreme proportions in the United States) will be used increasingly to control discontent and dissent. We are proceeding, even propelling ourselves, in this direction, even though we profess to fear this outcome. This is happening because we base our decisions and our dialogue on assumptions about ourselves, our fellow citizens, our economics, and our politics which are neither necessary nor correct but appear to be very deeply rooted in our culture.

Assumptions, the things we take for granted or hold to be true without proof or test, are an essential part of human thinking, communication, and planning. Assumptions are built into every statement or conclusion people make. They have to be. The world consists of an infinitely complex web of interconnected forces, and because the human mind cannot cope indefinitely with such complexity, and we do not know everything, our logic is confined to a very small segment of reality. We arbitrarily ignore the rest or assume that it is predetermined or irrelevant ("everything else being equal"). Or we assume that the unknown factors in any particular problem will take a certain form. (In doing this we are operating much in the manner of a scientist in a laboratory who sets up artificially restricted test conditions. Screening out most of the possible complicating factors enables the scientist to focus on a particular, narrow set of relationships. Assumptions allow us to screen out possible complications and focus on specific problems in the same manner.)

All human cultures are characterized by sets of unifying and simplifying assumptions that enable people to focus on their world and communicate and interact with one another. Members of a society can work together because they tend to share assumptions and have learned to focus on the same limited portion of a reality that would otherwise be too complex to comprehend or even conceive.

Although assumptions are necessary, they guide and limit further thinking; so they often dictate, or at least influence, the conclusions we reach or the paths we choose. The assumptions may be more powerful in controlling the decisions we reach than even the most careful logical analysis, because the logical analysis usually begins only after the assumptions are in place. Inaccurate assumptions lead to faulty conclusions, no matter now compelling or cogent the logic and how forceful the argument. Even if the best advocates in the country debate the issues and the wisest heads make the judgment and all act fairly and honorably, inappropriate or arbitrary underlying assumptions—the parts we often don't think about—will produce bad results.

Ideally, the simplifying assumptions we make are explicitly stated and commonly shared, so that they can be easily examined, evaluated, and changed if they seem to be leading to unacceptable results. Scientists are trained to make their own assumptions explicit and to seek out and challenge—and if necessary replace—the assumptions underlying each other's work. It is this process of constantly identifying and testing assumptions that gives science its value and its credibility. Scientific principles earn respect gradually and come to be accepted as "truth"—at least temporarily—only by surviving these challenges. Great scientific breakthroughs often occur because someone contests widely held underlying assumptions, "common sense," or "prior knowledge" and shows that they are not valid. For example, scientists in the fifteenth and sixteenth centuries dared to say that the earth was *not* flat, the sun did *not* revolve around it, and the logical conclusions based on those mistaken assumptions were wrong, despite "obvious" evidence and common assumptions to the contrary.

Few of us, however, are as willing or able to search out and examine the assumptions that govern our everyday lives. We are even reluctant to recognize that they exist. Because many, perhaps most, of our assumptions are held unconsciously, we don't realize the degree to which they guide our thinking; nor do we realize that many of the ideas we hold as "truth" are themselves assumptions. They become ingrained in our minds and we pass them on to our children without thinking. But, if we don't examine, question, and perhaps even change our assumptions, we can only debate endlessly and fruitlessly within the same narrow circle of ideas. It would be a bit like developing an ever more complex and sophisticated cosmology on the premise that a flat earth is the center of the universe. We can grant ourselves substantial additional freedom and power to solve our problems if we are willing to address our assumptions, recognizing even those that are unspoken or subconscious, and debate and examine them.

We need to be ready to evaluate books in any field (including this book) and to question the statements made by the authors; but we also need to identify and evaluate their implicit assumptions. We need to be able to question the statements and unspoken assumptions of our teachers as well. In turn, good teachers at every level should teach their students to root out and identify their own unspoken assumptions and those of their society as well as those of other people and other societies. That is what real education is: learning to

question in a thoughtful manner evidence offered by authority figures and the assumptions underlying it, rather than merely memorizing the facts or memorizing the glorious traditions of one's own
heritage without reflection. Learning to question thoughtfully has
to replace the kind of mindless rebellion which constantly simmers
and occasionally erupts in violence.

As citizens, we have to be able to tease out and question the
assumptions of our social and political leaders. We need to do so
selectively rather than simply by becoming discouraged by the vague
awareness that things make no sense and by rebelling or refusing to
participate in the political process. However, in complicated political
or economic dialogue the assumptions are not at all clear and the
language of our leaders appears designed to disguise their assumptions and befuddle our attempt at analysis. So the assumptions too
often go unspoken and unnoticed.

What assumptions are being made when someone tells us that
something can't be done or is too expensive? What assumptions are
being made when our leaders tell us, "there is no money for that"?
What assumptions are being made when we are told that a tax "cut"
will actually generate more revenue, that tax reform will help us all,
that affirmative action is stealing the jobs of qualified white men, or
that getting government off our backs will make society fairer and
enhance the freedom of all citizens?

Perhaps the most important and most recalcitrant assumptions
are those provided by one's culture. The assumptions are diffuse and
pervasive. They are transmitted to us before we reach the age of
reason by the elders we revere. Moreover, the same assumptions are
held by all or nearly all of the people who surround us. It shouldn't
surprise us that such assumptions can be very hard to identify, let
alone to dispute. Just as blinders on a horse keep it looking straight
ahead and prevent it from being distracted by other threats or temp-
tations, so the assumptions made by any group of people as part of
their culture keep their members looking in the same direction as
their fellows, *inhibiting their freedom* by limiting their perception
of choices. The shared assumptions of any culture may become evident only when one culture is compared to another. Knowledge that
transcends the assumptions of one's own culture is a powerful tool.

Americans, for all our protestation of freedom of speech, of
thought, and of action, are no exception. Our culture trains us to be
ignorant of alternative sets of assumptions, other options, and other

possible lifestyles. It even trains us to be blind to them when we see them. If we can't expose our assumptions to careful examination and modification or discard them as needed, we are no freer, no more progressive, and no less tradition-bound than any other people.

Our failure to recognize our blinders and comprehend their power more than anything else forms the basis for misunderstandings and intolerance. This is the essence of the tragedy. It is for this reason above all others that we need to be aware of the perspectives of other cultures. Knowledge of those other perspectives can encourage us to take off our blinders and enrich our lives, possibly solving many problems that seem insurmountable.

Solving our problems, understanding other people, living together comfortably, and making constructive changes where necessary demand self-examination. The tensions that divide us begin with assumptions that at best are unnecessary and at worst are just plain wrong.

One of our most significant, dangerous, and blinding assumptions is that misunderstandings, tensions, and inequities among people, as well as the failure and success of groups of people, are based on biology or "race." Such misunderstandings, in fact, are overwhelmingly rooted in the assumptions of cultures—our own and others. Culture generates racism because arbitrary assumptions lie at the heart of our inability to help or tolerate others or to understand them. The limits imposed by our own culture, far more than any limits of "other" people or their cultures, lie at the heart of our social problems. It is the role of *our* cultural assumptions in promoting the American tragedy that I will explore through most of this book.

My intent is first to expose and lay to rest some misconceptions about "human nature" and human biology, about culture, and about ourselves. I shall also challenge many other inaccurate assumptions and perceptions on which we in the United States base our decisions and policies.

Chapter 2 discusses what is actually known about human biological variation. It demonstrates that biological differences among human beings exist and are important when we consider the health and special needs of individuals, but they cannot explain most of the social problems usually blamed on them. I show that there is nothing in the theory of evolution (or creation) or in known patterns of human genetics and variation to suggest the innate superiority and inferiority of groups, a tenet dear to the heart of much historic and current American political philosophy.

Chapter 3 addresses the importance of culture (as anthropologists use the term) for explaining human differences and the tensions between human groups. It shows that the variety of human cultures is potentially of enormous value to us all, but that the culture of any group powerfully constrains the behavior of its members and their ability to understand or appreciate the behavior of any other group. As a result, the perception that others are irrational and inferior is perpetuated, robbing us of much of the potential richness we might gain from interaction with them.

In chapter 4, I discuss the much maligned concept of "cultural relativism." Cultural relativism is nothing more than the willingness to look at other people's behavior with an open mind, to learn before judging, and to think critically about one's own culture. Properly understood, cultural relativism is essential not only in dealing with others but for eliminating our blindness about ourselves. I demonstrate that other people's behavior often makes a great deal of sense in context and that our own cultural assumptions—"normal," "obvious," or "natural" as they seem to us—are often rightly questioned by other people. Their "failure" to comprehend or emulate our behavior may stem not from stupidity, ignorance, or cultural "pathology" but from vastly different beliefs that may be as valid as ours or even more so.

In chapter 5, I discuss some assumptions that limit the world view of "mainstream" American culture and generate intolerance and other tensions. I consider our strange definition of "freedom," our misperception of history and of human progress, and our narrow view of property, economics, and justice, among other topics.

Chapter 6 focuses on some of the unspoken assumptions that permeate current debates about the definition of "intelligence," the use of IQ tests, and the evaluation of performance in school and on the job. Many scholars have already challenged the interpretation of IQ tests and the data and arguments of *The Bell Curve* quite successfully. I also offer a critique of these data and arguments, but my approach focuses less on the structure, statistics, and history of IQ testing and more on the heritage of cultural chauvinism behind the interpretation of IQ data as measures of "intelligence." I also focus on the failure of *The Bell Curve*'s authors to take account of well-known human variables in performance which ought to affect the interpretation of test results. I discuss IQ tests as classificatory devices, focusing on their extraordinary but often hidden (or at least unspoken) grounding in specific cultural rules, criticizing the tests and their use but also discussing their place in American culture, the context that gives them their apparent meaning.

Chapter 7 discusses affirmative action and curriculum inclusion or multicultural education, focusing on the ways current debates are molded by our assumptions and by fine distinctions that we assume are logical but are really artifacts of culture.

Chapter 8 suggests that Americans must reexamine our own culture. It challenges the conventional explanations of cause and effect underlying fashionable predictions about our future and suggests that the needed solutions to our problems are very different from those our leaders are proposing. It suggests that we must actively teach knowledge, consideration, and toleration of other people and simultaneously teach a thoughtful version of our own history that is not reluctant to criticize the role the United States or certain privileged groups have played in history. We have to teach people about community and mutual responsibility. And without changing our basic ideals or constitutional principles, we must demand accountability from our politicians and place limits on the control of special interests. The wealthy (not just the working poor or working class) should be held responsible for contributing to society. Some of the enormous wealth now concentrated in the hands of a very few individuals could be put to much more productive use, for the benefit of all. "We the people," not the privileged few, should be the beneficiaries of our efforts.

CHAPTER TWO

The Innocent Scapegoat: Human Biological Variation and "Race"

THE BIOLOGICAL DIFFERENCES AMONG human beings and between "races" are all too often used as scapegoats—blamed for inequality and other social problems that are in fact the product of cultural differences and social and political pressures. Like most scapegoats, these biological differences provide a distraction that enables us to avoid looking at the real problems and searching for real solutions. Most of this book deals with the cultural and political factors that are at the heart of our problems; but it seems important first to describe what science actually knows about biological differences among people in order to put various misconceptions to rest. Most of what follows in this chapter is not particularly controversial, although it seems to have been ignored or forgotten in recent political discussion. This material can be found with only slight variation in any introductory textbook in physical anthropology or human genetics, a fact that makes it all the more discouraging that we don't use it in our public discourse.

Biological differences among people are real, and they can be very important in various specific contexts, particularly those concerned with health; but by and large the important biological differences are ignored in our zeal to use "racial" variations for political purposes. Liberals often ignore the real differences between people because they wish to appear to be color-blind; conservatives ignore the real differences because acknowledging them implies the need to look carefully at people as individuals and then invest in them. Both sides are wrong. Knowledge of these differences is important for improving our well-being. We routinely provide eyeglasses for the near-sighted and insulin for diabetics (who are, after all, manifesting biological differences) without attaching a social or political stigma to their need for aid. Many other human variations deserve similar consideration.

But the biological differences are *never* "racial," because they don't come in the kind of neat clusters or packages that the word "race" implies. Classifying people by color is very much like classifying cars by color. Those in the same classification look alike, superficially (if you ignore the detailed differences), but the classification tells you nothing about the hidden details of construction or about how the cars or the people will perform. For the most part, one biological variation cannot be predicted from the presence of another. Dark skin, for example, doesn't necessarily "go with" a broad nose, or "white" skin with a narrow nose, despite our stereotypes. More important, most human variation has nothing to do with either noses or skin colors. The actual patterns of human variations, including the real advantages and disadvantages they convey, make a mockery of popular images of "races" and of "racial" inferiority and superiority. In fact, they make such racist visions of the human species a scientific impossibility. I use the word "race" only in quotation marks and only to refer to categories used in popular discourse. These commonly used categories play a powerful role in shaping people's thinking and their behavior toward others. They also place powerful constraints on the freedoms and actions of all Americans. "Race" is a very important *social* and *political* category in our culture. In this sense, "race" is a political reality. For this reason, I refer to social and political categories such as "white" and "black" or African American. I also argue that people in some of those categories face special problems owing to their social position, not their biology. But "race," as the term is popularly used, never refers to biological realities.

The distinction between biological variation among people and "races" is an important one. It means that, although they differ from one another, people do not fall readily into biological groups and cannot be stereotyped; and differences between people, even those affecting their health and their abilities, come in highly particular mixes. Individuals undoubtedly have special health problems and specific abilities, but that is very different from saying that particular "races" are inherently healthier, smarter, or more capable than others.

What we know about biological variation and "race" can be summarized under the following nine headings:

1. Human variation is far more complex and intricate than most people realize.

Most of our folk classification of people and "races" depends on three or four highly visible distinctions such as skin color, the shapes of eyes or nose or lips, the texture of hair, or the length of limbs. But human beings vary in thousands of ways, many of them far more important than those. If there were any valid reason to divide the human species into biologically defined groups, any of these thousands of variations could provide as valid a basis for classification as color. Each variation would, however, divide the world's people in different ways. We could, for example, classify people by their blood type, which is completely unrelated to their skin color. In fact we do; we just don't consider it a "racial" classification.

Human beings differ in height and weight, breadth of hips and shoulders, and size and shape of their heads, their eyes, ears, noses, and lips, their limbs, chests, hands, feet, buttocks, breasts, and penises. Some people are long-waisted; some have small trunks and long limbs; some have relatively long shins, forearms, and fingers; others have relatively long thighs and upper arms. We have differing amounts of hair on various parts of our bodies, faces, and hands, and we lose the hair on our heads at different times. The hair comes in different shapes, colors, and textures. We have different amounts of fat, and it is distributed differently around the body. We have different numbers of active sweat glands and differ in the pattern and amount of sweat we produce. The list is nearly endless.

Everything I have mentioned so far touches only the surface of human variation. Most variations, including the most important ones, are not apparent. Some variations involve the size and shape of body parts we can't see readily, such as our teeth, and our hearts, lungs, brains, or other organs. Our bones vary in size and shape but also in the thickness of their dense outer cortical layers. Some women produce bigger placentas than others and some make larger babies. Slight variations in the normal design and function of our internal organs are known to exist and may be quite independent of the outward appearance of the organs. Lungs, for example, vary in size and volume but also in their capacity to diffuse oxygen into the bloodstream. Blood varies in pressure, as well as in the number and chemistry of the various cells, and in the amount and type of hemoglobin it contains. Muscles vary in the mixture of fibers they contain.

Other variations—in fact, most—are chemical and therefore not visible at all. Every person's blood can be "typed" not just to determine whether it is A, B, O, or AB and Rh positive or negative, but also to determine many other kinds of variation. In addition, hemoglobin, the red blood pigment that carries oxygen, comes in the "normal" form, the well-known sickle-cell form, the forms lumped together as thalassemia, and several other, lesser-known varieties.

Human beings also vary in the proteins that make up other body tissues. White blood cells (leukocytes) of the immune system display variations in proteins, the so-called human leukocyte antigens (HLA) that help determine whether the organs of one person can be successfully transplanted into another, much as the blood groups determine whether blood can be donated by one person to another safely.

The range of human variation is enormous, and much of it is still unexplored. As estimated in 1996 by participants in the Human Genome Project, which is attempting to map an entire human genetic code, there may be as many as 50,000–100,000 gene pairs designing the various proteins that are the building blocks of our bodies. Most of these are the same in all people, but as many as 15–25 percent are "polymorphic" and produce different forms of the same protein in different people. This means that just on this basis there are 7,500–25,000 possible directions of individual variation between any two people in basic protein synthesis alone. Because combinations of proteins and other factors are also involved, the number of potential differences between any two people is much larger.

These physical and chemical differences affect the way our bodies work. Our hearts pump different volumes of blood and our blood transports different amounts of oxygen. Some people naturally maintain a higher metabolic rate than others. We utilize energy differently. We metabolize cholesterol differently. Our ability to tolerate and work in heat, cold, and high altitude differs. We grow, mature, and age at different rates. Our ability to taste certain substances varies slightly from person to person, as does our ability to see, smell, and hear and our ability to digest certain common foods.

Some adults (actually, the vast majority around the world) cannot digest lactose, the sugar in fresh milk. A few people cannot digest sucrose or common sugar. Some people with a genetic irregularity called G6PD-deficiency (favism) can die if they eat European fava or broad beans, although most people digest them easily.

Chemical differences also make us more or less susceptible to a variety of diseases. Some individuals have genes that cause them to suffer cystic fibrosis, hemophilia, Tay-Sachs disease, thalassemia, or sickle-cell anemia; some, although not condemned to illness, seem to have an increased risk of getting multiple sclerosis, organic depression, diabetes, hypertension, rickets, breast cancer and other cancers, osteoporosis, obesity, atherosclerosis, stroke, or heart attack, all for reasons related partly to variations in genes and body proteins, not just lifestyles. Some people even seem to be more susceptible than others to germ diseases like tuberculosis, smallpox, bubonic plague, and AIDS, all for reasons related to their internal chemistry.

We have barely begun to explore this invisible variety, but it is as real as the most obvious superficial variations and much more important.

2. Most significant differences between people are the result not of genes alone but of genes interacting with the environment (or of the environment alone).

Human variation begins with the genes, or active portions of the DNA which each of us inherits from our parents. It is now very well established that DNA guides the chemical processes in our cells that help account for our characteristics. But, for the most part, genes don't work in a simple, direct way. Most genes don't simply "make" human "traits." Some genes don't do anything (at least most of the time), or perhaps we should say that they have no known function. Some regulate the activities of other genes, turning them on and off or providing the timing and context which define those other genes' function. Some genes make the proteins from which the body is built, most of which are not visible. In some cases, the proteins themselves are the traits that concern us. Blood "types," for example, refer to the presence or absence of different proteins. Hemoglobin is a protein, and the sickle-cell trait refers to a variation in the design of the protein.

But proteins often act primarily as enzymes or catalysts that we never see directly. They help regulate sequences of chemical reactions that in turn produce the traits, rather than producing the traits directly. Even in the case of supposedly simple, directly coded traits, such as blood type or hemoglobin, the important thing is not the name or the form of the protein but how it acts and reacts in particular situations.

Some chemical reactions are controlled by combinations of genes and therefore several proteins which interact with one another. Human traits like stature and skin color seem to be under the control of many genes interacting in ways that we do not fully understand. This is one reason that the inheritance of those traits (and in fact most visible traits) is not completely predictable. On the other hand, a single gene and the protein it produces might control a chemical reaction that has several results. Perhaps the best-known example is a genetic disease called phenylketonuria (PKU), in which the function of a single gene leads to a metabolic failure which can affect the growth, pigment, and mental development of an individual. If the action of one gene has several results, some outcomes may be "good" and some "bad." It was reported a number of years ago that among Morgan horses (show horses bred for beauty), one gene that breeders selected because it contributed to beauty also tended to result in the early death of the animals. One theory of aging, senescence, and death in all species is that genes that are beneficial early in life may have negative effects later in life. Human genetic design, too, involves compromises and trade-offs, genes that can have both good and bad consequences. This is one reason why it is not as easy as many people assume to identify "good" and "bad" genes—or "superior" and "inferior" genetic endowment. Many genetic human "diseases" actually confer advantages in some situations.

The main point is that the outcomes of our genetic endowment usually are not firmly dictated. We might think of genes as a recipe for building the body. As any cook knows, a recipe does not guarantee the quality or form of the final product. Certain genes may act differently in combination with other genes (when the mother's and father's "recipes" are mixed), producing unexpected outcomes. And a gene almost always expresses itself under the influence of a particular environment. Genes provide the recipe, but the environment controls the conditions under which the chemical reactions occur and may well supply chemical ingredients of its own in the form of other nutrients or poisons. All these factors confound the attempt to make simple predictions about the outcomes of a genetic mix or to identify exactly how genes contribute to our biology.

For example, many mammals, including some rabbits and Siamese cats, produce different pigments from the same genes when the temperature of their environment changes. In both rabbits and cats, colder temperature increases the production of dark pigment.

Similarly, many if not most human traits are the result of both genetic and environmental influences. It is important to note, however, that "environment" refers not just to the natural environment but also to the surroundings we create for ourselves, including the nutrition we provide, the germs we spread, the pollution we create, and the community, workplace, family, and social structure we provide.

Traits like stature, weight, and presumably "intelligence"—so-called continuous variables—which involve many genes are particularly likely to be influenced by environmental factors. ("Continuous" means that people cannot be divided into a few distinct classes—say, short or tall—on the basis of the variable but occupy positions on a continuum, so that the distribution is represented by a smooth curve on a graph and each person's height, for example, has to be assigned a relatively precise number.) Stature runs in families and is partly genetic, but it is also heavily affected by nutrition and disease, altitude, temperature, emotional health, and other factors. Many populations, including those in the United States, have grown taller when their diets were made richer.

Fat patterns and obesity also run in families and probably have a genetic component, and there is some variation in the ways individuals metabolize food, suggesting that there are real differences in people's chemical pathways, not just their eating habits. On the other hand, there are factors other than genes, such as childhood nutrition and learned dietary habits, that might explain a familial pattern of obesity. It is also possible that chemical differences related to obesity are themselves the results of environmental factors, behaviors, or dietary patterns rather than an independent cause. For example, nutritional deprivation in utero or in early childhood may predispose an individual biologically as well as psychologically to utilize food more thoroughly and to store more fat when a richer diet becomes available, predisposing the person to obesity in later years. A protein has recently been identified with which the body signals that eating can stop. This signaling device may vary from person to person for genetic reasons and may help account for different eating patterns; but we don't know what the other environmental influences on that protein are—and many of us overeat for social, cultural, or psychological reasons (such as anxiety or boredom), rather than because of any biological signal. Moreover, few people, whatever their genes, become obese unless they are eating a modern Western diet, rich in fats and processed sugars. Obesity of large numbers of people is a very recent phenomenon historically. Even now, it seems to be related to social class more than to any ethnic or "racial" or genetic variation. It was first a coveted sign of upper-class status and has become more recently a lower-class stigma.

Many diseases also result from a combination of genetic and environmental factors. For example, multiple sclerosis (MS) is associated with certain genetically coded proteins (HLA antigens) and occurs with different frequencies in different ethnic groups, partly, perhaps, because of the distribution of the genes for those antigens. So it is in some sense related to the genes. But the genetic factor is heavily influenced by environmental factors not yet clearly defined. MS is most common among people in cold climates and in modern industrialized countries. People of almost all genetic varieties have a much higher prevalence of MS when they move to such environments or adopt Western lifestyles.

Even well-known genetic traits may be affected by environmental variation more than we realize. Sickle-cell anemia is a thoroughly studied genetic disease, and its genetic basis is not in question. It has only recently been realized, however, that without medical intervention it may be a more serious disease in the United States than it is in the parts of Africa where it is common. Some recent and historic West African diets are rich in sources of a chemical known as cyanate which helps relieve the symptoms. But, foods such as manioc (cassava), which are rich in cyanate, are rarely eaten in the United States. So sickle-cell anemia is a genetic disease that is also exacerbated by a specific dietary deficiency in the United States.

Some human variations, of course, are largely plastic—that is, they develop during an individual's lifetime in response to his or her environment, behavior, or lifestyle. Some traits, like big muscles or low levels of body fat, can be developed by most people through training in a span of weeks or months or a few years, and may be reversed when behavior changes. Others, particularly variations in skeletal size and shape, can develop in response to natural environment or activity but involve a longer period of development and are relatively irreversible. Variations in head shape, for example were once thought to be excellent markers for "racial" classification, but they have long been shown to be plastic, changing relatively quickly over generations when families migrate to new places and the children grow up in new environments. It now appears that the barrel chests, large hearts, and blood that is rich in red cells that characterize some high-altitude populations will develop to some degree in anyone who goes to a high-altitude environment as a child, although some genetic factors may also be involved. But the distinction between what is genetic and what is plastic is not always clear. Surprisingly, the relative length of a person's (or other animal's) limbs is also affected not just by genes but by the environment in which the individual grows up; people and other animals raised in cold environments tend on average to develop shorter limbs.

Some supposedly "racial" differences may result almost entirely from differences in lifestyle or culture. Fertility (the number of children the average woman produces in her lifetime) is often thought of as a biological variable and even a "racial" trait. But variations in human fertility that we observe among *groups* of people (as opposed to individuals) mostly reflect the cultural choices people make about reproduction, birth control, and sexual behavior. Fertility is generally low in Europe and the United States because of birth-control decisions. It is higher in countries where more children are desirable as an economic asset and as protection for one's old age. Biological differences among groups in the natural ability to have children also relate mostly to such environmental or lifestyle factors as nutrition, health, exercise, and nursing habits. This natural ability, however, seems to be relatively high among affluent Western women who are richly nourished, whose diseases are controlled, who don't abstain from sex very long after a birth, and who bottle-feed their babies rather than nursing. It is not Third World or "nonwhite" women at all who are "naturally" high in fertility. To assert that some "races" are naturally more likely to reproduce—more fertile, as racist stereotypes often claim—is inherently absurd because it fails to distinguish among genetic differences, environmental differences, and cultural choices. It also fails to distinguish between inherent *ability* and actual *performance*—a fallacy that infuses a great deal of "racial" thinking.

3. It is extremely difficult to separate the roles of genes and environment as causes of variation, and the two are often so intertwined that the distinction is meaningless.

In many human variations, including height and weight—but also traits such as "intelligence" and behavior that are central to contemporary debates—genes, natural environments, and cultural choices are intertwined to such a degree that teasing them apart is extremely difficult if not impossible. There is no easy or reliable way to separate the various factors. We can employ statistical techniques to try to determine what proportion of the variation of any trait in a particular group of people or animals results from genetics and what proportion from the environment. By such tests, we can obtain a measure called heritability, which purports to describe how much of the variation in, say, stature comes from genes. Such estimates are then often used in attempts to show how much a particular trait is "genetically" determined. The problem with this is that the most we can ever measure by this method is the proportion of genetic contribution in the sample of people or animals tested under the circumstances of the particular test. We can never measure an inherent degree of control exerted by genes because genes interact with the environment and the same genes can exert more or less control in different situations. The size of the genetic contribution depends in part on how significant the variation in the environmental factors is. If environmental factors are held fairly constant so that the environment is the same for all, the observed variation will mostly be due to genetic factors and genes will appear to be a powerful influence. If the environmental variation among the samples is more pronounced, the influence of the environment will appear more powerful and that of the genes will appear to be less. The interaction of gene functioning and environments, in fact, is so intimate that many geneticists consider the whole distinction between nature and nurture, or heredity and environment, to be a false one. The gene-environment interaction, they say, cannot be neatly partitioned and assigned numerical values.

A common teaching illustration of this point involves planting seeds in a greenhouse. Suppose that we have one bag of seeds that are mixed as uniformly as possible, although the seeds are not genetically identical to one another. Suppose we plant some in a carefully constructed flower bed where growing conditions are uniformly excellent. The plants have identical environments in which to grow, but they will grow to varying heights. Because their environments were made absolutely identical, the different heights must reflect slight differences in genes. If we breed the tallest plants and grow them in the same environment, they will tend to produce taller offspring than those produced by the shorter plants—so their variation in height results from genes and appears to be highly heritable.

But suppose we take a second batch of seeds from the same bag and grow them in a second plot with uniformly poor growing conditions. *Within* this second group, the plants will also grow to varying heights, and the variation will reflect their genetic endowment because the environment, though poor, is the same for all. But most will be shorter than the plants in the first group. The differences *between* the two groups in this test will be almost entirely due to environmental factors (it has to be—we used the same seeds). And if we breed the offspring of the two sets of plants and rear them under the same conditions, the difference between the groups will disappear. So using exactly the same problem, and the same seed to test it, variation can appear almost entirely genetic or almost entirely environmental depending on which plants we compare. It is important to note that the measure of heritability didn't change just a little when we changed the conditions of the experiment (as if there were a central value set by genes and different environmental conditions only produced small variations around it, as would be the case if environment were only a minor component). The measure changed almost completely. Any initial result in one set of circumstances tells us nothing about the value of heritability under other conditions.

In the real world, of course, neither the genetic effects nor the environmental ones will be so clearly defined. But the principle still holds. We can't extrapolate heritability from one context to another. We can't provide a definitive statement about whether or how much a particular trait is inherently controlled by genes on the basis of any limited set of tests, even when we are looking at a characteristic as easy to measure as height. It is of no help merely to repeat the test or to do similar tests within the same limited range of environmental variation. The fact that the results can be replicated within the same range of conditions does not say anything about the reliability of results for understanding outcomes under other circumstances. In the same manner, no matter how many independent tests of the heritability of height or intelligence or any other trait we perform *within* the white American population or *within* the African American population, the results tell us nothing about the role of genes in explaining differences *between* the groups. Heritability could be estimated as a fixed, inherent value of genes themselves only if one were to get similar values in repeated tests sampling all possible (or at least an enormous range of) groups living in all possible environments. Such a result is theoretically possible but very rarely achieved or even undertaken among human populations; and no such result has ever been demonstrated with reference to human intelligence. (Note also that "groups" doesn't have to mean biological "races." The same principle applies to human groups as similar as our two handfuls of seed grown under different conditions.)

Diseases that have become prevalent in the past two centuries, like adult diabetes, hypertension, or breast and bowel cancers, demonstrate the same point. These diseases are all thought to have a genetic component because individuals are clearly not at equal risk. In the same natural environment some people suffer from one or another of these diseases but others do not—partly because their culturally patterned choices and individual habits are different, of course, but partly because of their genes. The pattern of risk runs in families to varying degrees in most American ethnic groups, and genetically identical twins tend to have similar risk of disease. Moreover, the risk may be statistically greater in some populations than in others for genetic reasons. (Thus, susceptibility to diabetes seems to be particularly common in some groups of Native Americans; susceptibility to hypertension seems particularly common in some groups of African Americans. MS is most common in Euro-Americans.)

But here's the catch: these diseases can be said to have a high heritability when we compare people who live in the same environment and eat the same diet. Under those conditions, we assume that the ones who get sick are the ones with certain genes. But heritability becomes relatively unimportant if (as with our two groups of plants) we look at people with different diets from different places or periods of history.

All the diseases mentioned become dramatically more common when people of any geographic origins adopt modern Western habits and diets. The immediate ancestors of the Native Americans with high frequencies of genes that predispose them to adult onset diabetes must also have had high frequencies of those genes; there is no way for the genes to have entered those populations on a massive scale in 75–125 years. But Native Americans rarely suffered from adult diabetes until their diets were altered after their conquest by Europeans. The difference between historic and modern Native Americans (or other populations) in the rate of diabetes isn't genetic at all; it is almost totally environmental. Similarly, whatever the genetic factors (if indeed they are genetic) that make some African Americans susceptible to hypertension or high blood pressure rising with age, the disease is confined almost entirely to populations (of any origins) now eating a typical American or Western diet, which is high in sodium, low in potassium and some other minerals, and high in fats. Native Africans eating traditional diets, like people of other parts of the non-Western world, rarely suffer from these conditions. So the pattern we see is mostly environmental.

This example also reinforces another important theoretical point. "Bad" genes, like those producing diabetes or hypertension, may be bad only in a specific environment or cultural context.

4. The processes that produce genetic change and evolution promote variety and short-term adaptation to specific circumstances. They do not produce steady improvement or "progress" toward perfection. They do not permit people or animals to be ranked on a linear scale of advancement or superiority.

Genetic variation begins, of course, when parents make copies of their own genes and pass them on to their offspring. Each child gets a different mixture of the parents' genes. The mixing of the parents' genes and the fact that genes interact chemically with one another account for much of the variation that can be seen in any family. Parents apparently pass on samples of their own genes randomly rather than "selecting" or otherwise controlling what is passed. Mixing the genes of two parents randomly permits more varied offspring to be born. Each sperm or egg is a fairly random sample of the parents' genes, and the combination produced by the two is unpredictable. Sexual reproduction is a way for parents to invest in a variety of children. It is *not* designed to perpetuate only the parents' "best" qualities, apparently because it is not possible to predict what the best will be when environmental conditions are subject to change. Spreading one's bets has been a more successful strategy than trying to reproduce perfection. Nature is apparently working hard to *create* variety by forcing us to mix our genes with others. It is ironic that some human groups are working so hard to deny or eliminate genetic variation.

If the movement of populations permits individuals to come into contact with individuals of a different genetic heritage, more variety may result. Breeding with people of other groups is a natural tendency, and it occurs whenever the opportunity presents itself. It is generally healthy in genetic terms for both the individual offspring and the groups to which they belong, despite the protests of "racial" purists. There is no genetic reason to expect that such interbreeding will produce disability or genetically inferior stock and no biological evidence that it does so. Biologists looking at other species, in fact, often talk about "hybrid vigor," suggesting that organisms with mixed heritage are *superior* biologically. Interbreeding also helps groups because it increases the variety of genes in each group. The known genetic dangers in the choice of mates are associated far more with breeding in too small and homogeneous a group. Inbreeding (breeding too close to one's own family) increases the risk of dangerous duplication of occasional deleterious genes. (Each of us is thought to be carrying some rare genes that are harmless but would be dangerous if an individual inherited two copies, one from each parent. Mating with a closely related individual, particularly a sibling, or one's own child, greatly increases the chance that the new child will get such a gene from both parents.) Outbreeding (breeding with relative strangers) poses fewer risks because the chances that both partners have the same rare gene is very small. This is probably one reason why most human groups have incest rules and other mechanisms that prevent close relatives from producing children together and why many very small groups encourage marriage outside the local community.

In addition to the random recombination of the parents' genes, copying mistakes or mutations inevitably occur in the processes of duplication and transmission. Some such mistakes are severely crippling to the offspring or even lethal, often long before birth. On the other hand, sometimes minor copying errors go completely unnoticed. Some errors, the most important ones for explaining variation and evolution, allow an organism to live but provide a slight difference from the norm, perhaps a slight advantage or disadvantage for the offspring under particular circumstances.

Mutations apparently occur mostly at random. They are not directed in a positive sense by any specific environmental force, although the environment may destroy the organisms that bear harmful mutations. The rate at which mutations occur can be affected by a variety of environmental factors, from cosmic radiation to chemical mutagens to caffeine. And, just as a typist will make the same errors repeatedly because there are only so many keys and so many fingers, so the same mutation happens again and again because the genetic "keyboard," too, is limited. So, given a long enough period of time and a large enough population, the occurrence of mutations and even the repeated occurrence of particular mutations are assured.

The processes discussed so far are about variety, not about perfection or progress. The question is why certain varieties perpetuate themselves in the genes of a particular population while others disappear—or why the same mutation or combination will disappear at some times and places and become more frequent at other times or places.

Part of the answer is what has come to be known (and misunderstood) as natural selection. Charles Darwin pointed out years ago that nature "selects" certain designs among plants and animals, just as a breeder selects horses with certain specific, desired traits and sees to it that those animals are the parents of the next generation, thereby concentrating and perhaps improving on the desired traits. Whereas the breeder selects for qualities like beauty, color, or speed, nature itself "selects" certain animals to be parents because they have traits that permit them to thrive and reproduce *in the particular environment they inhabit.*

The phrase "survival of the fittest," by which natural selection is often described, is widely misused. The "fittest" refers simply to the individual who is most successful at reproducing—passing on its own genes to children and ultimately to grandchildren, great-grandchildren, and so forth. An individual who has more descendants than his neighbor is "fitter," and the future population will tend to have a disproportionate representation of his genes. Fitness has no other meaning and no implication of overall quality, morality, or domination. "Survival of the fittest" refers to the idea that surviving long enough to reproduce is a necessary condition for passing on one's genes. But survival has never been a sufficient measure of fitness because one still has to attract mates, be fertile, and be sure that one's offspring are viable. Moreover, survival itself is a multifaceted challenge involving camouflage, resistance to various diseases, ability to obtain a wide range of nutrients, ability to withstand temperature extremes, ability to see, smell, or hear enemies, and hundreds of other problems, not just competition or dominance. The phrase also conveys the idea that what ultimately happens to individual members of this generation makes relatively little difference: the "survivors" are those whose genes are carried to future generations, and the fittest are those whose genes are carried on in more descendants than someone else's. If, even in the act of dying, you make or protect more offspring than your neighbor, you are more fit and you are, in this sense, a "survivor."

Natural selection means that populations in different environments may gradually accumulate higher concentrations of the particular genes that have helped organisms be fit in those environments, because their descendants, who carry some of their genes, become an ever-increasing proportion of that population. If conditions change, however, as they always do eventually, those genes may no longer confer an advantage.

It is important to note that the concept of fitness never carried with it the implications drawn by the so-called "Social Darwinists:" that it is "natural" and therefore proper for the politically powerful to dominate the less powerful. There is no necessary relationship between political power and fitness. There is no question that political domination can contribute temporarily to fitness if those with power use it successfully to monopolize reproduction. But that does not imply that they achieved their power through superior biological quality. And their political power does not imply that they are passing on genes of superior quality which will help their offspring in the future. Moreover, dominance has nothing to do with fitness if the dominated breed more quickly than the conquerors, as is often the case. The world's poor are reproducing faster than the affluent at the moment. If their populations continue to grow faster, they will be demonstrating their superior fitness in strictly Darwinian terms.

Fitness in the long run is an enormously complex balancing act. Any organism faces a vast array of challenges to its survival and its ability to reproduce. Fitness almost always refers to specific environments and sets of conditions, not to overall superiority. It generally reflects a design or adaptation that is beneficial for coping with specific problems. Different environments make different demands, and the demands change, so the factors that contribute to fitness change over time. But there is no sense in which natural selection anticipates change. Selection among potential parents always favors what is most useful here and now. Survival and fitness are largely a matter of being in the right place at the right time with the right traits. The future is left to take care of itself. There is no way to determine whether genes that have contributed to success in the past will contribute to fitness in the future, and most organisms eventually die out as a result. Nature has a very high extinction rate.

There is a classic example that biologists use to illustrate some of the limits of natural selection. British peppered moths come in two colors, black and gray. They constitute a single species because they breed together and produce fertile offspring. The balance of the two colors in the population has changed repeatedly in recent centuries. In this instance, fitness clearly depends heavily on the moths' ability to evade birds that use their eyesight to find their prey resting on tree trunks. The moths can escape being caught by being camouflaged and invisible against the tree trunks. Prior to the Industrial Revolution, gray tree trunks were common, and gray moths were relatively "fit" because they were harder for the birds to find. But, because tree trunks were first blackened with soot and later cleaned up owing to reduced air pollution, the "desirable" color kept changing. Is a moth better off ("fitter") being black or gray? It all depends on the color of the trees. Fortunately for the moth population, some individuals that are the "wrong" color or at least carrying one "wrong" gene generally survive. They provide the variety necessary to cope with the next crisis.

But which moth will be fit if a new predator comes along that hunts by smell or radar rather than vision? What if the new threat is chemical air pollution or disease or heat, not birds? Fitness will be based on very different qualities. Because desirable mutations are extremely rare and random events, they do not produce new genes specifically in order to cope with new problems; genetic variety has to be present (or an extremely rare mutation has to occur at the right time by pure luck). Or, perhaps the moth population too will simply become extinct.

The broad implications are twofold: we can never decide that one particular type is inherently more "fit," and eliminating genetic variety is dangerous. Selection relates to whatever aspects of the environment are most threatening at the moment, and the fitness of parents is always dependent on the qualities they need to survive, not the qualities their children will need—so the parents' design, no matter how successful, does not guarantee future success.

Evolutionary processes produce variety, not perfection, for the obvious reason that in a changing world, perfection doesn't exist. Most genes and most human variations are not simply "good" or "bad," although they may temporarily be adaptive or maladaptive— advantageous or disadvantageous *for particular circumstances*. Some human variations, viewed in the strictest biological terms, help to confer fitness in specific environments. But, is it better in terms of fitness to have diabetic or hypertension genes or not to have them? To carry the sickle-cell or cystic fibrosis or Tay-Sachs gene, or not? To have darker or lighter skin? The answer in each case depends on the environment.

The example of the moths brings up another important point. In the modern world, the environment for people as well as moths is often as much man-made as it is natural. So adaptive problems keep changing for people, too, no matter how buffered from the natural environment we may feel. We often talk as though natural selection ended when we became civilized because, as one 1995 newspaper column put it, "babies are not being stolen by lions any more." But human "progress" and "civilization" themselves generated many of the most important threats or selective forces in the modern envi-ronment, including many major diseases and chemical pollution, and those forces have shaped some aspects of human fitness and therefore of human variation. In the 1990s and the twenty-first century, AIDS, a disease not known until the 1980s, may become one of the most powerful selectors of who is fit. Perhaps more important may be resistance to the new wave of tuberculosis, or some other airborne disease (like a conceivable airborne variety of the lethal Ebola virus) that could spread much faster and more universally than AIDS. Le-thal epidemic diseases are largely products of civilization (because they can spread only among dense populations connected to one another by trade), and they are still very real possibilities in a world of cities connected by airplane routes.

It is only in the modern civilized world, apparently, that genes associated with hypertension, diabetes, breast cancer, or MS clearly have been a detriment to fitness. Genes that had no adverse effect before civilization—and may even have been beneficial—now threaten fitness. We have changed the environment and thereby al-tered the expression of our genes and the risks they pose. In the future, fitness may turn out to be measured by possession of a chemical variation that we haven't even noticed yet; it will probably have little to do with most of the qualities popularly associated with being "fit" or powerful. For example, we have now recognized a hitherto unimportant genetic variation in a few people that appears to resist AIDS. That minor gene difference could become a major determinant of fitness. It is also now well documented that sperm counts have fallen off drastically among men throughout large parts of the civilized world, presumably as a result of some (unidentified) kind of chemical pollution. Some men are affected less than others or not at all. That, not physical dominance, is the stuff of differential fitness or natural selection.

The processes that shape variety and change among animals have no plan or goal. Adaptation and fitness mean that some members of a population have the needed qualities to survive the most recent challenge or combination of challenges. Perhaps their children will have the necessary qualities to survive whatever comes next, but the success of the parents is no guarantee. Genetic diversity has always been the only long-term protection and it remains the best bet in a world in which the challenges are unpredictable and far from over.

5. A great deal of genetic variation appears to have no major adaptive significance, no advantage or disadvantage.

Natural selection tends to channel genetic variation in the direction of immediate, short-run advantage or adaptation, but other forces unrelated to the environment also affect the way populations of animals change. Survival and reproduction sometimes depend on luck, not quality of design. If, for example, a building or a cave collapses and no possible skill or adaptation can protect the people inside, luck or chance—who happens to be killed accidentally—can change the genetic distribution of the next generation. The example mentioned above—when a lion steals a child—probably isn't natural selection at all, in fact, because the lion distinguishes no variation among children—smell, strength, speed, or reaction time. The lion can catch any child and generally takes the nearest one. This is a matter of luck, just as a collapsing building falls on anyone who is walking by without regard for his or her genes. But those who survive, by virtue of their luck, not their quality, still get to pass on their genes to the next generation. Being a member of a dominant society and thereby being empowered to spread one's genes is almost certainly more a matter of luck than of genetic design because there is no evidence whatsoever to suggest that such dominance is related to any genetic trait.

The transmission of genes from parent to child also involves luck, as anyone knows who wishes to have a child of a particular sex or to pass on a particular desired trait. A family can have a "run of luck" in which, say, they get several daughters or several sons in a row, although the chances of having a boy or girl are always close to fifty-fifty.

Each parent passes only a random sample of genes to each child (apparently without regard to the contribution the gene might make to the child's fitness or the parents' wishes). By luck, the parent might pass a gene to several offspring in a row or to none at all. So, all or most of the children might get a desired trait that might help them to be fit in the particular environment; but it is equally possible that none of the children will get it or that an undesirable trait will be passed to one or even all children just by luck.

In this manner, by various kinds of luck, certain traits might become more common in a certain family or group as long as the group is small enough. This is what is called *genetic drift* or a "run of luck." Runs of luck, however, are possible only in a small sample. We can get "heads" four or five times in a row when flipping a coin just by chance. But over the long run things should even out. If we get twenty-five heads in a row, common sense tells us that we are not having a run of luck but that something other than luck is forcing the outcome. (We usually say that we are being cheated.) The same principle helps us distinguish luck and selection in evolution. A single family might have four daughters or redheads or taller-than-average children in a row, but if a town of several thousand average people had only daughters, or redheads, or tall children, it could be cause for serious concern. It would imply that more than luck was involved—that something was "selecting" children with those qualities. (There are parts of the world where the percentage of daughters is so small in very large populations that it can't possibly be a matter of natural luck, given the number of people involved. People themselves or some other "selective" force are interfering with the natural sex-determination process.)

On the other hand, a modern population of millions of people might have a high proportion of redheads, just by luck, if that population began centuries ago with a small group of people that just accidentally had a lot of redheads who passed the trait on to their descendants. This process is called the "founder effect" because the common genes are simply those that the founders of the population just happened by luck to have. The very high frequency of type O blood and near absence of type B among Native Americans may have occurred for a similar reason, as Native Americans are thought to be descended from very small founder populations from Asia. Other differences between populations may also reflect drift or the founder effect unless they occur too regularly on too large a scale to be mere chance.

Because many of the forces affecting variety and change are random (mutation, genetic drift, sperm and egg formation, sexual recombination), we can't simply assume that a difference we see among groups of people is an adaptation, much less that it confers any kind of superiority or inferiority.

6. Despite facile modern arguments about "racial" superiority and inferiority, demonstrating that a particular trait or variation confers an advantage (even in a specific environment) is extremely difficult.

How do we tell the variations that are or were "adaptive" from those that are chance occurrences? Although we can make the distinction only with great difficulty—and sometimes not at all—the attempt is important because it sheds light on important modern health problems. It also helps to dissolve our stereotypes by breaking down human variation into meaningful pieces. We are forced to look at one trait at a time.

Scientists begin by observing the *pattern* of the traits they want to explain—defining where or when they occur and do not occur. They can begin to study the function of certain variations (and explain the meaning of human variation in a larger sense) by studying the *distribution* of particular traits around the world. They usually focus on patterns that existed prior to A.D. 1500, when long-distance travel by large groups of people accelerated enormously. They then try to correlate the distribution of human traits to the distribution of various environmental factors that might have "selected" them until they get a good match. Matching patterns suggest *possible* causes.

But scientists have to supplement this study of distribution by analyzing the actual working of the trait to show precisely how genes affect its chemistry and how the trait relates to the environmental factors. Scientists need to show that there is a causal relationship between trait and environment (not just a coincidental overlap) and that the causal mechanism affects fitness and evolution on the scale observed. And they have to demonstrate that no other cause can explain the pattern equally well. Matching patterns or "correlations" are suggestive, but they are never sufficient to prove that one thing caused another (a point to which I shall return in chapter 6).

In a few cases, specific human variations have been studied to the point where there is little substantive disagreement about their genetic basis or their general biological significance (although the details are debated and refined and scientists continue their research). On the other hand, the precise genetic basis and adaptive significance (if any) of many of the best-defined and most obvious biological variations among human beings are still unknown or hotly debated.

When sickle-cell anemia was first identified and determined to have a genetic basis, scientists wondered why so lethal a gene had not simply been eliminated by natural selection. If potential parents with the disease die, or even lose more of their offspring than their neighbors, the gene should disappear. One clue to the understanding of sickle-cell anemia was the realization that the distribution of the gene in Africa matched that of Falciparum malaria (the most lethal kind of malaria), which suggested that the gene might be an adaptation to malaria. It was then shown that individuals with one copy of the sickle-cell gene suffered less from malaria. They were less likely to get sick, had less severe malarial symptoms, were less likely to die, remained more fertile, had more surviving children, and therefore were more "fit" than those without a copy of the gene. It was then shown that sickled cells resisted malarial parasites. A further piece of the proof came when the biochemical mechanisms by which sickle-cell hemoglobin discourages the malarial parasite were described. In addition, the chemical variations of hemoglobin and the genes that produce them have been described. We know fairly exactly how the genetic code for sickle-cell hemoglobin differs from the code for normal hemoglobin.

Scientists know that the sickle-cell gene, which produces potentially lethal sickle-cell anemia if an individual gets two copies, can be beneficial if the individual lives in a malarial area and gets only one copy of the gene. This fact keeps the gene going in malarial areas despite its disadvantages. But they know this only because the study of pattern and correlation was supplemented by detailed quantitative analysis and precise description of the causal links.

Similarly, the significance of variations in human skin color have been explored in some depth. The specific genes involved are not known, but a long history of adopting children and changing their environments from birth makes it very clear that, allowing for some variation as a result of exposure to the sun, skin color is largely genetic. The historic distribution of human skin colors provided the first clue to the understanding of their importance. It led to what is now known about the functions of melanin, the primary dark pigment, which all people share in various quantities and which largely controls the color of our skin. Research into skin-color variation has also contributed to knowledge of the effects of ultraviolet light on the human body.

If one looks at how people were distributed around the globe before the year 1500, it is clear that on average they were darker near the equator, and lighter at higher latitudes (closer to the poles), not only in Africa and Europe but in south and central Asia, southeast and east Asia, and even to a lesser extent in the Americas. (The lesser color variation of Native Americans is thought to reflect the fact that they have not been distributed in their present locations as long as Eurasian and African populations, having come from Asia only within the past 20,000–30,000 years.) That this gradation in color from dark to light occurs in so many areas of the world (and apparently developed independently in the various regions, as I will show) suggests that the distribution was the result of natural selection and not a result of random chance or the founder effect.

The distribution of human colors matches global patterns of temperature and of ultraviolet (UV) radiation, each of which is more intense near the equator than at the poles. It has been found that UV radiation is responsible for much of the damage to skin caused by sunlight, including sunburn and skin cancer. Skin cancer occurs late in life among Americans, rarely affecting their fitness; but light-skinned people in the tropics can be affected more severely and at an earlier age. Sunburn, which Americans think of as a minor, temporary problem, can be incapacitating or lethal for light-skinned people in the tropics who must expose their bodies to the sun all day. It can lead to infection and destroy sweat glands, leading to potentially lethal overheating. UV radiation can also cause the destruction of B vitamins, particularly folate, by a process called photolysis. Dark skin—skin with lots of melanin—is now known to block UV rays and to help prevent those risks to health, so dark skin confers an advantage in the tropics.

But UV light also stimulates the body's production of "vitamin D" (actually a necessary hormone) that facilitates the body's use of calcium, which is important for, among other things, the strength and rigidity of bones. Insufficiency of vitamin D can produce rickets or softening of the bones, which can cripple one's legs or distort a woman's pelvic canal, with obvious effects on fitness. In the absence of sunlight, people can obtain vitamin D from fish or, in the modern world, from artificial sources like fortified milk. But sunlight has always been by far the most important source. Light skin is now known to permit the penetration of more UV radiation and the production of more vitamin D, and therefore helps prevent these risks in environments where UV radiation is weak. Just as light-skinned people who work outdoors in the tropics are those most susceptible to sunburn and skin cancer, dark-skinned individuals in northern latitudes are most susceptible to rickets if they live in smog-bound high-rise cities like those of Europe and the United States, particularly if they work indoors. (There is no question that rickets afflicted such individuals in recent urban history. It is not so clear that dark skin would have been a significant problem in high latitudes earlier in human history as long as people lived and worked outdoors. Under those conditions the difference between the properties of dark and light skin, though real, may not have been significant enough to affect natural selection.)

In short, the array of human skin tones, which darken or lighten gradually with latitude, appear to be designed to balance the benefits and risks of UV radiation in areas where different amounts of UV radiation penetrate the atmosphere. The ability of the skin to absorb UV rays increases as the rays themselves decrease. So the natural distribution of human skin colors represented genetic adaptation to various environments in the prehistoric world.

All the effects of ultraviolet light were initially postulated on the basis of the observed distribution of the various diseases just described and have since been demonstrated in the laboratory or under live test conditions. Their relative historical importance, however, remains in dispute.

It is important to note that both African and European Americans seem to be slightly out of place geographically by the standards just described, so each may occasionally need minor health interventions, although of different kinds. The ancestors of African Americans were transported north, of course, and did suffer disproportionately from rickets when confined to smog-bound cities in northern latitudes. But stereotypical northern European Americans have also moved southward to a latitude more typical of Mediterranean Europe, the Middle East, or North Africa than of northern or western Europe, and they suffer an elevated risk of sunburn and skin cancer as a result. Philadelphia and New York are actually at about the same latitude as Madrid, Rome, and Istanbul, where people are typically darker than most residents of London or Stockholm. Houston is at the same latitude as Cairo, and Miami is about the same as south-central Egypt, Bahrain, and southern Pakistan, where people are typically far darker than white Americans. The fact that many Americans spend most of their lives indoors tends to protect light-skinned people from excessive exposure to sun; but it exacerbates the problems dark-skinned people face in getting enough sunlight. Our cultural pattern of sunbathing, predominantly by light-skinned people, is clearly maladaptive.

It should be noted that rickets can also be considered a dietary deficiency, because calcium intake is important to its prevention and people with enough fish or fortified milk in their diets may not need exposure to the sun to obtain vitamin D. Genes and environments interact in complex ways.

Based on the experience of black and white GIs in the Korean War, backed up by some experiments on animals, it has also been suggested that the melanin pigment of dark skin can be damaged relatively easily by frostbite in cold climates, so that extreme cold could itself have been a significant selective force for lighter skin at higher latitudes. Some scientists now think, therefore, that the world distribution of both UV radiation and extreme cold was involved in the evolution of human skin color variation. The relative importance of these factors remains in doubt.

Other such relationships between human variation and individual fitness in particular environments have been proposed, but most remain subject to debate. It is relatively well established that thalassemia and G6PD deficiency, like the sickle-cell trait, are genetic adaptations to malaria. Most other associations are more controversial. For example, the gene for cystic fibrosis is thought, but not proved, to have been an adaptation that conferred fitness by helping people survive cholera. Genes associated with Tay-Sachs may have become common among European Jews because they helped protect their bearers from tuberculosis. (Cholera and tuberculosis historically were both significant enough diseases to be agents of natural selection.)

Various proteins, including HLA antigens, appear to be associated with susceptibility to different diseases and may have been naturally selected for these reasons. ABO blood types may be among the factors that helped historically to protect some people from (and predispose others to) diseases including smallpox, bubonic plague, and cholera, although the connections are controversial. Genes that predispose some modern people to hypertension and diabetes may once have *improved* people's fitness in environments in which salt and calories were in relatively short supply. Now that those nutrients have become abundant, the same genes create problems.

The different shapes of human noses may be adapted to variations in temperature and humidity because long, narrow noses do a better job of warming and moistening cold, dry air and then retaining heat and moisture. People with linear ("lanky") body types and small people seem to have an advantage in hotter areas because they radiate heat more efficiently. On the other hand, a stocky build and large body size help people in cold climates stay warm and avoid frostbite because they maintain heat more efficiently, which helps to keep extremities warm. Altered circulation and metabolic patterns also help people in cold climates keep warm. A large chest, large lungs and heart, lungs that efficiently diffuse oxygen into the blood, and blood that is rich in red blood cells to carry oxygen all help people in the thin air of high altitudes to acquire enough oxygen to maintain their body processes and muscular activities. Large placentas help women to transmit more oxygen to a fetus. But these adaptations do not appear to be genetic, for the most part.

Some variations, including some that appear to be genetic, seem to be adaptations to particular *cultural* circumstances (alone or in combination with other environmental factors). All baby mammals (including human infants) produce an enzyme called lactase that enables them to digest lactose, the sugar in milk. Most adult mammals no longer produce the enzyme. (After all, once they are weaned, they are never again exposed to milk as a food.) Most adult human beings also stop making lactase, do not drink milk beyond middle child-hood, and may have trouble digesting it if they do (nausea, cramps, and diarrhea are common symptoms). The ability of some adults to digest milk is probably genetic, and the genes involved seem to be correlated, not surprisingly, with a history of dairying and using fresh milk as a source of food for adults, as much as it is linked to geography. The populations in which adults are commonly able to digest milk are mostly but not entirely European. So what white Americans take to be "normal" or standard human biology is a fairly rare trait of some Europeans and a few other people.

But even among adults in dairying groups, the practice of drink-ing fresh milk and the ability to digest it are unusual. Many groups, including those in the Middle East and North Africa, keep animals but typically convert the milk to yogurt and cheese, processes that use bacteria to digest and eliminate the lactose so it poses no problem for human digestion. Why do some groups drink fresh milk and retain the ability to digest it into adulthood—and why are so many of them (but not all) in Europe? It has been suggested that lactose is particularly valuable as an aid in the intake and utilization of calcium under conditions of reduced ultraviolet radiation and lowered vita-min D production. Perhaps sustained milk drinking and the ability to digest lactose developed commonly in high-latitude Europe for the same reason that light skin did.

On the other hand, it has been harder to make a convincing case that hair color, its degree of curl, or the shape and color of eyes correlate with any feature of the environment or that they function in a manner suggesting that they are adaptive. The pattern of occur-rence of these traits and many others is less well understood, and their appearance may owe more to historic patterns of genetic drift than to selection.

In sum, taken one by one, individual human traits can sometimes be shown to be adaptive to particular environmental conditions, but often such links can only be hypothesized or suggested tentatively and lack clear proof. Many traits have no known adaptive signifi-cance—and none of the known variations has the kind of universal significance that racism postulates. Moreover, problems inherent in trying to demonstrate that specific variations have adaptive signifi-cance show why facile racist pronouncements about the significance of human variation are nonsense.

7. The immediate practical significance of human variation is the effect of specific variations on individual susceptibility to a large array of modern diseases.

Whatever the historic reasons, many variations, not just the "disease genes," have ongoing importance for our health *under specific sets of circumstances.* These are the ones we need to address. Human beings are *not* identical nor are they all biologically "equal" under all circumstances. Nature does not provide equal protection insofar as adaptations to specific conditions are concerned. We have to recognize these inequalities and be ready to deal with them. Protection has to be adjusted for individual problems in the same manner that prescriptions for eyeglasses will vary from person to person. Further, because many so-called genetic diseases express themselves and cause harm most commonly under modern conditions that industrialized society has created, they are social problems, not individual weaknesses. Modern medical intervention is to a large degree not just progress; rather, it is remediation for conditions that have been created or exacerbated by society. It is not a gift, but an obligation of the society.

Pretending that everyone is equal or identical is dangerous because doctors may miss significant differences in illness and in the choice of proper treatment and because, on a larger scale, we may assume that any medical intervention developed for white Americans, like recommending milk, is naturally appropriate for all other populations. That is why public health workers try to identify risk groups, or groups of individuals whose biology (or cultural habits) predispose them to certain problems. There are specific genes that cause specific health problems or that help individual people to adapt or cope with specific environmental problems. Some such genes occur more frequently in some groups than others, and doctors have to know what they are. But saying that some members of various human groups are more susceptible to specific diseases is very different from saying that some are inherently inferior. Members of *all* groups show some such vulnerabilities.

Moreover, saying that certain diseases are associated with certain "races," rather than looking at the real array of people, is an inaccurate way of characterizing their distribution, as the individual genetic factors that create susceptibility are only very loosely associated with our social "races." It is far better to identify an association between disease and a particular trait, gene, or protein and then look for these traits and proteins (and now even the genes themselves) in individuals.

It is important to know which individuals and families have genes that predispose them to disease. Women whose families have a known history of breast cancer (or a known predisposing gene) have to be cautioned, particularly about their diet, weight, exercise, fertility, and breast-feeding patterns. People with a family history of hypertension or diabetes need to be counseled and monitored for these conditions. Some Jewish couples may need genetic counseling about the risks of Tay-Sachs disease; some other European Americans may need counseling about cystic fibrosis; some people of African and Mediterranean descent may need genetic counseling about sickle-cell anemia; European royal families get counseling about hemophilia. Those are responses to the medical needs of individuals, not "racial" stigmata.

As their history suggests, people with light skin are more at risk of sunburn and skin cancer than people with dark skin (a disability that may become increasingly important as the ozone layer is depleted). If I am responsible for the health and welfare of a group of people, whether as a doctor or a camp counselor, I need to know that those with the lightest skin are the ones who need particular protection at the beach or on an outdoor job. On the other hand, if I am an urban social worker, I need to know that, among residents of a smog-bound high-rise city without much sunlight, it is the people with the darkest skin that are at greatest risk of getting rickets. If I am sending troops to fight in a cold climate (as Americans did in the Korean War) or if I am running a ski resort, I also have to know that individuals with dark skin may be especially susceptible to frostbite. (But note that these distinctions relate to real, objectively measurable skin color, not to our social "race" classification.)

In addition to their possible associations with historic epidemic diseases, variations in ABO blood types are also associated with the risk of various cancers (including stomach, colon, cervix, and breast), as well as duodenal ulcers, gastric ulcers, diabetes, and ischemic heart disease. Like the Rh blood group, the ABO blood group affects not only the compatibility of blood for purposes of transfusion, but also the compatibility of mother and child. A fetus whose blood type is different from its mother's can suffer from a chemical reaction. (This is an important point to which I shall return in chapter 6.) Other invisible variations in our genes and proteins also affect our health. The genes that code various HLA antigens (or genes closely associated with those genes on strands of DNA) seem to be associated with susceptibility to diseases such as rheumatoid arthritis, ankylosing spondylitis (an inflammatory disease), Type I (childhood) diabetes, and MS. The point is that an enormous number of such variations, known and unknown, are important for our health. All individuals are affected by some, and all have different combinations of such genes.

The knowledge of all these patterns enables medical personnel to warn people about their risk and thus give them the chance to change their behavior; it enables doctors to take preventive medical care where needed. Preventive steps can be as simple as providing and using sunblock, or warmer mittens; it can be drug therapy; or it can be as complex as genetic counseling or gene therapy. Studying the chemistry of individuals who seem to be naturally immune to conditions that other people suffer can also help scientists to develop successful drug interventions because once they identify a specific gene that is associated with immunity, they can analyze and replicate the proteins involved. Soon it will be possible to copy and transfer the genes involved. Collectively, we can learn and benefit from human variety rather than denigrating it.

The knowledge of variation can also improve physicians' ability to diagnose illness because they look first for what is probable, and their judgment is improved if they are familiar with what is probable in a certain individual. But knowledge of human variety should ideally increase a doctor's awareness of *possibilities* and sensitivity to individual patients rather than leading to stereotyping.

The fact that most adults around the world do not digest fresh milk readily is an example of a variation in human design that we cannot ignore. We now know that it is misguided and dangerous to send powdered milk as a food to hungry people around the world (which was once U.S. government policy) and to use "fortified" milk as a basis for supplying special vitamins (especially vitamin D) to people in need, many of whom are not European or of European ancestry. Widespread, uncritical milk advertising or advertising targeted to inappropriate groups, as is now occurring, can be harmful. People who are lactose-intolerant are likely to reject the milk or, worse, to lose the value of other nutrients in their diets if milk produces vomiting or diarrhea. Using fortified milk as a source of vitamin D is particularly inappropriate because people with dark skin—those most likely to need vitamin D if they live in North American or European cities where there is not much sunshine—are often people who don't tolerate milk.

The point to emphasize is that we *do* need to know about genetic differences among people, but we also need to be aware that these problems, although important for individual health, are not the stuff of "racial" superiority or inferiority and that they do not justify fear or hatred. Such genetic differences are specific, specialized, scattered, and well mixed. They are the kind of things physicians correct or medicate or warn people about every day. The problems are individual problems, not markers of group status. We want our doctors to be aware that ancestry in a certain group raises certain possibilities and to use that knowledge. We also want people to be free to share knowledge of their ancestry without fear of being stigmatized. Understanding the real "inequalities" of natural design is extremely important for the health of all of us.

8. "Races" as depicted in the popular imagination do not exist and have never existed.

If variations are real and important, what does it mean to say that there are no "races"?

When we think of "races" we tend to think of three (or four, five, or even twelve) historically distinct divisions of humanity into which all people can be neatly slotted, whose separate origins are shrouded in mystery. Exceptions to this neat pattern are assumed to be recent products of interbreeding, or "race mixing."

The "race" model of human diversity is based on three major assumptions—all erroneous. First, it assumes that most or all differences among people, from color to fertility, are biological and inherited in one's genes.

Second, it assumes that the differences between human groups, if unsullied by recent mixing, would be sharp and distinct rather than graded—for example, that, historically, people were "purely" black, white, red, or yellow.

Third, the "race" model assumes that certain traits, like light skin, blond hair, and narrow noses, or dark skin, dark hair, broad noses, and predisposition to sickle-cell anemia, naturally cluster together as a "racial" package, so that, allowing for exceptions due to interbreeding, one can predict all of a person's attributes (visible and invisible) by knowing one trait. In short, it assumes that people can easily be stereotyped.

The idea of separate "races" essentially denies the existence of evolution or at least badly misunderstands it. Evolutionary biologists do sometimes talk about myriad local micro-"races" of animals or people, referring to the fact that each local population is slightly different from all others. The fact that the word "race" is used in these different ways only adds to the confusion.

Evolution works through gradual change and the gradual branching of family trees, combined with interbreeding between groups, resulting in an array of populations which resemble one other to varying degrees like the branches of any family. In fact, the major premise of evolution is that we are all part of the same large family.

There is no means by which this process could produce sharply distinct "races" unless each group had evolved in total isolation from the others (but mixing with perfect uniformity within itself) for tens or hundreds of thousands of years. And there is no reason to assume that this has occurred or even that it would be possible, given the configuration of the earth's continents and people's propensity to travel and to find new sexual partners.

Each human population adapts to various local conditions, mixes with other populations, and undergoes its own random mutations and drift, which make it distinct. But each also has an evolutionary history or family tree. It is likely to be carrying some genes and traits that reflect its origins just because they have never been lost, which complement those genes that reflect recent local adaptation or chance. As a result, each population is likely to share *some* genes with other closely related populations simply as a matter of family resemblance, much as siblings share many genes and traits even though as adults they may lead very different lives in different locations. To a diminishing degree individuals also share genes with their cousins, second cousins, and so forth. In the same way one would expect populations to have *varying* degrees of genetic similarity to those to which they are related historically. That is why it is possible to use DNA samples to trace family relationships among individuals but also to try to sort out the history of human migrations by looking for genetic similarities among human groups. "Neutral" genes (those that have no clear adaptive advantage or disadvantage) are the ones most likely to persist in a family line from sheer inertia. They are less likely than "adaptive" traits to be eliminated and replaced as a group moves from environment to environment. We can use the frequencies of "neutral" genes (or nongene segments of DNA, which are also transmitted from parent to child but don't affect the body) to identify branches of the human family.

But this is the nearest we get to "races," and it is not very near to the popular idea of "race." Close branches of the family tree have similar frequencies of some genes, but only some, and only some members of each branch will have those genes. Similarities between groups appear as statistics, not stereotypes, and the frequencies of traits will display graded changes, not abrupt boundaries. Moreover, most of the traits being measured are not visible and not the traits that are important for understanding how people function. Nor are they the traits used in folk classifications of "race." In fact, the family patterns suggested by the frequencies of these neutral traits often contradict the pattern of "obvious" "racial" traits we see. Besides, attempts to map the human family this way, which are always limited to comparing tiny pieces of DNA, have themselves produced contradictory or ambiguous results. Even the traits most useful for classifying human groups do not produce totally consistent divisions of the species.

As with any branching family, it may be possible to recognize side branches or cousins of gradually increasing distance by doing quantitative studies of the distribution of these genes. But there are no abrupt boundaries, no sharp biological distinction between people who are "family" or the same "race" and those who are not. Instead, we see only a series of more and more distant cousins. (Every culture, like every family, makes an arbitrary, conventional decision that cousins beyond a certain degree are not recognized as members of the group, but that does not affect the biological reality of gradual branching.) The organization of the branches of a family, moreover, varies depending on who is doing the measurements or who is taken as the starting point. Your family can be traced around you or your cousin or your second cousin and so forth; in each case the "family" will be different. Similarly, concentric circles of relationship within the human "family" can be traced around any population, but the circles change each time a new population is chosen as the focus. In addition, the circles often change when different genes are traced. And, like families, local populations have always had complex patterns of intermarriage which make it difficult to sort out relationships. So branches of the family are not "races" in the generally assumed sense.

Whether or not one applies evolutionary theory or recognizes a human family tree, there are many reasons, derived simply from the study of modern people, to discard "race" as a scientific classifying device. There is nothing in the distribution of people and their biology to suggest specifically three or four or five or twelve special creations. As I will show, one would have to assume millions of such creations, one for each local population, each only slightly different from its neighbor. (In fact, Darwin was perplexed by the nonsensical nature of assuming so many independent creations of other kinds of creatures with only trivial differences among them. This was one of the observations that initially led him to propose that variations had come into being through a process, not a series of acts.)

Anthropologists and biologists have never been able to agree on how many major "races" there are or where to draw the lines; nor have they ever known what to do with the enormous number of indigenous populations, largely unaffected by recent population movements or interbreeding (the preponderance of humanity), who appear to be exceptions to whatever "racial" scheme is employed. No matter what the "racial" classification, most people don't fit. To cite just one example, people in southern India may have very dark skin but straight or wavy black hair and narrow noses. The fact that dark-skinned people in India were so similar physically to Europeans in these and other ways was so troubling to earlier scholars determined to classify people into races that they often described them as Caucasians (along with European "whites") despite the fact that their skin color was not noticeably different from the color of many African "Negroes."

Further, individual populations are not homogeneous for the "racial" traits that supposedly characterize them. For example, the sickle-cell, Tay-Sachs, cystic fibrosis, hemophilia, hypertension, or diabetes traits never characterize more than a fraction of the members of any population. The highest recorded frequency of the sickle-cell gene in West African populations is 15–25 percent, and it is more commonly 10–15 percent or less. Even in a population "characterized" by the gene, most people do not have it.

As I noted at the outset of the chapter, there are far more kinds of variation than we usually recognize, and many are of equal or greater importance than the few visible traits generally used to classify people. Given all the genes that make a person and the amount of known (and unknown) variation in those genes, the small number that make any visible trait seem a poor basis for a "racial" classification. Even skin color, which is widely accepted as the primary basis for "racial" divisions, is determined by only an estimated 6–10 gene pairs out of 50,000–100,000 gene pairs that make up a human being, so it hardly seems a rational basis for classification.

Moreover, genetic similarities in visible or adaptive traits need not imply family relationships at all. Some obvious "racial" traits actually seem to have originated several times and to occur in populations that are not otherwise very much alike. Thus, parallel skin color variations occur repeatedly in different parts of the world corresponding to solar radiation, among people who otherwise have different traits and appear historically unconnected. Black Africans, black South Indians, and black Australians are not very closely related to one other, judging by their other genes. In fact, they appear more closely related to lighter-skinned populations in their respective vicinities. It is quite inappropriate to group people by color for any purpose other than recognizing common susceptibility to sun-related diseases. Similarly, the sickle-cell trait appears to have occurred by mutation and been incorporated into otherwise unrelated human groups, more than once, as there are very slight structural differences between sickle-cell genes and the resulting hemoglobin in different areas of the world.

The majority of genetic polymorphisms (different forms of a gene leading to variations between people) occur *within* each population rather than *between* populations. In other words, most forms of most genes are found in most populations. It is only the frequency of genetic variations that differs between groups, and in most cases the differences in frequency are fairly small. For example, the major ABO blood types occur in almost all populations. Only their relative frequency varies, and even then the ratios among the types are roughly similar in almost all populations.

Moreover, differences between groups are almost always on a graded scale, not absolute—that is, the frequency or intensity of traits usually changes gradually, not abruptly, from place to place. Americans are accustomed to observing that both "black" and "white" Americans actually come in a range of colors and that, at their margins, the groups are very similar and in some cases indistinguishable. In the United States, some sexual mixing between people of different colors is certainly involved. But the modern gradient of colors among Americans is simply a re-creation of the range and gradient of colors that is visible elsewhere in the world among indigenous groups who have relatively little history of breeding with outsiders (other than their neighbors) and whose color can't possibly be explained by the recent mixing of historically "pure" races.

Human beings all have the same pigments, primarily melanin. The only question is how much pigment each individual has and how it is distributed in the skin. If scientists measured each person's color, assigned it a number, and plotted the result on a graph, they wouldn't get separate clusters with a few people in between; they would get something like the familiar bell-shaped curve in which a few people are at the very dark end, a few at the very light end; and the vast majority are distributed smoothly across the middle of the curve.

If one travels from central Africa to northern Europe, the *average* color of populations gets gradually lighter, and people vary within each population. (Despite some rather silly recent squabbling, ancient Egyptians weren't "black" and they were certainly not "white." Like most of humankind, they were a variety of intermediate shades on the spectrum—which white Americans usually lump together as "nonwhite.") If we travel north from southern India into central Asia or from southeast Asia to east-central Asia, people also get gradually lighter. But we never cross a distinct line between "black" and "white." Geneticists and anthropologists call this kind of gradual geographic transition in some trait a *cline*. We might refer to it less scientifically as a spectrum. Clines result from several factors. For one thing, neighboring populations tend to be historically related in kinship networks which decrease in intensity with increasing distance, producing graded levels of genetic similarity rather than abrupt boundaries. Groups also typically continue to intermarry with their neighbors, sharing genes in a pattern of decreasing similarity with increasing distance. This also tends to produce graded patterns of similarity, not abrupt boundaries.

Moreover, environmental conditions to which populations adapt are themselves often gradual in their distribution. For example, the intensity of ultraviolet light and the temperature change progressively with latitude, not abruptly. Hence the force of natural selection for any trait may be gradually stronger or weaker, not just present or absent. Gradual differences in the intensity of ultraviolet light have selected the subtle gradations in skin color seen around the world.

The pattern of graded colors is not so evident to Americans because of a historical accident. After 1492, America was colonized by people from the lightest and darkest ends of the spectrum, so we tend to think in terms of distinct colors. But our vision of separate colors is inaccurate and gives us a false sense of the separateness of human groups.

We can also see clines in many other traits. Noses don't come either broad or narrow; they get broader or narrower gradually (and again, on average) from region to region. Eyes get rounder or more almond-shaped in gradual degrees as we move back and forth from East to West in Eurasia. Look at pictures of people from eastern Russia and western China and try to decide, from the shape of their eyes (or any other trait), which "race" they belong to. Here again, the historical accident of American immigration fools us because we have sampled the westernmost (European) and the easternmost (Eastern Chinese, Korean, Japanese) populations of the Old World.

Even traits that have simple genetic bases (so-called discrete traits, like blood proteins, that are either present or absent rather than graded in any individual) still display clines. We can trace patterns of increasing or decreasing frequency of the A, B, and O blood-type genes around world; and although the sickle-cell gene is either present as one copy or two or absent in an individual, it shows up in varying percentages of individuals in various populations so that any given population cannot be characterized by the presence or absence of the gene but must be described in terms of its relative frequency.

Perhaps most important in terms of our perception and tolerance of one another, different traits do not cluster together in neat packages. The various stereotypical "racial" traits—not to mention the much larger array of invisible traits—do not correspond to one another around the world. The vast majority of the 50,000–100,000 gene pairs that make up the human blueprint don't seem to have any correlation with the 6–10 gene pairs that are believed to affect skin color. A person's blood type may be so dramatically different from that of the "similar" person sitting next to him or her in an African

American church, a synagogue, an Episcopal service, a mosque, a Shinto shrine, or even a KKK rally that a transfusion could be lethal. On the other hand, the likelihood of getting a safe transfusion would not be altered very much if the members of those groups were shuffled and redistributed randomly, because the various populations involved do not differ very much in their percentages of the main blood types. Getting a transfusion from a poorly chosen person of my own color could kill me; but with a little care I can safely get a blood transfusion from someone of any other color.

In fact, given the huge number of gene pairs that make a person, the small number that determine skin color, and the percentage of other known genes that appear to be completely unrelated to skin color, geneticists have calculated that a European American is likely to have as many genes in common with many or most black Africans (or any other group) as with most Europeans.

A very few visible (and some invisible) traits do correlate *partially* with skin color because in some groups the genes are partly "linked" (near one another in the strings of DNA or chromosomes) and therefore tend to be passed together from generation to generation. They may also "go together" because the same chemical, such as melanin, affects more than one trait. In some human populations (but not all), dark skin, dark hair, and dark eyes tend to go together because melanin is involved in all three characteristics. Traits may also be partially correlated if they are adaptive to different aspects or portions of the same environments, such as heat, humidity, and ultraviolet light. But the correlations are far weaker than our stereotypes imply, partly because chance is involved and partly because different environmental factors correlate only partly with one another. Hot climates and high levels of ultraviolet radiation often go together on our earth and some people are adapted to both; but people living on high mountains may have a heavy burden of ultraviolet light without much heat, and they will have a different adaptive package. Similarly, heat occurs with or without high humidity and with or without the risk of malaria, and the adaptive human package varies accordingly.

All of us have to be careful not to see too much correlation between visible features and to assume that other features are naturally part of the package. For one thing, most of us see only a tiny fraction of the human "packages" that exist around the world. On a world scale, black hair and dark eyes may sometimes go together, but that doesn't mean that they always do or that other "racial" features also correlate. A look around the world tells us that even among indigenous peoples, narrow noses and straight hair do not necessarily go with light skin and that even hair color is not as closely linked to skin color as we commonly think. For example, people with very dark skin in Australia and New Guinea may well have blond or red hair and it may be straight or wavy, rather than tightly coiled. Such individuals are too numerous and are described too early in the histories of their respective homelands to represent a mixture of "races." Besides, from what we know about "mixed" marriages in the United States and in Europe, this mix of traits does not result simply from interbreeding of "blacks" and "whites." People of African-European parentage never combine really dark skin with really blond hair. So apparently some other gene combinations are involved in the Australian case.

Native Africans, for the most part, don't fit the "Negroid" stereotype. They are highly variable in color, gradually lightening from the equator north (and, less dramatically, from the equator south) but showing lots of local variety. In addition, whereas skin color is related to ultraviolet light, noses, if adapted to the environment at all and not just a function of drift, are adapted to a combination of humidity and temperature and therefore have a different distribution. So some Africans have dark skin and broad noses (particularly in hot, humid West Africa, where much of the American slave population came from), but those who come from cooler, drier regions but still with intense UV radiation may have dark skin and very narrow noses. And because body shape is related to climate factors other than ultraviolet light, dark-skinned people may have either stocky builds or very long arms and legs. The sickle-cell trait is a characteristic not of "blacks" or "Africans" but of populations historically living in (some) malarial regions representing only a fraction of the African continent; it occurs in proportion to the significance of malaria in the environment as well as to a series of historical factors. Most African populations don't have the trait at all. Nor is it confined to Africans or dark-skinned people. Some "white" people in areas of Mediterranean Europe also have the gene, as do some in the Middle East, India, and southeast Asia, not surprisingly in areas where malaria is present. Similarly, the ability to drink milk is not a European "racial" marker. Many individual Europeans and groups of people usually considered "white" (such as Middle Easterners) are intolerant of milk; and although milk-drinking ability is rare among adults in African groups, some dark-skinned African populations (showing few if any signs of "race mixing") drink milk as adults. Not surprisingly, they are pastoralists who keep and milk dairy cattle.

In summary, each local population is a mix of highly varied individuals whose traits are some function of their genes and their environments. The actual function is extremely hard to sort out and is almost never known. Specific genes for adaptation to a particular environment may be common in certain populations; but in fact the vast majority of genes, like those for blood type, are highly mixed within each population and differ from population to population only in statistical terms. Geneticists have repeatedly asserted that there is more genetic variation within most local populations than between populations.

Each local population has a unique package of genes that tend to fit its local environment; but each environment may present a different package of challenges involving temperature, humidity, altitude, disease, and so forth. Populations whose environments involve different stresses have different genetic mixes. Each local population also has its own genetic history, its own pattern of interbreeding, and its own history of genetic drift accounting for the varied distributions of traits without obvious adaptive value.

Nothing in all of this suggests that we can predict most of a person's attributes by knowing his or her skin color or that the human population is naturally divided into a given number of major "races" which are distinct from one another in the majority of their attributes. Nor is there anything to suggest that any variations or any groups are innately superior across the range of human environments, as opposed to being adapted to specific problems in particular environments that continue to change.

The problem is that we create "races" in our minds. In order for us to *see* how complex the mix of human traits is, how many different combinations of traits there are, and how unique each individual is, we have to be willing to look at each other carefully. We have a very unfortunate tendency to *see* stereotypes, as well as to think in stereotypes because we subconsciously "correct" the faces we see to fit the models in our heads. (This phenomenon is well known to psychologists studying facial identification and eyewitness testimony.) A quick glance tells a "white" person that another person is "black."

Because in our society nothing else matters, the rest of the face gets filled in automatically, not by real visual inspection, but by a mental computer program in which "all African Americans look alike." If even the most visible, measurable human traits can be misclassified in this manner, imagine how easily we can misinterpret each other's subtle behaviors.

9. There is no evidence to suggest that differences in behavior or general ability or "intelligence" between different human populations or "races" are controlled by genes.

Individual human beings clearly differ in a range of ways that influence not just their health but also their behavior and performance *on specific tasks*. Some of these differences are obvious, like variations in the size and shape of the body, physical coordination, the quality of eyesight, or the ability to digest foods or fight off particular diseases. There may also be variations in the design or function of the brain or in the chemical factors that motivate us, or that affect behavior or the ability to solve certain kinds of problems. Few of the latter variations are known; but other biological functions vary slightly from person to person and may even vary statistically from group to group. So, there is no reason to assume, simply as a matter of faith, that brain functions or other specific abilities do not vary as well. However, allowing for the possibility of such mental variations among people and proving that they exist are very different things. Proving that they are genetic in origin is even more difficult.

In recent years the disciplines of sociobiology and evolutionary psychology have revived interest in the idea that our genes play a significant role in structuring our behavior. These disciplines are based on two quite valid premises. First, any animal's behavior must, at some level, be grounded in the structures and chemistry of its body and brain and, ultimately, in its DNA; and second, those behaviors must, at some level, be subject to the same evolutionary forces that have shaped our bodies.

The disciplines are also grounded in several valid observations: for example, that our behaviors are molded, at least in part, by our physical structures—the shapes and capabilities of our body parts. Sociobiologists note that our behaviors are guided—rewarded or punished, reinforced or erased—by our nerve endings and sensations, our taste buds, and even our endorphins (natural brain opiates). They note that some behaviors such as the making and recognizing of certain facial expressions are universal among human beings and appear even to be shared with other primates and other mammals, suggesting strongly that the ability to perform or recognize these behaviors is connected to our common genes. They note that some of our reactions, like responses to cute babies and children's faces, appear to be universal among human beings, transcending local cultures. They note that biological categories within human populations such as sex and age appear to have some behavioral characteristics that differ from one another but also appear to be consistent across human groups and even related animal species. (For example, it is common not only among people but among other primates and even other mammals that the young are driven to play whereas adults prefer mostly to watch, protect, or rest, if not occupied with an important task.) They note, too, that a few specific genes have been identified which may influence broad categories of behavior or gross, pathological differences in mental function.

The premises and many of the observations of sociobiology are valid, and many researchers whom I respect have adopted its ideas as key premises of their work. But sociobiology, correctly understood, has very little if any bearing on the issues of behavioral *differences* at the genetic level *among human groups* and their political implications. Talking about groups or "races" is not the same as talking about different species. It is not the same as discussing universal human behaviors, or even the behaviors of people of different ages or sexes. Age and sex involve far more profound and consistent biological differences than the differences between groups or "races."

There is also a good deal of confusion within sociobiology about the level at which genes can be said to cause or define behavior. Most sociobiologists would not claim that, outside of a few oft-cited examples, such as the perception of faces or the inherent human capacity for language, genes control specific human behaviors precisely. Even Richard Dawkins, author of *The Selfish Gene* and an outspoken advocate of sociobiology, considered extreme by many, offers a metaphor suggesting that genes determine the overall goals and limits of an organism but that brains carry out the strategy and make the day-to-day decisions. They have to, as he points out, because genes can't act rapidly enough. His metaphor involves space aliens who must use intelligent robots to conquer Earth because they themselves are too far away to control day-to-day tactical decisions. Brains, he implies, are the intelligent robots of genes. Sociobiologists who postulate genetic control of specific behaviors seem to me to be naive not just about human nature but also about the way genes function and about the standards of proof necessary to make such an argument. In addition, the idea that genes control specific behaviors denies the existence of choice, planning, consciousness, strategy, and flexibility—the most important characteristics of the human brain. This notion denies what we actually know about our own biology. Behavioral flexibility is the hallmark of our species.

One of the difficulties that has plagued sociobiology since its inception is the problem of defining the behaviors in question. For example, a key tenet of sociobiology is that natural selection ought to make animals "selfish." The initial intended meaning of this statement is almost obviously true. If natural selection favors animals whose bodies are well designed to promote survival and reproduction, it should also favor animals whose instincts "selfishly" promote those same goals. If you throw yourself in front of a lion to save your neighbors or unselfishly give away food that your own children need to someone else's children, those neighbors and those other children will prosper and reproduce in place of you and yours, and your genes may eventually disappear. So, over the years, natural selection will weed out any genes that promote such unselfish tendencies. On this basis, a good deal of important theorizing has been directed at figuring out how various behaviors address selfish needs and why animals or people ever do what look like altruistic or unselfish acts.

The problem is that "selfishness" is not a precise scientific concept (in contrast to proteins, height, blood types, and other physical variations we have good cause to think are linked to genes). *Selfish* is also a word that has different meanings to different people. Like any word, moreover, it may have different meanings when translated into different languages. It also embraces different sets of behavior in American culture than in other cultures. So having selfish genes doesn't necessarily mean that one is a capitalist or a miser. In sociobiological terms it means that one is motivated to do what serves one's long-term reproductive interest and those of one's family *in a particular natural or social context*. As the natural or social rules change, so, too, should the selfish behavior. Selfish motivation might even demand generosity if generosity generated long-term benefits (as it clearly does in some human societies). A successful animal is one that can be flexible about how it serves its selfish instincts. Selfishness, like the drive to avoid pain, may be universal and genetic, but the behaviors employed, at least by people and other mammals, are learned behaviors adjusted for specific circumstances. The best work in *human* sociobiology tries to show how the general goal of selfishness leads people to use their brains to seek efficient economic or protective strategies (such as the best hunting strategies) which maximize their chances of reproducing *in a particular situation, environment, or social system.* The definitions of selfish behavior depend not on genes but on circumstances.

The difficulty of identifying such vaguely defined behaviors is exacerbated by the fact that we tend to read our own social habits into our definitions. Proponents of genetic theories of behavior have a strong tendency to mistake American stereotypes about behavior for what is "natural" and "human." Often they don't check to see whether the behavior is universal or whether its expression in the American population is conditioned by particular cultural circumstances. If, as the popular media reported in 1995, a chemical variation in the brain has been found that conditions impetuous, novelty-seeking behavior and a low threshold of boredom, this does not mean that there is a gene for skydiving or wearing a lampshade on one's head at parties. Even in our own culture, people might choose instead to be impetuous in their travel or their thought and writing or their architectural design. And in other societies with other opportunities and other definitions of what is normal, genetically determined impetuousness would take untold other forms.

Similarly, whatever real genetic differences there are in the behavior of men and women (and there are some), our definition of those differences is clearly distorted by American cultural expectations about the way men and women ought to behave. Genes may predispose women to adopt reproductive strategies of investing heavily in a few offspring because they can only have a few (another theme widely discussed by sociobiologists), but genes don't limit women to being housewives or cheerleaders. Any glance at other cultures shows that women can be burdened with far more physical tasks and entrusted with far more professional and managerial tasks than our culture permitted until very recently. Are men naturally more aggressive risk takers and women coy and conservative, or are these simply American stereotypes and expectations? Even if men and women do "naturally" differ, they will inevitably express their respective tendencies in culturally defined ways.

To cite just one example of a misapplication of sociobiology, an article in *Discover* magazine in February 1995 reported that in a survey of personal ads, men sought younger women with beauty, and women sought older men with wealth—thereby validating sociobiological theory. The problem, of course, is that these expectations are also part of our culture and they are constantly reinforced in the media. In other cultures (and at other times in our own culture), men have sought wives on the basis of the size of their dowries, or their ability to do hard physical labor, and won social approval for being successful in their quest.

How do we distinguish natural, genetically determined behaviors from cultural patterns? The only way to decide what is natural and what is simply American style is to look at a wide variety of other cultures. (It is especially important to look at those that have not already been substantially remade in our own image by colonialism and the modern global media. For example, it may be very difficult to get a view of sex roles in different cultures because European conquerors rapidly brought sex roles into line with Western expectations. Women may have been more powerful in many other societies until the conquerors addressed their attention and trade exclusively to men.)

It is also particularly difficult to assess behavior when looking at other societies, because it will appear in unfamiliar shapes and because even trained observers can be blinded by Western cultural expectations. Despite the naive efforts of modern psychologists to identify "human" behavior patterns in largely white middle-class American college classrooms, looking at other groups of people is exactly what we must do to test whether behaviors are biologically rooted. The only way to eliminate culture and traditional learning as explanations for behavior patterns is to look beyond the limits of our own (or any one) culture—but we rarely do.

Demonstrating that particular behavioral variations among human groups are genetically evolved adaptations to differing environments would involve very careful definition of the behavior plus all the steps that were necessary to prove the significance of variation in the sickle-cell trait or skin color: precise definition of the trait; proof of genetic inheritance of the trait; knowledge of the gene and protein chemistry that contribute to the trait; recognition of the pattern of occurrence of the trait; correlation of that pattern with environmental variation; knowledge of the mechanism by which a trait functions in the environment and its adaptive value (if any). But those steps are almost never applied to hypotheses about the genetic basis of differences in behavior.

Further, I have pointed out that the genes that build our bodies are actually catalysts, not the determinants of our traits; that the environment contributes to the production of most traits; and that most genes are not uniform within groups but distributed in various frequencies in all groups. I have also pointed out that most genes do not correlate with one another in different populations and, specifically, don't correlate with skin color; and that genetic variations produce only very small differences between groups of people. If, then, most known genetic variation does not follow simple "racial" patterns, why should we conclude that hypothetical behavioral genes would behave differently and cluster in "races"? "Racial" explanations of patterns of behavior fly in the face of the known patterns of genetics.

It seems much more likely that, whatever behavioral propensities are built into the human species, their expression is shaped by local experience. For example, the natural opiates in the brain may be biological and genetically designed, but they clearly respond to arbitrary social and cultural messages. We feel good largely because members of our society give us positive feedback about ourselves when we do things of which they approve. Perhaps the most important message of sociobiology is that animals and people are designed to respond to social feedback.

Intelligence

Like many sociobiological concepts such as selfishness, impetuousness, and gender-specific behavior, intelligence is very hard to define precisely. Intelligence is also a subject where we tend badly to confuse what is American style with what is natural. The expectation that intelligence ought to manifest itself the same way, the American way, in different situations and cultures (and that if it does not, people are naturally inferior) is extremely naive. Intelligence is also hard to link convincingly to genes, particularly to genetic differences between populations.

Because thought processes must in some sense be rooted in the structures and chemistry of the brain, and because brains are as likely to show genetically based variation as other organs are, there is no reason to deny the possibility that inherited variations play some role in differing capabilities. There is no question, moreover, that intelligence, as we define and measure it in Western culture, tends to run in families, suggesting that genes may play a role in its development. As I will discuss more fully in chapter 6, however, it is not at all clear that intelligence is *one* thing or that the components of intelligence are all related to one or a few specific organic properties of the brain for which genes are known or can even be postulated. As in the case of other postulated behavioral genes, showing that intelligence is the result of genetic inheritance requires showing not just that a pattern of inheritance exists but also that identifiable genes produce identifiable variations in chemistry and structure and that these in turn have some definable effect on cognitive development. We have no such knowledge regarding intelligence. Genes have to work through definable organic pathways. They can't produce abstractions.

Moreover, a pattern of family inheritance does not prove that genes are involved, as there are many other modes of family transmission. We would all agree that human beings inherit language, religion, wealth, and even patterns of thinking from their parents without the intercession of specific genes. Our knowledge of the processes of genetic transmission from parent to child suggests that genes would actually be a relatively inefficient way for parents to pass on intelligence to their children. Cultural transmission would be much more reliable. In fact, the very strength of family transmission of intelligence may be an argument *against* genetic transmission. Continuous traits involving multiple genes, like skin color or stature (or, presumably, intelligence) will "breed true" if both parents come from a population that is completely homogeneous for that particular trait (e.g., all very dark or all very light skin). As both parents have the same genes, sexual recombination doesn't produce variety. But if a population is heterogeneous and the parents have different mixes of genes, recombination can produce surprising results—children who are much darker or lighter or shorter or taller than their parents or siblings. The genes for intelligence, if they exist at all, would have to fit the latter pattern, as there is clearly a complex array of intelligence within any population. If children inherit their parents' intelligence as surely as they inherit wealth or religion, it must be because the mechanism in all three cases is cultural.

As anyone knows who has watched a child develop, human brains are like computers that need extensive programming to function. The programming takes the form of experience and teaching. For example, it seems pretty clear that the genetic structure of the human brain contains the capacity for language and perhaps even for a universal core grammar. But the child still has to be supplied with one or more languages in order to use his or her capability, and any child can be supplied any language.

The biological structure and inherent capability of the brain itself presumably depend partly on genes (although with few exceptions we don't know what genes are involved). But it also, with much greater certainty, depends on a variety of environmental factors during growth, such as the presence of toxins or poisons in the atmosphere or in the child's own or the mother's diet, the chemistry of the womb, and the quality of prenatal and childhood nutrition. The level of functioning that is achieved, as in any computer work, depends both on the inherent capacity of the machine *and* on the quality of the programming that is provided. We know that the programming and the nutrition that children receive vary markedly. On the other hand, we do not know of any genetically coded variation in the size or structure of the human brain that affects intelligence within the normal range. So the presumption that one's intelligence is (mostly) in one's genes is highly premature at best and probably wrong.

Trying to separate the genetic, organic structure of the brain from the social and environmental input in its functioning is a staggeringly difficult task. We haven't begun to sort it out despite the empty claims by some recent participants in the discussion. We are a very long way from demonstrating that it is the circuitry of human brains themselves that is unequal or that unequal ability runs in groups. We are not even very good at measuring mental performance (let alone inherent ability) objectively.

Like the postulated behavioral genes of sociobiology—and for all the same reasons—genes for intelligence cannot run in "races." Real, known genes do not display such a pattern, so why should the hypothetical ones? In addition, as I have pointed out, genetic differences among people do not generally confer overall superiority or inferiority in biological design. Most advantages conferred by genetic differences are highly specialized for particular situations (like resistance to particular diseases) and lose their advantage when circumstances change. Moreover, there are thousands of such potential advantages and disadvantages, and individuals receive a mix. Local populations in turn are a mixture of individuals and most have as much variation within them as there is variation between groups. The overwhelming evidence of known genetics therefore suggests that we have to talk about finely divided abilities, fairly evenly distributed, not about some monolithic superiority such as the word *intelligence* implies. If the vast majority of many thousands of human variations have no correlation with "racial" features, why should intelligence show such an aberrant pattern? There is no reason to expect that an evolutionary process (or a Creator) that bestows physical advantages in such an evenhanded, specialized, temporary manner, and mixes them up so thoroughly, would suddenly confer some monolithic mental or behavioral superiority on a particular group. Such an idea simply does not accord with what we know of human variation, genetics, and evolution. Moreover, as I will discuss further in chapter 5, there is no evidence of such group superiority in human history.

CHAPTER THREE

Understanding the Rules People Live By: Cultural Systems and Cultural Variation

THE LARGE-SCALE VARIATIONS IN BEHAVIOR that we think we see among groups of people are often mistakenly attributed to biology or "race," yet, as discussed in the previous chapter, "racial" differences among people don't exist. Specific biological traits may occur in higher percentages in some populations than others. But these differences occur in a huge array of combinations, and they account for only relatively minor differences among people, which are important (that is, confer significant advantages or disadvantages) only in special circumstances.

Most variation among human groups is in fact caused by *cultural* differences. Cultural differences are far more important, pervasive, powerful, and intransigent than most of us realize. They are also far more valuable for all of us than most people (including many multiculturalists) understand. Other cultures add beauty, understanding, and meaning to our lives and could add far more if permitted to do so. We would all be poorer without them.

I hasten to add that I am not throwing in my lot with those who simply replace "race" with "culture" as an explanation of other people's alleged "inferiority." Cultures, like organisms, are not superior or inferior; they are simply different from one another, different mixes of qualities, strengths, and weakness, in different situations. The point is not that other people's cultures prevent them from being as "smart," healthy, and wealthy as white American, Japanese, or French individuals. Cultures vary in challenging and potentially rewarding ways, and different cultures may do different things well, but they are not "unequal" in the sense that some are inherently better than others. The inequality is in the ethnocentric eye of the beholder. We often cannot imagine that other people might prefer their ways to ours or derive satisfaction from things that appear to us to be "quaint" and "primitive," but they often do; and our ways often appear irrational to them. Cultural differences are not explanations of other peoples' "failures"; they are explanations of the intolerance, misunderstanding, and racism that groups of people often display toward one another. Cultures act as barriers to communication and understanding, not as limits to overall ability.

It is true that for the past four centuries, northern European cultures and Americans have taken the lead in advancing science and technology. But our lead represents the direction in which we have chosen to put our energies, not our superior ability. It is not synonymous with superior quality of life. Our lead also reflects only 400 years of the 10,000 years or so since human beings first adopted farming as a way of life, and most of the advances of civilization were contributed by other people. Our lead is already clearly dissipating, as happens to all such temporary advantages in human history. As I will show in chapter 5, we have a rather narrow and optimistic perception of the costs and benefits of the advances we have contributed and of our own overall significance in world history.

It is also true that some cultures—most, in fact—have been less militaristic than ours and less able to defend themselves or to commit large-scale aggression. Many have disappeared from the human record and many are currently subject to our domination or at least our powerful influence. But that is not an indictment of their human, moral, intellectual, or artistic value; they are not necessarily deficient in anything other than military prowess. Throughout human history, political success and dominance have been largely the result of being in the right place at the right time to receive the mantle and accumulated technology of other powers as they decline, combined with a desire for expansion and conquest. Political domination is a fact of life, but it doesn't reflect cultural quality; we can't extrapolate overall preeminence from military strength. Our aggressive sense of our own superiority, justified by misplaced and misunderstood social Darwinism, does not seem a very useful or desirable prescription for our future, let alone that of other people. There is too much of value to learn from other independent cultures, too much knowledge and richness to be shared. In the long run, variety and constant cross-fertilization of cultures are the only hope for success, adaptation, and survival in cultural evolution, just as they are in biological evolution.

It is true that some people are forced to expend an inordinate amount of their energy surviving conquest, colonialism, and discrimination and that the effort required to survive may drain their store of energy and resources for other purposes. We see the world's others in the condition to which they have been reduced by conquest and then conclude that we are seeing their inherent inferiority. The full weight of political oppression can affect many aspects of a culture far beyond its most obvious physical and economic consequences. That some cultures have been driven to the point of extinction by such pressures is not an indictment of the inherent worth of the people or their culture.

The important point is that every culture, including our own, limits or channels the perceptions and actions of its members in arbitrary ways, so that members of different cultures behave differently. Our own cultural patterns are as arbitrary and as limiting as any others. Given the politics of the modern world, it is *our* arbitrary cultural assumptions and limits that are the most dangerous. For this reason, I want to call particular attention to the narrowness of the mainstream culture in the United States, as much or more than to the foibles of any other group.

Culture, Society, Nation, and State

The word *society* as I will use it refers to a group of people who interact with one another. It can refer to groups interacting for a few special purposes, as in the case of clubs or "secret societies," but anthropologists usually use the word to refer to people who interact a great deal for much of their lives and for most of their life needs. In either case, *society* refers to the group itself and to the system of interactions among members rather than to the individual people. It is more than a simple aggregate of people. This distinction is important because a society can easily be at odds with its own members and often is. Currently, American society is in precisely this situation.

Particularly in the ancient world and in parts of the world that haven't been modernized, the boundaries of a society were or are frequently dictated by space and distance; you can't interact with people you can't see or reach, so your society consists of your neighbors. In the modern world, with all its communication and transportation technology, the boundaries of societies tend to be dictated by political boundaries—lines on a map—or by the direction of transportation and communication networks, rather than by simple proximity. This means that society often involves interaction with people we don't know and cannot see. It also means that a society can include individuals who have complex ties to other distant societies. This fact can complicate the problem of addressing social needs. For example, the transportation and communication networks of colonized or newly independent countries, like Kenya of the 1960s, often were designed to serve the needs of the mother country (in this case Great Britain) and to facilitate interaction with the mother country rather than among local citizens. Many colonial citizens considered that their first allegiance was to Britain not their neighbors. These patterns limit the (former) colony's ability to solve its own problems. As another example, multinational corporations today operate in a kind of society of their own that no longer conforms to geography or to the society in which the rest of us participate.

Culture, in contrast to society, refers to the mostly unwritten rules and conventions of thought, communication, and behavior that people use so that they can interact in an orderly way. People who interact agree tacitly (and are taught or socialized) to obey a common set of cultural rules in order to make their behavior mutually comprehensible, just as they agree and are taught to use a shared common language. So, in brief, societies are the organized groups of people interacting; cultures are the sets of rules, formal and informal, spoken and unspoken, that govern their behavior.

In the prehistoric world, before or outside civilization, societies and cultures tended to have the same boundaries: the group of people who interacted tended to share a common culture and to think of themselves as one group. Civilizations (large-scale societies bounded and defined by central coercive power) appeared about five thousand years ago, and the relationship between cultures and societies changed. Societies came to be defined by space, transportation, codified law, and power (often conquest) rather than by proximity and shared culture, and the sense of cultural unity was often lost.

In the modern world, anthropologists and political scientists often use the word *nation* to refer to people who are bound together by a common culture and feel as if they belong together (as when we refer to the Lakota [Sioux] Nation or the nations of the Iroquois that had no central governments). *States*, or countries, on the other hand, are legally defined political units, societies bound together and bounded by laws, lines on the map, and the power of the government, regardless of the culture(s) of their citizens. We like to think of "nation-states," in which cultural unity and legal boundaries are once again the same, as the ideal form of society. But, a major problem and source of tension in the modern world, with its changing political alliances and boundaries often set by force and conquest, is that cultures and political units often do not match. That is, at least in part, why the French and Germans fought for years for the allegiance of Alsace-Lorraine and why the Serbs, Croats, and Muslims of the former state of Yugoslavia now say they don't belong together even though they were united politically for many years. Unfortunately, politicians often play up cultural differences, generating tensions among people who could otherwise coexist peacefully in one state despite their differences, as many peoples around the world do.

The "melting pot" ideal, still widely held in the United States, is the hope that all people who come to be part of our society and our state would come to share the same cultural rules—to become one nation. The reality is that they haven't and probably never will. Cultural differences have always been more pervasive and more important even within the melting pot of the United States than we like to believe. Moreover, as I will show, the barriers to blending, on all sides, are far more powerful than we acknowledge. For many groups, blending has never been an option, despite the ideal and their best efforts. Many other groups don't want to blend.

There are many sets of cultural rules operating in different social groups in the United States, and that is a major cause of our mutual misunderstanding and intolerance. Here, too, however, cultural differences that need not create a barrier to peaceful, constructive interaction are sometimes exploited by political leaders for their own purposes, generating greater intolerance. Many early American settlers found Native American cultures to be no barrier to coexistence or even fusion; and many Native Americans tried to become members of European communities. Such coexistence and blending were discouraged and ultimately destroyed, however, by larger political and economic forces, and now we are taught only about the "inevitable clash of cultures." In a larger sense, distrust of other cultures is something we are taught, sometimes very purposefully.

The diversity of cultures within the American population persists not just because the many cultures brought by generations of immigrants have not yet "melted," or because the mainstream culture has not diffused or been taught successfully to everyone "yet." Teaching the American way more aggressively or insisting on teaching only in English won't create one nation. It may have quite the contrary effect. Nor is the melting pot the best or highest American ideal, as I will show. Diversity persists because cultures themselves often are resistant to such change or the inclusion of others and resistant even to the diffusion of some cultural elements.

A major feature of any set of cultural rules (clearly visible since the Stone Age at least 35,000 years ago, when regional art and artifact styles first appeared) is that they are used to make boundaries. One goal of all cultures is to be different, to mark one's distinction carefully, and to exclude "others," sometimes by denigrating them and by discouraging cultural borrowing. That appears to be one of the major purposes of art and fashion in any culture. Cultural variations persist in the United States partly because the mainstream society defines itself by keeping others (including its long-standing minorities) out and also because the minorities in turn define their special status, their sense of self-worth, by developing and maintaining distinctive cultures and by *not* participating fully in the mainstream culture. Refusal becomes a matter of conscious or unconscious pride and the survival of the sense of self and culture.

It is important to understand that societies and cultures (so-called sociocultural systems) are commonly designed to protect their own integrity and the coherence of the group. Such systems will defend their members if possible, but will sacrifice them if necessary (hence the tension between a society and its people). The unity of the society and the sanctity of the cultural rules apparently are more important than the survival of individuals. The Vietnam War-era chant "Better red than dead" (i.e., better to accept the communist way of life than to die in a nuclear war) said that individuals are more precious than the system. But the slogan was anathema to many Americans because our culture, like most, teaches exactly the opposite. We are taught the nobility of giving one's life for one's country, one's nation, one's way of life. And of course society regularly demands mortal sacrifice in a wartime draft and in other ways.

Other cultures also have rules that tend to protect the sociocultural system even if they inhibit or threaten individual members. No society protects everybody. Societies may sacrifice fetuses or infants, girls, the elderly, the poor, soldiers, deviants, or transgressors. And they commonly set up rules that rank the well-being of individual members below the sanctity of the group. The power of patriotic sentiment—often obeyed to the point of death—suggests how profoundly cultural constraints can shape individual behavior even when they go against individual self-interest or the kind of genetic selfishness that may be programmed into us (as discussed in chapter 2). Cultures are very powerful, and they constrain our choices.

What Does *Culture* Mean?

Culture is one of the least understood words in the English language. It once commonly referred to what we might now call high culture—a knowledge of and preference for the things preferred by the upper class. Culture was more or less synonymous with "quality." We said that a person had "culture" if he or she knew and appreciated works by Shakespeare, Rembrandt, Keats, and Mozart; ballet; expensive wines and foods. But we also said that people had culture if they enjoyed stylish clothing or ornament. These things were valued badges of exclusive upper-class status and some of them—especially those that were only fleetingly fashionable—drew some of their attraction from the status they symbolized, not their inherent quality. So even by this definition, culture was more about defining exclusive membership and providing rules of interaction for an in-group than providing an objective measure of quality.

More recently, thanks to anthropology and the multicultural movement in American education, there has been growing awareness of a more generic meaning of the word *culture*. We now say that every group has culture; that there is more than one in the world; and that no culture is superior to another in all its aspects. We might, of course, agree that one culture produces more beautiful pottery, painting, poetry, or music or more science than another. We might agree that one culture handles certain specific problems better than another, or has contributed more in an area of accomplishment over a period of time. We have a new appreciation of variety, and a sense that we should explore that variety before deciding what is best. The struggle between multiculturalism and classics in American education is a struggle about the relative value of exploring this variety as opposed to learning, repeating, or rehearsing the traditions of the mainstream. Both are important.

But even in the context of this struggle, our sense of what culture means and what variations in culture can contribute to our lives is usually limited to the most obvious expressions of culture—the trappings: "ethnic" foods, music, dance, poetry, literature, and technology. Modern multiculturalism mostly celebrates variety in such cultural *details*. In fact, culture is far more important and cultural differences are far more profound than either side of the multicultural debate seems to understand. The real meaning of cultural differences is both exhilarating and frightening—exhilarating because it opens up enormous new possibilities that can greatly improve and enrich our lives, frightening because it suggests that dealing with others is more complicated and more subtle than we thought and because it threatens some of our comfortable assumptions about ourselves and about "truth."

In order to understand what culture really is we can begin with a simple analogy. We know that everyone must use a language to function fully in human society. Without a language, some major capabilities of the human brain have no program with which to operate. We know also that there are many possible languages and that the choice of language is an arbitrary convention or agreement—it doesn't matter what language people in any particular place speak as long as they agree to speak the same one. Any language involves arbitrary rules about how to speak, sign, or write which serve no purpose except to foster mutual comprehension. The rules help people to be consistent and predictable within their group. The arbitrary and conventional nature of language is demonstrated by the fact that every language changes constantly, though not so dramatically that mutual comprehension is lost. It is not clear that one language is "better" than another (although one language may have a larger vocabulary list than another *in specific areas* because the people who use it find those areas of special interest).

To get some idea of how difficult it is to rank languages in terms of quality, how much they change, and how arbitrary the idea of "correct" language is, recall that French (which in recent centuries has epitomized "high culture" among Europeans and many colonized populations) was originally a lower-class regional dialect of Latin. One might call it "ghetto Latin" except that it originated in a conquered province, not in an inner city. (You can almost imagine Roman nobility contemptuously dismissing the poor grammar and bad pronunciation of the ignorant colonials.) So using "proper" French or English grammar may help you to be admitted to certain social circles, à la *My Fair Lady,* but it doesn't have anything to do with good or bad (functional or dysfunctional) language per se. And even its capacity to gain its user social acceptance is fleeting: what is "proper" at any one time doesn't have much permanence as a badge of social status.

We also know that the various words and constructions of a language often do not translate readily into another language—not because the second language is inferior but because words and expressions in each language often have unique packages of meaning and nuance which have no exact counterpart in any other language. For example, the French word *honneur* does not have exactly the same meaning as the English word *honor,* even though we usually translate one as the other as the best approximation. The French and the English have slightly different things in mind when they use the terms. The qualities implied are not the same in the two cultures. Translating one as the other can lead to slight but potentially significant misunderstanding—even though there may be no better translation available.

We live in a world of infinite variety. In order to make communication possible, each language carves up that universe of variation and groups things into a finite list of vocabulary words, so it is not surprising that different languages don't always group things in exactly the same way. Each word represents a category or cluster of meanings. The word *blue* actually refers to a wide and arbitrarily bounded range of wavelengths of light along a continuum of wavelengths we call the spectrum. Although the word *blue* can be translated from one language to another, the translated word will not have the same boundaries because not all people or languages would agree on where blue ends and green or violet begins. And not all languages will agree that the spectrum comprises only six colors as we arbitrarily divide it. Many will have no single counterpart to our category "blue." Misunderstanding is obviously likely to occur. The same problems will attend the translation of any other word.

We also know that a newborn baby can learn any language (or languages) that its caretakers speak (or sign) to it. In other words, what language one speaks is determined purely by what one learns. There is no indication that any newborn baby cannot learn any language it is taught, or (except perhaps for deaf children) cannot learn to pronounce sounds correctly. There is no indication that the choice of language is in our genes, even if the human capacity for language itself clearly is. This proposition has been tested millions of times through the experience of adopted children, who grow up speaking their adoptive parents' language. Immigrant Americans often speak with an accent because they learned English as adults, but their children don't (except perhaps the accent of the region of the United States where they grew up). Similarly, the peculiar sound (to the American ear) of Australian English can emerge perfectly from the mouth of an Australian-born person whose roots are obviously African or Asian.

Even the sound system of each language is arbitrary. Children of any genetic group can pronounce the sounds of any language successfully. But of all the sounds the human mouth can make, each language uses only a limited number to convey different meanings. (Linguists refer to all the various possible sounds as "phones," using the term "phoneme" to refer to the much smaller set of sounds that convey differences in meaning and that people listen for or hear in any particular language.) What is particularly important in this context is that after childhood we cannot easily shift from one sound system to another. Often, adult human beings can no longer easily make *or hear* the free-ranging sounds of childhood because they have been trained not to do so and no longer have the flexibility to master any system of grammar and sound. Adult Japanese people find it difficult to speak English without an accent because (among other things) the Japanese language does not make the same distinction English makes between the *l* and *r* sounds, so that children in Japan never learn to hear or pronounce the two sounds distinctly or accurately by English standards. Similarly, speakers of Persian don't use the sound *w* represents in English and have trouble distinguishing between or pronouncing the English *v* and *w*. Even those who have spoken English for years occasionally confuse *wail* or *whale* for *veil* in oral communication. English speakers have the same trouble with French because we don't hear or learn to make the subtly distinctive sounds of the different phonemes that mean so much to understanding French. Most Americans not only have trouble making the sounds of other languages, we have trouble comprehending that other sounds exist, that the sounds of English are not the obvious, "natural" sounds of human speech. That is why we sometimes feel that foreigners are speaking gibberish. It is also why an English speaker trying to communicate in French with a French person (and not being understood) is likely to assume that his listener is being purposely difficult, snobbish, or rude. Because the English speaker is making every distinction in pronunciation that he can hear, he can't understand that the French speaker is waiting to hear a different set of sound distinctions in order to comprehend the intended meaning.

Culture is analogous to language in all these ways. First, everyone has a culture and must have one to be human. Culture is a human universal. Like languages, cultures change over time; like languages, they are coherent systems of interrelated parts; like languages, they are probably equal to one another *as structures* even though the political standing of their societies may differ. And, like the rules of a language, the rules of a particular culture are largely arbitrary conventions designed to add coherence and predictability to the interactions of a particular group.

Of course, all cultures must conform to nature and the biological needs of human beings to survive. If people don't eat, reproduce, avoid biological damage, and manage illness correctly (often within broad limits), they don't survive. But, there are many cultures that can make human beings sufficiently successful biologically to perpetuate the society and culture.

Trying to sort out the reasons for the variety of cultures is a complex historical problem similar to the problem of explaining biological diversity. Many of the differences among cultures reflect a history of adapting to specific conditions, just as some biological differences do; but many cultural differences, like many biological ones, are simply a reflection of random change, the history of individual groups, and the selective diffusion of ideas from one group to another. (And some, as I have mentioned, represent conscious efforts to be different from neighbors or conquerors.)

We also know that cultures are learned and are not in people's genes. A newborn child of any biological origin or genetic makeup can learn and become fully competent in its adoptive parents' culture without having any sort of cultural "accent" or limits—if it is permitted to do so. The child does not automatically display some foreign, genetically based cultural tendencies that betray its ancestry any more than it speaks with the accent of its genetic homeland (unless, of course, it is driven by social pressures to try to maintain or recapture its "roots"). Adult immigrants may never fully learn the American way of life; but their children grasp it readily if they choose, and may soon excel, just as they can speak flawlessly whatever version of English (or another language) they are taught. They can become fully integrated members of any society—as long as the sociocultural system permits them to do so (often it doesn't) and as long as their parents' sociocultural system does not discourage their integration too strongly (as it often does).

Cultures, like languages, also may not translate perfectly item by item into one another. There may be no clear, appropriate correspondence between the elements of two cultures any more than there is a perfect correspondence in meaning between words in two languages. For example, we may be able to identify the roles of teacher or doctor and the cultural rules which define each in another culture; but not only will the particular rules not be the same as ours, neither will the division of labor or the boundaries between the two roles. So translating the idea and reality of teaching or healing from one culture to another may be misleading. Similarly, we may identify the "religion" of a Pacific Island population, but that doesn't mean that the activities we are describing are exactly analogous to religion as practiced in our society or that they have the same purpose or fulfill the same functions. (This is one reason that people are often reluctant to change religion and often maintain their old religious practice, openly or in secret, even after they have converted to, say, Christianity. Christianity does not do all the things for them that the other religion did.) We cannot simply substitute one religion or one economy, one father role, chief, or even food from one culture for another because the bundles of meanings and purposes bound up in two religions or two chiefs or even two foods may not be the same. We have found that people offered modern medicine may prefer their own, even though the technological superiority of Western medicine seems obvious to us. Traditional African healers (often referred to as "witch doctors" or "medicine men") actually accomplish a number of important social purposes as part of their healing activities that Western medicine does not replace. They act as mediators, social therapists, psychotherapists, support groups, and so forth, doing things our doctors don't do or, for the most part, did not do until recently. If we simply try to substitute a Western doctor for a traditional healer, we not only miss these other social functions but also fail to comprehend the different but valid sense of illness and curing that the African groups have. The substitutes often don't quite match up to what they replace, even if they offer other benefits.

Lack of understanding of this feature of culture on the part of colonizers (accompanied, of course, by the use of force to promote change) did untold damage to colonized populations. New rules for families ended up weakening valid traditional family structures. Mistranslations and misunderstandings about ownership and land tenure (discussed more fully below) deprived indigenous peoples of their land and livelihood.

However, the similarity between culture and language goes further. Anyone who has struggled to learn a language knows that language consists not only of vocabulary but also of a series of rules, a structure for using the vocabulary that is usually called grammar. Grammar tells us how to order words to convey meaning, how to shape the words and fit them together so that others will know what meaning is intended.

Grammatical aspects of language, like sound systems and vocabulary words, are arbitrary conventions. We may agree to say "is not" rather than "ain't" when speaking "correctly," but we could, equally, prefer the reverse with no loss in meaning.

In English, words almost always go in the order subject-verb-object to convey meaning. "Man bites dog" and "Dog bites man" have different meanings. But English makes no clear distinction in form between subject and object. *Dog* and *man* each sound the same and are spelled the same regardless of how the words are used. But identical meanings can be conveyed in different ways. In Latin, the words may be arranged in a variety of ways; the subject is distinguished from the object not by order but by the ending attached to each word and the form of the verb. In contrast to English and Latin, Swahili uses prefixes to show relationships. Just as we become captives of the sound system of our own language, so we become captives of its grammar. We have a hard time imagining alternative ways to organize a sentence unless we have studied a foreign language. And even then, because Americans almost always study Indo-European languages, we have a hard time imagining a way to divide up reality other than by our arbitrary convention of dividing it into distinct nouns and verbs.

We accept the arbitrary limits imposed by grammar rules and sound systems in order to gain consistency. But the limits are not just those we accept consciously, the way we study grammar. Most of the rules are never consciously spelled out. Adults (even those who were poor at "proper" grammar in school) use a consistent grammar and shape words or arrange them in their learned grammatical order without thinking. Grammar rules act as "blinders" that limit our ability not only to use other languages but to recognize the possible existence of variation. The arbitrary rules of pronunciation, vocabulary, and grammar actually *limit* free expression—and that is their purpose: they tell us what words, what sounds, and what word combinations we may not use if we wish to be comprehended by our neighbors. Language limits our freedom to express and to comprehend the full variety of human expression in order to provide mutual comprehension within each society.

Cultures are like languages in this respect, too: they differ not just in their obvious trappings or specific items, their inventory or "vocabulary"—their foods and dances. They differ in more basic and subtle ways, analogous to grammar. What we might call the "grammar" of culture includes patterns of thinking, logic, perception, expression, the construction of "logical" categories, goals, values, ideals, morals, rhythms, emotions, and probably even psychological structure. And these grammars are just as arbitrary and just as constricting as the rules of language. Most of us cannot imagine cultural systems that are different from the one in which we were raised.

Cultural rules structure human thought and behavior (and limit our perception) just as surely as grammatical rules structure and limit language. Cultural rules act as blinders to keep us looking in the correct (i.e., the agreed) direction. These rules inhibit our freedom far more than political coercion does. Just as the learned sounds of English begin to seem "natural" and those of French "unnatural," so we come to believe that our arbitrary, conventional system of thought and conduct (our culture) is the only correct or natural way to behave. For example, as I hinted in my discussion of sociobiology in chapter 2, even scientists tend to assume that American sexual patterns or sex roles must be the "natural" "human" way, failing to explore the possibility that they are just cultural conventions (which to a large extent they are). Other "truths" that we hold as if there were no conceivable alternative are also conventional cultural rules, which deserve more thoughtful study. But without training we can't even perceive or conceive of the alternatives.

Comprehending how much of our own cultural system is arbitrary is perhaps the hardest lesson we have to learn. Just as learning English as a baby makes some sounds seem natural and others unnatural to us in later life—so that it is hard even to hear the distinction people are making in some other language—being raised in middle-class American culture (or any other culture) makes it hard to comprehend other people's thinking and behavior. Worse, socialization can make us blind to the very existence of alternatives, reducing our tolerance of other cultures and our ability to think critically about our own assumptions. We assume that people who don't speak or behave as we do are ignorant or stupid. We assume that they are trying to be just like us but are failing in the attempt.

What Cultures Have in Common: Shared Content and Structure

Human cultures are enormously varied. At the same time, because of universals in human biology (including brain structures) and broad similarities in the earth's physical environments, they share a number of features. All cultures provide solutions to certain common problems although they may accomplish them in different ways.

Over the years, in trying to understand what is universal to cultures and what is not, anthropologists and sociologists have made a number of attempts to define the shared content of different cultures or sociocultural systems. The lists vary but show a common core. (Members of other cultures would undoubtedly make other lists, dividing their world differently—if they bothered to make lists or divide at all!) I have freely adapted various approaches in order to convey certain ideas; but my framework of categories, arbitrarily dividing up a large and tangled complex of human behavior, is not intended to be exhaustive or immutable. It is intended only as a basis for thought and discussion.

1. All sociocultural systems provide for the biological needs of some of their members.

All societies, if they are to survive, must keep at least some of their members alive and feed and protect them (although few if any societies in history have protected everyone). Because people die, all societies also must find ways of replenishing their numbers. Almost all get new members by procreation; and all have rules or at least guidelines about when to permit or encourage members to have babies and how many they should have. (It is theoretically possible, of course, for a society to avoid procreating and get new members only by recruiting adults, as some religious orders do. But few societies chose this option.)

With minor exceptions, basic human survival needs are pretty much the same everywhere; but the common biological needs of human health and survival can be met in a variety of ways. For ex ample, people can obtain or produce their food through hunting, fishing, gathering wild vegetables, farming, or engaging in various kinds of economic specialization and trade. Their choice is dictated in part by the local environment. Hunting, fishing, and farming each can only be performed in certain places and the choice of prey or crops depends on the local environment; subsistence by trade alone is possible no matter how desolate the region if that region has a marketable resource (such as oil) and is connected to trade routes. Cities that are too large to produce their own food but located for the convenience of trade and transportation can support themselves by supplying special services to people who produce food.

The size and density of the population also helps determine the way food is provided. For example, farming supports more people per square mile than hunting does, and the style of farming is adjusted in part to population size. But many economic choices, including preferences for certain prey or certain crops, are arbitrary, dependent on other cultural choices, or a function of historical patterns.

In addition, every culture also has food rules that seem quite arbitrary to others. We have yet to find a human society anywhere in which people eat everything that scientists pronounce edible or don't find repugnant things that other people eat. (Americans aren't the only ones who consider certain food choices beneath us. Some African groups that eat things that horrify us find the practice of eating small mammals, as Daniel Boone and many American pioneers did, quite repugnant.) In fact, when groups with different cultural traditions are in prolonged contact with one another, they often use food choices, their "cuisine," as a way of establishing and reinforcing separateness and group identity. Thus steak and potatoes or the Thanksgiving turkey reminds mainstream Americans of our common heritage and reinforces our pride in being American, and, often, we choose to eat them even if other foods are available.

Every society also makes rules about maintaining health and hygiene with some seemingly arbitrary mix of empirical observation, superstition, politics, economics, and taboo, a subject to which I shall return.

2. All societies develop principles of ownership and exchange which both move goods and help define social ties.

We think of economic exchange as a market system in which goods are exchanged on a fairly impersonal basis for maximum gain or profit. But in many societies, exchange depends first and foremost on customary rules and expectations and preexisting social ties, and it serves to reinforce those social ties rather than to provide a profit. In this system, governed by reciprocity, the goods or services provided by one party may be exchanged for a diffuse, nonspecific kind of future obligation (friendship, assistance) and for affection and respect. They don't demand the immediate exchange of something of equal or greater monetary value. In some market systems (in parts of the contemporary Middle East, for example, or in other nonindustrial urban societies) there are specialized merchants who sell for money, but kinship or friendship networks are still relied on heavily to generate trust and the obligation to deal fairly. People buy from friends or kin instead of shopping for the best price.

In other societies, exchange may be centralized in a redistribution system, without a market or a profit motive but with a central collection point similar to the American tax system. People give or are taxed a portion of their wealth or production, which can then be redistributed to others as needed or used for group projects. An organizer or chief, although he may act as the collector, may not become wealthy. He may in fact be rich in prestige (and he may be very "fit" in biological terms). But he is often poor in material goods (rather like the person in our own society who collects from everybody else to make a group purchase but often ends up spending more out-of-pocket because the collections don't quite equal the cost).

Definitions of ownership, its rights and obligations, also differ markedly from society to society, just as they vary from context to context in our own society, depending on what goods are owned and who else is involved. For example, in American society, in which private property has an almost sacred connotation, the rights of exclusive ownership nonetheless tend to be more limited when dealing with friends and kin, who have a claim to share. It should not surprise us, therefore, that other groups of people for whom friends and kin comprise a larger portion of the society have less exclusive private property. It is important to note that organization by friendship, family, and kinship is not limited to the smallest or most "primitive societies." Many large historic and modern states retained kinship as a means of organization for many purposes.

Anthropologists have even defined the concept of "tolerated theft" to explain some economic behavior in small societies. People have a right to share or borrow your possessions (of certain kinds), and they exercise that right by taking things, often presuming on the social relationship—and you are socially obligated to tolerate the act even if it annoys you. But such theft is not anarchy. It has rules that are known to the members of the group. One anthropologist I know once wore a prized necklace while doing anthropological fieldwork, unconsciously counting on American principles of ownership to protect it. It was almost immediately "stolen" by someone who, according to the rules of etiquette in the group, admired the necklace, said, "Can I wear it?" and removed it from the anthropologist without waiting for an answer, rather like a pushy friend or sister in our society. (I say "sister" because even in American society, men and women have different rules for such sharing.) In this way, the necklace traveled all around the group, each person waiting the proper interval and then "stealing" it from the last, until my friend, using the new rules she had learned, stole it back, put it on—and later put it out of sight. In such groups, a hunter returning with a large kill would simply assume that other people, particularly kin, had the right to a share, like relatives at a family picnic.

Rules governing the ownership of basic resources such as water and land are even more varied. In the United States, we assume that farmers retain the ownership of land even when it is fallow. But many African farmers, before contact with Europeans, had a different set of rules. In many areas, land reverted to group or public ownership when not in use, and each family had the right to claim a piece of public land, farm it, and "own" it while they farmed it. Such systems created great confusion in European minds about who "owned" the land and whether it was "in use" or was available to be taken, sometimes as a matter of good-faith misunderstanding. The concepts of ownership and of fallow land were real in both cultures, and the appropriate words could be "translated." But both sides failed to recognize that the translations were not really conveying equivalent meanings. And, of course, because Europeans had the military power, they most often took the land anyway.

In Australia, the British used a legal doctrine called *terra nullius* (the land of no one) to claim the land of Aboriginal peoples. They asserted that because the Aboriginals did not farm or fence the land (didn't do the things the English recognized as establishing ownership), it didn't really belong to anyone and could be taken, despite the fact that the Aboriginal groups, although mobile, used the land, had defined areas that they exploited and cared for, and had their own rules of access. They just didn't define private property the same way the British did. European settlers in the Americas similarly saw the land inhabited and used by Native Americans as largely empty and open to claims of ownership by anyone who cleared and plowed it. They didn't recognize Native American systems of use rights or territorial markers. One has to wonder what the Native Americans thought Peter Minuit actually intended in his famous "purchase" of Manhattan Island for twenty-four dollars. The idea that permanent ownership of land could be transferred in that manner would have been completely foreign to the indigenous groups, and they weren't fools, as the story casually implies. Given the problems of accurate translation and what we know of indigenous exchange, they most likely thought they were being given a gift in honor of the friendship that had been established or in return for granting temporary use rights!

3. All societies have cultural mechanisms for decision-making and the enforcement of rules.

These functions, analogous to our government, legal system, and police, may be carried out in various ways. In small groups, decisions can be reached by consensus in democratic town meetings, as was true historically in the United States and occasionally still is. "Primitive" groups, therefore, often use what we consider the purest form of democracy.

The lack of *written* laws in small groups reflects the ease of communication and consensus, not ignorance. As I will discuss in chapter 5, written laws are necessary in large civilized conglomerates of people who never see each other; but small groups do better without them because unwritten rules have the advantage of flexibility to conform to individual problems.

In some societies, decisions may be formulated by leaders who can only state the consensus or mold it but have no power to dictate or enforce the rules. Such leadership is common to many organizations in American society. Or, rules can be determined by the authority of autocratic kings—largely a "civilized" and not a "primitive" way to do things, as only civilized groups give their leaders the power of coercion by force. European conquerors often made autocratic kings out of "native" leaders with more modest powers because they mistranslated the meaning of leadership as defined by the group—and because autocratic kings could better serve the Europeans' purposes while the Europeans provided military support.

A modern example of the inability to translate the idea of leadership from culture to culture became evident during the Iranian revolution of 1979 when American commentators tried in vain to find an English translation or equivalent for *ayatollah*, a title bestowed on the most learned and pious of Shi'a Muslims, to whom other believers look for guidance in political as well as spiritual matters. The term does not translate into any American categories. It defies our pigeonholes in ways that are crucial to mutual understanding and successful interaction.

Punishment for an infraction of the rules can be as subtle as the collective cold shoulder or ostracism or as violent as death. Or in a way less familiar to us, punishment can be accomplished by the eventual arrival of disease on the guilty party. We would call this a coincidence; many groups would not. For them, illness is an integral part of the political system. And, it is important to note that illness probably punishes evildoers at least as surely and as often as our police and judicial systems catch and punish them. (After all, unlike the police and courts, disease and death *will* certainly strike eventually and will punish the guilty.) In all sociocultural systems, the *perception* that the infraction of the rules will be punished is more important than whether punishment is actually and accurately meted out. Besides, punishment by disease is cheap to "administer" and implies divine involvement, perfect judgment, and an all-seeing eye (sort of like traffic control by airplane). It may help to avoid perpetuating social divisiveness by putting the blame for punishment on an outside force, and may avoid setting up patterns of individual or family hatreds or retribution. Such retribution as does occur tends to take the form of casting spells to create another illness, rather than physical violence.

4. Cultural rules organize shared communication.

Cultures define the rules of communication, including not only formal language but also a variety of subtler, less conscious means of communication, such as body language, the manual and postural cues by which we give additional meaning to spoken words. Some such gestures appear to be shared by all human groups, but others vary from group to group.

Words always have a formal meaning that appears in dictionaries, but most also have informal, but culturally defined, secondary meanings—connotations—that do not appear in formal listings but that one must know to communicate successfully. Culture also defines the conventional (colloquial) ways in which we express certain ideas; and it regulates how the meanings of words change in different contexts, such as when different subjects are discussed or when different persons are speaking. We all know that certain people can say certain things and be understood, while others using exactly the same words will not be understood or will be considered offensive—but few of us consciously work out the rules. (One rule that is clear is that members of a minority group can refer to one another affectionately using terms that are offensive when used by someone of a different group.)

During the Iranian hostage crisis of 1979–81, some Iranian Americans who spoke fluent Persian were appalled at the translations provided by American television—not so much because the basic words were mistranslated (although this is obviously a situation in which the imperfect correspondence of words might be critical) as because the translation missed or misrepresented various aspects of the context and nuance essential to true understanding. The respectful form, "Mr. [Jimmy] Carter" in Persian, as spoken by Ayatollah Khomeini, often came across as a disrespectful "Carter" in translation. And television audiences were bombarded with images of crowds and told that they were chanting "Death to Carter" or "Death to America" without being told that the chant was no more a literal threat or wish than "Kill the umpire!" or "Go to hell!" in contemporary English.

Shirley Brice Heath (in *Ways with Words*) provides similar examples of miscommunication in American schools (a context that will be important in the discussion of IQ tests in chapter 6). For example, when a teacher says, "Is this where this book belongs?" the students are supposed to go past the literal meaning of the question to the idiomatic meaning: "Put it away!" But not all American children are taught the idiomatic meaning at home even if they speak perfectly good English, so they respond in an inappropriate manner.

The subtlety of the cultural basis of communication helps explain why someone who has learned excellent French in a classroom instead of on the street still has a lot of difficulty communicating with Francophones who don't speak "correct" French any more than even the best educated of us speak correct English in our everyday transactions. It also helps explain why someone who has learned English in the "inner city" may have trouble in school or with IQ tests, where the conventional usage of words and expressions may be different from what he or she is accustomed to.

Culture also teaches us to use different metaphors in expressing ourselves. We commonly substitute a word or image with related meaning for the word or image we really intend ("He can't see the forest for the trees," "That is a whale of an idea"). In fact, our language is peppered with metaphors even when we don't consciously intend them. Members of our culture know the patterns and make the translation in their heads. People fluent in classroom English but lacking knowledge of current metaphors in a particular subculture will fail to understand. Moreover, they may not know when they are hearing a metaphor and when they are being given literal meaning. Meanwhile, we may become so accustomed to a particular metaphor that we forget its power to mislead.

In addition (and of great importance for issues such as IQ tests), we use conventional modes of symbolic representation to convey meaning in drawings, pictures, and poetic expression. It seems obvious to us that a drawing or photograph "stands for" a certain thing—because we were taught what it means, often before we can remember—but we forget how much culture intrudes. For example, to us "small" in a drawing means "far away," and a vertical line can represent a horizontal road extending to the horizon; but you have to be taught those conventions to get them right. In other artistic traditions, the size of a figure may signal its social importance rather than its distance from the viewer. People of different cultures tend to succumb to different optical illusions because the "illusion" demands familiarity with particular cultural conventions. In other cultures, as among some modern artists, the goal may be to capture the spiritual or visual essence of an object rather than to represent it naturalistically—making it hard for the uninitiated to recognize it. Or, if naturalistic representation is the goal, different attributes may be presented because no artist can portray everything. Interpretation of drawings relies on conventions that have become so common that we don't even think about them.

Communication extends beyond language and beyond symbols that are intellectually received. There seems to be a universal human need to express a sense of self, beauty, and the full range of human experience and emotion that cannot be easily verbalized. Such communication we refer to variously as art, music, dance, expression, creativity, poetry, and so forth.

Although artistic expression exists in every culture, these forms of expression are, in many ways, as conventional as language itself. They obviously vary markedly from culture to culture. Moreover, whether European opera, Japanese Kabuki theater, abstract painting, rock 'n' roll music, Balinese dance, or Aboriginal body painting, their meaning and value may be fully realized or appreciated only by people initiated into a particular culture.

Yet these are the aspects of culture that have been relatively easy for us to share. Americans and many other groups of people seem to have a common hunger to expand their expressive capabilities. Americans recognize, in this sphere more than any other, that other people and other cultures are able to express themselves in ways that we cannot. So historically mainstream white America added jazz to its classical music tradition, and some Americans enjoy Chinese paintings because they supplement the expressive capabilities of the mainstream culture. The modes of artistic expression of other cultures reach and touch us, even if we don't necessarily derive the same meaning and appreciation from those art forms as those steeped in their culture of origin. (This seems to be true of many Americans. It may be part of our cultural grammar to be receptive to outside inputs in this particular arena while being closed to others. Culture itself dictates what we will receive or reject from other cultures.)

In order to reach us and touch us, other people's modes of artistic expression have to be available to us. Sometimes we denigrate other cultures because we cannot see what they produced—because what they said or composed was not written down and what they painted was drawn on perishable materials. The Homeric poems have enjoyed enduring fame; but their renown is possible only because, long after the poet(s) lived, someone wrote down existing versions. These transcriptions probably were only pale shadows of the original performances, but if they had not been written down, we would never have known them. Oral traditions, stories, and epic poems abound in the cultures of literate and nonliterate peoples alike. Most have not been written down, or the written version has been destroyed, often by zealous European protectors of Christian culture. We cannot simultaneously value Homer and say that those other cultures produced nothing of value.

All cultures also create symbolic, supernatural worlds with which they enrich their lives, seek comfort or help with troubles, entertain themselves, unite their community, reinforce correct behavior, and attempt to facilitate their decisions and solve their problems. The symbolic world explains events and natural patterns that defy their (or our) rational analysis and provide a sense that people can manipulate things that are otherwise beyond everyday control. Such symbols have enormous power over people's lives.

5. Cultures provide rules that organize the specific interactions of particular people.

Cultures provide the definition of what sociologists call roles and statuses—the rules by which we sort out and predict one another's behavior as individuals. Roughly, *statuses* are the various positions one can occupy, and *roles* are the behaviors expected of a person in each position; but the term *role* is now popularly used to refer to both the position and the behavior. In a small society the definitions are relatively straightforward. Every other individual is personally known and the person's behavior can be predicted from knowledge of the individual's family, age, sex, and personality. Kinship is commonly a major determinant of status and role.

When we deal with large numbers of strangers we have to add more rules to help us keep track of roles. For example, students who have never seen me before and have no way of predicting how I will act have to expect that, as a college professor, I will act professorial in a classroom or my office—like a teacher and not a wrestler, a boyfriend, or a salesman, even though those are perfectly acceptable behaviors in other times or places. The only thing students need to know about me, at least at the outset, is that I am a professor. I play along, dressing and acting in certain ways (at least around the college) so that I can be identified as a professor. And I have to remember what role I am playing at any particular time—professor, father, fishing buddy, husband, neighbor—because my actions have to be different in each role. Each role, of course, is an *inhibition* of my freedom to act however I please. Any individual plays several roles: some, like "professor," are *achieved* through one's own efforts; others, like membership in a "racial" group or social class, are *ascribed* to the individual at birth. Once we have recognized that certain people have the status of father or college professor, or member of a "race" or class, and defined appropriate role behavior, the roles and statuses become the basis of expectation. In short, we stereotype people to make sorting and prediction possible. To this degree, the ability to group and pigeonhole people is an essential part of any person's adaptation to large-scale society; otherwise, we wouldn't know what to expect or how to act when we met many people. But such stereotypes become dangerous if they cease to be merely useful initial recognition signals for individuals, or guidelines for behavior *in specific situations* or roles and become permanent traps that automatically govern all of a person's activities, rather than just a special set. They also become dangerous when they are applied to *involuntary* membership in social categories like classes or "races." All blacks (or all whites) "look alike" to people of the other groups because in American society, historically, for most purposes, color was all one had to notice in order to pigeonhole someone and to know what behavior was expected—hence our tendency to see stereotypes, as discussed in the previous chapter. This is not because there were no real differences among individuals, but because no other characteristics mattered socially. As soon as we care enough or have culturally defined reasons to appreciate people's differences, individual recognition is easy because biological variation is so complex.

The statuses that exist in each society and the definitions we give to each role are somewhat arbitrary. Cultures divide up the range of human activities into different packages. All cultures have some of the same statuses, of course. All recognize "mother," for example, and almost all recognize "father," but the behaviors expected of an individual in each role vary considerably from culture to culture. In some societies, for example, the biological father acts as a casual friend and supporter of his children, whereas the mother's brother is the responsible provider, authority figure, and disciplinarian. When other cultures are compared to ours, the distinctions in the definition of fatherhood may be even more subtle.

A beautiful example of the problem of translating roles from culture to culture appeared in the film *Sahara* (1943), in which Humphrey Bogart leads a group symbolically representing the people fighting the Nazis. The ensemble includes one or two other Americans, several British soldiers, an independent-minded Frenchman, an Italian who can't decide which side he is on, and a black North African Muslim, who is portrayed with amazing dignity and sensitivity for that era. There is a very warm and human scene in which the African and one of the Americans compare their marriages. The American asks if it is really true that a Muslim can have four wives. The African says yes, but that he only has one wife. When the American asks why, the African laughs and says, more or less, "If your Bible permitted you to have four wives, would *your* wife let you?" They both laugh, sharing a moment of male bonding across "race" and culture at the expense of women, who are apparently difficult to get along with no matter where they live.

Of course, this exchange isn't really across cultures. It's all just American culture—in this case, the American definition of marriage—superimposed on everyone else. The fact is that in many societies, the purpose of marriage and the desires and relative power of spouses may be different from our expectations. A first wife often welcomes an additional wife to share the work. Economic cooperation rather than sexual exclusiveness may be the important part of a marriage; women may want their husbands to take additional wives to enhance their status, provide companionship, or increase the wealth of the household, as well as to meet the need for economic assistance or baby-sitting. The notion that a wife is primarily an emotional partner rather than an economic one—or that she has any influence on a man's decision to take a second wife—may or may not be true. Roles don't translate so easily. The assumptions that they do or should represents deep-rooted chauvinism and a kind of cultural imperialism.

The episode in the movie was a dramatic stab at liberalism toward members of another culture and "race." But it missed an important point. It tried to show that other people are really "okay" because deep down they are just like us. This is, in effect, what the assimilation of immigrants into the "melting pot" and the "integration" of blacks and whites in the United States stood for. The much more difficult but potentially far more rewarding challenge is to comprehend the real depth and subtlety of differences and to permit others to be different yet still coexist and enjoy one another.

Even within a culture, people may not agree completely on appropriate role behavior. People may get the core aspects of a role or status right but be uncertain of the marginal aspects of the role in a new cultural setting. And, of course, members of minorities may have to cope with conflicting role demands in their two cultures. A common problem that American parents of all kinds face is the need to balance their parental role as learned within their own families and communities with the parental role expected of them by members of the larger society who interact with their children. Teachers, counselors, the police, and others may have a different sense of how parents should behave toward their children than the parents and their children themselves have. Some members of minority groups may not be sure how the role is supposed to be played when they come up against official representatives of the mainstream culture—including people who have the power to take away their children if they feel that the parents are not behaving "correctly." Both parents and officials need to be able to adjust their expectations. The problems are likely to increase when either culture is changing rapidly so that the role definitions are in flux. Conflict in role expectations, which makes choices difficult, appears to be a major source of emotional stress. Any number of theories and observations in anthropology, psychology, biology, and medicine link such conflicts to anomie or disorientation, apathy, helplessness, and illness.

All societies are also forced to deal with people who simply don't fit the statuses to which most people can be assigned and/or who don't play the roles correctly. Such "unconventional" behavior threatens the integrity of cultural rules because if everyone emulates the deviant behavior, the social system may collapse. Unconventional people must therefore be isolated from others, "corrected," driven out, institutionalized, or killed. Or they must be put in special categories where their unusual behavior is defined as appropriate, not threatening. Many cultures give unusual people constructive and even honored roles instead of putting them in institutions.

People who do not fit neatly into the most common sexual categories seem to exist in every society, for various reasons, some of which are not clearly understood. Some societies simply define additional adult roles that allow people to do their unusual "thing" in a culturally accepted framework without stigma. Thus the "manly hearted woman" and the "berdache" (a man who has adopted women's work, dress, and family relationships) are both roles found in some Native North American groups.

Some cultures are homophobic; others tolerate and expect homosexual behavior in some individuals; some provide special statuses and roles that homosexuals can assume without dishonor; some take for granted or even expect that some people will be homosexual or even that most people will have homosexual relations at some time in their lives or go through homosexual stages of development. But these rules are, again, conventions, and there is relatively little to mark one set of rules as better than another. Moreover, we might well ask, better for whom—the individuals or the society?

Whatever the cultural rules and categories, rethinking them in the face of new (or newly observed) behavior threatens the shared assumptions of the culture—the glue that holds people together. Having finally recognized the existence of homosexuality, Americans face the problem of reconciling it with cultural values and categories that do not recognize it. But it is our system of categories, not the behavior, that is "unnatural."

So far, I have dealt with aspects of culture that have a fairly concrete meaning and are easy to recognize. The remaining features are more subtle but also more pervasive.

6. Cultures provide a shared, conventional definition of group and individual goals and values.

What are the good things in life and the virtues to which we aspire? How do we know if we are "succeeding"? How do we win other people's approval (which may be the most important human goal other than fitness itself)? We have to agree at least to some extent on what are valid goals in order to have some comprehension of one another's actions, just as we need a common language. But any of various definitions will do.

Individual wealth is a major goal in American society; but it was anathema to the vast majority of societies in human history, particularly those in which the society consisted almost exclusively of family, friends, and neighbors and in which sharing, cooperation, and respect were more highly valued. We also place value on getting ahead, winning out over others (whatever the task or prize.) But many societies actively discourage competition. Anthropologist Richard Lee has provided a powerful demonstration of what can happen in such a society to someone who gets to be too "big" by being overly successful or even excessively generous. Living among egalitarian hunter-gatherers, he used his Western wealth to provide a Christmas feast in the form of an ox that was far fatter than the animals the hunters could get. (Fat was very scarce and highly desirable in the group.) But instead of thanking him and joining in, people belittled his ox and ridiculed him for trying to be "too big." In Western society, anyone working as part of a team or in a union job in a potentially competitive situation knows about such pressure not to excel. One is likely to be accused of brown-nosing or trying to make everyone else look bad.

We can't assume that other people around the world or even within our own society are trying to achieve the same goals we seek, or value the same kinds of performance. They are not "failing" to match our success; they are aiming at different targets. In some cultures, spirituality and the achievement of an emotional and psychic sense of communion with supernatural powers are valued more highly than material wealth. Some people seek harmony and balance with nature; others seek beauty in nature or in human design. In some cultures, political power is the primary goal to which most people aspire, or it may be enjoyment of family or the bearing and rearing of many children. (With reference to issues raised in chapter 2, it is clear that neither "selfish" genes nor endorphins always respond to conflicting social stimuli the same way they do in our society.)

7. Cultures also provide shared definitions of appropriate and inappropriate means to achieve what one wants.

Every society has rules about how one may or may not try to achieve goals. As in any game, some strategies are legitimate and some are not. But these rules, too, differ from culture to culture, and they are arbitrary, often changing over time even within a particular culture. Our courts continually have to decide whether certain behaviors are legal. The definitions change, as do our definitions of what is moral.

What is the difference between clever business practices and cheating, for example? The boundary is clearly a social convention, not a clear and absolute moral principle, and different societies disagree about where to draw the appropriate lines. Moreover, we ourselves use different standards in different contexts. For example, a businessperson may be praised for using "sharp" practices against competitors but criticized or boycotted as immoral for doing the same with consumers. Most would also think that using these practices against friends or family was clearly wrong. In some small societies of friends and kin these practices might always be wrong, although some small societies value competition and sharp practices as much as we do. In some societies one is expected to best others in any transaction as a matter of form as well as profit—especially if they are not from one's family or neighborhood. In some societies people use witchcraft in their attempts to best others but would not consider using more direct methods. In some cultures people use physical force, although the situations in which force may be used are generally well defined. In some societies one gets ahead simply by hard work. In others, nepotism is the norm.

8. Cultural rules help define what we see and hear.

Human vision and hearing show little if any genetic group differences in range, quality, or capability. There is no evidence that biological differences account for the perceptual differences between groups. But just as every language has conventions that dictate which verbal sounds are significant and which we can ignore—so completely that often we can't hear them at all—so every culture dictates what we see, hear, or smell selectively. Our culture tells us which sounds and images to focus on consciously or unconsciously from the available array of sounds and images; and it tells us which parts of any pattern of sound or image are important. Even loud, disruptive sounds, like those of a nearby subway train, can be tuned out once it is clear that they are regular and unthreatening and of no importance to our lives. We often don't "see" things that are constant features of our environment. We tune out sights and sounds that have no meaning for our decision-making processes. Culture even has a significant influence on what we experience as pain. (It is well known that the brain can mask pain and that people of different cultures display different levels of pain in different circumstances. Pain is less intrusive if we expect it, more powerful if it surprises us. Cultures help define what is expected.)

Our "race" categories themselves are a good example of cultural patterning of perception. Our culture teaches us to focus on—to "see"—certain distinctions and to ignore or not see other distinctions that don't fit our cultural categories. We see human colors a bit like the way we see a rainbow. In both cases we look at a continuum of color but subconsciously divide it into a small number of distinct colors. We lump people into groups in culturally defined ways.

Each culture teaches its members to make selective use of the information presented to them by their eyes and ears, and the selection differs from culture to culture. This refers both to information in written and oral communication and to the information provided by natural objects or by the actions of other people. The result is that perfectly intelligent members of different cultures may be focusing on and reacting to different things even when they appear to be seeing the same thing or receiving the same message. An obvious example is that knowledgeable fans at a sporting event see a pattern while those of another culture experience only movement, noise, and crowding.

9. Cultures provide principles for understanding how the world works.

Cultures shape the way we think and the way we define, categorize and explain reality, and analyze natural systems—what we might call cognition. They define our science and our logic. This is perhaps the hardest point for people to understand—and the most important. Individuals in a society need to have shared rules about how to think, how to understand how the world works, how to explain why things happen, how to understand how other people are motivated, and so on. To use a little modern jargon, every culture teaches its own models or *paradigms* for explaining events. The rules or paradigms have to be shared to permit coherent communication and make people's behavior predictable. But systems of cognition, ours included, don't have to be "right" in some absolute sense, and frequently they are not.

Any system must provide a perception and understanding of the natural world that is accurate enough to help people to survive and reproduce. ("Primitive" people have repeatedly been shown to be excellent naturalists.) But beyond that, there is extraordinary leeway for a cognitive system to be arbitrary and conventional. Such arbitrary cognitive systems show up in many areas of our own thought.

For example, mathematicians know that there is no reason for mathematics to use a system based on the number 10 (base 10 or the decimal system). Other base systems would work as well. The decimal system was introduced to Europe from the Islamic world about A.D. 1300, and most of the world has now adopted it. Anyone who tried to use another system in popular communication wouldn't be understood. Mathematicians also know that the Euclidean geometry we all learned in high school is neither the only way nor the most accurate way of describing space on the earth's surface. It is in fact a holdover from "flat earth" thinking. But it is a common, consistent system sufficiently accurate for general use that we all agree to abide by for most purposes. Similarly, modern economics is to a large degree a system of interconnected ideas that reinforce one another in the manner of theorems in geometry. But it, too, may not be the only or the best system for describing the real world. How often, in fact, are its predictions accurate?

It is possible (and very common) for cognitive systems to be quite wrong—at least by "objective" Western scientific perception. I am not saying that there isn't a single correct interpretation of natural things, a "truth" that scientists can search for and ultimately discover—although some philosophers would say that. I am arguing that all human cultures, including our own, have gotten by for a long time on conventional ideas without knowing what that "truth" is.

For centuries, Western civilization proceeded on the presumption that the earth was flat and the sun revolved around it. People managed to solve their daily problems despite their misapprehension. Nineteenth-century American or European medical books (written at the height of our collective optimism about progress, science, and our own cultural superiority) sound just like contemporary books, describing "the truth" and the "latest and best" scientific knowledge; but to our eyes they seem incorrect, and often even funny. I have one such book in my office, a nineteenth-century tome that expounds at great length and with great pomposity about the latest scientific knowledge about the causes of malaria—but never once mentions mosquitoes, which as we now know are the agents that spread the disease. Civilization in the nineteenth century managed to survive without "proper" knowledge of malaria, even though the lack of knowledge undoubtedly caused some individuals to die. What makes us think that we have finally gotten everything right?

Many societies have theories of illness that do not recognize germs but instead focus on spiritual forces such as ghosts, witches, sorcerers, the evil eye, or the loss of one's soul to explain illness. This sounds a little less fantastic if you think of all these images as deeply ingrained metaphors or symbolic statements about conscience and social tensions. Sorcerers, witches, and the evil eye may represent the anger, spite, or envy of others; ghosts of the ancestors may represent the pangs of conscience; loss of soul may represent depression or discomfort with one's own behavior or identity, perhaps in situations of unresolved role conflict. These metaphors are not so hard to understand or even empathize with once we move beyond the narrow translation of the words into English equivalents and focus instead on the metaphorical implications. Many modern scientifically oriented Westerners experience disapproving glances from neighbors; and they continue to communicate with loved ones when they aren't present or even after they are dead, in dreams and sometimes in daydreams; and they often focus on evaluations of their own behavior in such "conversations." For most of us, of course, this is nothing mystical. We have neurological and psychological "explanations" for these phenomena (explanations which for the most part are no easier to validate than the actions of witches).

Such theories of illness based on emotional health and interpersonal relations can be very effective for explaining illness in both individual and social terms, even if they do not have all the power of our scientific medicine. Many illnesses in any population, from headaches to arthritis and some cancers, are *not* spread by germs. Moreover, in small-scale societies that are not in constant contact with civilization, even most germ diseases are not obviously "caught" from others, either. Some are chronic diseases involving germs that are always present, so that contagion is not obvious and "catching" the germ may be less important than the emotional state of the patient. Some are zoonotic (animal) diseases, which rarely spread from person to person and may provide no pattern pointing to human contagion. Under these circumstances, germ theory may not always be the most useful model even in objective "scientific" terms, and contagion will not be obvious, even to thinking, observant people.

A model of illness based on interpersonal relations may be both powerful and effective, for all its shortcomings. With such a model, disease loses its apparently random and mysterious quality and therefore some of its capacity to instill terror, all of which helps the patient's state of mind and therefore his or her health. Classification and explanation make us feel that we have some power and reinforce our sense of how the world works and that things are as they should be (just as it is always a relief when your doctor tells you the name of your ailment, even if he or she then says there is nothing modern medicine can do). Because everyone in a particular society agrees on the range of possible mechanisms, discussion and interaction are possible. The use of interpersonal tensions to explain diseases also serves important social purposes, as I have already stated, because it tends to regulate the behavior of both the individual fearing illness or being treated and others who observe and are thereby forewarned. Curers ("witch doctors" or "medicine men") come in and perform healing rituals. The patient gets a lot of hands-on attention. Social tensions are aired. Stress is alleviated. Sometimes the patient gets better. The society usually continues, whether the patient recovers or not.

Germ theory may be a more accurate and powerful way of dealing with some diseases, especially the epidemic diseases that spread rapidly in urban civilizations, which gave rise to the theory. Germ theory is well suited for certain civilized lifestyles in which large, densely populated settlements and frequent contact between strangers increase opportunities for contagion. Civilized life styles also make it more difficult to solve problems in interpersonal relations through intimate rituals involving the relevant participants. In the late twentieth century, however, germ theory lost some of its utility even in "civilized" countries when the concern with epidemic diseases was supplanted by other medical problems such as heart disease, hypertension, and many cancers, which do not involve germs. (The recent emergence of Ebola and AIDS is again diverting our attention to diseases caused by invading microorganisms.)

Germ theory can also be inaccurate and even misleading because, like any system of cognition, it can be overextended or maintained more by convention or social utility than by scientific observation or medical utility. Early in the twentieth century germ theory became something of a fad, used to explain many diseases, like pellagra, which were caused primarily by nutritional deficiency. The persistence of germ theory to explain pellagra suited the political agenda of governments that did not want the responsibility or blame for widespread malnutrition. In the case of pellagra, germ theory distracted physicians from treating the disease.

We, too, belatedly recognize that many major diseases (including not only obvious stress or psychosomatic diseases but even cancer, which has very real organic causes) may be affected by the emotional well-being of the patient. We explain such illnesses "scientifically" by noting that social stress can suppress the immune system through a known series of hormonal pathways, making stressed individuals susceptible to a range of illnesses. For all our scientific explanation, Western medical treatments come to resemble those that "witch doctors" have long practiced, treating the emotional state of the patient—the "whole" patient. We don't see the resemblance because each society uses its own cultural symbols and rules in effecting a cure. An African doctor may wear a special tribal costume instead of a white coat and stethoscope. But the purpose is largely the same.

We have realized also that many germ diseases don't depend primarily on catching the germ but have crucial social and emotional components as well. Some researchers dealing with the common cold, for example, announced in late 1996 that the emotional state of the patient may be a better explanation than germ theory for why some people get colds and some do not. Not so long ago, tuberculosis was a disease that many people "caught" in the sense that their skin tests indicated infection by the organisms—but relatively few got sick or showed significant development of the disease in chest x-rays. Getting sick from TB historically depended more on the quality of the body's immune defenses, and on the social and emotional state of the patient, than on catching the germ. (New and dangerous strains of TB have surfaced, and catching the germ may become more significant.) We now realize that many "germs" are around us all the time and that becoming ill with many organic diseases actually depends on the functioning or failure of the immune system, which we know is influenced by stress.

We also know, from scientific studies, that the immune system can be helped and illness reduced by placebos or by medical rituals intended to restore the confidence of the patient and help resolve social tensions. Much of our medicine, like that of witch doctors, has always been confidence-boosting ritual—even when it was not consciously perceived as such. Western doctors, belatedly, are now consciously re-examining their procedures and doing exactly what witch doctors do—adding personal contact, touching, psychotherapy, and social therapy to other treatments. But placebos and medical rituals only build confidence if they take the form that the patient expects—one reason for the persistence of folk medicines in our multicultural society.

In a sense, the witch doctors have turned out to be more accurate than the germ scientists in some cases, and their methods of curing— which are designed to alleviate stress and social tension—are sometimes more effective than combatting germs even in contemporary settings. Just as the patients of witch doctors sometimes get better (and sometimes don't), so the patients of our doctors sometimes get better and sometimes don't. Most often, patients get better largely on their own, in the natural course of things over time; some get better because of the reinforcement or tension relief or social therapy the doctor provides; some get better because of the specific medicine provided; some get better in spite of that medicine; some don't get better; some die. Our society, too, goes on regardless of the outcome, and most people continue to believe both in unscientific explanations of disease and in the efficacy of medical "cures."

The fact that all doctors and all sets of medical beliefs fail at least some of the time raises another important point about all cognitive systems. Such systems survive despite the fact that experience often does not validate them. Because we believe in our system, we credit doctors with the successes and find ways to rationalize the failures, just as people in other cultures do ("It wasn't the doctor's fault"; "I didn't take the medicine long enough or correctly"; "Medicine doesn't always work"; "She didn't take care of herself"; "I didn't go to the doctor soon enough"; "The diagnosis was wrong"; "The other sorcerer must be more powerful"; "Someone else must be casting a spell on me"; "I haven't appeased the correct spirit yet").

Every system of cognition is imperfect at explaining what is going on or predicting the future, but every society depends on sharing a coherent system of explanation; so every culture has built-in mechanisms for explaining its failures. The result is that the system of belief and cognition is largely impervious to challenge—and failures are blamed on secondary explanations or scapegoats *in order to permit the cognitive system itself to survive.* At a more dangerous level, it's common for people to say something like, "Our system works well—in fact, it is the best in the world—if only it weren't for the interference of the enemy tribe/ women/blacks/Jews/homosexuals." They say this instead of taking a good hard look at the assumptions of the system itself to see whether they might be improved.

Cognitive systems dictate not just what we think but *how* we think. For example, much of human cognition involves classifying and generalizing—recognizing that individual things are members of larger categories and applying the principles of the category to the thing. (This toy is like others in the category "round." Round objects roll. This toy must roll.) A major purpose of education is to teach us to make analogies—to recognize that individual items are members of groups, have common group characteristics, and can be understood on that basis, permitting us to enlarge our appreciation of each thing and make predictions about it by comparing it to others. The kinds of analogies we make shape the ways we perceive and think about things and what qualities we identify in the things we are studying. New analogies give us new ways to think. One of my primary goals as a teacher is to encourage my students to explore a wider range of analogies in solving problems than they normally use.

But the way we put things in categories—and therefore the way we think about them, the kinds of analogies we use—varies from situation to situation even within our own culture, and it varies markedly across cultures. There may well be absolute principles of classification, but which ones a given culture chooses to apply in a given situation can be arbitrary. As I will discuss more fully in chapter 6, other cultures may rank competing principles of classification in a different order than we do, and they may classify things on the basis of spiritual or other invisible properties or functional groupings that we don't recognize. Children growing up in a culture are taught which classifications they may not apply, just as they are taught which sounds not to make. Their "logical" mistakes, just like their grammatical errors, are often perfectly consistent logical extensions of thought or language that the adult culture arbitrarily refuses to recognize. For example, a child may logically add -ed to a verb to form the past tense, realizing that the particular verb is part of a larger class and having correctly perceived the common adult pattern in English; but in "proper" English that particular verb may have a different form in the past tense. We say *walked* but not *runned, goed,* or *comed.* The child may also classify things in ways the rest of us refuse to recognize despite the fact that the real or symbolic similarities involved are as valid as the ones adults use. Why aren't horses, cows, giraffes, and lions just big "dogs," as many toddlers maintain? Each one is, after all, a big mammal. What is the difference between flowers, which one is not allowed to pick, and weeds, which one can pick, even though some weeds are pretty? The point is not that as children grow up they learn to categorize more accurately, logically, or intelligently; the point is that as they grow up they are trained to say things and categorize things as adults do, even though the principles are largely conventional and may even be less logical than the ones children develop for themselves.

Because different cultures use different classification systems, intelligent people reared in different cultures or even different families may use different analogies, think differently, or draw different logical conclusions from one another. The arbitrariness of principles of classification is one of the major flaws in our attempts to measure intelligence across cultures or subcultures.

More important, if analogies give us new ways to think, and if exposure to other cultures increases the range of analogies we can make (as it must), then cross-cultural exposure is one of the surest roads to real freedom of thought and innovation. Narrow-minded insistence on the superiority of our own system will have the reverse effect.

10. Cultures provide a philosophy and a world view.

Some other dimensions of thinking that need to be discussed might compare better to our category "philosophy" or perhaps "world view" rather than "cognition" or "science." For one thing, every culture I have ever read about uses a creation story or myth to explain where people came from, to provide an overarching sense of how the world works, to reinforce pride in the sociocultural system (patriotism), and to reinforce proper behavior. The Gikuyu of Kenya have a creation story that is very like the biblical account except that Mount Kenya is viewed as the throne of the Almighty and the source of life. One Aboriginal Australian myth tells that people once occupied a completely flat world, without physical features, plants, or animals, until a great "rainbow serpent" created hills, valleys, rivers, and the various forms of life in his travels. According to another Aboriginal myth, Father Sky and Mother Earth had four children—sun, moon, sea, and rock—and then separated and never lived together again so they produced no more children. Sun and moon created clouds, wind, rain, stars, and storms. Rock created trees, birds, mammals, reptiles, and insects. Sea created oceans, tides, gales, and currents. All these creations lived in harmony until people appeared, with their dirty disruptive ways. Each story, told in full, teaches values, precepts, and moral and cognitive rules as well as providing entertainment—just as Bible stories do. This is one reason why the argument that American schools should teach both scientifically defined evolution and creationism makes no sense. How many creation stories should be included? There are thousands, each with the same claim to legitimacy as the one offered by what was, historically, one tribe (the Hebrews) among thousands.

Creation stories and other myths also include spoken and unspoken philosophies about how the world works and our place in it. Where Americans see a world ranked in various hierarchies, other people see diversity without rank. Where Westerners see an inevitable struggle and competition, others see balance and order as guiding principles. (One corollary is that, contrary to the opening assertion of *The Bell Curve,* most societies do *not* try to rank individuals on the basis of "intelligence.") Where Westerners see individual people acting alone, each responsible for his or her own actions, others see mutual interaction and interdependence among people and between people and the environment they inhabit. The Judeo-Christian tradition teaches that human beings have dominion over the earth, and our approach to world ecology and to other people is to try to control them and bend them to our purposes. Other cultures teach that we should try not to disrupt the balance of nature and that we are a danger to the earth. American mythology also teaches that we are moving toward some goal, inevitably improving ourselves (although the theory of evolution developed in Europe and the United States denies that there is either purpose or overall improvement beyond immediate adaptation). Our model also teaches that we should push other people aside and ignore environmental balance in our pursuit of that elusive goal.

In contrast, the Hopi of Arizona, like many other groups, see a world in which people are supposed to operate in harmony and balance with nature, a philosophy that may have more lasting value. As noted, some Aboriginal Australians taught that human beings were a potential danger to the land and had to learn instead to act as protective stewards of natural resources—a vision that may be a somewhat more accurate description of how the world works than our own mythology. But, whatever the merits of each philosophy, it is important to recognize that people like the Hopi and the Australian Aboriginals are not "failed" Americans or "unintelligent." They see humanity in a different way and pursue other goals. Such variations in philosophy explain historical patterns of world political dominance better than supposed differences in natural ability.

Finally, there are philosophies or world views that may never be consciously articulated in any particular culture because they seem to be obvious truths. Only an observer outside the cultural system may be aware of them. One such pattern is what anthropologists refer to as the image of limited good, the often unspoken assumption that the supply of all good things—health, wealth, happiness, even children—is finite and cannot increase. So if I try to get more and succeed, you by definition must get less. This way of thinking is thought to be particularly characteristic of peasants (or farmers sub servient to a central government), but it appears in the United States, too, as I will discuss in chapter 8. The image of limited good is the antithesis of the idea of economic growth, the equally conventional and arbitrary idea that we can increase the total of all wealth and therefore improve the condition of everyone. The ideas of economic growth and limited good may each be an accurate description of some areas of our lives at certain times and in certain places. Each is manifestly inaccurate at other times and places. The point is that culture manages our perception of the potential for growth and thereby guides our actions, quite independent of objective measurement. And these views of the world, like all cognitive systems, have a strong tendency to persist in the face of contradictory evidence. Most people, including Americans, hold an irrational combination of the two.

11. Culture provides arbitrary shared rules about emotional expression.

Some human emotional expression is universal and seems to be in our common genes and even in those of our primate relatives. For example, means of showing threat or appeasement are performed and recognized by apes and people alike. One of my favorite examples involves a picture of the late President Richard Nixon speaking about Vietnam. His formal speech had undoubtedly been worked over by any number of top professional writers to assure its perfection, and of course he was speaking in his own learned, conventional language. But his threatening posture and facial expression would have been comprehended by any people on earth speaking any language and by any chimpanzee or gorilla who happened to tune in. But they could not be seen by most members of his intended audience. The gestures were automatic and unintended.

Human cultures elaborate on these universal expressions or limit them for the sake of the smooth functioning of the society. It is common knowledge, for example, that people of some cultures are more expressive than others, and that some are more reserved. Americans often seem extremely emotional to the British, for example, but we appear just as cold to Israelis. It's a matter of training and expectation.

The distinctions involve more than a mere matter of degree. Cultures express different emotions and express them in different ways. People in parts of the Third World find American or European crying patterns unusual. They observe that adult American women cry sometimes but adult men rarely do, and that crying carries social messages about winning and losing arguments, meanings that have no counterpart in their own experience. All human babies cry, of course, as do all small children. Cultures differ as to when they take the crying privilege away from a growing child. Some cultures make everybody (or just boys) stop crying sometime in childhood. In many other societies no adult is allowed to cry, and no social meaning is conveyed if one does. People in these cultures find the ability of European women to cry amazing and may attribute it to magic. On the other hand, in many cultures both adult women and adult men cry.

Furthermore, some cultures don't simply allow people of a certain age or sex or other status to cry, they demand it. In these cultures, *not* to cry at the appropriate occasion—such as a funeral or when stepping down from political office, saying goodbye, or losing a game—is to show that one is not fully human. In such cultures, there is nothing unmasculine about crying, and it would be a mistake to place American values on the sight of a crying man. What we dismiss as excessive grief may be the norm and may be expected. People from such cultures seeing an American man who does not cry at a funeral may assume that he is extremely cold or that he did not like the deceased person. (As far as I know, there is no biological difference between men and women in crying ability as adults or between different populations in this respect. And a fostered child can adopt the expressive mode of its new culture.) Culture seems to be channeling even phenomena that seem to be firmly grounded in biology. All of this means, of course, that cross-cultural understanding, whether between heads of state or teachers and students in a multiethnic classroom, involves far more than just getting the words right.

Cultures also have highly varied rules about when the expression of sexual desires is appropriate and what sexual activities are legitimate. And cultures vary widely in their willingness to tolerate a range of bodily exposure. Americans are neither the most adventurous nor the most conservative. In some societies where physical seclusion is hard to find, privacy, if it is sought at all, may be in the eye of the beholder. The transgression, if any, may be not in those who have sex or expose body parts but in those who look at them. After all, many of us don't consider it indecent for couples to "neck" in public. We look away. And on many European beaches it is no longer indecent for a woman to bare her breasts, although it is indecent to stare at them. Similarly, in some parts of the United States a woman may now expose a breast in public to nurse, and the onus is on others not to look—a dramatic change in our rules. There is an often-told story of an anthropologist who was chided by Pacific islanders for looking at their naked bodies (one was supposed to look away for the sake of politeness and modesty). But, as the islanders said, it was all right "this time" because he obviously came from a less advanced society and didn't know any better.

In contrast, many societies, like those of the Middle East, have standards of modesty and sexual expression far more rigid than our own. In Iran of the 1930s, the governmental insistence that women uncover their hair as an expression of "modernity" shocked many women who regarded the new pattern much as American women might react to being told that they must go bare-breasted in public. There isn't, after all, any natural reason that uncovering one's breasts is any more immodest than uncovering one's hair. Women and men in some societies normally cover both; in other societies both sexes uncover both. In fact, in the past hundred years there has been a dramatic reversal in permissiveness about exposing the body. Europeans, who once tried to teach other people to cover up, now often play the opposite role.

In societies where families live in one room, children may grow up being exposed to their parents' sexuality and may play or practice sexuality long before either partner is fertile. Such observation and practice may actually ease the transition to adulthood, which is so difficult in our own society. Why is it that we consider natural and loving sexual activity, nudity, and breast-feeding obscene, but don't apply that term to the sight of a movie hero despoiling the flesh of his enemies?

12. Societies provide training in culturally correct behavior.

Because many rules in any culture are arbitrary rather than logical or sensible (or genetic), societies always invest a good deal of effort making sure that people learn the rules. They reinforce the rules of culture just as they work to get everybody to speak the same language according to the prevailing convention. In the same way that language is first learned at home from parents, siblings, relatives, and neighbors, so culture is first learned in the family and local community. And, just as children learn slightly different variants of the "standard" language depending on their home and local community, they also learn slight variations of the culture. In addition, the features of language and culture learned at home are mostly those that allow communication and effective interaction in the environment of home and local community.

Societies that are larger than a local community must share some elements of a common culture and must have ways to ensure that children learn those elements and become a part of the larger sociocultural system. Schools have been an important means of training children and adults in those aspects of the common culture. (This function is also performed by standardized legends, stories, and myths.)

American children learn the American way of thinking, values, permissible means to an end, roles, perception, cognition, and emotional expression in schools in our standardized curriculum. We reinforce them in our stories and legends (with their morals), which is why people from George Washington to Davy Crockett appear magically to display all the same virtues. And we transmit them through news and entertainment media, advertising, and many other ways. Other cultures do the same. Oral African stories teach morals, too. Parents punish "wrong" behavior. Ceremonies remind people and teach children what is expected of them.

It is important to note, however, that efforts to socialize the young (and one another) take an enormous amount of energy and may become ends in themselves. Conformity and loyalty to the system may become more important than rational problem solving.

13. *Sociocultural systems demand loyalty.*

Human beings, with their capability for symbolic abstract thought (or just daydreaming), can imagine themselves being somewhere else or doing something else despite their socialization. As a result, all cultures need to motivate people to observe the rules. Loyalty to a culture or nation is demanded as much or more than to a state.

A culture can be destroyed if its members adopt another culture completely, if group pride is no longer reinforced so that people become apathetic or lose belief in the system, or if they become so antagonistic to one another that they cease to interact positively. Cultural destruction of this sort can easily be followed by the disintegration of the society and decimation of the population itself.

Almost all cultures have a way of referring to their members as the "Chosen People," the "real" people, the "good" people or just "THE people," "*El Pueblo*," or "*La Raza*." Cultures teach that perception, and people everywhere believe it, including those we consider "primitive" or hold in disdain. Americans used to talk about our "manifest destiny" to conquer others, referring both to a sense of ourselves as the chosen people and to the sense that there had to be a higher purpose and an upward direction to our efforts. It is still common if not universal for Americans to assume that the American way is best or that truth, justice, and the American way go together. People everywhere are taught to think of themselves, their way of life, their town, their neighborhood, and even their high school or college as "the best." Believing that one is the best encourages people to participate without being too critical. Americans' patriotic pride stems from just such a cultural imperative.

Such pride seems to be essential to people's functioning in groups and even to their individual motivation. Without a sense that their cultural rules are good, even "the best," groups can become disorganized and individuals can slip into disorientation, as do many members of discriminated "minority" groups who have lost their sense of cultural value and self-worth. Many scholars think that the historic decline of Native American populations, Australian Aboriginal populations, and other conquered groups may have been facilitated by the loss of social and cultural cohesion that resulted from conquest, physical disruption, and dispersal—the ultimate loss of motivation to continue a lifestyle—as much as by physical violence and disease. Those members of a conquered group who survive, often as a lower caste or minority in their new society, must deal with a similar disorientation and lack of incentive even as they attempt to "integrate" into the mainstream culture.

An unfortunate aspect of the cultural pride and patriotism that is essential to the maintenance of any society is the definition of others as not good. That is, patriotism promotes or even demands chauvinism or ethnocentrism, disdain for people from the other high school, the other town, the other country, the other "race." A major challenge for modern society is to maintain patriotism and cultural pride without the antipathy toward others, the chauvinism, and the outright racism it encourages. However, anyone who has followed the changing allegiances of sports fans knows that chauvinism and ethnocentrism are malleable and can be redirected. Perhaps we can learn to treat other people or nations like neighboring high schools—with limited, fairly good-natured antipathy and rivalry—using the model of basketball or Olympic competition rather than war.

The most visible way in which people distinguish themselves from one another is to develop distinctive cultural styles. Group fashions in clothing, housing design, facial scars, tattoos, music, and speech serve partly to identify and reinforce membership in a particular group and are maintained for that purpose. People also develop values and styles of thinking that are purposefully different from those of their neighbors. (And as I discuss in chapter 6, part of the distinctive cognitive style of captive minority groups, which we consider to be "low IQ," is probably just such an intentional departure or separation from the mainstream culture.)

Every culture seems to reinforce patriotism by developing patriotic *symbols* to remind people of their membership. Many of these are visible: flags, distinctive clothing, masks, religious icons, and the like. Some are audible, like patriotic songs, phrases, or speeches; some, like Thanksgiving turkeys, are edible. All these serve as a reminder of things that are valued and as a quick, emotional patriotic "fix." So the culture celebrates group membership and flaunts its symbols (the flag, the Constitution, George Washington) as a constant reminder of its superiority. And it may well wave the flag or its equivalent precisely when patriotism is most threatened by divisiveness and perhaps when patriotism is least able to be defended on rational grounds. Many societies tend to hold their ritual gatherings and even do their group-oriented curing ceremonies when group tensions are high. It was no coincidence that patriotic celebrations of the American flag reached a peak during the Vietnam War, when the principles holding the country together were being severely challenged.

We tend to denigrate other people's symbols or to find them incomprehensible. But the significance of such symbols in all cultures can be better understood if we think about the enormous importance of flag symbolism in the United States. The American flag has become so powerful a symbol to many people that its safety is more important than that of the people it represents. The recent political initiatives for an amendment to protect the flag suggest that, to many people, allowing the flag to be desecrated is more dangerous than allowing millions of Americans to go hungry or to live without decent housing. By focusing on the damage to the cloth flag itself, of course, we deflect attention away from the weaknesses or intended criticisms of the system. But perhaps that is what symbols are for.

Hidden Purposes

As summarized above, any viable culture and the society it represents must accomplish a wide range of tasks. However, one of the things that makes it hard to understand what is going on in a culture is that many of these purposes are hidden or latent. Hidden purposes are often secondary to the avowed purpose of the behavior, but sometimes they are more important. Because they are "latent," they can be accomplished without ever being named or mentioned. So the curing ceremonies I have described may be intended to cure an illness, but they also resolve social tensions, educate people, remind them of the rules—and provide the occasion for a party. Similarly, we may say that we are going to war to make the world safe for democracy or to eliminate a dictator when our purposes also include expanding the power of our corporations, controlling trade, getting young men off the streets, sparking our own economy, deflecting attention from our own shortcomings, or just glorifying or reelecting a president. Culturally defined actions, like bills coming out of Congress, have an official title and purpose but also lots of "riders" tacked on, often hidden and having a different purpose. It is sometimes hard to separate the primary intention from the riders. And the riders may be the reason the bill is passed or defeated, or why the cultural behavior continues or is abandoned. So our plans to make war or to stop the war may depend not on our avowed purposes but on whether the secondary purposes have been accomplished.

This is one reason why it is difficult to change (or even fully understand) any culture, including our own. You have to change all the cultural "riders" as well as the avowed purpose of any behavior. This also helps explain why people of other cultures, as well as members of our own society, often resist what seem on the surface to be simple, commonsense changes. Those who would change cultural rules have to make sure that they are picking up on the hidden as well as the expressed reasons for doing things a certain way. But that may be difficult precisely because people don't want to express the other motives or aren't even consciously aware of the hidden reasons that are the real basis for a decision. Individual people act this way all the time. So do groups. Public dialogue in the United States is complicated by the fact that every group has purposes it will not express and even some that it cannot consciously perceive or articulate.

To take an obvious example, American medicine is supposed to cure people, and it should therefore absorb every available innovation in curing—not just the new technology but also other improvements in health care delivery. But medicine also employs a lot of people and uses a lot of technology that requires a substantial investment, and the secondary goal of maintaining that structure gets in the way of rational change. The real purpose of any bureaucracy is to protect itself; actually carrying out its avowed function may be secondary. In addition, practicing medicine and pursuing medical research in certain ways reinforce our system of values, cognition, and so forth. Hospitals turn patients away to maximize profits or just to maintain class or ethnic distinctions. We resist unconventional approaches because they violate our shared assumptions. "Socialized medicine" violates our sense of individuality and private enterprise, even if it might improve the health of many people. Doing medicine a certain way serves patriotism and cultural pride. It is apparently important to us to believe that American medical care is the best in the world. This is not true by many objective measures, including life expectancy and infant mortality. Even if it were true, that should not prevent us from learning new things from other cultures if curing, not patriotism, is our real goal. Nonetheless, the belief in our own superiority gets in the way of learning new things.

Medicine serves socialization and rule-enforcement purposes as well. Mothers use health warnings to socialize their children into correct behaviors that may or may not have any real medical effect ("don't play with those kids . . . they're dirty," which mostly means they aren't like us; and "stay out of drafts," whatever that means, perhaps just obey your mother). Many Americans want to use AIDS as a way of punishing homosexual behavior, which they consider culturally inappropriate (although it is apparently fairly natural behavior). AIDS is also a means of socializing people into good behavior and even of reinforcing a kind of patriotism: the society is saying (more or less) that the (heterosexual, monogamous, restrained) American way of sex is best, and AIDS proves it. Unfortunately, these secondary purposes interfere with the medical care itself. People who see AIDS primarily as vindication of their belief system may resist the promotion of condom use, needle exchange, or even medicines that can prevent or cure the disease because those techniques don't eliminate what they consider to be the underlying "deviant," "unnatural" behavior.

Our schools ostensibly teach children the skills and knowledge and provide the framework for thinking that they need to function successfully as adults. "Critical thinking" is a common goal among educators. But schools also serve a variety of other functions that help shape how they operate. Schools teach children to share the common American culture; to think like good Americans and to feel patriotic and *uncritical* about American values and American government. They also provide training in behavior styles that we take for granted as normal but which are in fact American cultural patterns. These include the idea of being ranked and graded, being competitive, and pursuing individual success, all of which would be anathema in many cultures.

Schools teach some things of which parents might not approve, sometimes quite unconsciously. In kindergarten my younger daughter had a teacher who insisted that children form two lines, a "boys'" line and a "ladies'" line, reinforcing the idea that distinctions between boys and girls were the most important way to categorize people (even at age five) and that, while boys would be boys, girls should already be ladylike.

Sometimes the things taught in school are so deeply ingrained in us that we don't notice them except by looking at how other cultures operate. For example, our schools not only teach ranking and grading, they also teach that some must fail. A "curve" must by definition have a lower end and an arbitrary cut-off point, below which some receive an "unsatisfactory" grade. But why in real life must anybody be officially branded in such a manner rather than merely finding his or her own level? We also teach that those who do fail have only themselves to blame. People in many cultures would not agree.

Schools serve a number of other purposes which interfere with our attempts to improve education. Particularly valuable in a society where families are isolated both from extended family and from neighbors, school provides experience in social interaction with peers that may be necessary for human psychological development (according to some theories), as well as providing valuable practice in getting along with others. (This secondary function is one reason that home schooling may not provide all of the necessary or desired functions of school, no matter how educated or how skilled as teachers the parents are.) Schools also act as baby-sitters and keep children off the streets and older children out of the work force. And education also employs many people and maintains several large-scale industries.

The secondary functions of education more than its "quality" are also some of the reasons that many American interest groups, churches, and the upper class want to educate their children in their own special schools. There are other reasons, of course; but in part, some parents want to promote special kinds of group membership such as religious or "racial" solidarity or purity. They pursue that goal even at the expense of giving their children rich and varied educational environments which by definition must include other kinds of people. Others want greater control over peer interaction and assurance that their children will socialize only with those of the same class. Still others want to protect their children from the disaster many people think our public schools have become, from the aggression of others and/or from the competitiveness of a ranked and graded instructional program.

If we want to change the educational system we have to be willing to focus on all the implications of change, not just on perfecting the quality of education in the narrowest sense. Indeed, we probably ought to face the fact that teaching students to think clearly isn't what we ask of schools. The secondary or latent functions are steering the ship.

Similarly, Social Security may protect older people from poverty, but it also encourages them to leave the work force and open the way for younger workers; it has contributed to a change in the structure of families by making older people more independent. It has created a potential source of government borrowing from the people and has even helped to shift the tax burden in the country downward (toward the lower classes). The tax, though mandatory, is levied only on salaries, not on the other forms of income more common to the rich; and it is levied only up to a certain amount of salary. Social Security also helped create a new sense of what government can and should do, a vision more far-reaching than Social Security itself, a vision Americans are bitterly divided over in philosophical as well as economic terms. So any debate about Social Security today must deal with allegiance to ideology and a host of secondary purposes, as well as rational planning for the elderly.

A great deal of what occurs in any culture seems to occur at this latent or unspoken level. Cultures regularly blind people to what they and their societies are doing and the reasons for their actions. People everywhere apparently are more comfortable when they are not fully aware of the implications of their own actions. This may be the single most important set of blinders that any culture imposes on people, a kind of selective lack of awareness of the reality of their own actions. Cultures commonly coexist with, and may even require, a fairly high degree of self-misperception on the part of their participants. It is a commonplace observation among anthropologists that what people do and what they say they are doing rarely match. Any member of a given culture has an incomplete and often inaccurate idea of what is going on; but even taken together, the descriptions of many participants may not conform to real acts, let alone their genuine significance. Americans are no exception.

People everywhere evade rules so that what they say they *should* do and what they actually do often do not match. Moreover, even when they admit to breaking the rules, people's honest descriptions of what they *actually* do and why they do it often still differ markedly from the observable facts. For example, we might say that people should not cheat on their spouses, and then admit that people do cheat, but still be wildly inaccurate, even in our private thoughts, in describing how often people do, in fact, cheat. A society may describe itself as polygamous when, in fact, most people have only one spouse. We define our culture and society as monogamous and invest a great deal of pride in our monogamy, although some people have multiple partners at one time and many people, even most, have multiple partners over the course of their lives. We consider our society a "melting pot" and a "land of opportunity" and like to think that each person's status is achieved through individual merit in open competition; but the reality in each case is different. No society lives up to its own image of itself—but because people are selectively blind to the discrepancies these can be hard to address.

One final point about cultural systems needs to be made. The pieces of a culture tend to fit together, albeit imperfectly. When one piece changes, others are forced to adjust. As the pieces tend to reinforce one another, the whole structure can become rigid and anachronistic, resisting useful change. Beliefs, values, and organizational systems persist beyond their objectively useful life. But, patriotism and cultural pride may blind people to the need for change.

A significant effect of this is that, in some sense, cultures age and die—or at least fail to maintain their hegemony or even their coherence over long periods of time. Cultures, like animal species, have a high extinction rate. As in biological evolution, variety and flexibility are probably the keys to survival. One of the clearest lessons of history is that we can't survive on pure patriotism.

We do change our systems, of course, but only within narrow, arbitrary limits based on cultural definition of what kinds of adjustment are permissible—itself a piece of our cultural "grammar"—or in ways that deny the perception of change. American culture is open to technical or scientific innovation but closed minded about creativity in social or economic realms. Other cultures are also selective about what changes they allow; but they may accept innovation in different spheres of activity. Many African religious systems, for example, freely add new deities to their pantheon on the basis of the pragmatic observation that someone else's gods appear to be powerful—or just to be on the safe side. (Many added Jesus to their pantheon in just that spirit and were surprised to discover that the white man's Jesus expected to be the *only* God.) But those same cultures may resist technological or economic innovations, often quite sensibly, if they appear to put people out of step with each other or with nature, which they may consider more important than efficiency or "progress."

CHAPTER FOUR

The Real Meaning of Cultural Relativism

CULTURAL RELATIVISM —roughly, the willingness to look thought-fully and tolerantly at other cultures—can help resolve many of our tensions and some of our problems. Even business leaders are now talking about the need to expand and supplement our "paradigms" (the standard models of our thinking, molded by culture and limited by our cultural blinders) to get the best results. Expanding and sup-plementing our existing paradigms—real freedom of thought—are what cultural relativism and anthropology are all about.

But relativism is a dirty word among some scholars, pundits, and politicians. It is easily dismissed because very few people take the time to understand what it means. Critics of relativism like Allan Bloom resent the idea that other people's behavior might be com-pared to—much less equated with or found superior to—our own. They fear that acceptance of relativism might create chaos and un-dermine our own (supposedly high) standards. They also fear that we might unthinkingly accept whatever other people do as part of our own lifestyle. They caricature relativism, describing it as the morally bankrupt assumption that no judgment of other people's behavior is possible. According to those critics, relativists believe that any behavior is as good as any other. According to those critics, relativism means that there is no truth, no morality, and no way to judge good and evil.

Those same critics often hold, even if subconsciously, the as-sumption that our own behavior doesn't need to be evaluated be-cause it is obviously correct or superior. But, too often we measure the "shortcomings" of others by our own cultural standards and fail to recognize our imperfections according to their standards—or even our own.

In their scientific research, anthropologists try to describe and analyze other people's behavior without being judgmental. This is necessary for the sake of clear-headed scientific study. Moreover, anthropologists often identify *particular aspects* of other people's behavior that they admire and might even wish to emulate. That is, we try to be open-minded about the possibility of learning something from other people. But few anthropologists abandon their right (even imperative) to make value judgments as thinking, moral people. And, few if any consider "ethnic cleansing," genocide, war, germ warfare, slavery, starvation in the midst of plenty, addicting young children to drugs, or infanticide to be acceptable just because they are part of the culturally patterned behavior of other people.

Cultural relativism does imply several other important things we must do which its critics deny or fail to comprehend:

Look carefully, think, and study before we criticize other people's behavior as ignorant, wrong, or "primitive."

Recognize that a culture isn't necessarily "deficient" just because it has different priorities and accomplishments from our own.

Put aside our own arbitrary cultural assumptions and prejudices—take off our own blinders—before we judge. Keep an open mind about what we might learn.

Try to understand the context and the latent purposes of what people are doing rather than looking only at the most obvious and superficial forms in isolation from the rest of culture. Look for the (fairly compelling) logic that often but not always underlies the way people do things. (Behaviors that look strange to us often make sense under the conditions in which people have to operate.)

Look for differences between people's actions and what they say or think they are doing, in any culture, including our own.

Recognize the fact that other peoples' "unusual" behaviors are often more successful in fulfilling their goals than we give them credit for.

And, acknowledge the fact that our own behaviors, too, are often based on arbitrary cultural conventions more than on logic, science, or nature.

The Commonsense Nature and Success of Other Cultures

Anthropologists have found that although many aspects of other cultures are arbitrary conventions, some aspects of any culture and some of the variety in human cultures can be predicted because they follow logical rules. Cultural choices are often strikingly sensible and successful in their context. For example, historically, "primitive" cultures have probably done as well or better than "civilized" ones in protecting the health of most of their members, a pattern that was not reversed for the most part until the mid-nineteenth or twentieth centuries. As I shall discuss more fully in chapter 5, the world's most "primitive" people, living in very small groups, are, despite undoubted hardships, surprisingly efficient, comparatively well nourished and disease-free, and even reasonably long-lived by historical standards (if not those of the late twentieth century). Many manage to exploit environments in which no one else could or would bother to try to live. The point is not that primitive life is a Garden of Eden. It isn't. The point is that for most of history and for most people, civilization probably made things worse. It is the modern world's civilized poor, captives of the modern "world [political] system," not "the primitive," who are markedly malnourished or disease-ridden.

Human beings have repeatedly found that certain things work well in certain natural environments, with certain sizes or densities of population, or with certain types of social groups, and they have repeatedly adopted similar, sensible solutions to common problems. In other words, there are often good reasons for at least some cultural differences and good reasons why people resist change or even why they should not change.

A great deal can be predicted about a culture, for example, by knowing the size of the society that developed it. Much "primitive" behavior is sensible adaptation to small group size and relatively low population density. In fact, "primitive" behaviors are often the way members of large societies behave when they are in small groups. Alternative cultural forms are often much more successful than we think. Of course, we have to avoid judging the inherent capacity of other cultures to solve problems when we ourselves or other world powers have recently contributed to their problems by expropriating land, water, or other resources; redirecting local economies to serve fickle world markets; or restricting people's movement, as is the case for much of the Third World. The superiority of our own cultural system is not as obvious as we like to believe, except in its political or coercive power and in the sense that some of what we do is necessary in the context of the very high population densities that define "civilization."

Hunting and gathering and "primitive" farming economies are actually reasonably efficient in caloric returns for the time or labor expended, as long as population densities are low enough. Under these conditions they may compete successfully with more "advanced" systems. Moreover, they often represent sustainable systems or systems whose gradual erosion of the environment is very slow by modern standards. Walking into a supermarket with a large bankroll of inherited money is clearly the most efficient way for an individual to get food. Farming in a rice paddy that someone else has already developed at the cost of great labor may also be very efficient, as is modern American farming once water, fuel, energy, fertilizer, seed, and all mechanical needs, transport, and storage facilities have been provided. But next to these techniques, hunting a large animal when you see one (even with a spear) may be the most efficient way to get food that human beings have ever invented (in terms of caloric return for hours spent). The fact that most of us don't hunt to support ourselves says as much about the increasing difficulty of finding such animals and our own enormous numbers as it does about technological "progress." In any case, "primitive" people commonly have very good intuition about the relative efficiency of the options available to them and it is often this sense, not ignorance, that shapes their choices.

Moreover, "primitive" people are commonly relatively clean, particularly in comparison to the urbanized members of historic and modern civilizations. They may not bathe a lot, but their natural lifestyles discourage the transmission of many of the very germs and parasites that force the rest of us to wash frequently and to develop sophisticated systems to eliminate our waste and garbage. Moreover, when they are free to exploit large areas with reasonable resources, they get well-balanced diets that are surprisingly rich in protein, vitamins, minerals, and fiber and relatively low in calories. Their diets are better balanced than the diets of most of the modern world's population.

Other aspects of cultural systems are also predictable and appear quite sensible if we know the size of the population and whether the people fully share a culture and consider themselves "one nation" by kinship or think of themselves as interacting with strangers. Reciprocal (nonmarket) styles of exchange (discussed in chapter 3), which may seem foreign to us, make a great deal of sense once those variables are taken into consideration. People who live in small groups tend to use a (reciprocal) system which is often written off as "primitive communism" and assailed, like all "communism," by American politicians. (A letter to the editor in the *New York Times* in early 1995 actually said that the United States was justified in pushing some small tribes in South America out of the way because they were "communists"—one of the most ignorant, chauvinistic, and bigoted suggestions I have ever heard.)

The "communism" referred to—which *is* communism in the truest sense, not our distorted perception of it—is actually in use in most American families and plays a major part in "family values." Even in our capitalistic society, we do not typically behave as capitalists at home. Within the family we expect to share and to give on the basis of affection, family ties, need, and ability to provide, not profit. Most of us would consider this a morally "higher" type of exchange than that in the marketplace. Parents don't sell food to the highest bidder among their children (or sell it to strangers who can pay more). They distribute it "fairly," invoking some mix of cultural principles of evenhandedness and differential need. (Even American families, of course, hold somewhat irrational cultural notions of what "fairness" means relative to real nutritional needs.)

Parents don't expect much from their children in return, at least in the near future. What American parents haven't bought gifts at birthdays and holidays—not to mention providing food, clothing, and shelter for a child for the rest of the year? The return? A handprint pressed into a clay plaque and wrapped in a smudged, sticky sheet of paper ("I made it myself in school"). From each according to ability, to each according to need, the whole thing bound together by kinship and affection and the vague, unspoken promise of future reciprocity—the promise that care will be returned later when and in whatever form it is needed as the child grows and becomes able and the parents age. If one understands that in small-scale societies people typically are all kin, one can appreciate the inherent rationality and dignity of a system of exchange based on personal relations, sharing, and vague future obligations rather than on markets and profit.

Understanding the Context of Other People's Choices

Cultural relativism means that we have to consider any behavior in its context to comprehend why it occurs. Such understanding may lead us to reevaluate and even appreciate behaviors that initially seem bizarre. They may be serving important but latent purposes that are not obvious to us (and sometimes not even to the people who practice them).

One of the most frequently cited papers in anthropology describes the introduction of a seemingly trivial technological change to a tribe of hunter-gatherers. It explores the rich but hidden ramifications of such changes and the interconnectedness of a cultural system. Lauriston Sharpe's "Steel Axes for Stone Age Australians," as the title implies, explores the social consequences of missionaries' gifts of steel axes to people accustomed to using stone. Every account I have seen says that steel axes (unlike many "improvements") do represent an advance in efficiency compared to stone axes. Moreover, steel axes don't pollute the environment or have unforeseen health consequences, so there is no obvious sense in which the gift was anything but just that, a real gift. And it was appreciated as such by the recipients. The problem was that people didn't think about the other meanings of the stone axes. Stone had been procured through male trade networks across the Australian continent. These also served as networks of other traded commodities, as well as of communication, alliance, mutual obligation, and economic insurance. The stone axes were also a status symbol, which, for better or worse, reinforced the status of men and their power in their families. Steel axes came from the Christian missionaries and only from them, ignoring and hence undermining the political networks of the people; and they came not to the leaders or elders of the group but to anyone who was willing to come to the mission, often women and younger men. The axes rewarded and empowered people who had previously lacked influence and even people who deviated from cultural norms. The steel axes improved cutting but they undermined the trade partnerships, social relationships, and symbols of the group. It was as if benevolent Martians had landed in the United States and began to hand out gifts of great value, conferring great power, to children and street people. (This example makes another point. People who are willing to take the lead in participating in a colonial situation or even talking to anthropologists or missionaries are often fairly unusual by their own cultural standards, as are people who are willing to deal with foreign governments or outside corporations. Such people don't represent the societies from which they come, and we can't reasonably say that we have reached an agreement or signed a treaty or contract with a particular society because we have dealt with such people. We can't assume that such contracts should be legally binding. After all, I can't buy your house for twenty-five dollars by getting one of your children, your neighbor, or the family maid to sign a contract just because you were not home and that person came to the door.)

Many components of any culture serve several functions. An African giraffe hunt and the social interactions involved in the distribution of the meat are depicted in *The Hunters* by John Marshall, an educational film well known among anthropologists. I often ask my students what would happen if we outlawed hunting in that society and instead offered to supply beef from a truck (or provide jobs). Such a scene has been played out over and over again in various forms in colonial societies. The nutritional value of the beef would be about the same as the giraffe it replaced, although there are a few ways in which giraffe meat is probably healthier than domestic beef. But hunting is not just about nutrition; it is also about pride, being a man, and having a valued job to do, about exercise, leadership, group entertainment, social bonds through sharing, and many other values that farmers and craftspersons in our own society would appreciate. Beef from a truck isn't an adequate substitute any more than most of us would accept the nutritional equivalent of a Thanksgiving turkey provided in the form of Spam. The loss of the nonnutritional value of the giraffe can be almost as devastating as the loss of the nutritional value, given what we know about what it takes to maintain the coherence of a culture.

We might do well to apply this lesson about looking at things in their context to American culture as well. In what ways, beyond the obvious, did cars, electric lights, or personal computers—and the cultural baggage that comes with each—change the values of society? How did they alter the structure of families or communities, sex roles, and so forth? Are we paying a price that no one anticipated, a price that no one fully perceives even now? The results that are *not* obvious often turn out to be the important ones. What is the cultural meaning of the automobile beyond its obvious purpose for transportation? What has the automobile come to symbolize in American culture that makes it so hard for us to consider alternatives that other people use with great efficiency?

Cultural Relativism and Purposeful Change

Trying to make changes in people's behavior without such analysis can be frustrating because people won't go along. It can also be dangerous if people do go along—or are forced to do so—but no one has anticipated the full range of consequences. Both kinds of negative consequences have happened with many of our well-intentioned attempts at "aid."

Robert Desowitz, in his charming book *New Guinea Tapeworms and Jewish Grandmothers,* provides readable and often humorous accounts of attempts at medical assistance gone wrong for precisely these reasons. An attempt to eliminate a tapeworm parasite from people in New Guinea failed because the campaign involved changing the behavior of the group in ways that they refused. The behaviors in question involved cultural values that were not fully understood by the doctors. Thorough cooking of pork was necessary for health, but the ritual uses of pork prevented it—and the ritual was considered more important than health. In other instances, "good" medical practices were thwarted by the reality that people's working day had a very different schedule from what doctors were used to, and their economies placed different demands on them. Medicine came up against several additional barriers: authority and communication often radiated in different patterns than they do in Western society; people had conflicting social and role demands; the symbolism people perceived in Western medicine violated their own symbolic values; and "bad" health practices (like undercooking pork or cigarette smoking) often had symbolic meanings that overrode health considerations.

Most important, Desowitz points out that the Western doctors came with a lot of cultural baggage of their own, along with their scientific medicine. It wasn't just the cultural assumptions or latent purposes of the "others" that got in the way, but also those of the doctors. The Western doctors perceived themselves as superior and as having "correct" answers, and they assumed that their cultural style, not just their medicine, had to be transferred. They assumed that people would "naturally" see the logic of their position once it was offered. When transferring technology or teaching it to others, we find it hard to separate the essential parts of our own culture, in this case the medicine, from the cultural baggage attached to it. Desowitz's book offers the valuable insight that many of the unexpected cultural issues and problems of dealing with health in the Third World have counterparts in American culture, a moral that everyone, especially medical personnel, needs to understand.

On a larger scale, many anthropologists and ecologists question the work of such organizations as the World Bank for their failure to take into account the rich array of things that are going on in any culture and the potentially negative secondary consequences of the changes they make. The bank appears to assume that economic "development" and technological "progress" are obviously right, and thus it works primarily with individuals from those cultures who see benefits (including personal profit) in progress. But building dams and irrigation systems may bring malaria and other insect-borne diseases, as well as schistosomiasis, an almost equally devastating disease that is transmitted in standing water. Dams destroy land and displace people. In addition to their possible ecological damage, these technological "improvements" also change land tenure systems and the distribution of ownership, dislocate communities, undermine traditional values and symbols that once held communities together, and create new poverty and a new class of disconnected people even as they make some people very wealthy. Not all the damage can be measured with economic statistics. We have to study, think hard, and consult broadly with the intended recipients about whether to offer changes in their lives. And, if, collectively, we decide to implement changes, we need to make sure that we have the consent of the people and that the changes serve the real needs of all the people involved, not just our needs or the needs of those who are eager for change. In addition we ought to be ready to help correct the inevitable negative consequences as well as to celebrate the achievement.

The understanding of cultural relativism is also essential for dealing with behaviors in which we may wish to promote change after careful thought. For example, female infanticide and female circumcision are still widely practiced in various parts of the world. Female circumcision is common in parts of Africa, the Middle East, and Southeast Asia and is now spreading to the United States with immigrants from those regions. Female infanticide, which is fairly common in South Asia and other regions, is also practiced in the United States—mostly in the form of the abortion of female fetuses after amniocentesis. The point is that people don't do these things because they are ignorant, evil, or immoral (even if we consider the behaviors themselves to be). They do them in response to powerful pressures or incentives built into their economic and cultural systems. If we wish to change the behaviors, among others or among ourselves, we have to identify those pressures and incentives accurately and address them.

Although some Western families may abort female fetuses as a matter of casual sex preference, in most parts of the world, female infanticide is grounded in powerful systems of economic rules of ownership and inheritance, established sex roles, and marriage patterns that make daughters very expensive (because one must provide a dowry for them) and of relatively little use in one's old age (because they move away when they marry). Sons, in contrast, receive dowries from their wives' families and are sources of labor, income, and lifelong support for their parents. Unless some of those rules are changed or grinding poverty is eliminated, there will be a powerful incentive to continue eliminating female infants.

Such behaviors have certain functions in the cultural system. If we want to understand or replace them, we need to know what those functions are and devise means of satisfying them (both the conscious and unconscious ones). Those who would eliminate abortion, prostitution, drug abuse, single-parent families, and crime in our own system would do well to learn the same lesson. Those behaviors also are responses to social pressures and incentives, not just to ignorance, obscure criminal leanings, or even "low IQ."

Female circumcision is a good example to consider in a little more detail because this topic has received attention from public media and tests the boundaries of cross-cultural tolerance and cultural relativism. We have to begin, of course, by recognizing that in our society we perform male circumcision, and that for the most part our reasons are not well defined rationally or scientifically. We are told that it doesn't hurt, but all the while the babies scream. Why do we do it?

Ancient Hebrews and modern Jews and Muslims circumcised male children as a symbolic sacrifice, to reinforce their manhood, to initiate boys into membership in the group, to mark them as members of a group, to set that group apart, and to define a limited range of marital and sexual partners for their women. The Hebrews or Muslims, of course, would not necessarily have mentioned all these reasons if asked. No culture consciously describes all of its purposes. Circumcision even provided status and income for those who performed the operation. This may seem a trivial reason, but practitioners (like the people who sell American cigarettes) are often a vocal and powerful lobby for the continuation of any practice.

Circumcision has spread widely beyond Jews and Muslims in the United States, and even though the practice is often questioned, Americans continue to circumcise their male children for similar reasons or perhaps because we fear the psychological scars to boys who don't look like their fathers or their peers. So the custom is self-perpetuating, whether it has any real value or causes real harm. And yet, there is little evidence that male circumcision produces lasting pain or illness or threatens life, or even that it interferes with urination or male sexual performance or enjoyment. (There has even been some suggestion that circumcision helps to prevent penis cancer in men and [perhaps] cervical cancer in their female partners. But whether or not these speculations prove to be true, they are so recent that they can't possibly provide the rationale for the historic practice. Yet the publicity and the *belief* that these speculations are true have probably contributed to the perpetuation of the custom.)

Female circumcision involves (at a minimum) removing the hood or prepuce of the clitoris in an operation analogous to the male procedure. But it can also involve excising the whole clitoris or even trimming a woman's labia and sewing them shut, to be cut open only when she is married and her husband desires sexual access—and perhaps even then to be sewn shut again if he intends to travel. This more extreme form of the practice provides a chastity belt of the most drastic and irreversible kind, and it serves both symbolically and anatomically to control female sexual urges in cultures which assume that female sexuality might otherwise be both uncontrolled and dangerous. (Cultures differ markedly in assessing whether men or women are better able to exercise sexual restraint despite the absence of evidence of any underlying biological differences between human groups. Only fifty years ago it was assumed in the United States that all restraint had to come from chaste women's moral strength because everyone knew that men were incapable of restraining their urges. But even the British disagreed with Americans' perception, resulting in a certain amount of confusion and strain when GIs met British women during World War II. The recent change in the sexual habits of American women obviously is controlled by cultural patterns, not by their genes.)

Whatever the pattern of female circumcision, the operation, usually done at puberty, is very painful. Moreover, it can leave a woman for the rest of her life with only a tiny hole through which to eliminate urine and menstrual blood, a loss of sexual satisfaction, constant pain, especially during intercourse, extraordinary difficulty in childbirth, and a very high likelihood of infection. So why is it done? And why, more mysteriously, do older women perform the surgery, young girls submit, and both try to evade attempts to suppress the practice? It is not something done by cruel and vicious men to protesting but helpless women and girls. Some of the people who fight most strongly against attempts to eliminate female circumcision are in fact often older women and the girls themselves.

For the older women, performing the operation is one of their few avenues to prestige and livelihood—it is their special role, and they cling to it both as an economic necessity and as a basis for their status in society (just as, say, the manufacturers of cigarettes persevere in producing their product, despite all evidence of the damage it causes, for fear that no other role with equal rewards will be available to them or that their lives will change in unforeseen ways). The older women also have a lifelong belief in the sanctity of the custom and find it threatening to question the belief so late in their lives— just as cigarette manufacturers apparently can convince themselves that their product does no harm because to admit otherwise is damaging to their self-image.

The girls who are circumcised participate, usually willingly despite the pain, because they equate the operation with growing up, being a member of the group, being real women, proving their value, proving their devotion to their parents and to their husband's honor, getting a license to marry, and being acceptable on the marriage market (just as cigarette smoking, almost always unpleasant at first, seems necessary as a social marker to some American teenagers). Marriage in such societies isn't just an extended sexual dalliance, as it may be among wealthy career-minded Western men and women (a style and perception of marriage that then trickle down to others in our society). In the societies in question, marriage is an economic partnership that is necessary for survival. The need to be acceptable in the marriage market is a very real concern in societies where women have few other options and the men they want to marry often have strong feelings about the condition of their wives. Women's sexual pleasure is low on everybody's list of priorities (as it was in the United States until about forty years ago). Men associate the operation with the purity and fidelity of women, the honor of their families, and the purity of the family line in societies where inheritance through the male line controls most property, making illegitimacy a pronounced concern.

In one of the most human and readable accounts of cross-cultural interactions I have ever read, *Dancing Skeletons*, anthropologist Katherine Dettwyler describes a conversation with a Malian (West African) woman about the custom of circumcision. The Malian woman, herself circumcised ("of course"), absolutely refuses to believe that Dettwyler can be happily married and respected, able to have children—her husband, in-laws, and parents still honored—if she has never had the operation. It's hard to figure out who is more incredulous about whom! But it is very clear that the superiority of the American way isn't at all obvious to the Malian woman—and also that, for a Malian woman, trying to change the pattern can be very threatening.

This custom doesn't fit my idea of moral behavior, and like most anthropologists I would not include it in a list of behaviors I respect just because it is someone else's culture. But we still have to understand what is going on if we want to change it. No one will thank us for liberating them. Perhaps if older women had another role . . . if the choice of husbands was wider . . . if girls had other choices about their futures (such as careers or travel) . . . if the right people (the generation of women in the middle? the men?) could be reached. . . . If tobacco farmers could grow a different crop . . . if they could be offered other employment . . . if tobacco companies had the chance to reinvest their assets . . . if tobacco-state politicians could find some other issue on which to run for office . . . if the children who take up smoking had some healthier way to assert their independence and adulthood. . . . Changing people's customary and culturally patterned behavior requires awareness of context and of the secondary benefits associated with a particular behavior. The same principle applies to American perceptions of American minorities. For example, what we see as laziness or ignorance, reflected in poor school performance or teenage pregnancy, may actually be purposeful behavior fulfilling various cultural functions, even if those functions cannot always be articulated.

The same principles apply in dealing with problems on an international scale. Why can't we simply stop people from making so many babies? I have already pointed out that fertility often involves purposeful behavioral choices, not innate reproductive ability. Nor does it imply thoughtlessness, or stupidity. We might do well to ask *why* people make babies. This is not as silly as it sounds, because people everywhere know how *not* to make babies, by avoiding sex or even while being sexually active. Whatever the reason, there is evidence that fertility has gone up during the evolution of civilization, and it appears that in many parts of the world fertility has increased as a result of European colonial domination. So it is hardly as though our "civilized" intervention is needed to stem high fertility that is otherwise a natural characteristic of "primitive" people.

Although most people know about methods of birth control, abortion, and infanticide, it is possible that by providing easier and more attractive methods we can help people lower their birth rates. But the important point is that most people involved, including those in the United States, *want* children. To understand why, we have to understand what children provide for them, in unspoken as well as spoken ways.

This isn't the place for an extensive analysis, but a few things are pretty clear. First, children themselves are entertainment, and providing alternative entertainment, like television, cuts down on reproduction. Second, children are possessions that provide a sense of ownership and also warmth, emotional support, and uncritical love, particularly for people who have nothing else. Third, whether we are talking about people in a foreign land or unwed mothers in New York, children change a person's status in ways that may be considered desirable, so having children may be especially important to people whose political and economic circumstances yield no alternative means of achieving improved status. Fourth, particularly on farms, children can share the labor and thus provide productive wealth. And, children everywhere are potential sources of security for their parents' old age. In poor countries or in places where parents are not protected by a social security net, having many children ensures that some will live long enough to provide support for the parents later in life. Helping children survive is another important way to encourage people to cut down voluntarily on reproduction.

Perhaps partly for the same reasons, parents given the opportunity to accumulate a little wealth often voluntarily reduce their own reproduction rates. An improved standard of living—permitting people to share in economic wealth and growth—often acts as birth control. Poverty seems to cause high fertility more than the other way round.

Cultural relativism might also lead us to put the problem of population growth in a better perspective by seeing it from alternative points of view. For many people in the world the problem is not population growth itself but the absence of accompanying economic enfranchisement. In the "primitive" world, each additional person is one new unit of economic demand. One more mouth to feed means that so much more land has to be farmed or so much more food gathered. Parents feel the impact and the system adapts (albeit often with very slight diminishing returns, depending on how quickly and completely each new child earns his or her own keep and depending also on technological adjustments). People can see the relationship between population and food and can exercise rational restraint. And they feel or perceive themselves to be in control. That fact alone may help restrict fertility as people see the consequences of having to feed an additional mouth; but it also ensures that those babies who are born will have access to resources.

In the modern "civilized" world, where almost all wealth is privately owned, the poor exert little or no demand for resources. The world's food problem isn't a problem of supply but a problem of demand. The economic principle of demand combines need or desire *and the ability to pay.* (We may all covet a Ferrari automobile, but most of us will never be able to afford one. So we are not part of the demand for Ferraris; Ferrari doesn't count us when it decides how many cars to produce. For all our desire, we don't expand its market.) It is the lack of demand, not a lack of food, that is at the heart of the issue. The poor may want food, but they have no money, so they don't increase the demand for food or stimulate food production, nor do they force the world market to redirect itself to their needs. So they remain hungry despite the fact that there need be no shortage. After all, if the problem is that there isn't enough food, why are so many farmers out of work, so many farms abandoned, so many farmers paid to keep their land fallow? Sometimes the government buys the crops only to keep them in storage. Farming remains such a low priority for land use that we build or pave without regard for the quality of soil. Land is devoted to specialized luxury crops; other land is devoted to subsidized tobacco farming, when tobacco is basically a dangerous drug; land is devoted to growing sugar that the world doesn't need; land is devoted to the inherently inefficient practice of growing fodder crops for cattle—or birdseed. If the world's poor were able to generate a demand for food, farmers would have the incentive to grow more food instead of these unnecessary crops. But of course, it is precisely because there is no such demand that the rest of us get to eat so much beef so cheaply or devote so much land to recreation. We have a stake in other people's remaining poor.

Conversely, in the American free-market system, the rich are entitled to exert disproportionate demand (thousands or millions of times their numbers). It is, to a great extent, their large and accelerating demand, not the growing population of the poor, that stimulates the destruction of world resources. The Amazon rain forest is being destroyed not primarily by the people who live and farm there but by the outposts of wealthy civilization seeking resources. In Central America, where I have worked, it is not the growth of the Mayan population that threatens resources—many Maya don't own any land. It is the demand of relatively wealthy North Americans for beef, stimulating the more profitable but ecologically more wasteful and destructive production and export of cattle by wealthy landlords. Sometimes a little cultural relativism opens our eyes to the real nature of our problems. We can't resolve the food crisis without putting aside our blinders.

Cultural Relativism, Moral Imperatives, and Essential Conformity

What does cultural relativism imply about morality? It certainly doesn't deny it, as its critics imply. But it does say that we should not confuse what is moral with what is simply the American way or even the Christian way. Cultural relativism means that we must try to distinguish between things that are morally reprehensible or wrong and those that are just not our cultural or religious *style*. Most people in any culture have a powerful tendency to confuse the two. But in a world full of many cultures we cannot afford the confusion.

Distinguishing universal moral imperatives from cultural conventions is a complex problem that has been debated at length by both anthropologists and philosophers. People might agree that war violates moral imperatives and that styles of art or dance are purely cultural conventions. Those same people might still reasonably debate the relativity or universality of behaviors and "moral" precepts nearer the middle of the spectrum. Moreover, what appears to be a moral absolute in one culture might itself be a cultural convention in another. For example, we used to think that covering the body in clothing was a moral imperative except in certain limited contexts— although other people would hardly agree and despite the fact that our "absolute" standards are themselves changing. Americans also tend to consider the rights of the individual as absolute, whereas other cultures value the honor and obligation of families and communities far more and consider our emphasis on individual freedom to be extreme if not immoral.

A perfect resolution of absolute and relative morality and values may be no more attainable than any other ideal. But making genuine efforts toward distinguishing the two and being sensitive to the problem are essential to tolerance and to world peace, justice, and order. Morals and values are not necessarily correct just because they are ours or because they are traditional.

I personally would begin (perhaps with my American blinders focusing my attention on individuals) by placing behaviors that do real harm to real people in the realm of moral absolutes and putting behaviors that harm only American (or other) cultural conventions to the other side. For me, letting people starve is a moral issue; desecrating the flag is not. In a gross way, the distinction is not too hard to make. But "real harm to real people" itself requires definition. For me, behaviors that inflict physical harm on people, cause their deaths, leave them hungry, or expose them to physical dangers or diseases involve the clearest moral absolutes. And because with some exceptions human biology is fairly standard, it is relatively easy to develop universal moral standards to deal with common biological needs. Everybody, regardless of culture or nationality, should have the right to eat, to have peace and freedom from abuse, to enjoy health and health care, and so forth. That should be our highest moral imperative. I would say that behaviors that interfere with those rights are morally reprehensible, regardless of the culture in which they occur.

To me, avoiding psychological and social harm to others is also the stuff of universal morality (although it ranks below physical harm, if the two must compete). But here morality is harder to define because psychological and social needs are subject to cultural definition. I would say that there is a universal need for people to be able to participate in social systems that satisfy their own psychological and social needs in that they provide fulfillment and positive social feedback from others. People should have the right to define those needs for themselves—except that their needs can't involve harming others. We need to respect the dignity of others in their own terms and in their own cultures and societies.

Because symbols and conventions are also very important to people's lives (and even to their health), respecting other people's symbols should be a universal principle of behavior, again with the exception that no group's symbols and conventions should be allowed to harm others. However, arbitrarily imposing our definitions of cultural values or symbols on others, as we often do in the name of morality, is the antithesis of morality. Proselytizing by the sword and conquering or exerting economic pressure in the name of religion and perhaps even broadcasting our symbols to an unwilling audience are immoral. Doing harm to others in the name of Islam or Christianity, capitalism, communism, or even "freedom" is immoral.

Avoiding real harm to people is the bottom line. If people in some foreign country maim or kill their daughters (some do, as I have pointed out), I think it ought to stop. But what of the fact that people in some cultures may marry more than one spouse? Polygamy, in which a person may have two or more legal marital partners at one time, is "immoral" by our system. In some societies it may be abusive to women, in which case the abuse, per se, ought to stop. But polygamy may, in fact, be highly moral in the larger sense I have described, and it may be favored by both men and women. It is often a pragmatic system guaranteeing that all people are protected by marital ties and given an opportunity to have children. In societies without welfare systems and social security nets, marriage and children are the primary basis for all social entitlements. One purpose of the levirate, a custom known in biblical times in which a man was supposed to marry his brother's widow, was to guarantee that widows continued to have all the rights due to a wife: nurturance, food, and shelter; sex; bearing all-important children; and the appropriate social and economic interactions. Polygamy, whether through the

levirate or other means, also solves one social problem often implicated in female infanticide: the fear of having too many unmarriage-
able daughters. Thus the issue is whether the system promotes the
welfare of individuals, not whether it conforms to our own arbitrary
values.

In college I developed a friendship with a Nigerian student
named Sam, who was raised in a polygamous household. Sam
couldn't afford to go home, so he used to come to my house for
vacations. Once, at the end of a visit, we all prepared to go back to
college: my brother, myself, Sam, and another friend. At the door,
Sam stopped to say goodbye to my mother and thank her. And he
said, probably perceiving the isolation of American housewives of
the period, "It must be very lonely for you when your children
leave." My mother replied that it was lonely—but that it must be
worse for Sam's own mother, who wouldn't see him for ten years
(until he had finished medical school). Sam laughed and with a mixture of sadness and humor said, "Yes, she misses me—but, you see,
she isn't lonely; she has the advantage of all the other wives and all
their children to keep her company." The human need for company
is universal (and that is where the absolute morality lies). The mechanism for fulfilling the need may vary. Insisting that ours is the only
proper way seems to me highly immoral.

We also have to recognize that our obligation to act in a moral
manner, by our own standards, cannot be limited to those who look,
act, and think as we do. No system of morality can permit us to
harm others by doing things we would not do to one another. Other
people have the same rights we insist on for ourselves. It can't be
moral to allow chemicals or medicines that are banned in the United
States for safety or health reasons to be dumped or sold in other
countries. It can't be moral to smuggle drugs, even in the name of
freedom and democracy. Nor can it be moral to allow our companies
in foreign countries to use child labor or to pay wages that we consider immorally low here. We have to maintain our own standards
of morality while recognizing the standards of other people. Ethics
is more than a weapon with which Democrats bash Republicans or
vice versa.

Real morality does not grow from American constitutional precepts or religious symbols; it grows from the real needs of other
human beings, which, at their core, are universal. However, all cultures and religions also measure morality in terms of adherence to

their own specific rules, values, and symbols. And because some conformity is necessary to run a society, all cultures are justified in doing so—up to a point. But we have to recognize that, in this (latter) sense, morality is as arbitrary, as much a convention, as any other cultural pattern. We tend to confuse the two meanings of morality, appealing to "moral" principles as absolutes when we are in fact defending arbitrary cultural conventions. Learning how to tell the two types of morality apart would be an important contribution to mutual tolerance and peaceable world order.

Absolute morality aside, we also have to distinguish between essential and nonessential conformity, between cultural rules that require complete compliance and those that don't, because while enforcing compliance in the former case, we can tolerate and even celebrate variety in the latter. Of course, we have to require compliance with standard driving rules, regardless of where or in what culture someone originally learned to drive. And, like any culture, Americans have many other laws and expectations defining what people may or may not do, which must apply to all people regardless of their place or culture of origin. At the same time, we have to recognize that many of our laws and expectations are conventional and no more moral in an absolute sense than the choice of the "correct" side of the road to drive on. That is, we have to see that all people conform in certain ways without conveying the message that their prior failure to do so reflects inherent immorality or inferiority. We don't after all, assume that a British or Japanese citizen, trained to drive on the left, is inherently inferior. We just make them change sides of the road.

Most of us recognize, however, that some things don't have to be standardized, by law or by custom. There seems to be little need to insist on uniformity in what people eat, as long as we make sure that they have the ability and the knowledge to eat a balanced diet. Much would be lost and little gained by standardizing eating habits.

The difficulty comes in deciding how to deal with gray areas of freedom and conformity. The U.S. Constitution is dedicated to the proposition that the government may not use law to specify people's religion; and I can think of no reason that religious conformity is necessary or desirable for us to function as a society. But there seems to be a strong undercurrent of feeling in the United States at the moment that we ought to be demanding more religious conformity focused on Christianity and "family values."

One of the most perplexing issues has to do with linguistic conformity: the insistence that there can be only one standard language in the United States, English. Clearly, conformity in language would make communication easier, but it would rob some of us of our individuality and our culture, and it would rob the rest of us of some of the richness that we gain in our lives from enjoying diversity. Besides, the way we go about insisting on the use of English tends to imply that there is a symbolic or even moral imperative involved, not just a practical need. Our insistence on using only English and the *manner* in which we go about it denigrates large portions of the population and serves to divide, not unify, the country. If we insist on standardizing, why not make every American child learn two languages, English and another of their choice? This would remove the stigma that dual-language education now carries. It would make every child more aware of the existence of others and also improve communication among us; and it would make everyone's skills more marketable in the world arena. Most other modern countries demand competence in two or more languages above a certain level, and many of the world's most "primitive" people speak several languages. The American myth that no language other than English is necessary should rapidly evaporate as the international economy becomes more important.

If we do not teach two languages, perhaps we can at least communicate the idea that it is useful for everyone to learn the same language, which in our country, for historical reasons, happens to be English, without simultaneously conveying the false sense that English is naturally superior or that speaking only Spanish (or any other language) is a lifelong stigma.

We have to be able to decide which conventions are truly moral, which (although arbitrary) are essential for the continuation of our society, and which are merely conveniences, matters of style, or even prejudice. I suspect that if we did make such distinctions, the most important rules would gain more compliance because resistance and resentment would be reduced. People understand (or think they understand) when conformity is essential, as in driving on the correct side of the road, and when it is not, and they resent unnecessary demands to conform. We may have to teach people why certain kinds of conformity are essential if the reasons are not obvious. Perhaps we should drop some such demands for conformity altogether.

We can maintain our belief in something very like the Golden

Rule as a principle of action—but it requires a slight modification. "Do unto others as you would have others do unto you" is beautiful, particularly in a small and homogeneous world in which people share a culture. But the rule is not quite sufficient in the modern, multi-cultural world. Perhaps we should update it in the original spirit but in the face of broader knowledge and say that we should treat other people as *they* would have us treat them—as our own preferences might not always be shared. Assuming that other people naturally share our preferences or moral precepts (or "ought" to) misses the intention of the original phrase. It violates the Golden Rule. Real morality involves understanding that other people may actually want different things than you want and being ready to adjust your behavior to recognize those differences. Real tolerance doesn't mean permitting other people to be like us; it means permitting them to be different.

To give an obvious example, it is important to honor someone else's religious beliefs, but we need to do so in ways *they* appreciate, not just in our own style—honoring the Sabbath on Friday, when visiting, rather than Sunday, if that is what our friends do, or wearing hats or taking off our shoes if their practice demands it.

As a more subtle and important example, we need to recognize and honor the ways in which other people's cultural grammars, their emotional and moral systems, may place different demands on them from the ones we are accustomed to. We have to recognize, for example, that some cultures demand much more (or less) emotional expression of grief or pain than we consider appropriate, and not denigrate other people's behavior. We have to recognize that cultural differences demand that people play certain roles in unfamiliar ways—that, for example, a son reared in a another culture may owe his mother something different than we would owe in similar circumstances or that marriage may have various meanings in different cultures. Perhaps we even need to recognize that members of an oppressed group may face particularly strong culturally defined needs to express their pride or to build pride by being exclusive in ways that members of the majority in power need not and should not be permitted to do. (After all, it does the majority little harm if a small group somewhere wants to have an exclusive club. But if the majority excludes others, or if finance and power are conveyed within such groups, then the practice is very damaging.)

It is not sufficient simply to allow an African, Native, or Asian

American to participate in the mainstream culture if this requires them to "do as we would have you do" and deny their own identity and culture. It has to be possible to participate without excessive conformity and without having to deny one's heritage or to assume all the inessential and arbitrary conventions of the mainstream culture. This is one of the things African Americans said in rejecting integration, the idea that they would finally be allowed to be "just like white folk." They didn't want to be "just like white folk"; they wanted only the chance to support themselves and to have freedom of movement and respect on their own terms. They were objecting, rightly, to the insistence on unnecessary arbitrary conformity (as well as to the fact that even conformity didn't get them in the door). (Their terms did not have to include a different set of driving rules because common sense showed the need for conformity in that area.)

It is essential—and very rewarding—to honor people for what they are even while demanding necessary conformity. Friends we make from different regions, walks of life, religions, ethnic groups, and colors or "races" add richness to our lives and breadth to our experience, our perceptions, and our options. They offer us not only their ethnic foods and dances and their holidays, but also their values and understandings, their definitions of human roles, and even their perceptions of the world, of events, and of history. Cultural relativism involving exposure to other cultures—learning from "others" who are themselves free to act, feel, and think according to their own cultural precepts—is an important road to a rich life and real freedom. There is no freedom unless we are aware of, and have accurate information about, alternative courses of belief and action. Ultimately, cultural relativism is about freedom of thought.

· CHAPTER FIVE ·

Some Assumptions of American Culture and the Problems They Generate

CULTURAL RELATIVISM IS ESSENTIAL to accurate self-perception and self-understanding. It can help us solve our own problems as well as increase our tolerance and understanding of others. This may be the most important meaning of relativism and the most crucial contribution of anthropological knowledge. By studying other cultures we learn that *every* culture has arbitrary, conventional rules about behavior and arbitrary beliefs, logic, and emotions. We also learn that every culture acts for reasons that are hidden and sets up sometimes imperfect and incorrect perceptions of what is going on. What people say and even think they do is not always what they actually do or why they do it. American culture is no different from others, no better and no worse in this regard. We, too, make our decisions within a narrow framework of cultural assumptions or cultural blinders without even realizing that the blinders are there. And, like other cultures, ours is characterized by a huge gap between the way we describe ourselves and the way we act.

Our failures are only human, and I do not mean to suggest that other countries or cultures are less chauvinistic or more moral than the United States. But because of American power and influence, we are in a position to do unprecedented harm to others as well as to each other. That obliges us to learn what our own arbitrary conventions and false perceptions are and how they relate to our biological and moral imperatives and to the needs of others. We have to be willing to think about these conventions and even change or compromise the arbitrary parts where it seems appropriate to do so, rather than just pursuing them blindly. Some of our arbitrary assumptions and false perceptions lie at the heart of our intolerance and the problems we face.

We in the United States, of course, also have the same need and the same right as any other society to set cultural standards and demand conformity that permits us to interact coherently. We have the same need and right as any other culture to reinforce compliance and patriotism. But we should not lose sight of the fact that this is what we are doing. We should never confuse cultural standards that permit coherent interaction with natural superiority or higher morality. We should never cease to distinguish the necessary from the purely conventional, purely patriotic, or merely convenient. And we should never sacrifice our willingness to balance the needs of conformity and patriotism with other social needs, values, and goals. We shouldn't sacrifice the health and quality of life of the players involved for the sake of cultural symbols. Nor can we fail to continue to examine alternative and potentially better ways to do certain things.

We need to remember that "civilized," "modern," "healthy," "clean," "efficient," "industrial," "moral," "advanced," and "good" are not synonyms for Western, or American. We need to see that sometimes the qualities and values implied by each of those words contradict or compete with one another. We need to see that, although the parts of any cultural system are interrelated and mutually reinforcing, resisting change, we can learn those relationships and make thoughtful changes in our own system by incorporating parts of many cultures without buying the whole package of any one. We can recognize and even adopt the valuable perceptions and conventions of other cultures much as we selectively borrow their art or inventions, without having to adopt the entire lifestyle. Recognizing the inherent value in some "foreign" or "primitive" ideas doesn't mean that we have to live in mud huts.

With care, we can change our system without threatening the whole. We can selectively adopt what we have learned from other cultures without discarding the valuable pieces of our own system. Selective modification is, in fact, the only way for any system to survive. Thoughtful change is the best way to protect our culture as a whole. It is the mindless pursuit of certain purely conventional values that is likely to lead to the collapse of the system or to violent backlash. Extremism promotes extremism.

Unfortunately, just as being trained from birth to speak English makes it hard for Americans to comprehend or even recognize the existence of an alternative system of sound and grammar, our cultural principles often prevent us from considering other options or from even conceiving that such possibilities might exist.

Fifty years ago, most Americans undoubtedly considered our food the best in the world and would have been highly suspicious of attempts to get us to eat new things. That kind of ethnocentrism is not surprising, given what is probably natural, biologically driven caution about new foods and given that cultures motivate people to conform even in choices of food. But, in the United States in those days, except in a few cities or particular ethnic enclaves, Chinese food was hard to find, pizza was just appearing, tacos and other Mexican foods were still on the horizon, and Japanese, Thai, Indian, Middle Eastern, Ethiopian, Vietnamese, and other cuisines were almost unheard of. I think that most of us, even in the small towns of Middle America, would now agree that our cuisine has subsequently been enriched enormously by the addition of these "foreign" tastes.

Similarly, 150 years ago people would have said that our music, deriving from the classical traditions of Europe, was the best music there was. But the Western musical tradition has certainly been enriched since then by an infusion of African and African American musical traditions, producing blues, jazz, and rock, which have profoundly increased the range of musical options available, to the apparent enjoyment of a very large segment of the population. We have also enjoyed the enrichment of "foreign" techniques in painting, sculpture, graphic design, and architecture—and foreign contributions to our corporate efficiency, electronics, computer design, automobiles, factory design, medicine, martial arts, and meditation techniques. The list is very long. In medicine, for example, not only have we gotten a better sense of the natural functioning of the human body, not only have we begun to emulate "primitive" concern for the psychological and social being of the patient as a means of curing, we have also found it rewarding to try to identify the active chemical ingredients of "ethnic" medicines. With a mix of cultural chauvinism and profit motive, however, we don't usually give credit or compensation to the ethnic source. We don't recognize what might be considered other people's contributions or their intellectual or cultural property rights because they haven't been patented or copyrighted in our particular style or in our courts.

It stands to reason that other aspects of our culture can also be enriched by exposure and honest, open-minded attention to various aspects of other cultural traditions. We might broaden our thinking about our economics, politics, and social organization. We might also make more encompassing our perception, emotions, cognition, and values, and even areas of science. We might well benefit, for example, from emulating the sense of family and community responsibility, polite behavior, and respect for one another and the elderly that many "primitive" cultures commonly display, even if we don't wish to imitate all of their constraints. We might do well to learn from the ability of other cultures to "employ" everyone, to provide meaningful lives for elderly people and people with disabilities, or to find meaningful roles for young adults and ease the transition of adolescence. The problem is not that other cultures have nothing but food and dance to offer; the problem is that we have been unwilling to look beyond these obvious components.

American cultural values, rules, and systems—ranging from hygiene and health care to private property, from the pursuit of profit to the celebration of "freedom," and even to our perception of history—are, to a large degree, simply arbitrary conventions. They are not clearly "correct" or divinely inspired; nor are they the only, the most efficient, the most modern, or necessarily the "best" solutions to natural or social problems. This is not to say that they should be abandoned wholesale, nor that our system is bad. It is simply that our cultural patterns are not so obviously inviolate that we need never review and adjust them for pragmatic reasons or compromise them to fulfill other important goals. It is possible to hold values thoughtfully, in moderation, rather than wave them as patriotic flags which blind us and automatically forestall all discussion of alternatives.

Health and Hygiene

For example, health and hygiene are important values and there may well be objective ways to measure them. Americans pride ourselves on being the "cleanest," the most "advanced," the most scientifically sophisticated in such matters. We measure the hygienic "failures" of others by our standards and often don't even notice our own shortcomings. But American perceptions of health and hygiene, like those of other groups, are often mere cultural conventions with no real scientific value.

Americans like to think that we are clean and other people are dirty, but other people have the opposite perception, often with equal justification. How, they ask, can you blow your nose in a piece of cloth or paper, put it in your pocket, and use the cloth again? How can you eat with the same hand you use to clean yourself after urinating or defecating or blot yourself with paper instead of washing thoroughly? How can you sit and expose the skin of your buttocks to the toilet instead of squatting so that only the bottom of your feet or shoes comes in contact with the ground? (a posture that may reduce germ transmission and may, in any case, relieve constipation and make bowel movement easier).

How can you jump in and out of the shower so fast, other people ask, when real cleaning takes a long time and involves real scrubbing? How can you have a dog in your house—and how can you allow it to run free, poking its nose into whatever it finds in the back alley, or drinking from your toilet, and then allow it to come to beg at the dinner table or lick your hands or your face? (Not long ago, serious researchers thought that dogs were implicated in spreading a virus that caused multiple sclerosis, explaining why MS is principally a disease of Western society where dogs are allowed in homes. So this was no idle criticism. This theory about the origin of MS is no longer widely held, but the potential of household pets to attract and spread germs is very real.)

It is important to note that the matter of toilets is not a question of being "primitive" or "civilized," of holes in the ground or latrines as opposed to modern toilets. In many parts of the affluent civilized (but not Western) world there are fancy tiled bathrooms, with immaculate porcelain toilets, flat on the ground, which flush but have no seats, just places to put your feet—and have faucets near them rather than rolls of toilet paper.

Small bands of mobile hunter-gatherers who move on when their campsites get dirty might well ask how we can bear to go on living in areas where our garbage builds up, rats and insects proliferate, and (until fairly recent history) feces accumulated. They might also ask how we can breathe air polluted with chemical fumes. And, as I have mentioned, the small groups and frequent movements of hunter-gatherers do help protect them from the diseases that make our sanitary precautions necessary. So while they may appear to be unclean by our standards, such groups may suffer fewer dirt-related diseases than we do. They certainly suffer less than the poor of the civilized world.

Almost all nutritionists and health researchers agree that, except where special health problems exist, breast-feeding babies is healthier for both mothers and babies than bottle-feeding them infant formula in terms of cleanliness, nutrition, economy, the infant's immunity to disease, its mental development, and the likelihood of future cancer for both mother and child. There is even some evidence that breast-feeding or not exposing an infant to formula improves a child's IQ. But through much of the twentieth century middle-class American women haven't nursed their infants, for reasons that often are nothing more than arbitrary cultural style. (Breast-feeding comes and goes, partly as a matter of pure fashion, a bit like skirt lengths or the shape of automobiles; but the use of infant formula, here and in other countries, is also heavily influenced by aggressive and often misleading commercial marketing of the formulas which the U.S. government has been extremely slow to regulate.) And, although the barriers are now coming down in some places, our society has imposed all kinds of arbitrary rules that make breast-feeding difficult, such as our culturally defined sexual obsession with breasts and fairly arbitrary cultural standards of decency, which treat breast-feeding in public as if it were indecent exposure. We also have refused until very recently to structure the workplace and other public places to permit breast-feeding in private, and we have refused to schedule women's work to permit nursing even though women all over the world manage to combine nursing and work. Can we learn to distinguish between situations in which breast-feeding is truly incompatible with other job demands and situations in which it is merely "improper" by some arbitrary cultural standard or is prevented simply by cultural inertia?

Having taught women everywhere that breast-feeding was "uncivilized" and unacceptable and that bottle-feeding was superior and healthier, American health authorities now have a moral obligation to teach or reinforce breast-feeding in the Third World, where its superiority over bottle-feeding is even greater than in the West. Breast-feeding is particularly valuable in places where there is little money to buy formula, where there is no way to sterilize bottles, and where water for mixing formula may be impure. Breast-feeding also clearly reduces the fertility we claim to abhor. Yet we don't teach breast-feeding because selling infant formula in the United States and in the Third World is highly profitable. How can we simultaneously push infant formula on the Third World and complain that birth rates are too high?

Our sexual fetish with women's breasts and particularly with large ones is itself cultural. People in many parts of the world don't consider women's breasts a focus of sexual interest, or they have different preferences. Our fetish is becoming a medical problem. Our preoccupation is beginning to resemble the historic Chinese preference for tiny bound feet among women, a practice that now seems bizarre and horrible to us. However, in both cases the preoccupation with particular body parts has resulted in artificially altering those parts to the point where they may lose their real function and may even be deformed beyond the known human range. In both cases, the deformation can threaten the health of the woman. By exporting magazine and television images we are exporting the large-breast fetish to people whose sexuality has survived millions of years without it.

Despite undeniable technological advances, particularly for problem pregnancies, American styles of giving birth often have little to do with scientific knowledge and a lot to do with fashion and politics, as Jessica Mitford described in *The American Way of Birth.* From the perspective of other cultures, many of our practices seem ignorant and dangerous. Scientific principles support some of these critiques. For one thing, we require women to give birth horizontally or even upward rather than making obvious use of gravity to assist them, as many other cultures do. And the timing, place, and style of the birth process and the instruments used speak to the convenience of doctors and the proper cultural "staging" of birth, not to the health of mothers or children. Whether midwives might assist more births and do so more often in the home (which has some significant benefits for normal deliveries) has been at least as much a political question about who controls the birth industry as a question about how health can best be served.

There are serious questions, too, about whether decisions about open-heart surgery (mostly for older men) are being made with the benefit of the patient in mind rather than for reasons that are purely a matter of cultural style, of overcommitment to technology in medicine, or of consideration for the benefits to doctors.

We tend to define health problems in purely American terms,

assuming that American experience is a sufficient basis for judgment. For example, we used to take it for granted that it was "normal" for blood pressure to increase with age. It isn't, and in non-Westernized places it doesn't. We take it for granted that vitamin pills are an essential part of health care, when in fact people who have wide access to fresh foods (as most "primitive" people did until conquest) usually have no need for supplemental vitamins. We assume a level of obesity and a risk of adult diabetes that are far above "natural" standards for people who don't eat Western diets. We have begun, belatedly, to realize that patterns of health around the world can help us get a better sense of the causes of disease and identify ways in which our own lifestyle, not "human nature," is the cause.

It is increasingly recognized that the two great hallmarks of Western medicine, germ theory and surgery, valuable as they are, are overstated and overused, and we are moving back in the direction of understandings and techniques long shared by other cultures. Yet, we are still fascinated by high-tech solutions to complicated but often very rare medical problems, particularly those of very premature birth or very old age, which are often very expensive. In contrast, we are unwilling to invest in relatively inexpensive preventives for more common and more important conditions. In the twentieth century our enormous progress in health and life expectancy almost certainly owes more to measures in public health than to heroic individualized medicine. But, we tend to ignore or disdain the former while we worship and reward the latter. We don't even try hard to prevent the conditions that later require the high-tech interventions, such as deficiencies of maternal health and nutrition that often contribute to the complications of premature birth. So we develop very sophisticated and expensive methods to correct flaws in the occasional defective fetus but don't bother to promote cheap prenatal nutritional supplements or breast-feeding, which would save or improve the lives of millions of children at a far lower cost. Until quite recently we did not pay much attention to the diet and exercise patterns of middle-aged men which contribute to heart failure and high blood pressure—diseases that could largely be avoided by proper preventive actions. We see ourselves as heroically "attacking" and "conquering" health problems, not preventing or avoiding them or balancing the body to make use of its own health-restoring capabilities (which are very real even if they are sometimes overstated by practitioners of alternative medicine).

Most important, we insist that medical care is too expensive and takes too large a share of the economic pie (what better to spend it on?), but won't take obvious steps to distribute health care dollars rationally. We don't take the steps that almost all other modern countries have taken to ensure that medical care is available to everyone, leaving a substantial portion of our population uninsured and without medical care. As a consequence, people put off seeing a doctor, often with the result that treatment becomes more expensive. An estimated 40 million Americans are without health insurance. Visitors from foreign countries, where any of us could get medical care without question, worry about traveling in the United States for lack of common health insurance coverage.

We do not have health care statistics proportional to our wealth or even to the amount we spend on health care. Neither American life expectancy nor infant mortality are commensurate with our economic status. I once heard a representative of the Bush administration on *The MacNeil-Lehrer NewsHour* scoff at such numbers by saying, in effect, that the numbers didn't mean anything because they embraced the poor and the nonwhite who dragged our averages down. Well, perhaps. But those people count. They are part of our country and of its national statistics. Besides, they don't drag the average down because they are genetically predisposed to premature birth, illness, or even poor hygiene. They drag it down as a result of the physical and psychological conditions in which they have to live and the fact that in our system it is difficult for them to get medical help.

Because the poor then become major reservoirs for diseases like tuberculosis, which can spread to the rest of the population (a very significant contemporary concern), we in the mainstream are not even rationally protecting ourselves if we fail to protect the health of the poor. We are even slashing our investment in health care and research at a time when we are at a great risk of new epidemics.

Freedom and Individualism

The American concept of freedom, on which we pride ourselves even more than on our hygiene and health, is also bound up in cultural rules. Ironically, it actually restricts many kinds of real freedoms. The word *freedom* has become so distorted and abused that it is more an empty buzzword than a reality. Like any American, I value my real freedoms and do not propose to give them up lightly; but our current concept of freedom nevertheless does require reevaluation on at least three counts: cultural constraints, absence of limits, and selective application.

Cultural Constraints

First, much and perhaps most of our "freedom" is an illusion. At best, we are free only within certain sets of cultural constraints and culturally defined perceptions. Like a horse with blinders on, we are "free" to look anywhere we like as long as it is straight ahead; we remain blithely unaware that our freedom is restricted by the fact that we cannot see alternatives. This, not government regulation, is by far the biggest constraint to our freedom. The only remedy is education in the awareness of alternatives. Awareness of other cultures—real multiculturalism—is the best possible way to enhance our freedom because it takes the blinders off.

On any given day in the mid-1990s, perhaps one-third of the students on the college campus where I teach are wearing baseball caps, some with the visors forward, some backward. If you ask the students why, they will tell you they just feel like wearing a baseball cap, that this is a "free country" and they can wear what they feel like wearing. They are, they say, freely expressing their individuality. They interpret the fact that so many of their peers are expressing their individuality the same way as simple coincidence—and they are incredulous that anyone should dispute anything so obvious or question their interpretation. But five years ago no one wore a baseball cap to class, and five years from now no one will. The students think that they are expressing themselves freely and individually because they can't see the constraints of fashion and conformity operating on them.

Of course, they aren't the only ones. "Free" women slavishly adopt hemlines and styles of dress that fluctuate with monotonous regularity; they are not fashion "choices." Upper-class men, free-thinking captains of industry and free enterprise, all wear almost exactly the same thing—and this virtual uniform has scarcely changed in any direction in at least fifty years. Male college professors wear a uniform of baggy pants, worn sweaters, and, of course, a beard. People who break those rules might lose their status among their colleagues, so they can't defy the convention even if they can think of alternatives. For the most part, however, we don't even conceive of alternatives or perceive the real limitations to our freedom; we simply assume that such dress is right and natural. We assume that men naturally wear trousers and women wear dresses, but there is no biological basis for such a preference, and in many cultures the pattern is reversed for one sex or the other.

The danger is that more than clothing may be affected by fashion or unconscious consensus. For example, free thought and free speech are similarly constrained, not by law but by what other people are thinking and saying. It should be very clear that our textbooks are not at all free to explore alternative visions of American history (a point to which I shall return) because the standard version seems right and natural to so many people.

We are not free to discuss using or seriously taxing the enormous wealth concentrated in the hands of the very rich or even to admit to the existence of class differences in the United States. In a much more general way, we are not free to discuss important ideas or to consider alternative solutions to our problems if those ideas or solutions touch, even remotely, on any of our cultural taboos, like communism or even socialism—or if such a connection is even hinted at by cynical opponents. It is much easier to express fascist and racist sentiments than communist ones, although communism is the most benign of the three. Are Americans free to contemplate the possibility that Cuba's economic problems result not from communism but from the fact that Castro inherited an economy badly distorted to serve the purposes of its former colonial masters? Sugar was not one of Cuba's major indigenous crops, and a monolithic focus on so specialized a crop is a colonial pattern, not a primitive one or even a communist one. Are Americans free to consider the extent to which Cuba's problems may also result from our own unrelenting and overpowering economic embargo— opposition that we have just redoubled by laws restricting the freedom of companies *in other countries* to trade with Cuba? Do Americans know that despite its economic problems, Cuba's health care system is highly regarded in Latin America and elsewhere outside the United States? The rate of infant mortality in Cuba, despite the country's poverty, is closer to that of the United States than ours is to that of Japan, and the Cuban rate is lower than the rate for black Americans.

Our freedom to make decisions is severely restricted if we don't get accurate information and fair presentation of a full range of options, from our teachers, our news reporters and media analysts, or our politicians. We are not free if we are informed of only a narrow range of opinions and if we can vote only for one of two candidates who are very close together in the political spectrum, each promoted by a party heavily indebted to special interests. We are not free if special interests and the wealthy can exert influence on government decisions far out of proportion to their numbers. We are not free if the candidate we elect devotes his attention to the special interests and to getting re-elected rather than to governing the country in the people's best interest. We are not free if we are ignorant of history and of the consequences of our choices. We are not free if advertisers can manipulate our desires and our opinions in ways we don't understand. We are not free when American incarceration rates are five to ten times those of other Western countries—all of Europe, Canada, Australia, New Zealand—and even four times greater than Northern Ireland (which is in the midst of a revolution) and greater than South Africa. Blacks in the United States are incarcerated at four times the rate of South African blacks, and even whites in United States are incarcerated at rates double those of European countries.

Even the best news program on American television, *The News-Hour with Jim Lehrer*, is, for all its free-flowing discussion, blithely unaware of cultural blinders controlling and limiting discussion. Despite the often lively debate, everyone on any particular panel is arguing from within the same narrow range of cultural assumptions. Even those who are critical of others from the right or the left begin with most of the same assumptions. Because those assumptions are our blinders, no one notices. So we never hear other facets of the issue, and our discussions of social policy go around and around in the same small circles. Does anyone on the program ever question whether Americans have the right or need to be intervening in other countries or whether our supposedly humanitarian democratic motives disguise other purposes? Does anyone ever ask pointed questions about the distribution of wealth in this country, which we take to be natural, or the pattern of taxation that underlies many if not most of our economic problems? *The NewsHour with Jim Lehrer* does try to bring in representatives of American opponents (in recent years, for example, Iraqis). But they tend to be upper-class or upper-middle-class individuals, usually Western-educated, who largely share the assumptions of American culture, capitalism, and class structure, even if they want to prevent the United States from controlling their countries. And almost every one of these guests from an opposing country represents the position of central government or large corporations, not of the "little" people who make up most of any population. The only person I can remember on the news who really challenged American cultural assumptions was the Iranian Ayatollah Khomeini, who, speaking in the early 1980s, simply refused to accept things that Americans assume are true or obvious and insisted on addressing mutual problems from a wholly different set of values, categories, and, perhaps, cognitive rules. Instead of trying to understand his intent, most Americans—and American commentators, including one psychiatrist on national television— simply assumed he was unbalanced.

Our "free" market economics also exists within very tight sets of cultural constraints that dictate what is permissible. Those constraints need to be examined rather than just being held as "natural." Who wins in any market depends on the rules of the marketplace— and there are always rules. Change the rules and you change the winners. Corporate lobbyists work very hard to change the rules of the marketplace in their favor (and invest enormous sums that might otherwise be used to improve the company's service or product or to meet obligations to society). If the market is "free" and market forces are naturally unfettered and inexorable in their operation, as economists love to claim, why does industry need such lobbyists and why do advertisers spend such enormous sums to mold market behavior? Why are the rest of us taught that the free market follows its own course and can't be tinkered with? Why don't we become lobbyists and advertisers ourselves for our common good? Why aren't we free to manage the market for our own benefit? Better yet, why don't we insist that government exert its moderating force on our behalf? This is presumably why we pay taxes.

One of the problems is that Americans see government and its policies as the only limit to our freedom, failing to notice how powerful the other constraints are. Freedom requires checks on the power of one's neighbors and on the power of big business, and perhaps "big religion" as well. We talk about laissez-faire and a "free" market as promoting freedom when constraints within those systems themselves, such as entrenched ideas, preexisting wealth and power, prejudice, monopolistic practices, and even concentrated buying or selling power may be far more serious limits to freedom for most of us than are government regulations. We talk about "freedom of opportunity" considering only governmental but not private or cultural constraints on opportunity. We pride ourselves that the U.S. Constitution has eliminated a few of the most obvious legal obstacles to individual success but fail to note how formidable other constraints in the system, like racism and preexisting inequalities of wealth, can be. We celebrate the legal freedom we afford new immigrants to join the American melting pot without noticing that other forces make it extremely difficult to join the mainstream unless you "look right" and your name isn't too peculiar. As Benjamin DeMott has pointed out in *The Trouble with Friendship*, the myth of upward mobility does particular harm to the poor because it leads us to fail to understand the constraints under which they operate. We assume that they are free agents responsible for their own destinies—who could grasp their own bootstraps. We fail to recognize that the bootstraps exist in structures and freedoms they are denied. We overestimate the freedom of the lowest classes, assuming that they can emulate our patterns of upward mobility without the social means to do so. We demand that they display equality of responsibility without giving them equality of opportunity, power, or freedom from constraint.

Laissez-faire ("getting the government off our backs") doesn't create freedom for most of us; it just permits those who are already powerful to further limit what freedom and opportunity the rest of us enjoy. For those of us who are not wealthy and powerful, a fully representative and responsive government would be a major force for freedom by limiting the coercive powers of those who are wealthy and powerful and the organizations they control. In fact, business has become so big that only big government can balance it. The recent fashion to decentralize government and "return power to the states" is an anachronism that plays directly into the hands of multinational corporations because if corporations are larger and more powerful than governments, they can manipulate markets and play regions against one another for even greater profit. (This may well inspire some of the advertising and lobbying on behalf of returning power to the states.)

Good government can also increase our freedom and our well-being by offering options and solutions to problems that have no immediate dollar profit associated with them. Health, education, and the environment are important despite the fact that no one has fig-

ured out a way to wring a monetary profit out of solving the problems associated with them. The government could provide universal
health insurance similar to that found in other Western countries—
insurance that covers everyone including people who move to a new
town, change jobs, are unemployed, or have a major illness. Such
government-sponsored insurance would greatly add to individuals'
freedom to change their locations or their lives, or just their freedom
not to worry about catastrophic illness. Because this insurance system would not face pressure to maximize profits, it could insure
people in high-risk categories and people already diagnosed with
serious illness. The same government could generate new opportunities for many of us, such as encouraging education through GI Bill
-type benefits or creating conditions favorable to small businesses
that may show no immediate profit. Paying taxes in support of the
solutions to those problems is part of our freedom.

Governments, despite their own propaganda, can also support
media that offer more balanced information than what is provided
by competing private interests. Despite its limitations, *The News-
Hour with Jim Lehrer* still enormously expands the range of opinion
most of us can get from commercial television, and it is able to do
so because it is broadcast on public television and is therefore less
dependent on private sponsors and under less pressure to take a certain line or to package the news in short, flashy segments to improve
ratings and profits. Anyone who thinks that we will gain "freedom"
and "get government off our backs" by ending funding for public
television doesn't understand what freedom is and what constrains
it. All this is not to deny that governments can be oppressive. It's a
question of balance. At the moment the threats to freedom come
mostly from the private sector, as is true periodically.

Absence of Limits

The second major problem with our concept of freedom is that freedom has become such an overwhelming American symbol that we
can't imagine compromises or limits. We value freedom, but we also
value health, prosperity, peace, family, community, and human life.
These values demand some balance; freedom can't just be unlimited.
All societies require the freedom of individuals to be constrained by
the rules of the group. Moreover, all require individuals to be constrained by the specific rules of the statuses and roles they adopt. In

particular, people in power should legitimately lose some freedom. They lose some of the rights to which ordinary citizens are entitled. For example, it is now clearly understood that employers and college professors have *less* freedom to approach their employees or students for dates or sex than do other people. This ought to apply even more clearly to people who wield the power of high office. For people with power to fall back on their freedoms and rights as ordinary citizens as they often do to cover their abuses in office seems to me to be an unconscionable mockery of our freedoms. It should also be clear that the alternative to unlimited freedom is not mindless adherence to social directives from a dictator, as it is often portrayed. The alternative is for people to agree collectively on what limits on freedom are necessary to accomplish our other goals and maintain our other values.

The American vision of unlimited individual freedom, born more than two centuries ago on the frontier of wide open spaces and isolated, self-reliant people, has become something of an anachronism. The temporary conditions of the expanding frontier allowed a few Americans to experience (and others to celebrate) something approaching the ideal of unrestrained individual freedom. It is "primitive" people living in small groups, sparsely dispersed over the landscape in the manner of pioneers, who can walk away from one another and whose societies often lack coercive force. They are relatively free in this sense (although they, too, voluntarily limit their exercise of freedom in order to benefit from family and community).

Civilization by its very definition requires a far greater degree of interdependence than that experienced on the frontier. Civilization is a style of organization made necessary more by the large size of a population and the intimate interdependence of the people than by anything else. It requires limits to individual freedom. We should thoughtfully and cooperatively negotiate those limits instead of waiting to be told what they are. If everyone is to enjoy individual freedoms within a community, my freedom must be limited by yours, and both of us must restrain our exercise of freedom in the name of the community. The very wealthy and powerful who advocate unlimited freedom (from government) have the resources to insulate themselves, to control their own environments. And often, having enjoyed the benefit of the freedoms society allows, and done their damage, they move away. Most of us can't move away or isolate ourselves, so we have to manage our social and natural environments through what one prominent conservative, Garrett Hardin, called "mutual coercion mutually arrived at."

Because we impinge on each other in a crowded world and in a civilization defined by interdependence, freedoms can never be absolute. Freedoms are always reciprocal, and the balance must always be negotiated. If some individuals are free to drive recklessly, the rest of us are not free to drive safely. If some people are free to blast their stereos, the rest of us are not free to enjoy peace and quiet; if some people are free of "big government" regulations on the purity of food, the rest of us are not free to eat safely; if some are free to pollute a lake, the rest of us are not free to swim in it; if factory owners are free to move "their" factories at will, the rest of us are not free to be secure in our jobs; if we, the majority, are free to exclude you, the minority, then you may not be free to travel, to eat in public, or even to earn a living.

In a more general sense, it is important to distinguish between "freedom to" and "freedom from." These two freedoms are reciprocal: if I am free to do certain things, you are not free from their consequences. If you are free to hoard wealth, I may not be free from poverty or even hunger. All laws must balance the two kinds of freedom. I think that "freedom from" should be given greater weight than it is; but in certain areas of our lives, we are aware only of individual "freedom to." The American concept of freedom tilts sharply toward the freedom of the aggressor. For example, laws almost always seem to favor people who want to "develop" or "improve" things rather than the community or individuals who will feel the impact of the change. Perhaps that is because we tend to assume that change is good because it moves us forward, even if it isn't clear where "forward" is. In other cultural systems, the values may be reversed, and the (often conservative) good of the community almost always takes precedence over individual freedom to initiate. This tends to retard "progress," of course, but it also retards the many negative aspects of change and progress. Perhaps the right balance is somewhere in between.

The concept of individual freedom is important and cherished in our society. But it is too often treated as an inflexible principle, a nonnegotiable absolute rather than what it really is—a right granted by a particular culture in a particular social contract, whose precise boundaries are therefore negotiable and should be

carefully evaluated. Even our most civilized and libertarian counterparts elsewhere in the world often think that Americans are a
bit extreme on this subject. We teach our children not just that
their freedom is important but that it is the overriding principle by
which they should run their lives, so the automatic response to any
complaint about someone's behavior or request for civility is, "It's
a free country." Unfortunately, we never teach them what the benefits of real freedom could be—or what responsibilities freedom
entails.

American colleges face the dilemma that, having finally dropped
their overprotective cosseting of their students ("in loco parentis"),
they have failed to develop alternative means to teach students that
they have any obligation to the community or society in which they
live. Apparently their parents haven't taught them that, either. In
American society the idea of freedom has become so rigid a symbol
that it inhibits our genuine freedom to reconsider and if necessary
renegotiate our social contract. "Freedom" has become a constraint
or set of blinders.

We all recognize, if we think about it, that freedom is not absolute. We are not "free" to choose which side of the road to drive on
or to decide for ourselves which color stoplight says "go." Driving
rules do impinge on our freedom, of course; but all sane individuals
recognize that the trivial impingement is necessary for everyone's
safety. One is not free to discharge a firearm or even swing one's
fists wildly in a crowded room. Yet in other contexts where society
may also have compelling or at least significant interests in setting
limits, merely raising the battle cry of "freedom" trumps all other
discussion.

Does the society have the right to curtail the movement of a
homeless person with tuberculosis who poses a serious threat to
spread the disease? Advocates of "freedom to" say no; proponents
of sound health care in the face of a potential epidemic far more
serious than AIDS—"freedom from" the threat of disease—may say
yes. (Perhaps we should make a distinction between the right of a
young Hmong woman in California to live or die with her cancer
in the manner of her own choosing—which offends our medical
principles but endangers no one else—and the right of people to
travel freely while spreading contagious disease.) Do we have the
right to curtail sales of certain weapons or restrict the time and place
of hunting because of potential harm to others? Libertarians, ever

protective of "freedom to," say no; promoters of public safety and "freedom from" harm say yes. Do we have the right to restrain a factory owner from abruptly moving away? According to principles of capitalism and the freedom of capital to move, the answer is no; according to principles of social debt and responsibility and human welfare, as well as freedom from abrupt unemployment, it is yes. Do we have the right to restrict pollution and even the use of private land if the use of that land can poison people or waterways? Do we have the right to limit the pollution of our media with messages of hate, intolerance, and lies? Principles of free speech incline one to say no but perhaps here, too, we need to compromise with other values (particularly because in reality we compromise the principle of free speech all the time).

Our debates about free speech involve both aspects of freedom discussed so far—questions about the balance of individual freedom and social needs and also questions about the limits to our freedom which are not in our laws but nonetheless powerfully affect us in ways many of us do not usually think about.

In a simple sense, the chosen American position on free speech is very clear. The First Amendment to the Constitution says that Congress shall make no law prohibiting free speech, and, in recent years at least, the Supreme Court has tended to take this prohibition very seriously. In our system, in theory, anyone can say or write anything without fear of government censorship, and others are free to listen or to read whatever is written. In practice, particularly in wartime, but also at other times, the government has often limited speech. It has limited not only speech that was thought to threaten civil order or the war effort, but whatever was considered to threaten the coherence, legitimacy, and power of the government, to threaten patriotism, to suggest communism or socialism, to threaten the status quo, "law and order" (or perhaps just the privilege of the upper class). In contrast, where speech threatens only minorities, the consensus is that the right of free speech is more important than the comfort of the community.

However, the Constitution does not guarantee free speech. It only says that Congress (and by extension other levels of government) may not limit it. And it certainly does not say that people are obliged to broadcast, publish, or otherwise disseminate the free speech of others. A few years ago a new round of Holocaust denial appeared (claims that all of the evidence of Nazi atrocities was a hoax). Silly as that is, we believe that people have the right to say it. But, according to historian Deborah Lipstadt (in *Denying the Holocaust*), many college newspapers published the claims on the misguided ground that the First Amendment required them to do so. Contemporary racists and anti-Semites have the right to say what they like. That is not at issue. But major media are not obliged to publish or broadcast racist garbage (as many now do), nor are they required to give it equal time. After all, we can't give equal time to every possible view, so the principle of "equal time" is always invoked selectively. Only the "major" presidential candidates get to debate on national television. The same media that find time for "free speech" of a racist sort are apparently much more loath to find time for ideas which merely question our basic economic assumptions. Various groups of citizens (as well as public opinion) have the power to grant or withhold the dissemination of ideas and they exercise that power. The mere act of selecting what to publish or broadcast is an exercise of such power and it takes place all the time. Some judgment by citizens is always involved.

Conversely, although the law and the government may not limit free speech, social and political pressures of various kinds limit speech, and the power to do so tilts very heavily toward groups and individuals in power or simply those who hold power at critical bottlenecks in the communication system.

Consider the ongoing debate about whether to teach evolution or creationism in public schools. Creationists claim the right to speak, and that right is not in question. They also claim a right, which they say should be guaranteed by government mandate, to be heard in public schools, in science classrooms—which is a very different claim. They argue that they are being excluded, their freedom curtailed by a political monopoly of evolutionists. It seems to me (and I am of course an evolutionist) that they have been given a free, fair hearing. The word *science* refers to a kind of free market of ideas—not a perfect free market but probably the closest thing to a real free market that exists. People throw in ideas, other people try to knock them down, in a kind of intellectual king of the mountain. The surviving ideas, the ones that can't be knocked down (yet), are taught as science until better ones come along. No one has succeeded in knocking down Darwin's theories in 135 years (although they have been challenged many times and have occasionally been modified). In contrast, every argument made by creation science does get heard and considered, and almost all get knocked down immediately by the forces of that marketplace because they lack scientific substance. So what creationists are asking for is not equal access, but politically privileged access to a market in which they have already lost repeatedly. Yet, despite its history of scientific challenges successfully withstood, we are not free to include evolution in our elementary and high school textbooks (or therefore, practically, to teach it at all at those levels) because a relatively small group of determined creationists in certain key states wields excessive power in the choice (and therefore the design) of high school textbooks. Citizens, for better or worse, have a great deal of power to control what gets said or heard in this "free" country. We need to give some thought to how that power is and should be exercised. We have to stop pretending that we can't and don't limit freedom of speech when in fact we do. We need to make sure that when limitation occurs, it is done carefully and thoughtfully.

There is one other issue in the discussion of free speech that merits attention because it has enormous consequences for the problems under discussion. I refer to the "right" of major corporations to use the principle of free speech to undertake massive and lavish lobbying which clearly affects and often determines the votes and actions of our elected officials.

American courts decided many years ago that corporations were equal to individual people in terms of their rights, including the right of free speech. Given common sense and the disparities of power between corporations and people, that seems like a strange way to create "equality." But, clearly, those decisions still hold, and corporations, then, have the same right as any other individual to express an opinion about pending legislation. However, to argue that the right of free speech allows them to lobby in the manner they do seems clearly a distortion of that right, beyond reason. Such excesses in the name of free expression may be permitted by legalistic interpretation of the law, but not by good sense or human decency.

This interpretation completely ignores the fact that freedoms are reciprocal—that the freedom of one impinges on the freedoms of others. The massive lobbying of corporations makes the free speech of citizens essentially irrelevant to the legislative process (and therefore robs us of our right to be heard). It makes our free speech meaningless—effectively depriving us of it—and it deprives us of the freedom to enjoy the government that was envisioned by the founding fathers, in its ideal form. A good parallel is that if one person with a very powerful amplifier were free to broadcast with enormous power and volume over any wavelengths she chose as a matter of self-expression, she would drown out the broadcasts and the enjoyment of music that other people ought to be free to hear. We do in fact regulate broadcasting to prevent that. Such regulation is a (quite legitimate) inhibition of free speech. Freedoms need to be balanced. At the moment, however, the power of wealthy special interest groups is clearly out of control and is a major factor in problems that face us. It needs modification by courts with a sense of community and balance. Why not adopt the principle that anyone, person or corporation (if corporations are legally persons), can submit one written brief (devoid of cash presents, personal audiences, golf trips, or sexual favors), and no more, in an attempt to influence any particular piece of legislation. That would allow us to enjoy free speech unfettered by the extreme power of a few. It might help to level the playing field a bit.

The point is not that the answers to these questions about freedom and free speech are clear or easy; the point is that they have to remain subject to thoughtful discussion and to be decided on the basis of the real needs of real people, not steamrollered by an American cultural icon or fetish. We also ought to be able to explore new ways of answering those questions and solving the dilemmas they pose, by studying how other societies deal with some of the same problems.

Selective Application

The third major problem with our concept of freedom is that the idea of legal freedoms is almost always selectively applied (like the "freedom" slave owners once enjoyed from government constraints on slavery—combined with government force constraining the freedom of the slaves to object). The freedom of the rich and powerful is still given more weight than that of the poor, that of whites more than nonwhites, that of men more than women, and that of husbands more than wives.

We tend to recognize the "freedom" of the rich to take the money of the poor in ways available only to the rich (many that are very dubious ethically, monopolistic, or even clearly illegal—price-fixing, sweatshops, embezzlement, bribery, graft, insider trading, price gouging, deceptive advertising, deceptive labeling, legal sleight of hand, withholding information about the known dangers of a product, and a host of others). At the same time, government constraints protect the rich from poor people who try to get money back using the only means available (including petty theft, panhandling, and even strikes). We punish the poor severely for infractions of the rules, but rarely the rich. If, compared to petty thieves, wealthy embezzlers were punished to a degree proportional to the size of their crime, most would never get out of jail.

In the 1870s President Rutherford B. Hayes considered it improper to use federal force to protect the basic rights (and lives) of free black American *citizens* who wanted to earn a living and to vote but were being attacked by radical whites (see Eric Foner's *Reconstruction: America's Unfinished Revolution*). But Hayes did consider it appropriate to use federal force to put down strikes that threatened property or profit. In fact, there has always been a curious selectivity in our determination of when the government should stand aside and permit "free" expression or "freedom" of action and when it should intervene. It has curtailed the freedom of strikers and demonstrators to protest against the abuse of wealth and power with great regularity; and almost as frequently it has failed to intervene in matters that involved the safety of the poor or minorities. Even in the 1960s the government was extremely slow to protect the civil rights, safety, and even the lives of blacks or of civil rights protesters, black and white, among its own citizens. The record is long and well documented.

This selectivity is built into our system so deeply that many people can't see it, and therefore many people, rich and poor, come to support the image of laissez-faire freedom and equality that Americans like to project. But no one with any property actually wants a *real* (as opposed to selective) laissez-faire system because such a system would permit other people simply to attack them or take shares of all wealth. Laissez-faire may work nicely in small groups where people are constrained by personal knowledge and friendship. But in a large and heterogeneous country where people are strangers, true laissez-faire leads to anarchy. Anyone who believes that "getting government off our backs" is essential to personal freedom ought to be prepared to do without the prevention of violence and protection of property, law, and order that government provides. Surely so-called libertarians don't mean that other people are free to assault them on the streets. They take for granted, unconsciously, that government will continue to provide the protections they need, failing to recognize that those protections are as negotiable as any other. The people now moving to Utah, Idaho, or other western states to get away from government regulation will surely yell for help if the land they have invested in is attacked by bandits or corporate loggers or even unscrupulous lawyers—or a foreign power. If they don't yell for help, they will just lose. Are these new Western pioneers completely self-sufficient (no oil, no plastic, no metal, no cloth, no purchased food, no guns or other manufactured goods, and so forth)? If not, they must rely on the government to protect the industries and the national and international trade routes that supply them. In fact, they want government "off our backs" except for the things they expect governments to do for them; they want selective freedom for themselves but they want government to limit the freedom of others. On a much larger scale, many conservatives at the national level want government "off our backs"; but they also want the government to regulate the sex and reproductive lives of others or to provide corporate subsidies and otherwise protect property and corporate interests.

We apply the concept of freedom even more selectively in the international arena. We do not recognize the freedom of other people *not* to participate in our "free market," nor do we permit them to withhold their desirable land and resources from that market. We do not permit them to assign resources as they see fit or to fashion a government of their own choosing. We have used force and economic power to convert land or other resources to our desired uses and to prevent them from being reclaimed for indigenous use. We have forcibly "opened" other countries to participation in our trade networks as exporters and consumers. We have prevented other people from using their own systems of land ownership or even their own religions. We have hunted indigenous people to extermination to claim their resources. Many times we have used our governmental power and our military might (when "necessary") to restrict those freedoms. For example, we have used large-scale force, the threat of force, or covert action to oppose attempts by other countries such as Guatemala or Iran to redistribute land or revenues from resources to their people more equitably, at the expense of our corporations. We intervene even when the reforms are being carried out by duly elected democratic governments which seek all the things the United States ostensibly stands for.

certain resources to be public property but permit something made from them to become private, as, for example, when we permit commercial logging or mining of public lands. Consider, too, that the government always retains eminent domain (the right to take privately owned land as needed for public purposes).

In all these cases, private property is limited by the need or desire of the larger society to preserve historical sites or wild lands, avoid overcrowding, maintain safety, uphold community standards, build roads, and so forth. In a democratic society we collectively limit private property rights. I think most of us would agree that the principle of limited ownership is essential to our social organization, even if we argue about specific applications of that principle, as we often do. The point is that there is lots of room to think about the boundaries of ownership without denigrating the idea of private property itself, and we do it all the time. Yet our blinders prevent us from taking a rational approach to some such problems.

As a way to understand private property as a cultural convention, consider the example of two Stone Age hunters who have just killed a mammoth. They have used some combination (and such success is *always* a combination) of skill, intelligence, cleverness, single-minded focus, ruthlessness, perseverance, strength—and luck—to score this economic bonanza. But the Stone Age hunters don't get rich, and the reasons why they don't are instructive.

The first reason is that, in their society, cultural rules demand that their success be shared. They can't hoard the carcass any more than we can hoard a Thanksgiving turkey. With the support of prevailing values and ethics, their friends, neighbors, and relatives (i.e., everyone in their society) simply help themselves or make requests for more that can't be refused. If the hunters tried to turn them down (sort of like not serving second helpings at Thanksgiving), no one would help them defend "their" property. Other people would insult them or shun them, their efforts would be ignored, and if the hunters persisted, they would ultimately be abandoned or told to leave the group. Because social approval and membership in a social group are very important to almost all human beings, these are serious threats that have a profound influence on behavior.

The rationale for sharing is partly that people are friends, neighbors, and kin, but it is also partly that each hunter can cover only a limited territory and is therefore helped by other hunters, even if those others are unsuccessful on a given day. (This kind of sharing and cooperation seem to be a constant feature of human social organization. They help define our species.) Everyone knows that hunting is chancy and relies on reciprocal exchange involving future obligation rather than immediate trade to balance out the risk. Everyone also knows that he or she may someday need assistance of other kinds. Sharing sets up the right to expect the protection of others in case of accident, ill health, feuds, war, and so forth, much as holiday reciprocity sets up the expectation of future cooperation in our own society. In short, by sharing, the hunters reaffirm their rights to a social safety net that provides other services and promises protection in times of need.

The unspoken rationale for sharing also includes the realization that the hunters' success is based at least in part on shared group knowledge about where and how to hunt and how to make bows, arrows, or poison for arrows; it is also based on the assumption that other people do other essential if less "profitable" things, like gathering vegetables, curing the sick, or carrying and caring for children. In short, there is a recognition that individual success is built on—and protected by—the contributions of other members of the group, and that success may be transitory. Other people deserve a share or have to be allowed a share as insurance for the future. But, most important, there is an agreement that the rights and needs of other people to eat take precedence over any "right" to private ownership or hoarding of the carcass.

Even Bill Gates, who has scored an economic bonanza in our own society based on a similar mix of skills, determination, and luck, needs and gets a social safety net. Such a net covered him long before he became wealthy, would have continued to cover him if he had not been so successful, and will continue to cover him if he loses most or all of what he has. That safety net, too, is ultimately built on sharing, so the society that provides it has a right to demand that he continue to share, even were he to feel that he had outgrown his need for the net. Moreover, no matter what his genius, Gates's success, like that of the hunters, is heavily grounded in the ongoing institutional support and cultural knowledge that his society provides. Gates didn't invent computers or software all by himself, even if he did develop a useful and profitable new method of packaging and marketing software. He built on the basis of a great deal of existing hardware and software, much of it provided by publicly funded research. He also made extensive use of the technical and social infrastructure provided by his society. For this reason as well, society has a right to an ongoing share of the wealth he produces.

But most Americans embrace the myth that whatever private property a person has was gained entirely on his own, aided only by his own wits and the capital he had previously developed. In fact, Americans erroneously attribute both success and failure much more to the personal qualities of individuals than most cultures would. And not only do we believe in private property, but we agree that the right to private property *always* takes precedence over the right or need of others—even their need to eat. We will defend property, no matter how it was obtained or how much of it has accumulated, even against the demands or needs of hungry people far more readily than we will defend the right to eat. (This position would be outrageous to most "primitive" people, whose moral sense in this regard may be more advanced than ours.)

There is another point. In the Stone Age example, the mammoth will rot fairly quickly. The hunter can't possibly freeze it, dry it, salt it, or preserve it in any other way. And he couldn't carry it with him even if he could preserve it. So the "wealth" is transitory. Were he allowed to keep the entire carcass for his personal use, the hunter would have nothing left in a month, no matter how big the carcass. There are few ways to "bank" the wealth or convert it to some permanent, storable form other than as reciprocal obligation or prestige. Prestige is a wonderful commodity, and many societies rely heavily on it as a means of balancing an exchange system. A successful individual can seek and amass almost any amount of prestige in exchange for wealth, but prestige can't be hoarded. It is transitory and needs to be renewed, so even a successful individual has a constant incentive to earn favor. Yet prestige, unlike hoarded wealth, does not undermine the real economic needs of others. Instead, it helps them because helping others is often what garners prestige. Moreover, because the real payoff for most human beings is social approval, prestige is a powerful motivator.

The difficulty of accumulating wealth in the Stone Age is partly a statement about nature, mobility, and a lack of storage facilities. But it is also a statement about the hunters' society and cultural system. By choice, not ignorance, they do not employ money or other systems to store or transport this type of wealth—i.e., wealth representing food or basic resources—in a permanent form. People in such societies often have portable symbolic wealth like stone axes or scarce beads which can be exchanged for other symbolic wealth or prestige. The hunting society could easily decide that it would repay the hunter with a certain number of special beads that he could wear around his neck and redeem for meat when someone else was successful or even use to buy land. But they don't. Food and land are kept outside the "money" system. Their cultural convention is to honor the kind of diffuse social obligations just described, at least where food and land, rather than beads, are concerned.

For private property to become a significant part of a sociocultural system, society as a whole not only has to acquiesce in honoring private property, it also must actively develop and honor systems for the perpetuation of private wealth. In order for wealth to be owned and kept, there has to be some system to transfer it into a permanent, storable, movable, and convertible form.

Bill Gates's software programs are useless unless he can convert them into food, shelter, transportation, and other essentials for himself and his family and unless he converts what is left into goods whose value is symbolic but that win him public approval and admiration, such as fine art. But no matter how much wealth Bill Gates accumulates in any form, he can consume only a limited amount. His remaining wealth would dissipate quickly or be taken by others if it were not for various mechanisms for storing and preserving it. In earlier times, preserving accumulated wealth typically meant building physical protective devices such as fortified storehouses and castles. But such wealth was still bulky, hard to move, hard to defend, and often perishable. More recently storage has meant the elaboration of an enormous series of social, legal, and economic institutions whose purpose is to make wealth ever more condensable, convertible, storable, and movable—and far more easily concentrated and kept in individual hands.

Permanent private wealth exists because we design institutions to maintain it, not because it is a natural or inalienable right. This is an enormous industry and a very profitable one. Our society invests a great deal of energy (and wealth) in protecting private assets and allowing them to be moved and perpetuated by devices ranging from vaults, police, and guard dogs to all-purpose money itself, as well as traveler's checks, bank accounts, gold, diamonds, real estate, stocks and bonds, stock exchanges, "futures," "options," letters of credit, wire transfers, credit cards, inheritance laws, corporate structures, and a host of other mechanisms. Many of the institutions for storage and movement of wealth are nominally private and are very profitable, but all depend on the coherence of society and its infrastructure and the protection of government to maintain them.

In short, society as a whole helps to protect, preserve, and move—as well as produce—the capital that becomes private wealth. Society, in the service of creating and perpetuating wealth, also provides its natural resources, its accumulated wisdom, its formal education, its systems of information storage and dissemination, its communications networks, its labor, its division of labor (which provides that other people take care of other necessary functions), its highways, its legal structure and police powers, its economic institutions, its railroads, its military defense and security. It even helps to increase corporate wealth by using governmental power to open foreign trade, sometimes forcibly, and providing enormous business subsidies (corporate "welfare"). Many if not most of the great fortunes have resulted from cooperation, connivance, assistance, sweetheart deals, contracts, and special protection all provided by government. Society is left to clean up the wastes created by a factory and the human "waste" of discarded workers that can be created by corporate decisions.

Why doesn't American society, which provides so much support for any private venture and invests so much in the generation and perpetuation of private property, insist that the wealth be shared rather than protesting taxation as an unfair imposition on successful people? If in the name of economic and technical efficiencies we continue to recognize rights to private property and the accumulation of property (as I think we probably should), why don't we recognize the enormous amount society contributes and demand a reasonable share? Why do we count what society contributes to the poor so heavily (when they actually get relatively little) but perpetuate the myth that the rich do it all themselves and deserve to keep it all? The government provides far more services to the rich than the poor.

Yet, by our system, private owners, even of major corporate structures, still claim absolute ownership. If, after receiving the benefits and support from their society which I have just enumerated, factory owners decide that they are tired of a certain location or are not getting enough profit from it, or want to get cheaper workers outside the country, all they have to do is say they intend to move. They invoke "private property" as if it were a right unencumbered by any social or economic obligations to others. Everyone then agrees that they have a "right" to move despite the legacy of unemployment, social disruption, and perhaps pollution that they leave behind. There is no sense that they have any social or economic obligation to others, including the workers and the community that have built the success. To keep the owners from moving, the local community might even be forced to offer yet more concessions, benefits, and support but without recognizing its right to a current and future share of the wealth generated and a share of the enterprise itself. Even a sports franchise whose success is synonymous with the name of a particular city and built on the loyalty of local fans apparently owes nothing to the city or its fans. Cities can be squeezed into competing for franchises with ever more attractive and costly concessions at the expense of their taxpayers.

According to our cultural rules, this kind of private property has too often become an absolute and inalienable right of an individual or corporation. Instead of invoking the negotiable social contract, the society conveniently forgets its own contributions. Few private corporations would knowingly allow someone they had trained, nurtured, and equipped (or even just employed) simply to leave, taking private possession of a valuable product that he or she had developed while working at the company. In fact, many companies demand a large share, if not all, of any such product when an employee leaves. Yet our society, which could claim sponsorship, inspiration, and nurturing that is far more important than that offered by any corporation, regularly gives away its share of such wealth. Why doesn't our society protect its interest in developed wealth in the same manner that any corporation would?

In all of our discussions of American economic problems, the enormous wealth owned by the very rich (but developed and maintained with the backing of the society as a whole) is never mentioned as a legitimate resource for the rest of us. Apparently it is not a negotiable item in our culturally blinded deliberations. If we want to balance the budget, why assume that it must be done only by cutting costs (or by raising taxes on salaries)? Why not balance the budget by first deciding what government must spend to meet its obligation and to address human and social needs and then telling the privileged how much we must take to "balance" those costs?

Our tax system illustrates our cultural blinders concerning the extent to which wealth is socially generated and our bias in applying the right of property in a manner that favors the rich over the poor. Although Americans constantly discuss ways to modify our tax system, we seem completely unable to have a discussion of tax reform that would actually shift more of the tax burden from the working class toward the rich. We don't have to settle for either raising or lowering taxes, even if those are the only options our leaders usually present us. We can redistribute the tax burden or shift it among the different economic groups. In fact, most recent changes in tax laws have had the effect of shifting the burden even more onto the working class. That could be reversed. Every proposal for simplified or "flat" taxes that I have seen in the past few years just happens to increase the tax burden on the lower middle class, as if simplifying taxes automatically produces this result. Growing numbers of the "little people" see that they are being taxed too heavily and take action where they can, but usually in the wrong ways. They vote down local school and community taxes, which harms their own children and communities. Too often they support any politician who promises to cut taxes, failing to notice that the specific tax cuts proposed usually reduce the taxes of the rich proportionally more than those of the poor—and usually save by taking benefits from the poor and lower middle class, not the rich.

Logically, the last dollars that should be taxed are the ones working people need to maintain a basic standard of living. Yet because we are governed (and our opinions molded) by the rich, we allow working people's wages to be taxed first and most consistently. And as we simplify and reform our tax structures, "flatten" taxes, create loopholes, and try to eliminate taxes on investment and savings, we make those wage earners carry more and more of the tax burden. Why not, instead, focus taxes more heavily on the enormous amounts of money many people have above and beyond their basic needs? If we must have a simpler, flatter tax system, why not do it by setting a fairly high tax rate and eliminating all or most deductions, but then offering a massive, perhaps twentyfold, increase in the personal exemption? For that matter, without all of the trouble of restructuring the whole system, why not simply add a massive increase in the personal exemption to our current tax system and increase taxes in the upper brackets to offset the losses in revenue? There is plenty of wealth and income above the level of personal exemptions to pay all the bills. Borrowing an idea from other cultures, we might even consider taxing not income but wealth itself—

that is, the amount an individual or family has accumulated above some threshold level, which would also put the tax burden more squarely where it belongs. We can get a sense of the power of the upper brackets by noting a fairly simple fact. Based on figures from the *Los Angeles Times* cited by H. R. Kerbo in his 1996 book *Social Stratification and Inequality,* the tax *break* that the Reagan administration gave to the richest 1 percent of the population saved them more money ($70 billion per year) than is needed to pay for the entire American welfare system—with $20 billion left over for schools or other priorities. We don't have to put welfare on the backs of the working class, and we don't have to reform welfare by pitting those on welfare against the working poor, as is now happening. All we have to do is demand a reasonable part of our own money back. Supporting welfare does not mean taking all of the wealth of the rich or even greatly increasing their taxes. It would mean only rescinding their latest tax break.

If we wish to reward real merit or important innovation, as we should, why not alter the tax structure so as to recognize the distinction between innovation of technological or social value and income that is simply an ongoing reward for past success or that comes just from the buying and selling of assets or the manipulation of existing capital? Or we could allow those who earn money by their own creativity to keep it, but then tax it all before members of the next generation, who may have contributed little, can inherit it. We could consider making more use of the nonmonetary (or non-tax-related rewards) that other cultures use so effectively. And perhaps we should remember that innovation comes from people dedicated to tasks. Would higher taxes stop Bill Gates from trying to improve his products?

In this context, we have to get over our shared misconception that numbers provide an objective measure if calculated with great precision by someone in authority. In fact, once one leaves behind the story problems of grade school, most numbers in the real world are built out of estimates and even arbitrary assumptions. During 1996 a government commission was engaged in recalculating the cost-of-living allowance used in determining tax brackets and social security payments. The new estimate was widely publicized as providing a "more accurate" estimate, which, just coincidentally, increased taxes and decreased projected Social Security benefits, thus enhancing government revenue mostly at the expense of the working class. But the notion that the new calculation provides a "more accurate" estimate is absurd. There is no correct real or hypothetical single number which defines the cost-of-living allowance because there are too many different ways to measure it, so one cannot claim to be estimating it "more accurately." There are only different estimates calculated using different assumptions or different data. The assumptions of this group make its estimate relatively low. But we could easily compute a hundred other estimates, all equally "accurate," but all different. The choice of assumptions is political, or at least blinded by cultural assumptions, not mathematical, and we should stop pretending otherwise.

The Profit Motive

The profit motive has served as an important engine for economic growth in recent Western history. There is no question of its value, at least if "growth" and "progress" are the goal. But economic profit is not the only possible human motivation and it is not sufficient for all human purposes. What is profitable is not necessarily good for society or the people, although that is what is assumed and taught. As I hinted in chapter 2, we could structure social choices so that even innate selfishness was played out in other ways that are productive in social terms. Most human societies, including a majority of those that made substantial contributions to human "progress," have gotten along perfectly well without considering profit as their single significant motivator in the manner that Americans do.

I noted in chapter 3 that chiefs in many societies using a redistributive economy work hard themselves and organize the work of others in order to be able to give away material goods. Such chiefs can be identified or distinguished from their fellows not by their material wealth but often by their relative poverty and the esteem with which they are regarded. And, in many societies (including our own to a diminishing degree), individuals are honored for the substance of their accomplishments, not for the monetary rewards they have garnered. Sports heroes and musicians and even artisans and scholars may be honored for their skills and not just their wealth—but we seem to pay less and less attention to such achievements.

The increasing attention paid to profit in our society is in fact one of our arbitrary cultural values. We allow economic profits to motivate us above all else. Such a pattern is not natural or inevitable.

We socialize our children to value material goods, to measure success in economic terms, and to rank people on the basis of wealth. We could socialize children to place a higher value on respect, family unity and honor, tradition, pride in craftsmanship, the creation of beauty, responsibility, and concern for others. We could teach them to seek the approval of their peers through these mechanisms, any of which could provide the motivation for doing some tasks as well as or better than the profit motive.

The national obsession with the profit motive distorts our perception of ourselves and our fellows. Why should those who are more interested in art, literature, beauty, family, friends, nature, knowledge, the environment, the education and health of our children and our neighbors' children, and the care of other people simply allow those with no ambition other than profit to take everything and destroy what we value in the process? And, why should we participate in the myth that their profit and wealth reflect their superior "intelligence" or ability, hard work, or thrift, when it may reflect only their narrow-minded ambition, greed, ruthlessness, disregard for morality or law—and, in fact, most often just reflects their inheritance? Why, moreover, are we willing to agree to the notion that nothing can or should be done unless it generates a profit? Not everything that we ought—or might even want—to do is profitable, and profitability should not be the only measure. Even if we accept the profit motive, why do we accept the premise that *unlimited* profit needs to be offered as the only possible incentive to production?

We have to be willing to ask ourselves whether economic profit should be the only basis for exchange and interaction; whether the pursuit of profit should continue unfettered by other concerns; whether profit should be the only incentive we recognize; whether we should continue to recognize the profit motive but limit or tax profits at a higher rate or demand accountability for the real (e.g., human and environmental) costs before the profit can be measured; whether we should try harder to teach some other values, or to define the areas in which profit is not an appropriate incentive.

There are certainly specific contexts in which the unlimited pursuit of profit is inappropriate and should more actively be discouraged, even in our system as it now stands. We don't expect doctors to base medical decisions on potential profit, but some do, and the newly dominant HMOs and drug companies are distorting doctors' priorities in the name of profit. We used to hope that our sports heroes would put loyalty to their fans ahead of higher salaries. We used to hope that the owners of sports franchises would put loyalty to the cities that nurtured their teams ahead of greater profits. We used to hope that truth and justice would win out over profit in legal affairs; and that fair practices toward customers would limit the pursuit of profit by merchants. We even hoped that our major corporations would be loyal to their workers, would deal with consumers fairly, and would put something back into the community. Where corporations once felt some responsibility to their employees and their customers, as well as some to their stockholders, they now seem to consider only their stockholders (and the management itself). The present drive for short-term profits has produced an economic trend—a fad—of "downsizing" and unemployment in the name of greater "efficiency," even in the midst of prosperity. Even potential consumers are now being eliminated because they can no longer afford the product. We are building the lower class. Unless it is our intent simply to force such people out of the work force without any support, we are also adding dramatically to the costs society must bear, even though we say we want to end welfare.

What are we to make of the recent move to profit by patenting the genes of other people? In our search for solutions to various health problems we are scouring the genomes (the full set of individuals' genes) of groups of people around the world that we otherwise dismiss as genetically inferior, to find genes that can fight a disease or prevent some other problem. The patent, and therefore the profit, will go not to the people who have the gene but to whoever identifies it to the satisfaction of an American (or Australian, etc.) court. As in many things, the profit will go to people who know how to do the paperwork, not the people who produce the needed good. Aren't there some things that belong to people by nature and, if shared, should be shared for human good, not patented for profit?

Wartime is another context in which the unlimited pursuit of profit is inappropriate and dangerous, even in a society so strongly governed by the profit motive. Is there a reason why, in wartime, when society feels free to call on its sons and daughters to give up years of their lives and risk their health and their lives, we cannot demand that corporations and their stockholders or the people who (privately) sell government bonds sacrifice much or most of their profits to the same cause? Like soldiers, corporate owners, stockholders, and employees could be put temporarily on a draftee's wages, their profits temporarily sacrificed to the same cause to which poorer people sacrifice their normal wages, their bodies, and their lives. But, in fact, wars tend to be highly profitable for the contractors involved, and this may be one reason why we fight so many. If wars were really a matter of national defense and security, this would not be the case.

In addition to contexts where profit is inappropriate, we can recognize situations in which making a profit ought to be illegal—or is illegal but goes unpunished.

During Congressional hearings addressing the Iran-Contra scandal in 1987, for example, one of the people involved, Albert Hakim, defended himself by saying alternately that he was carrying out secret policy for the government and that he was just being a good American businessman trying for a little profit. This outrageous mixture of motives aroused little ire. Hakim had wrapped himself in the profit motive like wrapping himself in the flag. Yet the very combination of motives lay at the heart of the fiasco. The whole operation should have been illegal, demanding significant criminal penalties, but no such penalties were invoked. (The term "Iran-Contra scandal," incidentally, provides a very good example of the use of cultural symbols to place patriotic blinders on us. Iranians and Contras were each potentially involved in the transactions, of course, but neither in fact was integral to the scandal from an American point of view. It would more appropriately have been called "the United States government–CIA–Reagan Administration–Oliver North scandal." It was the behavior of American officials that was scandalous and illegal. But the terminology skillfully deflected attention away from "us" and toward "them.")

Despite vague and fairly toothless rules, we do not seriously question the mixture of the profit motive with patriotism and public service in our politicians; yet these motives are potentially in conflict, and the pursuit of profit by public servants weakens us nationally and internationally in addition to undermining the credibility of government. Should we let our Congressional representatives profit from their association with corporate lobbyists and then make decisions affecting those lobbyists? Politicians do such things, of course—in fact, the practice is rampant—and that is what lobbying is all about. Why isn't it illegal?

Should we permit an ex-president, already rewarded with a generous pension and expenses for life (precisely so that he doesn't have to demean his office by going back into private business), to sell his services to a foreign country at a very inflated price? Doesn't that tarnish our image as a great country, not to mention setting up an obvious conflict of interest for future presidents? Doesn't it send a powerful message that *anything* in our society is for sale? All social roles and statuses involve sacrificing some freedom of action. Shouldn't privileged statuses demand well-defined limits, even in a "free" country? Doesn't voluntarily accepting certain privileged social status, like a position in government, carry with it certain restrictions on freedom and profit, even if those values continue to be primary themes of American culture? It seems reasonable to insist that people not pursue financial gain while serving in elective office— and it seems reasonable that in the process we might educate our children about integrity and the limits of the profit motive.

In sum, the profit motive is not a "natural" human drive; it is a value taught by our culture. We can socialize our children in ways that modify or limit this motive, and we can provide other rewards so that people will perform jobs that are not profitable in dollar terms. We can also regulate and harness profit-seeking more effectively. It is not radical to suggest that we need to rethink our rules and limits. What is radical and dangerous is to insist that profit should continue to dominate all other human considerations.

Efficiency

Economic growth, "efficiency," and "progress" are badly abused conventions. Americans pride themselves on living in the richest nation on earth, on having developed a system of technology and invention that provides most people with more material goods than individuals in other times and places have ever had. We also pride ourselves on having a system in which economic growth and ever-expanding wealth seem almost assured. But this system, too, needs reexamination and perhaps moderation.

One problem is that the American definition of "efficiency" is very narrow. We tend to refer to efficiency as an absolute measure that is inherently desirable; in fact, we need to specify exactly *which* efficiency we are talking about. Efficiency is not an absolute, but a *ratio* between any of various measurements of input and output. The measure of efficiency depends on what measures are being compared and what (unspoken as well as spoken) supporting assumptions are made. Different efficiencies are often in competition with one another. Something that makes the most efficient use of time, for example, does not necessarily make the most efficient use of such other resources as space, energy, or scarce material; in fact, it commonly wastes those other commodities. Driving fast to make efficient use of one's time is an inefficient use of gasoline. In agriculture, historically, the efficient use of land was often in opposition to the efficient use of labor; and even now, the most efficient use of human labor is very wasteful of other sources of energy. "Efficient" American farmers can produce many times more food for each hour of work than do Third World peasants working by hand; but they are in fact extremely wasteful of energy. For each calorie of food derived, our "efficient" farming requires the investment of many times more energy obtained from all sources than does any "primitive" system. If we export our "efficient" system, it can be very costly for others who do not always have the means to buy fuel and chemical fertilizer. Moreover, if we change our assumptions and measure *all* the human labor invested, including building tractors, refining petroleum, producing chemical fertilizer, storing and transporting materials and fuel, instead of just the farmer's time, it is not so clear that our farming is even particularly efficient in the use of human time and energy. So we have to be careful to specify what we want to maximize and to consider the alternative forms of efficiency and the various ways to measure it before we choose our methods.

Americans have fallen into the trap of measuring efficiency only in terms of dollar profits. Moreover, we measure only *private* profit, without considering other values, and then conclude that we have measured "efficiency." In addition, we measure efficiency only for the task at hand, although doing a particular job in the most efficient manner is not the same as making efficient use of the material or natural resources or human resources of a whole society (or perhaps even a whole factory). Nor is maximizing profit the same as meeting the needs of that society effectively.

Feeding people, giving them the opportunity to participate and support themselves, and maintaining their human dignity ought to count when we assess efficiency. So should preserving the safety and beauty of the environment, the quality and safety of the product itself, and a host of other considerations. Making farming more "efficient" typically forces people off the land, perhaps into unemployment; it typically decreases the nutrient value and safety of the food grown (because crops have to be specially bred and then fed and protected with chemical fertilizers and insecticides); and it may have far larger environmental costs than farming in more traditional ways. Addressing those problems would almost certainly be more efficient for the society, if not for the farm itself. It would almost certainly increase our "efficiency" with reference to public needs and public costs, ultimately benefiting everyone.

And, even if we agree to confine ourselves to thinking about labor efficiency and dollar profits, we have an odd way of measuring productivity and costs when we estimate efficiency. We measure the output of factories and the size of private profits without evaluating the background costs in dollars (let alone in quality of lives) to the society as a whole. Of course a factory can be "efficient"—that is, profitable to its owners—if the rest of us absorb the costs of its pollution, transportation, discarded labor, and so forth in our taxes or in the reduced quality of our lives. Its "efficiency" results from the fact that we don't count those costs.

Examples abound in the public sector as well. Crime is terribly costly to our society and so is punishment. Although putting people in prison appears to be the most efficient short-term solution to crime, it is remarkably inefficient because it encourages future criminal activity and is very expensive. Moreover, the need for so many prisons is almost certainly related to our narrow definition of economic efficiency, which excludes many people from the work force. Surely the best way to make most people obey the law is to make them feel that they, too, have a decent stake in the "system" and in the protection of the same laws. Apparently lacking any sense of this, New York State, in the name of efficiency and cutting costs, is cracking down on crime by building more prisons to accommodate its ever-growing number of prisoners, while at the same time it is trimming social services and trying to eliminate public universities which serve the poor. It is far more costly to keep someone in prison than in college, and four years in college clearly have a more positive effect. Neither prisons nor universities will do much good, of course, if the economy is restructured as is now occurring so that many jobs which in the past paid reasonably well no longer exist. This concept of "efficiency" seems extraordinarily narrow and short-sighted.

Economic Growth and Progress

We also have to ask very seriously what constitutes economic "growth" and what it is good for other than satisfying a fairly arbitrary American cultural definition of human purpose and helping the rich get richer.

There is abundant evidence that, throughout history, "growth" has not improved people's lives anywhere near as often or as consistently as we assume. We are living at a time when economic growth or improvement for corporate interests is accompanied by declining standards of living for most people. Contrary to popular American belief, we don't all gain from "growth." We don't all share, even if the whole pie gets bigger. Can we reevaluate our cultural obsession with growth in ways that permit us to separate the useful parts from the dangerous parts? If growth doesn't improve the lives of more people, what good is it? What else are we trying to accomplish? Shouldn't those who gain from economic growth, or the effort it takes on the part of the society as a whole, have some responsibility to those who lose as a consequence of the process (because they are forced out in competition or because they want to do something else)? By the very nature of our civilized system we are tied together, the gains and losses intimately bound to one another.

I am deeply concerned that the politicians and economists who lead us appear to be going round and round in a closed circle of assumptions that reinforce each other but blind them and us to other problems and alternative perspectives so that they do not focus on what ought to be the real human goals of the enterprise. Real economics isn't about charts and paper dollars or even about growth; it's about producing and distributing real goods to real people in reasonable relationship to their needs. What is "good" for the economy is not the same—or as important—as what is good for people.

Part of our faith in growth comes from a false sense of progress through human history. We have a profound belief in "progress" and we are willing to put our faith in it, blindly, as a cultural image, even though we don't actually pay much attention to whether or how we measure it. Our faith results partly from the fact that we usually recite only the history of privileged classes and technological advances rather than exploring the realities of life faced by the common people.

Changes in the structure of cultures and societies through historic and prehistoric time have led, through competition, toward bigger political units and the accumulation of material goods. But cultural evolution is no more about progress than biological evolution is. Bigger political units have been successful in the last ten thousand years or so of political competition; but it is not at all clear that they have been associated with improvement in human lives prior to the twentieth century, or that they will be in the future.

The data from scientific and historical sources (reviewed in my book *Health and the Rise of Civilization*) call into question much of our sense of progress, at least if progress is about people's health, nutrition, and quality of life. (What else is it about?) For most people, the quality and quantity of nutrition have probably *declined* through history; only for the affluent populations of the twentieth century have they improved. As I suggested in chapter 4, most of the world's most "primitive" hunter-gatherers, measured earlier in this century, had diets that were better balanced and richer in protein and vitamins than those of all but the most affluent citizens of the modern world. And the hunter-gatherers' caloric intake was at or above modern Third World standards, even though those hunter-gatherers remaining to be measured had been pushed into some of the world's poorest environments. This comparison applies not just to the Third World, but also to the working classes of the world's most affluent countries. The nutrition of the working classes of eighteenth- and nineteenth-century urban Britain was far worse than that of most "primitive" groups. Worldwide, the trend in human stature, probably associated with nutrition, was more down than up until the twentieth century, when the trend was reversed for some people.

Historical and ethnographic data also suggest that "progress" and "civilized" lifestyles have generated or intensified most of the health problems that most people can think of, even if some diseases and health problems have existed throughout human history and some have been eliminated. Germ diseases have become more common and more widespread as human groups became larger and more intimately connected by rapid transportation. Malaria and schistosomiasis increased when people began to farm and to irrigate their fields. The great epidemic diseases, like measles, smallpox, typhoid, typhus, influenza, mumps, and cholera, spread widely primarily under "civilized" conditions once large groups of people were connected by trade. Bubonic plague was a disease of the most populous cities of its day and the cities most intimately linked to large-scale trade networks. In short, it hit the most civilized, most developed communities. Venereal syphilis by most accounts appeared and spread for the first time in sixteenth-century Europe. It is also civilization and its trade patterns that generate the risk of AIDS and Ebola, the new drug-resistant strains of tuberculosis, and a string of other once-localized infections that can now be spread by people traveling by airplane and in urban interactions. With the exception of AIDS, we are now enjoying a hiatus between major epidemics. But there is good reason to assume that there will be others. Consider how long it is taking us to develop techniques to fight AIDS, which actually travels very slowly. Some killer epidemics that are airborne rather than sexually transmitted may spread very quickly, like influenza. We think of modern civilized science as curing or eliminating diseases, and it does. But civilization and "progress" also *create* the risk of disease by providing the context in which diseases can spread. Those conditions still exist, and as we "grow" and "develop" we create more.

Historically, the transmission of epidemic diseases was a major weapon of European expansion, particularly in the Americas and in Australia, where populations previously unexposed were destroyed more by diseases brought from Europe (which most Europeans had as children) than by the superiority of European technology. The conquest certainly didn't reflect superior European health, nutrition, or hygiene.

The major noninfectious scourges of the twentieth century—diabetes, hypertension, atherosclerosis, multiple sclerosis, coronary heart disease, and some common cancers—seem to be generated or at least exacerbated by modern dietary habits (super-refined food) and modern pollutants. Despite what most of us were taught, the increasing incidence of these diseases does not result simply or primarily from the fact that people live longer. In fact, hypertension, diabetes, and breast and bowel cancer are strongly linked to the very features of food processing that make our food industry so "efficient" and profitable. These diseases rarely occur in "uncivilized" populations. Primitive people must be doing something right, and it would be well worth our while to look at their lifestyles and consider adopting specific aspects. When we "civilize" such people we introduce all of these health risks to them—and when we further "advance" our own society it is likely that we will add additional risks to our own lives.

Life expectancy is approximately the *average* number of years the individuals in a population live, reflecting not so much how long individual people live as how many people reach old age. Life expectancy has not shown the progressive improvement through history that most people assume. Most Europeans had life expectancies indistinguishable from those of the Stone Age well into the nineteenth century; and life expectancies of working-class people, especially those in many European cities, were well *below* any reasonable Stone Age estimate as late as about 1850. In India despite a history of British rule, the life expectancy was at or below Stone Age levels as late as about 1920. Infant mortality in major cities generally fell below Stone Age levels only in the twentieth century; many major American cities around 1900 had infant mortality rates well above the average for "primitive" tribes. The orphanages of seventeenth- to nineteenth-century Europe (which some of our politicians want to emulate), were commonly the places where polite society let children die, off the streets and away from public scrutiny. Well-documented patterns of infant and child mortality in many of these institutions would have shocked almost any primitive population. Every act of "progress" or "modernization" threatens the well-being of many people.

Civilization is not inherently good for people or their health. The only way civilization benefits people is by sharing its wealth and investing in public health and well being. Civilization *without* investment in human welfare, such as eighteenth- and nineteenth-century English cities (where nutrition levels, life expectancy, and human stature were among the lowest in human history), is probably the worst environment in which people have ever lived. This occurred of course at the height of English wealth and power. We need to study potential "advances" or profitable schemes more carefully. We need to look much more carefully at the costs and benefits of "progress": who pays the costs, who reaps the benefits.

In addition, we should not confuse political dominance with progress. The modern dietary privilege of Americans does not rest only or even mainly on "progress" or our ingenuity as farmers. Increasingly, it rests also on our economic and political power to take the food of others (as when relatively nutritious subsistence farming in other parts of the world is replaced by specialized cash crops that we desire). It is important to recognize that the ability of Europeans and Americans to move wealth and military power rapidly over great distances has done untold damage to people in other parts of the world, contributing significantly to our prosperity but to their poverty. But we assume that our "free" market and our mechanisms to move wealth (backed by military might) give us the right to own property and dominate the market, even where people did not want to play by our rules. Many Maya in Belize own no land because when the Spanish came in as conquerors (followed by the British who displaced them) they abrogated the Maya land tenure system and gave or sold the land to one another. The modern owners use the land to grow cash crops or beef, which they sell to American fast-food chains, while the Maya are malnourished for want of usable land.

Progress and modernization, in a Third World country, too often mean rebuilding after colonial occupation and along lines that benefit international commerce and the world system, not the people. For this reason, many countries amass huge debts. Colonial powers and their modern counterparts build railroads, roads, and communication systems to meet the needs of international commerce, not those of local people. We demand that poor countries pay interest on loans made to them to "modernize." Moreover, we expect them to view paying off the debts as a higher priority than feeding the people. Our progress is built partly on other people's hardship.

Imagine what it would be like if people arrived in our neighborhoods with the military power to back up their demands and announced that henceforth only their currency could buy anything or pay taxes. All our money and our socially defined rights to land and resources would be useless. Only they would have the power to buy, and they would therefore, magically, own everything that had once been ours. If we wanted to buy anything or even pay taxes we would have to work for them. It sounds like science fiction, but this scenario was enacted repeatedly during the era of European colonial expansion.

Or imagine that, without conquest, people arrived with bushel baskets of thousand-dollar bills and could buy anything they wanted, causing enormous inflation in our currency and rendering our paltry salaries and savings meaningless. This, on a very small scale, is exactly how many Americans feel about Japanese or other "outsiders" who have never been to the United States before but somehow, almost magically, seem to have thousands of dollars to spend and who buy up "our" land or art and inflate "our" prices by their ability to spend lavishly, making our few dollars worth even less.

What if the strangers told us that the products we produced for trade at the behest of a former colonial power were no longer being purchased by people half a world away, so that we had no way to earn money or buy food? Perhaps they would tell us that the products we desired were no longer available or that their prices had risen precipitously because people half a world away no longer wanted to sell. They might even say that a commodity we desperately needed (like fuel for our tractors for the new "efficient" agriculture) was now much more expensive because people somewhere else had decided as a matter of fashion to drive large gas-guzzling cars—and they had so much money that they could buy up all the gas they wanted even for such a trivial purpose.

All this is a tiny fraction of what happened in Africa and other parts of the world under colonial rule and what continues today in these areas. In various parts of Africa, for example, the British took over the land by force and proceeded to sell it to one another at prices in English pounds, currency to which Africans had no access, and at levels impossibly far above the wages Africans were permitted to earn. This has happened over and over throughout the Third World, and this—not ignorance or "primitiveness"—is a major reason why people in much of the world are hungry and malnourished and why, once independent, they are now perpetually indebted to the Western nations. The same mechanisms, of course, greatly increased the buying power and the value of European money by giving its possessors access to, and monopoly power over, world resources. A political stroke of expropriation, not just a miracle of indigenous European economic growth, accounts for many of the vast disparities of wealth that now exist. So people in Central America who are hungry export their beef and people in Africa with vitamin A deficiency export the oils that they need to consume in order to absorb the vitamin. We continue to direct the economies of other countries for our own benefit. The 1991 Iraqi war wasn't about our respect for the territorial integrity of Kuwait (itself a colonial creation of the twentieth century, not an ancient country); it was about who controlled the oil we wanted.

All this demands of Americans a bit more humility about ourselves, our history, and our superiority. It also demands a bit more caution about our future. We can't assume that progress and improvements in our lives are guaranteed by technological advances (which are often very costly to health).

In addition, the improvements in health that we *have* seen, such as the unquestioned dramatic increase in life expectancy in the twentieth century, come primarily not from new discoveries, but from social investments in people's environments, their education, their nutrition, and so forth. The great discovery of the germ that causes cholera would have been meaningless without massive investment in restructuring water supplies and sewage systems, particularly in cities. But we are often way behind our own medical and technological sophistication in implementing solutions. We can't simultaneously take pride in our "progress" in health while denigrating and cutting off government investment in such solutions. The idea that disease control is one of the government interventions or frills we can cut back on (apparently on the theory that we have eliminated disease) is even more dangerous than it is absurd. Yet we are cutting that part of big government in the name of economic progress while preserving defense spending, although the threat of attack by disease is far more real than the threat of military attack.

The point is not that we should give up "civilization" for "primitive" life. We couldn't do this even if we wanted to. There are far too many of us. And most of us, myself included, would not want to. The point is rather that we should give more thoughtful consideration to the nature and meaning of the progress that we cherish. The health benefits of progress come only from the wealth that society diverts and invests to deal with health problems—ours and those of the countries whose economies we have dominated and which, in any case, like our own cities, are likely to share their health problems with us. Civilized structures, not dirt or individual poor hygiene or ignorance, are responsible for most modern health problems around the world, and so civilization has an obligation to make the investment. And, because our wealth, health, and well-being have been achieved partly at the expense of Third World people, we have an obligation to divert more resources to solve problems that we have helped to generate.

Manifest Destiny

The idea of manifest destiny is Americans' version of the universal "Chosen People" myth. Our version suggests that it is human nature and the human mandate to charge ahead toward some goal, like an Olympic runner, and that we are the ones selected to bear the torch on behalf of humankind.

People everywhere have a perception of world history that is distorted by their biases. Our rendering of history is no worse than that of any other culture, but our vision nonetheless serves our chauvinism, our intolerance, and our racism.

For one thing, in our version, what happens to other people doesn't count, so we can celebrate the birth of "freedom" and "equality" as if they were universal goals or achievements without paying attention to the fate of Africans or Native Americans or even their descendants who became American citizens. Our children are taught a version of history that makes racism and intolerance easy to maintain. The American version of world history appropriates all the great events in human progress, reinforcing our cultural pride. Then, in a bizarre logical twist, we refuse to offer full participation in our society to the descendants of the very groups that are responsible for those events. The Old Testament is "ours," even as Jews may be excluded from full membership in our society. The classical Greeks and Romans or the Italians who gave us the Renaissance are part of "our" tradition, but their descendants were often denied entry to the United States or relegated to an inferior status when they tried to immigrate early in the twentieth century on the grounds that they were not up to "our" standards. African American athletes manage to contribute to "our" glory and our medal count in the Olympics while they, or at least their less famous relatives, are still being denied full citizenship.

Textbooks and popular images have conveniently forgotten other civilizations which predate (and contributed heavily to) the Greeks, including the Egyptians, Persians (i.e., Iranians), Indus Valley populations, and Chinese, as well as other independently derived civilizations like those of Mexico, Central America, Peru, Ecuador, and Chile. Sometimes we acknowledge their historic greatness even as we denigrate their modern descendants. The "cradle of civilization" in the Fertile Crescent is part of "our" history, but people of the Middle East are demeaned.

Moreover, we conveniently forget that the Renaissance itself derived not only or directly from Greek and Roman inspiration but also from Islamic North African (often dark-skinned) Moors and Arabs. These groups advanced classical scholarship and dominated learning in western Eurasia between the decline of Rome and the European Renaissance, a period far longer than the current period of European domination. (At best, Islam is given credit for holding onto the torch and not dropping it or letting it go out, until Europeans were ready to run forward with it again.)

It is conveniently forgotten that the purest of the pure, Northern Europeans, the only group whose status in our elite is never challenged, were a comparatively backward people who contributed relatively little to the rise of civilization and did not assume any form of world leadership until about four hundred years ago. Besides, many of the ancestors of Anglo-Americans were not the intellectual elite of their mother countries but rather the poor—riffraff, malcontents, and convicts—the very people who are dismissed as unfit today.

One obvious lesson from taking a long-term and broadly encompassing view of history is that cultural and political "leadership" changes rapidly for reasons that can't possibly be genetic. A second obvious lesson is that it is the cross-fertilization of different groups of people with different traditions that promotes the flowering of culture. A third is that our own "lead" is surely temporary.

Isaac Newton once said that if he could see a great distance, it was because he was standing on the shoulders of giants; and he may have known or should have known that some of those giants were not European. Why, then, do Americans of the twentieth century, largely lacking Newton's own giant scientific stature, spend so much time patting themselves on the back and rewarding themselves for their "natural superiority" and their "vision" without realizing that they, too, are standing on the shoulders of others?

To see our place in history more accurately and benefit more fully from the accomplishments of our predecessors, as well as contemporaries from other cultures, Americans also have to get beyond treating our country's history as a cultural icon or a creation myth. This approach to history feeds our patriotism but stifles thought, self-perception, analysis, and tolerance toward others.

Consider, for example, what the word *colonial* means. It refers to societies created when one country or people is dominated or taken over by another. This often but not always takes the form of sending settlers to live in the new land and develop it in the interests of the dominant country. Several sets of people—the various indigenous inhabitants of the colony, the new settlers, and the people of the mother country—have to interact. The interaction is complicated because the groups have separate interests—in fact, each group is likely to be subdivided into several factions and social classes. That is, the indigenous people are not all alike, nor are the settlers, nor are the powers-that-be of the mother country. The interactions are fascinating, particularly because they also involve complex intercultural misunderstandings as well as intracultural tensions.

But most American schoolchildren never get the slightest inkling why our own early history is called "colonial." They assume that the word simply refers to a time period before the American Revolution, characterized by things like buckled shoes and three-cornered hats like the ones they make for school pageants. At best, the idea of colonies conjures images of a unified and peace-loving population of Europeans moving into previously unoccupied space—as if the Native Americans were not really there. At worst it conveys the image of wily Europeans like Peter Minuit buying the land from Natives Americans, who were too foolish to know the relative value of land and beads.

The reality is that, rather than unfolding like a morality play peopled by saints, our colonial history included a variety of ethnic and cultural disagreements, class struggles, racism, and brute force, much like other colonial situations. The shifting alliances between various British or colonial American interests and Native American interests are compelling, as are the class tensions among the colonists and the struggle for power between the elites of the colonies (our "Founding Fathers") and those of Britain over who would rule and who would profit. The latter were struggles in which the common people had relatively little interest. The Founding Fathers ran a revolution for the sake of their own social-class interests and then wrote a Constitution designed primarily to preserve property and privilege rather than human rights. The supreme colonial American hero, George Washington, far from being a modest farmer who "heeded his country's call," was an extremely rich man, by some accounts the richest in the colonies. (After all, Washington was not given regal

Mount Vernon as the gift of a grateful country after the revolution; he inherited it from his family well before.) Washington was fighting British restrictions on his own vast property claims. Like Benjamin Franklin, Washington was a large-scale land speculator. He wanted to invest in land on the western frontier which the British government had recognized by treaty as Native American land to be preserved for Native American ownership and use. The British tended to see the various Native American groups as sovereign neighbors and were in part defending their property rights and their sovereignty. Washington stood to gain enormous personal wealth by having the colonies declare independence from British rule.

My point is not to vilify George Washington but to emphasize the complexity of his situation and his motivations. The danger in allowing Washington and other revered figures to be sanctified in retrospect is that it prevents us from thinking critically about leaders or about our political system, then and now. As things stand, schoolchildren and in fact all citizens, are taught that historic political leaders are faultless ideal people who are impossibly far above them. Washington's mantle of seeming perfection reinforces uncritical approval of modern leaders who do not deserve it, or at least it reassures people that our system is great, even if we don't think that we are getting great leadership now, or even within memory. Instead, we have to teach children that they *always* have the right and duty to be informed, to question, and to expect answers that accord with common sense and the experience of real people. If we don't teach our children to tease apart and evaluate the mixed motives of our historic leaders, how can they possibly be free to make good judgments about modern political candidates? If we don't teach our children about the complexity of historical events, intolerance is infinitely easier to maintain.

The American Revolution ought to be viewed in the light of situations like the messy, ugly struggles for power between European governments and European settlers that characterized twentieth-century Algeria, Rhodesia, and South Africa. Portraying our Founding Fathers as impossibly noble men who were motivated only by a vision of abstract "freedom" and "justice" badly misrepresents the facts of our history. It also creates superheroes in place of mortal individuals and stifles thoughtful analysis and criticism. It also severely underplays the contribution of Native Americans, people of Spanish descent, African Americans, and women to our history and makes people cynical about history itself when they realize that they have been taught a distorted version of events.

A comparative analysis of colonial encounters also provides insights into the meaning of events and the motives of actors that can help us understand those events as well as our own historic legacy. As Albert Memmi has vividly described in *The Colonizer and the Colonized*, colonial situations tend to force people into certain roles. They create their own special players.

Memmi, a Tunisian Jew who suffered as a double outcast under French colonial rule from his birth in 1920 to Tunisian independence in 1956, provides a powerful portrait of the influence of colonial society on its participants which not only sheds light on our history but is relevant to the history of our intolerance. The oppressed or colonized groups, he said, would be forced to become angry, uncooperative, sullen, and depressed. (Memmi was speaking of French North Africa, but his remarks obviously apply to Native Americans, African Americans, and Hispanic Americans as well.) He gave two reasons: that colonized people were forced to deny their own identity in order to survive; and, that even after self-denial, they were put in a classic double bind of contradictory demands. Colonial society demanded not just that one have certain skills, speak the right language, act European, or even learn to succeed under the new rules. In addition, one had to *be* European (which was, of course, impossible). Colonial society also demanded that everyone share the values of the ruling class—which meant, among other things, that members of oppressed groups were supposed to despise people like themselves. They had to learn self-hatred. And, while demanding compliance with its values as well as its actions, the larger society still would not allow oppressed groups full membership. Despite our image of a great melting pot, American history is replete with examples of African Americans, Hispanic Americans, and Native Americans (like Cherokees in Georgia) who did assimilate and become successful by the standards of the ruling society, only to be threatened, exiled, ruined, or even lynched by a society determined that they not succeed. African Americans, of course, faced such pressures through at least half of the twentieth century and still face them occasionally, in the form of burned churches or in subtler forms. The old idea that all such people needed to do was join the "melting pot," as Allan Bloom reasserted, is manifestly untrue in the face of such history. It is hardly surprising that members of "captive" or colonized minorities are ambivalent about trying to enter the mainstream or that they lose interest in trying.

Psychoanalyst Erik Erikson (in *Childhood and Society*) provided a touching description of a small African American boy who found that he could not be Red Ryder (his comic-book cowboy hero from the 1940s and 1950s) even in his fantasies, because Ryder was white, and the boy had learned that he couldn't cross that line. White children of the era who played cowboy happily ignored the fact that their hair color didn't match Red's. Hair color is not a difference we consider significant. But our culture had taught the black child—and as a young child he had already absorbed the lesson—that a skin color difference was a line that could never be crossed, even in one's imagination.

Perhaps just as important, Memmi said that colonization also leave an indelible mark on the ruling class of colonizers. He pointed out that the people from the mother country who participate in the colony have to be relatively eager for profit, and relatively insensitive to the rights of indigenous people and to the damage they might do to those peoples and their lands. This means that the colonizers were often more racist than the people they left behind in the mother country and more reluctant to give up what they considered their natural privileges. Often, as the underprivileged members of their own societies, they revel in their newfound privilege and superiority. Applying Memmi's analysis to American history leads one to question whether the Pilgrims, Puritans, and other early Euro-American settlers were just seeking religious freedom, as our textbooks insist, or if this was just the most noble sounding part of the "freedom" some of them wanted.

What is most important, Memmi argued, is that colonizers have to *become* racists if they are not already, because only by racism and the denigration of others can exploitation be justified. Moreover, Memmi argued, colonizers have to work to remake the colonized to suit their economic needs, dehumanize them to make them fit the racist image, and create caste barriers they cannot cross. Racism, he said, comes not from the failures of the powerless but from the self-justification of the powerful, who need to dehumanize the populations they dominate in order to justify their domination. If their own cultures, like those of Europe after the Enlightenment, otherwise professed freedom and equality, the need for racism to explain why some people were not accorded those things would be all the greater.

In more recent history, seeing the United States as the epitome of progress and civilization, destined to control North America from sea to sea and then to lead and control the world economically and politically, Americans interpret all of our military actions as "defense," including defending Texans from Mexican aggression in order to annex Texas, and defending "settlers" from Native Americans whose land they were usurping. We no longer have a Department of War, just a Department of Defense. Yet, the United States has been involved in at least two dozen wars or military or police actions in the past two hundred years, all of them on someone else's territory. We haven't had to defend the United States proper since 1814. (In World War II we did have to defend Hawaii and other colonial outposts in the Pacific, but at the time Hawaii was effectively a colony with a military base, a token of our own expansionism; statehood was barely on the horizon.) All those actions, whatever their avowed purpose, resulted in expanded territorial, political, or economic control of others.

Our biased perception of our military history and the myths we maintain about the uses of our military make it very difficult for us to understand the fears and reactions of other countries; but a careful look at the record makes it very clear why we are feared.

Today, despite its avowed interest in peace, the United States maintains the largest military force in the world by a large margin and continues to build it beyond any rational defensive need. The ostensible purpose now is to have a military capable of fighting wars in two places simultaneously—but of course that doesn't mean being able to defend both Ohio and Arizona; it means being able to control both Southeast Asia and Southwest Asia. What would we say if some foreign power invaded us to protect its "national interest" in Kentucky or Ohio, or to protect some of its nationals who were living there or trying to do business (perhaps running a Toyota factory)? How can we claim to be "defending our country" or "defending" American interests in other peoples' land and resources, as we do with reference to Middle Eastern oil? Do other people have the same right to commandeer *our* resources? Besides, if our need for oil gives us the right to interfere in other countries, shouldn't need first give us the right to commandeer the wealth of our own elite?

Putting ourselves in the shoes of any of these other people, is it so surprising that American soldiers, American embassies, and even American civilians are cursed, reviled, and sometimes attacked by suicide bombers or by crowds? Having committed ourselves to a political and economic style that demands military intervention—but having grown up on John Wayne movies in which heroes don't get hurt and even bad guys die bloodlessly—we then turn around and claim that if the other guys actually harm our soldiers or use the weapons available to them, they somehow aren't playing fair. How can anyone complain that the Vietnamese didn't treat downed American bomber pilots "fairly"—or are the rules of war supposed to be obeyed even by the civilians living on the battlefield who are not themselves protected? We also insist that it is obscene to air the images of the damage of war on television, but we apparently do not consider it obscene to conduct war itself.

In the same vein, when viewed in the light of knowledge obtained by comparison to other systems, the events in our history offer useful lessons that could be applied to current problems and situations. They even become a good deal more comprehensible as the actions of real people who respond to real and contradictory pressures, as we all must. Historical events represent actions that we must think about, evaluate, and discuss, leading to honest evaluation of our own assumptions, rather than just being symbols that we must memorize. In short, looked at from this perspective, the events of our history teach us to think rather than just providing propaganda.

Egalitarianism

Another of our patriotic historical myths that contributes directly to intolerance is the myth that the United States has a "classless" society, or at least that class is not a salient feature of our social organization. Americans hold the belief that we live in a meritocracy and that success is equally open to all so that wealth reflects nothing but the merit of individuals. Class is not supposed to enter into our political discussions, and any politician who brings up the subject is immediately chided for unnecessarily generating tension. But, in fact, the classes have been pitted against one another throughout our history, and class distinctions, not "racial" ones, should be the single most important factor in our economic and political discussions.

As the myth goes, the American continent, which had been largely empty of anyone of importance, was settled by honest, hard-working Europeans of modest means who managed to carve farms out of the "wilderness," establish towns and cities based on small commerce and crafts, and create a society in which, if there were some rich people and some poor, at least there were not too many of either, nor too wide a gap, and everybody had a fair opportunity to become rich. New immigrants were welcomed and given a similar chance to better themselves. With the Industrial Revolution, opportunities simply expanded and the new wealth allowed everyone (of reasonable competence, sobriety, and initiative) to become wealthy, or at least part of the new middle class.

But, in fact, we have been sharply divided by "race," ethnicity, and social class from the outset. The boundaries of these categories have been very difficult to cross; and as described by Howard Zinn (in *A People's History of the United States*), the struggles between groups have been a major feature of our history.

A close reading of American history shows that European settlers came from a wide variety of backgrounds and that many European social-class distinctions were carried over or reproduced in colonial society. Inciting the American Revolution and drafting the U.S. Constitution were the actions of the rich, and they served primarily upper-class interests. It was not "one nation" that chose to separate from Great Britain, nor was it "we the people" who wrote the Constitution. It was a moneyed class. The Declaration of Independence, the Revolution, and the Constitution did nothing about either poverty or slavery. And after the Revolution, the country did not permit all European immigrants (such as the Irish), let alone blacks, Hispanics, Native Americans, or women, to assimilate into our "classless" society.

The struggle about how taxes should be distributed began almost immediately. Historical incidents like the Whiskey Rebellion, which most American students are taught to dismiss entirely as the work of crazy men with stills and cornpone, actually represented an early attempt to resist the efforts of the Founding Fathers to build the nation's tax base on the activities of the poor rather than taxing the rich. The Civil War was of interest primarily to the wealthy on both sides; and the Industrial Revolution produced a new and badly impoverished working class in the United States, just as it did in Europe.

Class differences are with us still. Statistics widely reported in 1990s (for example, in the *Statistical Abstract of the United States* published by the Department of Commerce in 1993 and Kerbo's 1996 book) indicate that the wealth differential between rich and poor and the proportion of the country's wealth controlled by the richest people are greater in the United States than in any other affluent country. Almost all observers agree, furthermore, that this concentration of wealth at the top and the disparity between rich and poor are increasing. Far from being a society without classes, we now have the widest class stratification in the "free world." One percent of the American population owns almost 40 percent of our wealth, and 10 percent of the population owns 70 percent of the wealth. This means, of course, that the country has far more wealth than most of us can conceive and that most of our careful discussions about government funding, which ignore that wealth, make no sense. We have an enormous amount of wealth and income that could be taxed in order to solve our financial problems (and we would have enough even if we left the bottom 30 percent of the population out of the tax base altogether).

Moreover, striking as those figures are, they understate the differentials of wealth in the United States. The figures suggest that the average member of the richest one percent of the population has about sixty times the wealth that the average citizen has. In fact, the richest Americans may have wealth that is *ten thousand* times or more what even a reasonably high-salaried individual can save in a lifetime, and several million times what the poor can ever accumulate. The earnings of such a wealthy person from modest interest alone could easily be *five thousand* times what a minimum-wage earner is paid for working forty hours a week, fifty weeks a year. To pretend that American society is classless distorts our political dialogue beyond reason.

Historically, class divisions have not been without their social and political benefits. It is common knowledge among anthropologists and archaeologists that all past civilizations depended on class stratification. Certain major social tasks, from the valuable construction of irrigation ditches or medical research to the socially insignificant and wasteful building of pyramids or modern monuments to wealth, can be accomplished only through the centralization of at least some wealth and power. Historically, this centralization has been accomplished through class stratification. But anthropologists also know that the benefits of being civilized are very mixed and very unevenly distributed. "We the people" don't get all the benefits, and such "civilized" structures as class divisions, coerced labor, and slavery work against, rather than for, the welfare of most people.

Class divisions are not divinely ordained. They are a function of social choices. We undoubtedly need concentrated wealth and power to serve many purposes, including legitimate defense. We can't all become independent, because there isn't enough room and because we do want the services provided by our fellow citizens and our government. But we ought to be willing to examine our assumptions about privilege—its importance, its power, and its reasonable limits. The questions remain: How much centralization of wealth and power is necessary for what purposes? Who gets to use it? Why shouldn't most of that wealth belong to the community? We ought to be building irrigation ditches or their modern equivalent, not pyramids or other forms of conspicuous consumption whose only purpose is to glorify the rich and powerful. We the people ought to have a much larger voice in how the wealth is spent, and we ought to be able to spend for public purposes while maintaining a reasonable standard of living for all. We can do this even while permitting the successful to accumulate reasonable extra wealth. The myth of a classless society gets in the way of approaching these ideals.

Justice

Americans believe in justice. We say so every time we recite the Pledge of Allegiance. But, like many other things we believe in, the concept is not as simple in design or execution as we casually assume. It is easier to pledge than to do. One problem, of course, is that despite the glib wording of the Pledge, "liberty and justice" don't always go together. In fact, often they are in opposition. If I am truly free, nothing guarantees that you will get justice. The tension between the two is something that has to be reconciled constantly by thoughtful people (not by judges alone). It can't just be recited.

In addition, Americans don't seem to agree about what the words "for all" in the same Pledge mean. "All" means "all of us," presumably, but few Americans seem to be willing to include all other Americans, let alone the other people of the world, in their definition. In our multiethnic country, trying but not fully succeeding in being "one nation," we don't seem to agree on who "we" are. It has been easy throughout American history to define our neighbors as "others" who do not merit justice, whatever the definition of justice is.

A bigger problem is that we have contradictory ideas of what justice itself embodies. Some people equate justice with absolute equality; some equate it with the freedom of the "fittest" to take whatever they "earn." Some people equate justice with the idea that the society should provide at least minimal guarantees for everybody. Some people think justice means that people should get things according to the station in life they were born in. Some people, including the framers of our Constitution, thought that justice protected the rights of property, not the rights of people. Most people think that justice has something to do with equal protection under the law, a fair trial, and legal equality, if not economic and social equality. For some, that is all that justice means. Clearly these issues need further discussion. My own view, based on the principles outlined in chapter 4, is that a just society is required to provide the necessities of decent life, as well as respect, for all people. That is essential. Beyond that, it can recognize and reward the special contributions of a few; but that is a luxury.

I also think that we tend to rely too heavily on law and government to produce justice, forgetting the role that individual good sense and conscience have to play. Every society we know has laws, written or unwritten, and the laws must be obeyed. Despite the protests of libertarians, anarchy doesn't work, especially where large numbers of strangers must interact. Moreover, our laws must form a system that is coherent, consistent, and predictable. The body of the law and "precedent" (respect for what was said and done previously) are essential because they make the system predictable. Precedent in law is simply one form of contractual conventional agreement—one of the sets of cultural rules about what to expect—that makes all human social life possible.

But real justice has to extend beyond the formal system of laws. Law itself is an arbitrary social contract. Its purpose ought to be to serve human needs, not to perpetuate its own integrity. Unthinking adherence to precedents can lead even the best and most consistent logic into convoluted blind alleys that serve no one. The law alone is not a sufficient source of justice. Any set of laws, including our own, exists within an arbitrary and often unspoken frame of cultural assumptions which constantly needs to be reevaluated. If the assumptions are misguided, inappropriate, inaccurate, or out of date, the laws will be bad. Our goal ought to be a system of law and justice that can see beyond the narrow circle of its (and our) assumptions and our arbitrary cultural values. Its purpose is to serve higher social and human needs, which are often subtle. Moreover, real needs may vary from group to group within the society (as a function of ethnic distinction or of minority status itself, for example).

The law has to earn the respect we give it by its wisdom and compassion. To the extent that the law does earn people's respect, it will almost certainly gain greater compliance. Otherwise, both precedent and the sanctity of law are simply additional sets of blinders that impede us from making good choices. The fact that an action is legal should not be sufficient to win our approval or even our acceptance.

We have to remember, too, that the abstract principles of the law mean little unless they are applied wisely to the realities of a situation, accurately perceived. Too often, it seems, the law is interpreted only in terms of its own system or symmetry without regard for the fact that circumstances are irregular. For the law to maintain, for example, that removing affirmative action rules will "level the playing field" or make us a "color-blind society" again (even though it might do so in strictly legalistic terms) would be utterly absurd to any honest observer of the treatment of women and minorities in the United States. A society based on the rule of law, especially law heavily slanted to favor the powerful, exercised without a knowledge of circumstances and without common sense, fairness, and compassion, simply perpetuates or expands the privileges of the powerful and creates the conditions to which I alluded in chapter 1.

Equally important, we have to remember that the law is only one set of principles, the minimum, by which we live. Ethical principles involving human needs and consideration for one another must also be consulted.

Making the law serve real human needs and real justice is a problem that plagues all societies, but particularly large-scale multi-ethnic states. In small communities, where face-to-face encounters of people who know one another and share similar values are possible, justice may be relatively easy to maintain or restore through the intercession of kinsmen, friends, elders, or local courts run by people who know the individuals involved. Customary principles of unwritten law are interpreted with broad prior knowledge of the specific people and circumstances. The goal is to find a settlement satisfactory to all that will permit the individuals to go on with their lives and permit the group to maintain its cohesion. Often no attempt is made to determine guilt or innocence, as that would simply per-petuate social tensions. For most such people, the idea that justice could or should be impersonal, distant, or "blind" would be absurd. They would want the judge to be someone who knows everyone, not someone who knows no one. And they would want the decision to reflect the specific circumstances, not just abstract principles.

The abstract law of large countries cannot so easily deliver justice. One reason is that formal written law cannot concern itself with all of the small day-to-day injustices that afflict many of us as individual citizens. Its machinery is too massive and too slow, and too expen-sive to mobilize. It responds far more readily to the problems of major corporate interests and wealthy individuals who can afford to pay for lawyers' services. In addition, the law of large countries can-not be written with enough subtlety to recognize individual people or to anticipate all possible injustices or to decide every case accu-rately. It must use—and therefore reinforce—broad categories of people. The law stereotypes us. And, as written law (as opposed to customary law in small societies or informal resolution in our own society), it cannot be flexible enough to recognize the variables in every case and get them right. It must, therefore, be interpreted by good people with justice on their minds. Even then, the law will not decide everything correctly. (The first writing down of laws, histor-ically, was not an episode of "progress." It was a concession to the increasing size and complexity of human groups.)

We as citizens have to recognize that part of the price we pay for living in a large civilization is small disappointments, small imper-fections in how the law is applied. We tend to want to throw out any law that disappoints our sense of justice even in small ways, rather than recognizing that justice for others, individual interpre-tations of the law, occasional misjudgments or misapplications, im-perfect enforcement, and the inflexibility of written law itself all mean that we will occasionally be disappointed. If we threw out every law that produced such minor inequities and disappointments, as many wish to do with affirmative-action laws, we would have no laws left.

A further problem about relying on law to produce justice is that law must concern itself with two other principles, order and power. Both are clearly more central than justice to the purpose of law in large-scale societies. In any society, order is more important than justice, because it is order that helps perpetuate the society. Order is a necessity, justice is a luxury in many ways, unfortunately, and laws are written and enforced accordingly. But we could work toward making laws address both order *and* justice.

Many of us find the concept of "trial by ordeal," practiced historically in our own culture and in many others, to be a quaint symbol of irrational minds. In such a system, guilt or innocence is decided by a physical test in which knights win or lose in battle, an accused woman bound hand and foot sinks or floats, or the accused is or is not burned by hot coals. How, we wonder, can justice be done in this manner?

But trial by ordeal plays a significant part in maintaining the social order because doing something official about infractions, teaching others about them, and then putting the issue to rest are more important than ensuring justice. The ritual itself drives home the important social teaching, and the judgment appears to be the judgment of God, not of mortal and culpable people. So the trial puts an end to the matter and to vengeance and recrimination. Determining guilt or innocence correctly is secondary. Sometimes the right person is found and punished, sometimes not. Either way, the society goes on.

Although we like to think that trial by arguments before a jury of one's peers is a better approximation of justice than trial by ordeal, often, perhaps most often, it is not. The criminal trial of O. J. Simpson raised serious doubts about the system in the minds of many Americans; but others, particularly members of minority groups, have known for a long time that determining real guilt or innocence often is not a central part of American judicial proceedings. The Sacco-Vanzetti trial, the Lindbergh kidnapping trial, and the trial of the Scottsboro Boys, among others, have had far more to do with latent functions, including the maintenance of order, the reinforcement of group values, propaganda, symbolic punishment, prejudice and hate, and the education of others, than with the determination of guilt or innocence. Our society, too, goes on, whether or not the guilt or innocence of the individual has been accurately determined, with some sense that a lesson has been taught or learned and an episode put behind us, even if there are lingering doubts about the verdict.

In short, systems of judgment serve many purposes. Justice is only one, and it is not necessarily the purpose that guides our efforts, even if it is the one we are most conscious of. So unjust outcomes continue to surprise us, when in fact they are the obvious result of a system that actually has different, unspoken goals. If we really wish to make justice the outcome of our efforts, we have to be conscious of the multiple purposes of our institutions, the multiple levels on which they operate. We have to sort through those purposes to make certain that the structure of our legal system is really focusing on the right goal. Whether or not one likes the verdict of either Simpson trial, it should be clear that justice was not the only or even the primary goal on either side.

In any large-scale state, stratified into social classes and combining a variety of economic specialists and ethnic groups (i.e., in any state in which people do not feel voluntarily united as a nation), power is also more necessary than justice, because it is the threat and occasional use of coercive force that maintain order. Unfortunately, this necessary apparatus of social control at best competes with justice as a goal of law. In addition, once the mechanism of power has been put in place, it can also be diverted for private good. It becomes a mechanism by which some people advance themselves individually. There is always a tension between the use of power to ameliorate social problems or to promote justice and its use for personal or small-group gain. The people who get power often decide that justice isn't so important after all, as any number of modern as well as historic memoirs of government service attest.

A further problem in the United States (or any country) is that, like most cultural codes, the code of law exists on several levels, so that perception and reality don't agree. This permits hypocrisy or slippage between what we say we do and what we actually do. There is a danger that we will do things in the name of the sanctity of the law when, in fact, we are just acting out our prejudices. The hypocrisy is sometimes obvious, particularly to the poor and powerless, whose interests are rarely served. It contributes significantly, I suspect, to their disdain for the law and for law enforcement personnel.

Most laws exist at the level that is formally written, but there are other levels of any law which are implicitly understood, intended to be taken seriously, or actually punished. We all know that the posted speed limit is not intended to designate the speed at which people drive or the level of speeding that will actually be punished. What we don't know is how fast we can go before the police will pull us over and whether their reaction is consistent from day to day or driver to driver or "race" to "race." In fact, it is rarely consistent. Similarly, tax accountants know that IRS computers will not flag for an audit slightly inflated claims, and, like drivers, tax preparers depend on their past experience, their knowledge of current conditions, and the social status of the particular taxpayer to estimate the extent to which claims can be inflated with only slight risk of apprehension or with only a minimum penalty. The rest of us don't have (or can't afford to pay for) this expertise and therefore pay more tax or risk more severe punishment. The result is that accountability and enforcement are unequally applied because law enforcement officials can always revert selectively to the official letter of the law and because we are not all equally privy to knowledge about the unspoken levels of enforcement. "The system" exploits the discrepancy between the levels of meaning in law enforcement to focus unequally on some groups of people (typically the nonwhite) and on certain spheres of activity (typically those involving the poor).

Because such multiple levels of perception and enforcement characterize nearly all cultural systems, it is hard to know what to do to correct this problem. But two things are clear. First, under our present system, people need access to legal expertise, which is as much about providing advice for navigating the unspoken levels of the legal system as it is about formal law itself. Equal protection under the law demands equal access to such advice. If we eliminate legal services for the poor, we compound their problems because we remove the last vestige of their ability to use and understand the system we ask them to live by.

Second, the frequency with which people break—or are seen to break—the law depends in large degree not on their morality but on their sophistication in recognizing exactly where the law will intervene and how to get around it. Conservatives often suggest that the poor, the nonwhite, or other outsiders break the law frequently because they lack moral development or intelligence. Lack of sophistication in legal matters and lack of awareness of options (and sometimes greater real need) are probably far better explanations. At least we should not stigmatize the poor further by asserting that they are dumb or immoral when they are just acting based on their imperfect understanding of the system and the options that exist.

In the United States the problems of obtaining justice through law are also compounded by a number of historical patterns. At the most superficial level, the U.S. government sows confusion by using the word *justice* when it really is referring to order or even to power. Bombarded by such messages, we tend to lose track of what justice itself actually is. The Justice Department has been a major lever of governmental power but only rarely one of justice throughout much of the twentieth century. The individuals we entrust with power in the name of justice often betray the trust. (Examples abound in descriptions of the role of the FBI in twentieth-century "law enforcement" and politics.)

The problem is exacerbated because, while we maintain the fiction that the law is a great and neutral set of organizing principles that demand equal compliance by all, many of its principles were, as I have already pointed out, developed with specific class interests in mind or even for personal profit by the Founding Fathers and others who were hardly disinterested. In fact, the entire system of American law springs from assumptions in English common law which are markedly skewed toward protecting property, not people. Laws continue to be written and interpreted primarily by members of the upper classes and slanted toward their interests. And the law is continually shaped by advocacy, most often representing those who are already powerful. As is becoming increasingly obvious, in any legal proceeding the quality of advocacy may be more important than morality or common sense.

Judgments of guilt or innocence depend heavily on the popularity, wealth, and "race" of the accused and the politics of the times. Levels of punishment are wildly unpredictable and unequally applied. People who abuse positions of public or private trust and power, use financial influence to rob us of millions of dollars, or threaten the integrity of government itself are rarely punished as severely as common criminals. Corporate and white-collar crime injures society far more than street crime but is often punished less severely than burglary; white-collar criminals don't do "hard time." Zinn has pointed out that almost no one went to jail because of the Iran-Contra affair of the early 1980s except an individual who in protest removed a street sign honoring one of the villains—this despite the fact that the affair was one of the most significant challenges to American constitutional government in the twentieth century. Are people who accidentally overhear the Speaker of the House breaking his own recent promise to the House—in the midst of an investigation into the legality of his own activities—and who tell someone what they heard (illegally, as it turns out), really the most important villains of the episode? We repeatedly use legalisms to deflect attention from real culpability.

The media reinforce unequal application of the law. Why do American media give so much attention to the need to punish a few welfare cheats? Why does this one form of cheating among so many arouse so much ire in taxpayers? And why do we permit a legitimate desire to stem welfare fraud to become a call to end welfare? Why can an American president offer a baseless quip about welfare queens and harm so many people? The cheats do exist, of course; but those who cheat represent a tiny fraction of those on welfare (most of whom are people in real need). Fraud should be curbed, but for the most part it represents only the opportunism that occurs around the fringes of any valid program, and trying to end the cheating by tightening enforcement may be more expensive than the cheating itself. And on a national scale, welfare fraud just isn't a very significant economic problem. Why don't we seriously punish the powerful people whose crimes cost us far more? We certainly don't threaten to eliminate banks or business or government (or "end banking as we know it") because some bankers cheat, let alone because some people write bad checks.

The law can and does protect people, but it can also act as a shield for inequity, injustice, brutality, and racism. If it fails to pay attention to the real needs of real people, the law is not so much legal as legalistic—involved only with form and not with substance—just as it was long ago when the Supreme Court once decided that, according to law, based presumably on Constitutional precepts and precedent, African Americans were not citizens or even real people and therefore had no rights that whites were bound to respect.

Some recent confirmation hearings should put to rest the myth that, even now, the Supreme Court represents a set of wise "elders" deciding thorny issues in their collective wisdom for the greatest good, even if that is what schoolchildren are taught. Justices should be selected for their wisdom and compassion and their ability to see beyond the limits of our cultural blinders and legal definitions, not just for their politics or even for their ability to offer nicely reasoned constitutional arguments. In fact, the Supreme Court ought to act as a court of appeals empowered to get outside the narrow circle of the law itself and to see beyond the limits of our cultural assumptions. Justice, not just constitutionality, ought to be the basis of its decisions. It ought to recognize other social and cultural factors and to determine when legal justice is not sufficient and other principles of justice must be invoked. Yet the serious consideration given to some nominees in recent years suggests a clear preference for fine legal scholarship over wisdom or compassion. One recent successful nomination was a victory for cynical manipulation of the American ideal of broad representation. The nomination was in fact designed to discredit that ideal. Cynicism, political ideology, and packing the court with politically safe votes have clearly been shown to be more important than selecting wise, compassionate people with common sense—or than obtaining justice.

The arguments in the late 1990s about redistricting along "racial" or other lines in Georgia, in which redistricting to (presumably) increase the representation of a minority was held to be less legitimate than redistricting for political advantage, show just how far the Court can stray from compassion and good sense, and how far purely legalistic arguments (nice reasoning from faulty assumptions) can lead it astray. Can the right to abortion really turn on a "right to privacy" that some can find buried in the Constitution and some cannot? The ongoing debate about abortion involves the potential for a great deal of real physical harm or death to adult women and to fetuses, no matter how it is resolved. It can cause pain by violating the emotional values of those involved and of many who are not involved except as a matter of their faith. Balancing the harm and well-being of the different players is a complex and difficult task. Yet that is what we have to do and we should make our decision explicitly on that basis. Searching for a guide in the Constitution or torturing its prose to come up with such a guide seems to me not only futile but harmful. There is no discussion of the issue in the Constitution; those who claim to find one are generally trying to use the sanctity of the Constitution to deflect responsibility for a hard decision. Hiding behind the Constitution allows them to be less than forthright about stating the views they hold anyway. Even if a discussion or hints about abortion policy had been included in the Constitution, the idea that it should govern our lives two hundred years later, when both medical and social circumstances have changed dramatically, seems absurd. The Court should put aside a legalistic search for precedents and face the hard twentieth-century choices with real people in mind.

The law is an arbitrary, negotiable contract, and we can insist on negotiating it with real people's interests in the balance. Why isn't the principle of measuring real harm to real people the major principle in Court decisions? We might even question whether legal expertise ought to be the necessary or the only qualification for all members of the Supreme Court. Lawyers, like economists, engineers, anthropologists, or specialists in any other field, become focused on the particular system in which they operate and are blinded to some degree to competing sets of principles. In our court system, this monolithic focus on legalism in the narrow sense is getting in the way of focusing on real issues. Certainly it is necessary for some justices to be lawyers or to have legal advisers; but perhaps others ought to be chosen to represent a wider range of social needs and areas of expertise, as a reminder of what goals are truly being served. Moreover, we might ask whether, even among lawyers, we need to focus so heavily on those representing the practice of upper-class corporate law rather than reflecting a broader array of the American people and their problems.

Finally, our use of the Constitution is part of the problem. The Constitution is a bit like a Rorschach blot in which people see what they want to see. Perhaps it would be more meaningful to say that it is like the traditional origin mythology of any society that reinforces group patriotism and teaches principles of behavior but can be retold and reformulated to suit changing goals. Therein lies its value.

But we cannot pretend that the Constitution holds the answers to specific contemporary problems or that reading it with greater and greater precision will tell us what those answers are. The Constitution was written more than two hundred years ago in a world in which many present-day problems could not even be imagined. And, it was written by wealthy men who considered the right to own property and even to hoard it more important than the right to eat. (Which right, after all, does the Constitution, as it is commonly interpreted, protect?) It also defended the "right" to own slaves but perceived no rights for the slaves themselves and few for women or the poor. The Constitution and the courts that interpreted it also failed to uphold the rights of African Americans as human beings, let alone as citizens, through more than half of the twentieth century. So the idea that a document more than two centuries old can serve as a detailed and accurate guide to contemporary decisions is clearly inappropriate. Pretending that it serves this purpose dulls our thinking about contemporary problems and hides the responsibility of individuals and those advocating specific political agendas for shaping decisions. We have to make ourselves and our representatives and judges accountable for our decisions rather than blaming them on the Founding Fathers.

The Constitution and other precedents properly represent a model, a set of ideas out of which reasonable people might fashion reasonable responses to current problems. But pretending that the Constitution provides specific answers to modern problems and teaching our children that the Supreme Court is above reproach and criticism makes us as tradition-bound as any culture we deplore and prevents the law from serving its real purpose. Hiding behind the Constitution, rather than using its important ideas constructively and selectively, prevents us from taking full advantage of the flexibility inherent in our system. It serves mostly to blunt thought.

I don't think the American mainstream is trying very hard to promote justice. If we are, we are so blinded by ingrained cultural assumptions and class interests that we aren't doing it very well. A society that pretends to be a democracy, rooted in equality and rationality, has to do a better job of clarifying and implementing those values. The contradictions between our stated goals and the reality of our acts which exist in the system play a large role in generating the frustration and cynicism that many Americans feel. But because questioning the system itself has always seemed too threatening to the maintenance of our system of beliefs, we have been forced to redirect our anger toward handy scapegoats. That means that we not only have to choose people to act as scapegoats; we have to invent ways to justify our choice.

CHAPTER SIX

Justifying Inequality: Cultural Assumptions About Intelligence and Competence

AS WE HAVE SEEN, CULTURAL blinders largely govern our perception of social problems and their solutions. Reviving a shopworn but popular argument in *The Bell Curve: Intelligence and Class Structure in American Life* (1994), Richard J. Herrnstein and Charles Murray attempt to justify inequality and our use of scapegoats. They try to prove that some of the realities of American life—differential job performance, differential income, class, poverty, crime, morality, family values, illegitimacy (and discrimination by "race," although they don't say so explicitly)—are grounded in inherent biological differences in human mental ability. Their book and the publicity surrounding it have given disrespect for people who are "different" or poor a scientific veneer. With an overwhelming array of numbers, charts, and graphs, they purport to demonstrate that some people and some groups, particularly among African Americans and the poor, really are inferior in innate intelligence. Herrnstein (who died soon after the book came out) and Murray argue, in effect, that these people have earned their marginal status in society, that they have what they deserve, given their limited merits, and that efforts to help (or even share with) them are misguided. But, in their zeal, Herrnstein and Murray completely fail to grasp the cultural basis not only of test performance but of intelligence itself and of people's contributions to society; and they do not consider a host of other factors in human biology and culture that affect performance.

Many scholarly reviewers have found their arguments to be shallow and self-contradictory (see, for example, the collections of essays edited by Steven Fraser and by Russell Jacoby and Naomi Glauberman, both published in 1995). *The Bell Curve* clearly crossed the line from being controversial or questionable scholarship to being misleading or even intentionally deceptive in its authors' use of evidence and arguments. But the book was nonetheless dangerous enough to prompt many scholars to respond publicly.

The danger came not from the merits of Herrnstein and Murray's claims but from the inflammatory nature of those claims and the wave of publicity that surrounded the book's publication. Unlike most scholarly books, it received enormous media attention (including cover stories in *Newsweek*, the *New York Times Magazine*, and the *New York Times Book Review*) and got amazingly gentle handling, before it ever had much serious scholarly review. Various critics have since wondered why arguments that were neither particularly new nor particularly well supported suddenly became so fashionable—and fashionable is the right word. The *New York Times Magazine* called Murray, the surviving author, the "most dangerous conservative" (conservatives probably ought to have called him the most embarrassing). Moreover, the book was drawn immediately to the attention of conservative politicians and pundits, who shared its views and who waved the book about as long as they felt that it served their purposes and until they began to get the sense from scholarly reaction that it might discredit them.

But a more important danger was that the book played into and reinforced certain American cultural biases. Superficially, it appeared to provide scientific support for a number of shared American cultural myths. The real importance of the book lay not in its overt claims to science but rather in its latent function of reinforcing white American patriotism and chauvinism. It appeared to demonstrate that things really do work the way American values and "know-how" say they do, and it purported to demonstrate that being a good American (read white, middle-class, male American) and doing things "the American way" are the secrets to success. It reinforced the idea that we live in a meritocracy in which anyone who is clever and hard-working can get ahead. And, it appeared to demonstrate that, despite the discontent of liberals and minorities, the system really works. The only danger the authors foresaw was that, as natural merit was freed to seek its own level, the gap between the (smart) rich and the (dumb) poor would naturally and inevitably become impossibly wide.

Despite the authors' claims that they bravely explored forbidden ground in the search for truth, the book reverts to familiar stereotypes and effectively scapegoats minorities and the poor, the people least able to defend themselves, focusing attention on them and their failures while ignoring problems and issues in other parts of society. The assertions in the book—and the IQ tests it relies on so heavily— also constitute one version of the very widespread cultural pattern by which all human groups "prove" their natural superiority over all others. The popularity of *The Bell Curve* is a classic example of a culturally defined cognitive pattern (a model describing how the world works) that doesn't have to be right, only widely shared, to have important cultural results.

Moreover, the book and the IQ tests themselves serve primarily the same function: to validate our social system of selection and discrimination and to give it a veneer of legitimacy. Although they undeniably open doors to the few members of the lower classes who succeed at them, the tests, as I will show, can't possibly measure what they purport to measure. They do reassure us, however, that we live in a free, competitive, individualistic society in which success is based on a person's merit—never mind that, aside from "race" and sex, most people's social status is based on what their ancestors achieved, and that that accomplishment had to do with specialized insights, insider knowledge, luck, or skirting or breaking the law, as much as or more than raw intellectual power. And never mind that there are other virtues like hard work, teamwork, communication, ambition, and pride in craftsmanship that contribute to success, as anyone who has ever worked on a large project knows.

It is these myths concerning intelligence and success and their biological and cultural bases, not just the conclusions of *The Bell Curve* itself, that I want to explode. Others have questioned the book and the tests. I want to challenge the reader to look beneath some of the shallower and more harmful conventional American cultural assumptions that contributed to the popularity of the book.

Herrnstein and Murray's work includes the following propositions:

1. There is a real, biologically based entity called "intelligence" that exists in what might be called the "hard wiring" of the

human brain, not in the cultural programming (or what might be called the software), and all human groups recognize it and seek to define and measure it. [The latter point is manifestly untrue.]

2. "Intelligence" is a *single* thing, a unified core capability underlying most other specialized capabilities, rather than simply an amalgam of whatever specific test results we care to combine.

3. Such intelligence can be realistically and fairly measured by IQ tests [without regard for the cultural background of those tested].

4. Intelligence is highly "heritable"—i.e., it is determined principally by our genes. Using methods like those I described in chapter 2, the authors propose that genes explain about 60 percent of the variance among individuals in intelligence. [They admit at one point that they don't know whether there is a 60 percent heritability of variance *between groups*—the key question. But the damage has been done and the 60 percent figure hovers like a ghost in all of their arguments, including their discussion of group differences. Without such a figure, most of their arguments evaporate. Note that in this context, "groups" refers not just to "races" but to classes, income levels, regions of the country, and so forth.]

5. Because intelligence is in our genes, IQ scores can't be altered substantially during one's lifetime by any kind of social intervention, and evidence to the contrary can be dismissed.

6. Human "races" are differentially gifted in IQ at least in statistical terms. [The authors admit, however, that there is variability in intelligence within each "race" so that an individual's IQ can't be predicted based on his or her "race."]

7. Intelligence as measured by IQ is strongly correlated with the incidence of poverty, crime, marital stability, illegitimacy, and other lower-class failings. And because it is largely genetic, IQ must be the cause, not the result, of those behaviors or the social situations that promote them.

8. Because IQ and intelligence are genetically based, they can be used as independent correction factors mitigating any attempt to show a relationship between environment and any social outcome. For example, apparent discrimination "disappears" once intelligence is taken into account.

9. Attempts to alleviate social problems through social assistance of various sorts, including existing affirmative action and welfare supports, are misguided. [The authors do suggest that such programs might work better in other forms—and I agree—but the premises from which they would offer modifications are demonstrably false.]

This line of reasoning, so appealing and so obviously "true" to many people steeped in American cultural values, cannot be supported by scientific evidence, despite Herrnstein and Murray's abundant graphs and statistics. As I have already shown (chapter 2), no genes have been identified which affect variations in intelligence within the normal range, and there is not even a very strong case for postulating them because no physical or chemical variations which might be genetically based have been found in the brain associated with variations in intelligence within the normal range. Genes (particularly those for complex traits with continuous distributions, like height) almost never function to determine "traits" or outcomes in the complete absence of environmental inputs, and determining what proportion of variation in any trait is contributed by genes, other than in a specific sample tested under well-controlled conditions, is inherently impossible. Genes and environment interact, and the mix of the two can change from situation to situation so that heritability, the popular measure of genetic contribution on which Herrnstein and Murray rely, is always specific to a given situation. Moreover, the "heritability" of intelligence has been tested only over a very limited range of circumstances, if at all, so that we have no means of measuring the inherent power of postulated "intelligence" genes. (This is a simple statement about how statistics work; it is not a political assertion.) Moreover, the patterns of family inheritance of intelligence on which genetic models rely don't actually demonstrate that the inheritance is genetic since so many other mechanisms of family transmission are known. In fact, as I pointed out in chapter 2, genetics shows us that genes do not reliably transmit characteristics from parent to child because parents pass on random selections of their genes, the genes of the parents mix, and genes act differently in the presence of other genes and variations in the environment. So, even if something like intelligence runs in a family, it relies heavily on cultural transmission (wealth, nutrition, leisure, expectations, intellectual focus, respect for schooling, etc.), not genetics alone.

The notion that there is a genetic basis for differential "intelligence" in human groups larger than families has even less scientific basis. As I demonstrated in chapter 2, "races" as predictable clusters of biological traits do not exist because there are thousands of genetic loci, of which only a fraction of 1 percent relate to traits that we think of as "racial" or that are associated with particular groups. And most traits, even the popularly recognized "racial" characteristics, don't actually occur together in neat packages and don't correlate with skin color. So if intelligence does correlate with color to any significant degree, it almost certainly does so for social, not genetic reasons. Furthermore, as I pointed out in chapter 4 and as is readily apparent from a broad reading of history and prehistory, European world leadership is an extremely transitory phenomenon. The assumption that it is based on genetic superiority is untenable on historical as well as biological grounds. In addition, the historical record hardly suggests that Europeans have demonstrated superiority in moral or social qualities, even though Herrnstein and Murray suggest that intelligent people are superior in those ways as well.

Further, postulating or even knowing that something is under genetic control says nothing about whether it can be changed. Some kinds of bad eyesight are at least partly caused by one's genes, yet the problems can be corrected with eyeglasses or surgery. Adult diabetes is influenced by genes, as are the risk of skin cancer and the likelihood of developing hypertension, yet all these defects are correctable through medical interventions, without stigma, as long as the society is willing to make the investment. When biological correction is not possible or not effective, we make special adjustments in the physical and social environment to make it easier for people to live with their problems. We make such corrections for members of the society all the time, with no sense that helping them is inherently unjust or shameful or that it marks inherent inferiority. And because such genetic flaws, taken together, are fairly evenly distributed, there is little reason to find any group "inferior" in some larger sense. Besides, even if genes account for 60 percent of human variance in intelligence (as Herrnstein and Murray postulate, incorrectly, and at their most pessimistic), that still leaves a powerful 40 percent for environmental influence and manipulation.

In addition, there is a great deal of evidence (some of which Herrnstein and Murray cite and then ignore) that IQ, whatever it measures, can be altered by changing the environment in various ways, including improving health and nutrition of mothers, fetuses, and children; breast-feeding; reducing exposure to toxic lead; improving parent-child communication; providing special educational programs; providing foster homes; motivating students to work hard; increasing self-esteem; improving teachers' regard for students; and raising teacher expectations for students. There are undoubtedly others.

There is also a lot of evidence for the whole American population, for American ethnic groups, and for populations wherever tests are given that IQ is changing in ways that can't possibly be genetic because they happen too fast. It is widely recognized that average IQs are increasing fairly rapidly. These changes in IQ clearly must have more to say about relationships between testing and real performance, or about social patterns of learning, than about biologically rooted "intelligence." The genes of a large population don't change that fast unless there is a very dramatic episode of natural selection such as an epidemic. It is also widely recognized that African Americans are slowly but steadily gaining on white Americans in IQ. And, if you believe the tests, various other groups have made astounding gains in short periods of time. Some immigrants (e.g., Italians, Poles, Jews), large numbers of whom had IQs so low that IQ testers considered them mentally defective when they arrived in the United States early in the twentieth century, now hold their own or excel, as do the once-"defective" Chinese and Japanese. And it is a source of wonder to hear the "geneticists" of intelligence like Herrnstein and Murray fawn on Ashkenazi Jews and Asians, the current winners of the great IQ race, considering that the former were sent back to Nazi Germany seventy years ago to die because, partly on the basis of IQ tests, they weren't worthy of admission to the United States, and the latter were once held in great disdain. (The Japanese in the period after World War II were widely "known" to be capable of imitation, never of innovation.) Could these groups have evolved biologically so much in sixty years?

Studies of inheritance in identical twins (i.e., twins that are genetically identical because they grow from the same fertilized egg), the usual way scientists attempt to measure heritability, are badly flawed in their basic structure. People who believe in the power of heredity like to show that identical twins "reared apart" still make similar scores on intelligence tests; therefore, they argue, their intelligence must be in their genes. In a more general way, pairs of identical twins, pairs of fraternal twins, members of families, and unrelated pairs are compared across a range of environments on the assumption that if identical twins are more similar to each other than the other pairs are, the similarity reflects their identical genetic makeup. In fact, however, identical twins "reared apart" have almost invariably spent the most critical developmental period in very similar environments, so environment as well as genes is likely to contribute to their similar endowment. For one thing, identical twins are always reared in the same womb, an environment where major environmental influences on brain development occur. Moreover, because they are chemically identical, they will have a similar reaction to the chemistry of that womb, more so even than other siblings or nonidentical twins. Fraternal twins—really just siblings who happen to be born at the same time—can have different blood types and certainly have other protein differences that distinguish them from each other and distinguish each from the mother. As I indicated in chapter 2, we know that even a difference as subtle as blood type can cause a chemical reaction between mother and fetus that can harm the fetus or affect its development, so the chemical similarity of identical twins—which is of course in their genes—might have a significant effect on the fact that their mental development is comparable. That is, they might develop in a similar way not because their "intelligence genes" are identical but because their responses to the womb or later environments were the same. The important genes may not be those for brain design at all but those that control identical reactions to chemicals present in the environment. Unlike the postulated but unknown "intelligence" genes, this explanation of the similar development of identical twins involves well-established chemical mechanisms. At the very least this means that it is extremely difficult to separate the genetics of intelligence per se from the genetics of chemical similarities affecting development. Unless we separate identical twins right after conception and implant them in different mothers, there is no way to distinguish the genetic and environmental components of their early mental development. Comparing identical twins to fraternal twins or non-twins doesn't separate the two components because the essence of being identical is itself both genetic and environmental.

Moreover, twins reared separately after birth are rarely reared very far apart. The number of well-documented cases of twins reared apart in the scientific literature is quite small, and the comparative similarity of the environments in which they were reared can be shown easily. Often they are placed with relatives in the same town, go to the same school, and virtually always are reared in the same social class. Moreover, identical twins, more than even fraternal twins, tend to be treated in a very similar manner by the people around them. This is important because, as in the example of the plants discussed in chapter 2, the more similar the environments, the more important the genetic factors or "heritability" appear to be in explaining the observed variance. So under these conditions we will see high heritability not because it is an inherent property of intelligence but because the nature of the samples keeps environmental variability small. Yet if we construct very dissimilar human environments, like the two trays of soil in the plant example, the observed differences will result much more from environmental factors.

By definition, identical twins are almost always reared in the same social classification of "race." Because "race" identification becomes a very significant part of the individual's environment in a number of ways in the United States, this is no small matter in assessing genetic and environmental contributions to intelligence. Two individuals reared in different "racial" environments (which in this country are almost always markedly dissimilar) are likely to display different patterns of "intelligence" regardless of their genetic endowment.

Defining "Intelligence"

There is a great deal of controversy about whether intelligence is in fact some unitary "thing" that can and should be measured on a linear ranking scale. Linear ranking—the idea that someone is always first, someone second, and so on—is itself a kind of American folk belief to which many other cultures don't subscribe. This means that we should be especially careful in assessing scientific conclusions that purport to demonstrate linear ranking, lest we succumb to a peculiarly American model of thinking, when we think we are discovering "the truth." The ranking may be in our perception, not necessarily in what we are studying.

Proponents of the unitary intelligence idea like to refer to g (for general factor of intelligence) as the symbol of that core intelligence which can be measured and ranked by IQ tests. They suggest that g, computed by a sophisticated mathematical factor analysis of various test scores, lies at the heart of other abilities and that people have different amounts of g. Critics, notably Stephen Jay Gould, instead argue that intelligence is made up of many separate things and that g is nothing more than a number concocted by mathematicians which could easily change if underlying assumptions were changed. Gould offers a good explanation of this point in *The Mismeasure of Man*, but his explanation is complicated, for most of us, by the mathematics involved. I will try to explain the point with a couple of simpler analogies that capture the basic ideas involved, although they miss some of the mathematical subtleties. My analogies, however, also add some cultural subtleties to the discussion.

Let's take a simple mathematical concept that everyone is familiar with: the average. We can easily calculate the average height, say, of women in a natural population by measuring the heights of many individuals, totaling the measurements, and dividing the total by the number of women measured. The number we get, say 5'5", gives us a reasonable picture of the group of women that we can compare to another population in which the average height of all women may be 5'7" or 5'3". Although calculating the average is not as good as knowing all the individual heights (which tells us more about each population), the average is meaningful. Height always refers to the same commodity measured in the same way; the women in question are comparable beings; each woman counts only once; the women's heights are fairly similar; and the heights in question tend to cluster around the mean, approximating a normal ("bell"-shaped) curve. Most individuals are close to the mean in height, while a few individuals are very tall or very short. So the average tells us about most women. Given all those factors, most of us would agree that the average has real meaning for describing the women of a natural population.

The problem is that I can also calculate an average of any numbers I choose, whether or not they make up any reasonable set. For example, in my living room, the carpet is one-half inch high, the couch is 25 inches high, the lamp is 60 inches high and my stereo speakers on the wall are each 90 inches high. The "average" height of all my living-room furniture is then 53.1 inches. The calculation makes the arbitrary assumption that the speakers deserve to be averaged separately, so the pair of speakers counts twice, despite the fact that the couch, which covers much more floor space, counts only once. Changing that assumption changes the average, so the average itself is a bit arbitrary, as many averages are, and that is part of my point. The average we get depends on which things count as separate and which way we add the numbers up. In this case, as in the calculation of g, there is more than one reasonable way to define the basic units to be counted. But, more important, most of us would say that this whole calculation was nonsense, despite the trappings of science, because for most purposes, there was no unity to the items averaged, so there is no meaning or reality to the figure of 53.1 inches. The objects in the room don't cluster around that height the way women in a population cluster around their mean. The mere fact that we can do a mathematical calculation, no matter how sophisticated, does not necessarily mean that we are measuring or calculating a real thing. Clearly, whether an average (or any other mathematical computation) means anything depends on one's initial assumptions about the objects in question—whether, for example, they are considered to be related and comparable to one another. That may, of course, be a much closer and more difficult call than my fairly broad example suggests. We cannot prove that g is not real; but the mere fact that g can be given a number doesn't prove that it is a meaningful entity. From the point of view of someone looking at a human head from the outside, it may seem obvious that all mental functions are related. From an internal perspective it would seem clear that the brain, like the rest of the body, involves an enormously complex set of processes, interacting and even competing with each other, which may be no more similar than apples and oranges or rugs and chairs.

The other analogy that may be instructive for understanding what is wrong with measuring g or IQ is to compare intelligence and health. Both are desired qualities and each has some vague intuitive reality and unity in our minds. That is, we think of each as a desirable "thing" that can be evaluated. But suppose you go to a doctor for a physical exam and at the end he says, "You got an 84." That is probably better than getting a 74 in our system of reckoning. But what does it mean, and what good is it? So you ask the doctor what an 84 means and he says, "Well, you got a 90 in lungs, an 85 in heart, but only a 77 in left leg. So I averaged them." (He apparently counted the three scores equally.) You have now learned considerably more about your health from the three specific scores—meaningless as such numbers are—than from your average score. You might be pleased that it was only your left leg, not your heart, dragging your average down, and you might want to be given an average weighted to reflect your more vital organs. But, as should be obvious, you don't want numerical scores, you don't want an average, and you don't want a ranking. You want the doctor to identify and deal with your specific problems. What do we gain by assigning a number except ranking (the American obsession)? One thing is clear—we don't get health care. IQ tests or other tests of g are silly, as they are now most often used, for exactly that reason. When working with large groups those who administer the tests are so obsessed with ranking that they forget to teach or heal. But there are individual psychologists and teachers, looking at individuals, who often can and do use the tests, broken down into their component parts, to help people deal with specific problems, just as good doctors look at patients one at a time and deal with their specific health problems instead of just ranking them.

Like Gould, I suspect strongly that there is no reality behind the mathematical computation of g, just as there is no meaningful average in the heights of my furniture or in the health scores of various parts of my body. I don't think we gain anything from measuring g because in human ability, as in health, we find out little by averaging scores. And I am virtually certain that if g does exist as a meaningful mathematical amalgam of various abilities, we will still find that g itself is culture-bound—that it is specific to the skill and ability mix inculcated by a particular culture and therefore varies in its individual components and mathematical composition from culture to culture rather than being a universal measure of "intelligence." Why should we assume that biological evolution has defined the human brain around a set of American categories of mental performance? Given what we know about cultural patterns of perception and cognition, we can't take it for granted that the intellectual patterns and processes of people raised in mainstream white American culture are universal (or that these are obviously the "best" such patterns and processes). We can't it take for granted that the structure of the mind, the psyche, or any other aspect of the functioning of the human brain has, or ought to have, the same structure in different cultures. Nor is it clear that what IQ tests measure is synonymous with the problem-solving skills that most of us, let alone people in other cultures, actually use. (In fact, as I will show, there is reason to believe that it is not.) If IQ tests have validity for predicting success in white middle-class culture, it is not because they measure an inherent, universal, biologically rooted "intelligence" but because they measure the particular, arbitrary constellation of skills that white middle-class culture teaches, uses, and measures.

Testing IQ

More than a century ago, the original designer of IQ tests, Alfred Binet, intended using the tests for something like what we would consider good health care. He wanted to find a way to identify the specific learning problems of individual students (or just the gaps in their training) for the purpose of remediation. He specifically warned against using the tests to try to rank people on a general scale.

But the tests were quickly taken over by people (mainstream scientists, not quacks, at least by the standards of their day) who clearly employed the tests for not-so-hidden social and political goals like reinforcing class structures and keeping immigrants out, as well as pigeonholing people in job categories. The history of such political uses of "scientific" intelligence testing is long and sordid, as Gould pointed out very effectively in *The Mismeasure of Man.*

In some cases, the overt bias of earlier tests astounds us now. In an era before widespread radio and television, for example, illiterate rural Americans and brand-new immigrants were asked to identify baseball players—as a measure of inherent intelligence, not cultural knowledge. Poor people were asked to complete unfinished drawings of a tennis court (where a few, at best, might have served as ballboys). Immigrants to the United States were asked to identify attractive faces; the "correct" answer was a northern European ideal, while some other options looked much more like many of the immigrants themselves. These questions were administered seriously by professional testers of intelligence. As recently as the 1980s, questions manifestly dependent on household habits (identify a thimble) or on education (where is Egypt?) were considered to be measures of aptitude or intelligence. What is a perfectly intelligent midwestern American of modest means supposed to do when the word *regatta* appears in a test question? Moreover, the definitions of "correct" and "incorrect" answers to a question were often highly arbitrary, even within the American cultural repertoire. The tests often came with explicit instructions for graders about which answers were correct and which were incorrect; the amount of detail necessary in such instructions provided a good indication of how subtle the distinction between correct and incorrect could be. When the tests were given to children in other environments, the arbitrary definition of correct answers could produce bizarre results. Children growing up in the Middle East who identified a camel rather than a rabbit as an animal they might see in their yard were deemed incorrect, just as suburban American children who gave this answer would be. One marvels at the strength of the testers' own cultural "blinders," and how naive, how blithely unaware of even the most obvious cultural differences (or thoroughly unscrupulous in the use of tests), one must be to make *and perpetuate* such mistakes.

Many of these early efforts have been disowned by modern scientists—but, clearly, scientists can be as blind to their own cultural assumptions as anyone else, and science serves a variety of secondary social agendas. Scientists who disown what now seem like transparently silly assumptions by their forebears still make their own, as I will show. Herrnstein and Murray, rather than looking at the problems of the early work, try to rehabilitate their precursors and freely cite these earlier results when the outcomes suit their case. For example, they reinforce the idea of the "racial" inferiority of black Americans by "showing" that the inferiority is also shared by black Africans. (Their single-minded focus on "race," using a definition that is at least fifty years out of date, apparently blinds them to the fact that most African Americans have large numbers of genes from European ancestors and are genetically quite different from black Africans, who are themselves a very diverse group genetically.) The black Africans, in turn, were given tests like the ones just described, many of which the original testers clearly intended for different purposes and/or later disavowed. Herrnstein and Murray even argue that black "inferiority" cannot be a result of the oppressive American environment since "Africans" show similar patterns. Never mind that most Africans were taking the test through filters of linguistic or cultural translation. Never mind also that many results came from South Africa, which, at least until very recently, was perhaps the only place in the English-speaking world with a regime more oppressive to blacks than the United States.

Item Content of Modern IQ Tests

But I want to focus on the cultural structure of modern IQ tests (and of thought processes), and on the unspoken assumption that, if intelligence exists and is measurable, it will naturally manifest itself in ways sanctioned by American culture.

Let's consider first the *item* content of IQ tests or standard aptitude tests. I do not claim to have made an exhaustive review of all modern IQ tests, but I have reviewed many, and I have taken several tests of the SAT or GRE format that Herrnstein and Murray consider fair surrogates, read old IQ and SAT exams, coached students for a variety of such tests and reviewed their results, read and listened to defenders of the IQ tests, and read many critiques. I find that IQ test questions persistently demonstrate the kinds of cultural blinders I have been discussing, often in ways that even the best-intentioned testers don't seem to notice. I have chosen some examples that are particularly obvious, but almost any IQ test or aptitude test question can be dissected in the same manner, for the simple reason that it is no more possible to write a question without culture than it is to write one without language.

Contemporary tests include many items that are more subtle than the early examples but still demonstrate naiveté about what people in other cultures (including American minorities, city children, and the poor) are familiar with. The test taker is asked, for example, to answer questions about cows or pigs or acorns, seemingly innocuous common American items. But many inner-city children and even some college students have never seen such things and react with astonishment when they first see one. (To observe this, ride a school bus with a group of inner-city children going on their first vacation in the country—or take college students on an archaeological excavation outside the United States.) Test takers may also be asked to notice that a cute suburban house has an incomplete chimney. But how many city children have seen such a house? More important, how many have lived in or visited such a house or been close to one for long enough to make it an object of real interest and scrutiny. How many are likely to think about what a chimney is and whether it is complete?

The mere existence of cows, pigs, acorns, and suburban houses somewhere in the general environment, including the dissemination of their images in television and print media, is not enough to make them fair test items if they have no meaning to some of the individuals being tested. We all learn things better when they have real meaning to us. Moreover, people need not be completely ignorant of such items to be penalized on the test. They will also do badly if their responses are less than automatic, because the tests are usually timed. Those who have to think harder about parts of the question—if, for example, they have to stop to conjure up the image of a suburban house—will score lower on tests than those who don't.

Consider a question that appeared on the SAT test a number of years ago: how many posts would you need to put up a barbed-wire fence along a 100-foot side of a field if you had to put a post every 10 feet? The correct answer is 11 (not 10). The question is not primarily about math, of course, it's about fence building. And anybody who has made a fence—a child from a farm, for instance—wouldn't miss the question, provided that he or she thought of it as a practical question. It's in the child's culture. A student from any background who stops to think twice or make a drawing also sees the need for the eleventh post. But the tests put a premium on speed (and rapid, shallow thinking), and the test environment encourages students to focus on their mathematical thinking, not their practical skills, so perfectly intelligent people who had never put up a fence might miss the question or take longer to get it right. Knowing things intellectually or being able to figure them out is not the same as having them ready and familiar, at the forefront of one's thinking, ready for instant use. The latter often depends on actual repetition or practice—familiarity, not capability. IQ tests mostly test the familiarity of the knowledge. We all "know" lots of facts (if we stop to think) that we don't automatically use because we don't practice them.

Despite this particular example, white middle-class students from college-educated families face relatively few questions outside their cultural expertise because other college-educated, middle-class, white suburbanites write the questions. But some people aren't so lucky—and on a much larger scale, that is one major problem with the item content of IQ tests.

Test vocabulary also favors people in the middle-class mainstream and probably favors people from certain regions of the country. Anyone who has traveled around the country knows that common English words often have slightly different meanings in different areas or subcultures. (Is a milkshake a drink with ice cream? In Chicago it is; in Boston, you have to order a frappe. What people call a soda in some parts of the country is "pop" or "cola" in others—to cite two obvious examples. Other instances may be more subtle.) Moreover, as I have suggested, words frequently have secondary, idiomatic meanings or connotations that are not formally taught, do not appear in dictionaries, and are not known to people outside the mainstream. These meanings are often regional or temporary in their use, much as the word *terrorist* is now associated in many American minds not just with someone who commits acts of terror but with a person from a Middle Eastern country. These secondary meanings affect our use of words, often unconsciously. To solve word problems, one may have to be familiar with these nuances, which must be absorbed through exposure to the culture of those who write the tests. It is unreasonable to assume that the words on a test have the same meaning and the same nuances to different groups of Americans. In fact, I suspect it would be very difficult to find words or examples that one could say with certainty did not at least have some regional nuance. The problem would be particularly important if the same test were used in other English-speaking countries, where identical words often have very different meanings. Speaking English is not a sufficient common bond to make tests comparable. Moreover, one has to be confident in one's recognition of meanings. Anyone who does not speak the English of the American mainstream on a regular basis could be at a significant disadvantage.

The Cultural "Grammar" or Structure of IQ Tests

IQ tests, like languages and cultures, have a grammar as well as a vocabulary. The examples I have offered so far are all questions in which the cultural *vocabulary* is biased; that is, the questions refer to items from the mainstream culture which may not be familiar to all. Well-meaning testers try to correct the test "vocabulary" by using items from a wider variety of cultures or by using more culture-neutral items (although no items can be wholly neutral because any culture has a pervasive influence on the meanings we attach to objects and on our attention and our perceptions).

But the biases extend beyond the content or the specific items selected. The biases also involve other arbitrary American cultural rules and assumptions about thought itself. Our cultural *grammar* as well as the *items* of our culture are built into the tests. Even if the items are changed to suit a particular subculture (as minority parodies of the IQ tests occasionally attempt), the structure of test questions usually still embodies the arbitrary cultural logic of those who wrote them. The tests are still biased toward people who share that logic. Even critics of IQ tests often do not understand this point, because most of us are not conscious of the cultural rules that mold our thought processes.

One way to get a sense of how hidden cultural assumptions affect the correct answers to test questions is to think about common childhood riddles and why they are funny. A favorite riddle of mine asks how a mother who has seven potatoes and three children to feed should divide the potatoes in order to be fair. The mathematical answer is that each child gets 7/3 potatoes or 2.333 potatoes. Of course, the *correct* answer to the riddle is that the mother should mash the potatoes. Getting this answer right is not a function of being smart or knowing math, it is a function of understanding the peculiar rules of riddles (which vary from culture to culture). Riddles are funny precisely because they violate the commonsense rules the culture normally uses. You have to know when and how you are supposed to break the rules in any given situation. If you are presented with a riddle—or the situation leads you to suspect one—you are supposed to know that you are looking for a "trick" answer. But the trick answer itself must satisfy a certain specific definition of humor: it must "make sense" within the riddle context. Not just any nonsense answer will do. (Most of us never figure out the rules of riddles or other forms of humor, we just catch on to the pattern after a while. Some people, who "have no sense of humor," never get the pattern even though they may otherwise be very smart.)

Note, too, that in many households, and in some cultures, common sense and "fairness" might not dictate an equal distribution of potatoes at all—that is an American assumption. A different idea about what is "fair" would make the riddle and both the straight mathematical answer and the joke answer puzzling rather than funny. It would be obvious in such households that the older children—or the younger—or the boys—or the father (rarely the girls!)—would get most of the potatoes, just as we take it for granted, arbitrarily and somewhat irrationally, that the potatoes should be divided equally among the children and that the father should get the biggest piece of steak.

Another riddle in American culture, perhaps the best known, is "Why did the chicken cross the road?" But this is a riddle in reverse; it doesn't work unless you are into the "trick" culture of riddles. Then the perfectly straightforward answer, "To get to the other side!" seems humorous for its lack of a twist (or its double twist).

In each case the correct answer is funny by being surprising, breaking the expected pattern, yet fitting a secondary (joke) pattern. To get the answer right, you have to understand the special rules of riddles—and you have to know whether the special rules apply in a particular context and you have to do it automatically. If you are too busy trying to understand the rules or find the trick, you don't get it.

Sometimes if you know a subject too well you don't get the joke because understanding the joke requires ignorance. Sometimes getting the "right answer" to a question depends on a lack of knowledge about the subject, too. One telling example, itself a joke, involves a teacher from Chicago who goes to teach in a rural town in Wyoming. During math class, she asks a student a straightforward question: "Johnny, if there are ten sheep in a pen and two jump out, how many are left?" Johnny says, "None, Ma'am." The teacher says, "Why, Johnny, you don't know anything about math, do you? The correct answer is eight." He replies, "I know my math, Ma'am—but you don't know anything about sheep." For practical purposes, the correct answer *is* none. Johnny's mistake was thinking like a rancher, not a mathematician—providing the practical answer in a context in which he was expected to provide a theoretical mathematical answer. What if you were asked to find the sum of three and a half footballs plus two and a half footballs? The mathematical answer is six. But the correct (practical) answer (five) depends on knowing that two half footballs usually cannot be added together to make a whole.

These questions are considered jokes, but they illustrate a problem with some questions on IQ and SAT tests. It may be impossible to separate the strict mathematics from the cultural content of the question and (especially under the time pressure of standardized tests) to know whether to provide the mathematical answer or the cultural one. One has to know when and how much to flesh out the bare mathematical bones of the problem with common sense and reasonable assumptions (which, in real life, we all do all the time in ways we are trained by our culture). What seem like obvious mathematical questions may actually depend on the known or unknown properties of the items discussed, cultural assumptions and perceptions of the items, the context of the question, and the expected style of answer. All these additional conditions are part of the culture of the tests.

A few years ago, a question circulated in the media as an informal test of intelligence. "What word has the letters *kst* in the middle, in the beginning, and at the end?" The correct answer is *inkstand*. But that is really a riddle, not a test of intelligence at all, because to get it right you have to recognize the double meaning of parts of the question. You must also recognize that, by the particular rules of riddles, you are expected to play with double meanings in the phrasing of the question rather than to answer seriously. If you are into the riddle culture and realize that you are playing by those rules (and, of course, if you understand English grammar and recognize obsolete vocabulary) the answer is not so hard. But most people assume that they are constrained by the rules of serious inquiry, so they miss it, desperately straining to find a word in which the letters *kst* occur three times. Whoever developed this question as a test of "intelligence"—reportedly a group priding itself on superior intelligence—wasn't smart enough to understand that this is a matter of initiation into a special culture, not intelligence.

The point is that all questions, not just riddles, have built-in rules that dictate how one is supposed to answer. All questions, serious or funny, are in fact "trick" questions in the sense that one has to know in what framework to supply an answer. And although the comparison to humor may at first seem strained, test taking is a highly artificial situation which requires rules that are different from those of everyday common sense, just as humor does, and that may be viewed with great suspicion and caution by those who are not part of the mainstream culture.

Like many other students, I have missed questions on tests by trying too hard to figure out what the "trick" was or giving the question a more sophisticated interpretation than the tester intended. As a college professor and a parent, I have found that it is very hard to give "correct" answers to the inquiries of my students or my children. I must constantly judge what level of answer the child or student wants and can hear, understand, and use. Like a parent who responds to a child's question, "where did I come from?" with a sophisticated explanation of sex and reproduction (when all the child wanted to be told was "Kansas" or "New York City"), I occasionally find myself answering a deeper question than the student intended to ask, or the reverse. Correct answers are specific to various contexts. And I have been immersed in American mainstream culture for my entire life. Imagine trying to understand what context or level you are supposed to respond to if you are not a fully integrated member of the society.

The same principles apply, more subtly and more perniciously, to the questions on intelligence and aptitude tests. If you don't automatically understand which rules apply and are busy looking for the trick in the question, or if you have an inherent distrust of the mainstream culture or of the testing situation, you may not score well even if you "know" the answers. You have to know American test culture and be comfortable with it. Tests, like classrooms, have cultural rules of their own. Many children in the American mainstream have often absorbed test culture through practice and guidance. Sometimes families that can afford it invest a good deal of money to provide opportunities for their children to become familiar with the test culture in advance. Other children may have to stop and think more—and the tests penalize stopping to think. (One very likely explanation of the reported widespread rise in IQ scores is that gradually more people are becoming more familiar with test culture. That is certainly more plausible than assuming that they are all getting "smarter.") But the biases clearly remain.

We also have to consider the *presentation* of the questions on a test, as well as their content and design. Identifying the missing parts of a cow or pig in a drawing (a common test item) involves a bias in content, as I have described, because many children have not seen these animals before or have had no reason to focus carefully on them. The common four-legged quality of most animals may not be obvious to perfectly intelligent people, particularly children who have never seen or had reason to focus on a variety of animals. However, making the correct identification of missing parts in a drawing also requires knowing the *drawing conventions* used. How can one identify "what is missing" in a line drawing of an animal? Almost everything is missing! The real question is rather: according to American cultural drawing conventions, what is missing that is not supposed to be missing? Any drawing or representation of an object leaves out lots of details while emphasizing other details that have come to stand for the item in our culture. We know, for example, that Bugs Bunny is a rabbit because of his exaggerated ears, even if the rest of his body is not rabbit-like in the least. Drawings of cats have to have whiskers, round heads, and pointed ears, even if the rest of the body looks like a snowman. Bugs Bunny is an exaggeration, of course, but in any drawing the artist must be selective about which lines or contours to present in order to convey meaning. The choice of the significant features to present is cultural. Nonliterate peoples, particularly those whose art does not attempt to be naturalistic, are likely to have trouble dealing with our two-dimensional pictures or drawings, even if the objects they represent are familiar. Our inaccurate abstractions may leave out the distinctive features that other people look for to identify objects, just as English leaves out the sound distinctions that French makes. When I first looked at Australian Aboriginal art I saw only an artistic jumble. But someone literate in these conventions can often see a story; and once I had been shown how various real-life items were represented in the abstract, I could sometimes "read" the art, too. (But I would certainly fail an Aboriginal IQ test based on such representations. I wouldn't know what was missing, even if it was perfectly obvious to an Aboriginal.)

Drawing conventions also vary in different contexts within our own society. Sometimes we draw animals in pure profile showing only two legs; sometimes we show four legs; occasionally we show three legs to suggest a particular angle or pose or movement. Identifying the missing leg(s) is really a matter of knowing (immediately and automatically) not just that cows have four legs but that in a particular drawing style all four are supposed to show. Some civilizations (like those of ancient Egypt or Assyria) routinely showed five legs, (front *and* profile) in one drawing. Others showed multiple arms or legs to convey motion or power. (Is Shiva, the multi-armed Indian deity, missing any arms in any picture you have seen? Did it ever occur to you to count? Are there conventional rules by which Shiva is "correctly" portrayed with more or fewer arms depending on certain circumstances, so that someone literate in Indian culture would know whether one was missing in specific circumstances?) American cartoonists often use similar conventions to show movement, speed, surprise, and other qualities. I may not be able to tell "what is missing" in comic-book drawings of superheroes, or what action is being depicted, but my fourteen-year-old nephew always knows.

One question that has appeared in IQ and aptitude tests, as well as in various scholarly discussions of the tests, shows a drawing of two cats silhouetted in front of the sun/moon. You are asked to identify what is missing. To get the correct answer, you are supposed to note that one cat has no shadow. But to get the question right you have to know what the simple drawn figures stand for and how European and American artists conventionally present three-dimensional spatial relations in two dimensions. Our drawings of the sun and moon are conventional, not accurate. So if you are not literate in those conventions you don't understand the scene at all. But you also have to know that the sun/moon placed higher on the page is supposed to be not only above the cats but in the distance—and that a squiggly line (the "shadow") below one cat is supposed to be a shadow *behind* it. The graphic style is unknown to many cultures and may be relatively unfamiliar to anyone who grew up mainly watching live action television rather than reading picture books and cartoons. (Remember that some cultures use the size and placement of figures to indicate importance or social relations, not geographic position.)

An example, reprinted in *Newsweek* in 1994 in an article largely sympathetic to *The Bell Curve*, unintentionally illustrates another kind of hidden bias in the vocabulary and grammar of the tests. It is a simple analogy problem of the type all schoolchildren face repeatedly: "A has the same relationship to B as C has to?" (This is often symbolically abbreviated a:b::c:? requiring additional familiarity with our conventional system.)

Simple logic, right? A and B in the example were *acorn* and *seed* and C was *oak*. The correct answer is supposed to be *tree*, so that "*Acorn* is to *seed* as *oak* is to *tree*," *acorn* and *oak* each being specific examples of the categories "seed" and "tree." The content is biased, of course, even though it appears relatively harmless: those items are not obvious examples to children who rarely see trees or acorns, who rarely read or think about them, categorize them, or contemplate how trees grow. I can testify that many inner-city children going to the country for the first time are astonished that things like corn actually have to be grown, and that milk (which they get from the store) comes from cows.

But there is at least one more subtle bias (and possibly many) hidden in the structure of this and all analogy problems. We think that analogies test simple logic. But analogy problems are questions about the *categories* in which we put things. The categories determine the logic. By definition, an analogy exists only if pairs of items can be put in the same group. But, as I suggested in chapter 3, categories are cultural conventions, not revealed truth. Other cultures categorize things in different ways and would therefore set up different analogies and get our test questions wrong, or find the "correct" responses nonsensical. Their answers would not suggest that they were less intelligent than we are. Remember, we ourselves categorize objects in many often conflicting ways: by size or color or material or function or place of origin or by things that complement each other or operate on each other in certain tasks (like a needle, thread, and a torn shirt, as in a sewing basket). We even classify things together that share mystical or symbolic or purely cultural qualities that can't be seen by an objective observer outside the culture. For example, we group together the items of Protestant or Catholic or Jewish liturgy or the paraphernalia of baseball. (A bat, ball, glove, and spikes "go together," but only if you know the game.) Different classifications are used in different situations, but there is no way to say that one is obviously "correct" in the abstract. The only way to know which categorizing scheme applies in a particular context and how the different modes of classification are ranked is to be initiated into the local culture. (Should this robe first and foremost be classified with other pieces of cloth, with other articles of clothing, with other red objects, with manufactured as opposed to natural objects, or with other items of the Catholic liturgy?) Intelligent people from other cultures might have different but perfectly logical categories based on their symbolic interpretations or based even on different perceptions of function.

In the acorn example, the correct answer is based on the assumption that *seed* is an inclusive category and that *acorn* is part of that category, just as *oak* belongs to the category "tree." But it is also common usage, even in educated American mainstream culture, to consider an acorn a nut and to consider "nuts" a category distinct from seeds. What is the answer to the *Newsweek* puzzle then? What if the question referred to walnuts or avocados rather than acorns? Both are seeds from trees, and identical analogy problems could be set up; but most of us wouldn't immediately recognize them as seeds or recognize that the analogy was based on their placement in the "seed" category. (Botanists may have a firm, formal definition that delineates the category "seed"—but most of us use a far more flexible folk classification based only on the usage common in our immediate environment. How many of us would correctly and immediately classify a tomato as a "fruit" or know that a peanut is not a nut?) Again, one doesn't have to miss the right classification completely but only be delayed or confused by an alternative possibility to be penalized on an IQ test.

Cross-cultural studies have shown that the way people classify things depends on many variables, including the situation, the question asked, the types of objects presented, the familiarity of the objects, and the amount of *formal, literate, Western schooling* people have had. This implies that Western culture teaches certain styles of classification. The studies show how what appears initially to be the test takers' inability to classify in a certain way can disappear once the tester learns the cultural rules of the group or asks the right question or gets past alternative styles of classification that seem more important to the people being tested. So analogy problems are not merely tests of logical ability; they are also tests of literacy and facility in American culture.

North American-trained doctors have often had trouble communicating with Latin American patients. The doctors are taught to work with the categories "germ" and "antibiotic." But many Latin Americans who are familiar with diseases and antibiotics have a classification system they consider more important: the opposition of "hot" and "cold." This system of classification derives from the humoral system of classical Greece and Rome via colonization by the Spanish, not from "primitive" Native American folk belief. In the system some diseases and some antibiotics are classified together as hot, some as cold. The categories are only loosely related to what we consider the commonsense meanings of hot and cold as temperatures, and they apply to a very wide range of things, many of which we don't associate with temperature. (This broad application of hot and cold may make more sense to us if we remember that we also use the words *hot* and *cold* to refer not just to temperature but to spiciness, passion and emotion, colors, and styles of music, among other things, even if we group these things only very loosely. In mainstream English, some kinds of jazz and the color blue can be "cool," other forms of jazz, the color red, and sexiness are "hot." And we, too, have one illness that we still refer to according to this system, the common cold.)

The critical principle in the Latin American medical system (and more broadly in such cultures) is balance. One should always balance heat and cold, so one is supposed to oppose a hot disease with a cold medicine and vice versa. Adding a hot antibiotic to someone already hot with disease is considered silly and dangerous, and patients will reject such a suggestion or even experience psychosomatic damage, even when the North American doctor is convinced that the prescription is the right one.

To further complicate things, the classification of specific medicines and specific diseases and other items of culture as hot or cold can vary from village to village, so one has to learn different cultural rules of classification in each place. In any case, Latin American medical logic comes from different categories than ours, and we find their categories hard to master. In fact, their medical logic is secondary to the balance principle itself—they think primarily about balancing many kinds of hot and cold, not primarily about antibiotics and germs at all.

We have great difficulty keeping the categories straight—so we are uneducated and perhaps unintelligent by their standards. If they constructed an analogy test we would be expected to recognize immediately that the most important categorizing principle, the basis for the analogy, was the "temperature" of items rather than the categories we would normally use, and the correct answers would be very different from what we expect.

Perhaps our classification is "better" because it is more "scientific," although germ theory, too, is inaccurate in many of its applications and our medicine is just rediscovering balance and moderation. But even if the Latin American system is less accurate or even wrong, people are still socialized into it. Their individual responses say nothing about their "intelligence," only about their training. One would not say that Isaac Newton was less intelligent than twentieth-century physicists because he lived in a more ignorant world and therefore knew less. But he would have done very poorly on most of our IQ tests.

Two final examples come from a 1995 professional presentation on the campus where I teach by a psychometrician (psychological tester) *extolling* modern IQ tests. I don't know whether the examples he discussed actually became part of official tests. But they exemplify the subtle problems that can still infect all such questions.

One question involves identifying a picture of one of two famous scientists, Sigmund Freud or George Washington Carver. The question makes a gesture toward "fairness" by permitting identification of an African American scientist or intellectual or a white one. The question of course discriminates against anyone outside American or Western culture. But, even among Americans it is hardly fair, because the biases run far deeper than the designer of the question envisioned. First, the category "scientist/intellectual" itself may be significant to more members of white American culture than of African American culture. Whites might therefore culturally be more likely than African Americans to recognize such an individual, regardless of his or her color.

With respect to this particular example, reasonable people disagree about whether Carver is as identifiable in African American culture as Freud is in mainstream white culture. The only way to tell would be through widespread scientifically controlled polling. But that is not the point. The point is that we can't just "translate" the question or the example into another color or culture and *assume* that it has the same meaning or is equally valid. How well any individual is known in any culture depends on cultural values, nuance, and emphasis, not on people's intelligence. In any case, surely this question measures exposure, not intelligence.

But this example has another bias that is much more subtle but much more important. It may or may not apply to African American/white differences but it certainly applies more broadly. The problem is that there are various ways of learning and "knowing" things or people. The style and means of knowing are also part of a cultural pattern that varies from group to group. This question favors people who learn *visually* and people whose teachers used portraits and picture books to instruct. In a culture in which parents tell stories rather than read aloud from picture books, and in which oral tradition is important, where people are illiterate or do not watch educational television, or where people learn about a hero of science in church sermons, people might know scientists like Carver or Freud very well but be less familiar with their pictures. If church sermons in the African American community reinforce knowledge of Carver (which some do), is it done with pictures? Even in mainstream American culture, in the age before widely distributed photo magazines and television, how many people knew what their heroes looked like, even if they could recite their life histories by heart?

More to the point, can we assume that all people in the modern world who are equally smart obtain their information in the same way, or that they should, or would choose to? Or that we would want them to? Most of us have had colleagues in school or on the job who have different patterns, styles, and schedules of learning.

These differences often enrich what we can do collectively. None of us possesses the full range of human skills. We rely heavily on the varied abilities and perspectives that others supply.

Another potential IQ test question in the 1995 presentation involved two sets of cartoon figures. The respondent is asked whether any figures from the first set are repeated in the second. The correct answer is "no" because, although two pseudo-human figures are very similar, the diagonals on their tunics are reversed. The figures are supposed to be nonsense figures without cultural content. The use of cartoon figures supposedly eliminates cultural bias, but the figures are actually very similar to the art of some areas of West Africa, and people from this region, accustomed to scrutinizing similar figures, probably would do very well on this question.

But what is actually tested? The key question is whether one perceives *and considers it worth noting* that the diagonal stripes are reversed. Anyone from a culture in which sex or social class is indicated by the direction of the stripes on peoples' clothing would get this right because they would have learned to focus on this distinction. But most of us have been taught by our culture to tune out such distinctions. For example, most of us probably don't notice whether a man wearing an earring has it in his right or left ear. Yet some American gays notice because to them the distinction conveys important information (or did; such patterns change, even within one culture). Perhaps a better-known example is that Americans are often aware of whether a person is wearing a ring on his or her left hand. If it is on the right hand, we ignore it. If it is on the left we check to see which finger it is on, because a ring on the fourth finger conveys an arbitrary cultural meaning that symbolically indicates marital status. Rings on other fingers have no particular meaning. We focus on what our culture tells us is important.

In order to simplify the bewildering array of information and noise reaching us, we all learn to tune out things that have no cultural significance and to focus on those that do. (This is one reason that unsocialized children often "notice" things their elders ignore.) The psychometrician who presented the example involving the cartoon figures said that a "very smart" girl got it right. (Most of the adults at the presentation got it wrong.) But the girl, who may indeed have been very smart, didn't get the question right because she was smart. She got it right because she hadn't yet learned what to ignore—and because she had probably practiced on puzzle books that challenge children to identify exactly such trivial details in drawings. Adults have other distinctions to worry about.

Different cultures teach different rules about what to tune out, just as English-speakers learn to tune out the subtle distinctions in vowel sounds that French speakers are taught to hear. So this question, too, is a test of cultural habits, not intelligence. But a critical point is that cultural differences in what we perceive and what we tune out affect our reaction to *all* IQ questions and to all real-life situations, not just to test questions explicitly about perception. Our experiences are constantly passed through cultural filters. We pick up on different aspects of the same item or situation so that items on tests or everyday situations have different meanings to different people. People who share the mainstream culture have an advantage because they see things the same way their testers (or employers) do, not because they are smart.

Thus, even those IQ questions most carefully constructed to be "fair" or "culture-neutral" can readily be shown to be culture-bound and biased at a multitude of structural levels. And, as with an onion, peeling away the layers of bias leaves nothing. The bias is not something that can be scrubbed off the surface. No matter how hard we try to frame questions objectively, we are testing cultural awareness, not intelligence. There is no such thing as measuring pure thinking ability because all tests (and probably all thought itself) build on cultural categories and examples, just as all language builds on conventional rules of grammar.

IQ tests (and other similar standardized tests) can be used to measure the extent to which an individual has learned the vocabulary and the rules of classification of a particular culture. Just as classroom tests are used to discover who has absorbed which facts and concepts from the curriculum and to adjust teaching patterns in response, IQ tests that are designed to measure the learning that educators consider to be most important could be a valuable tool for diagnosis—as they were originally intended to be. But that is not, for the most part, the way the tests are used. For the moment, perhaps the best use to which such tests could be put would be asking groups of students to identify and discuss the cultural biases in each question as a means of understanding American culture and its assumptions. That would be a real learning exercise.

This deeper analysis of cultural bias in the tests refutes *The Bell Curve*'s assertion that differences in test scores of blacks and whites do not represent cultural bias in the tests because the questions African Americans miss aren't the ones with bias. Instead, according to the authors, African Americans miss the questions that test pure thinking ability, the ones most related to *g*. Therefore, they say, the lower average test scores of African Americans must reflect a real cognitive deficit, not a difference in culture.

But if you are a tourist in Paris, it is relatively easy to learn French vocabulary and the specific items of French culture—the kinds of superficial content that surfaces as bias in tests in obvious ways. It is much harder to learn the subtle cultural rules of thought and behavior, the underlying grammatical structure of a culture—or even to recognize their existence in real life situations (or in test questions). It is very hard, for example, to tell a joke successfully in another language or culture, because one may not know the special rules that define humor, even if one is otherwise fluent in the language and has a large vocabulary. But these are the things that reveal deeper and more subtle bias in the tests. I would expect minorities to do better on questions with the superficially content-biased cultural items and do worse on items with more subtle structural biases based on cultural grammar—the ones which are quite mistakenly believed to reflect pure abstract thought. This is apparently the pattern that occurs; but it doesn't reflect minority ability, just less participation in some of the subtler and more deeply buried aspects of the mainstream culture.

All this suggests, incidentally, that cross-cultural comparisons of IQ (like Japanese-American comparisons, which Herrnstein and Murray discuss) have no significance whatsoever. To make a meaningful comparison one would have to submit large, matched, representative samples of American and Japanese students to the same test. But that is impossible because one group would have to take the test in a foreign language or in translation, and the test can't be easily translated. The words don't translate accurately; they may not have the same meaning in the two languages or the same importance in the two cultures. Nor will the issues and nuances in the individual test questions be conveyed. The questions don't have the same meaning or the same importance in two cultures. Members of different cultures may perceive and focus on different aspects of a question. You can't just change the items in a problem—say, an analogy—into items familiar in the other culture because the categories that define the analogy may not be the same or have the same importance or familiarity. But if you don't use directly translated tests, how can you be sure that a score of 100 on one test is equivalent to a score of 100 on the other? The only way to develop a fair cross-cultural test would be to know or assume in advance that samples of Japanese and Americans were of exactly the same ability and then design a test that accurately reflected that equality. But, of course the only way to know that the samples of Japanese and Americans are similar is to test them. At this point the problem and the solution have become hopelessly circular. It is a basic premise of scientific method that one can't simply presume an outcome and then "test" it using one's own presumptions. One must have an *independent* way of testing assertions. What independent test can show that observed differences between Japanese and Americans in IQ test performance reside in the people tested (let alone in their genes) rather than in the tests themselves?

Another issue has to do with so-called reaction-time tests, in which the participants must both provide an answer and make a physical movement. According to Herrnstein and Murray (based on the work of Arthur Jensen), these tests show that whites have faster cognitive reaction time than blacks and that blacks have faster physical reactions—and, they say, as each group excels at some part of the behavior required for the test, the tests aren't biased, and neither group displays more test anxiety than the other. So, if you time reactions to questions, whites start to move faster and blacks move faster once they start. (Or, as critic Leon Kamin put it sarcastically, apparently white men can't jump, but they have faster computer chips in their heads.) There is little question that individuals vary in physical reaction times, and there is no reason to doubt that they also vary in cognitive speed. But measuring such differences in "natural" or genetically determined speed in an unbiased manner may be impossible. And showing in an unbiased manner that "races" differ in these ways is impossible, the very effort inherently misguided. Other critics have pointed out that, even on tests comparing reaction times, the results are more mixed than Herrnstein and Murray indicate. Moreover, given what we know about human genetics, any such group difference is almost certainly cultural.

Reaction speed has a lot to do with confidence, whether or not the confidence is justified. It also has to do with facility acquired through practice, with familiarity, and with motivation. People who have to pause momentarily while taking a test (or doing any other task) because of cultural uncertainties about the content or form or underlying meaning of any of the questions—or inherent distrust of the situation—will be slower than those who are at ease. Given what we know about subculture patterns in this country it is quite possible, even quite likely, that, on average, African Americans and whites have had different patterns of practice in cognitive and physical skills. They are likely to have gained different degrees of familiarity with mainstream cultural issues or physical movements, acquired different patterns of cognitive or physical facility, and achieved different patterns and levels of confidence in their physical and cognitive skills. It seems likely that these factors explain group differences in reaction times. Each person does better on skills he or she has practiced most. Group averages are skewed accordingly.

Any televised high school quiz show will prove the point. Usually wrong answers aren't penalized, so the format rewards the individual's willingness to make fast guesses. The shows are not necessarily dominated by the "smartest" or the most knowledgeable students. (They are certainly not dominated by the most careful or thoughtful students.) They are dominated by those who have the personality or the inculcated social behavior pattern to jump in even when they aren't sure of an answer. Willingness to jump in fearlessly in verbal or cognitive matters is almost certainly a cultural product, taught mainly, it would seem, to white boys.

Four other significant biases of IQ tests remain to be discussed. These are areas in which the structure of the tests clearly reflects deeply rooted American cultural assumptions—but in which the structure of the tests misrepresents reality even in our own American experience. First, most tests put a great deal of emphasis on finding simple, clear-cut, right-or-wrong answers. But the idea that answers are simple and clearly right or wrong (like the "facts" we are constantly taught in school) violates the reality most of us face regularly. Thoughtful judgment about complex questions is a far more valuable commodity in the real world than snap judgments of factual "truth," but IQ tests don't recognize thoughtful judgment. The "intelligence" (or, if you like, the g) that IQ tests measure is a very narrow and shallow ability without much application to the real world. Whatever happened to thought and wisdom?

Second, the tests put a great deal of emphasis on finding those simple answers quickly. We assume that speed is a sign of intelligence. In some other cultures, in contrast, speed in answering is a sign of a mind too simple to reflect seriously on problems that intelligent people know are complex. Even in our own culture, speed is rarely an element in most significant decisions.

The way wrong answers are penalized (or not penalized) on the tests is itself a cultural convention which loads the tests in favor of certain styles of answering. If, for example, all wrong answers are punished equally but only lightly, speed and guessing are favored. Real-world problems often involve far more significant penalties which are far less evenly distributed and less predictable and which require people to be more thoughtful. The emphasis on speed in our test culture, of course, is in keeping with other aspects of our culture in which quickness is valued. It even appears in the instant reactions and sound bites, rather than thoughtful answers, that we expect of our politicians. But it is not a good way to get useful answers.

Third, the tests emphasize individuality and competitiveness. Members of many cultures would find such competition anathema and might be reluctant to participate or to excel, so their performance would suffer. Immigrant children of many cultures in American schools are often surprised that they are supposed to do their exercises alone rather than cooperatively. But even in the American corporate world, cooperative efforts and interactive decision making are more common than tests of individuals in complete isolation. Individuals are judged, but they are judged on the basis of their contribution to team efforts. Different individuals can make valuable contributions in different ways. Some of the most dedicated college professors I know are trying to build team effort back into their classroom exercises to prepare students for real life.

Finally, doing well on the tests involves not just knowing the content or even the cultural grammar of questions; it also involves focusing on the additional cultural rules of test taking just described. One must know how to balance speed and accuracy, when to guess, when to skip a tough question, and so forth. This knowledge is usually a matter of good coaching. It has been my experience, in coaching students and reviewing their results, that their "failures" are often of this latter type, not a lack of knowledge, and that their scores can be improved dramatically by coaching in test-taking technique.

In sum, rather than testing "intelligence" or aptitude, the tests measure an arbitrary and narrow set of cultural expectations. "Standardized" tests should be called "standardizing" tests because they force people into very narrow and unrealistic patterns of knowledge, thought, and behavior.

The merits of any of the objections that I and others have raised to using standardized testing as a measure of intelligence can be debated. Collectively, however, they suggest very strongly that one cannot just assume the fairness of test questions, and one cannot judge questions for fairness in any simple way. One can't presume that in such a large and varied country (let alone in other countries) the cultural knowledge necessary to perform well on the tests is homogeneous or equally shared. Nor can one assume, just because the tests generate numbers, that they accurately measure any real thing— or the same real thing in different people. What the tests attempt to measure seems to be markedly at odds not only with other cultures but also with our own real-life experiences. The burden of proof is on those who insist that the questions fairly test "intelligence" and that a measure of "intelligence" is meaningful. They haven't begun to prove it. The outcomes of their efforts are far too dangerous to be used as uncritically as they are when so many obvious flaws in the logic abound.

Individual Test Performance

Beyond looking at the content and structure of questions, the forms of the test, and the stated and unstated rules of test taking, we have to think about the use of tests themselves and how people understand and react to them. Why do psychologists, political scientists, and others who spend half their lives studying the complexities of the human mind and its motivations still assume that, when faced with a standardized test, everyone simply puts forth his or her best intellectual effort unhindered by conscious or unconscious reservations, distractions, rage, or other such limits so that the results reflect sheer brain power?

For one thing, we are all plagued individually and culturally with selective focus, limits, distractions, and blind spots unrelated to our intelligence. People do well in areas that excite their interest and give them confidence but do poorly in areas that bore them, make them angry or anxious, discourage them, undermine their confidence—or simply violate something in their definitions of themselves. We all also have arenas in which we define ourselves as incapable and therefore do not perform well. Our parents and our peers consciously teach us (as does our culture) to focus selectively, to disregard what they consider noise, and to keep attuned to their goals and values and expectations for our lives. And, of course, both culture and parents adjust their teaching according to sex, "race," and class, deciding what we need to know or don't need to know on the basis of what they want from us. If the parents' goal is to help their daughter become an engineer, they need to spend time exercising her capacity for solving abstract mathematical problems. If they want her to become a wife and mother, they don't. Similarly, if their goal is for their son to become a doctor, they don't need to push him to excel at basketball. But if being a doctor is an impossible goal, basketball may seem like an important potential avenue to success and an important thing to practice.

But parents and teachers also educate by unintentional example. Children absorb their interests and attitudes simply by being around their parents, and that helps to structure their focus and their selective blindness. For example, my parents, as part of their Ashkenazi heritage, believed strongly in the power of written words and in the importance of school. They pushed all of their children to value education and do our best; but they also led by example because they themselves had the skills and commitment. They also taught us that the mechanics of cars and appliances could be left to somebody else so we never developed these skills. But perhaps, more important, on the few occasions when we were confronted with car trouble or other mechanical problems, it was very clear that my parents, who otherwise appeared all-powerful in my child's eyes, were anxious and helpless, and I learned this too from their example. To this day, despite having developed many mechanical skills, I cannot look under the hood of a car and focus on the problem at hand. I see only a jumble of wires, because I can't look without feeling anxious. I also observed my parents' impatience and anxiety with the instructions for any mechanical device, and I still cannot read such instructions calmly. One's ability to focus can be very irregular and can be governed quite powerfully by irrational things.

Ability lies in where we learn to focus our attention without anxiety, not in our general intelligence. I suspect that many perfectly intelligent people (people who may be far cleverer and more proficient as auto mechanics than I am) see only a jumble of words when they face a standardized test, perhaps because they have absorbed a family legacy of anxiety about school or written words. There is good reason to suspect that people from different cultures consistently approach testing situations with different levels of enthusiasm, motivation, and clear-headedness. Many people learn from their parents to hate, fear, distrust, or devalue written words, schooling, or exams, just as I learned to fear automobile engines. I suspect that this is part of the real reason for "math anxiety" and for the fact that some women may not focus as well on math as their male counterparts do. We tend to do what our role models do, and those role models are often same-sex parents. So girls perhaps hold back from math, defining themselves as helpless, partly because their mothers did (just as I learned from my father to fear automobile engines) and because they somehow learned that feminine identity involved mathematical helplessness and anxiety. After all, we are only one generation into a culture that permits women to do math seriously, and most contemporary mothers were reared the old way. (Another reason, of course, is that girls are often told very aggressively by their teachers, their peers, or the media that they do not belong in an advanced math class and have no chance to pursue careers in math. It isn't just parents who influence us.)

On a much larger scale, almost all Americans, most of them presumably perfectly intelligent, are fairly helpless when it comes to acquiring foreign languages because it is something that few American parents, and few elementary or secondary schools, value or teach. (We also don't recognize multilingual ability as a sign of intelligence, at least on our tests, despite the fact that in many cultures it is both an essential skill and an important measure of ability.)

Why should poor, nonwhite parents teach their children that school and IQ tests are important places to focus their attention rather than hurdles that induce anxiety? As I have pointed out, doing "white things" successfully or trying to join the melting pot hasn't given most African Americans access to the rewards that mainstream culture can offer. The message is still very clear that excellence is likely to be less valuable, or not valuable at all, if one is black. Often it brings trouble. So why bother? And in any case, how well can parents for whom education was of no value motivate and guide their children to be proficient in school?

Focus, mood, and anxiety are likely to be particularly important for anyone subject to racial discrimination. During 1994, in successive issues, the *New York Times Magazine* ran a fairly positive article on Charles Murray, co-author of *The Bell Curve*, and shortly thereafter reported on incidents of racial discrimination at Denny's restaurants. Apparently, African Americans with professional dress and demeanor, including members of the Secret Service, could not go into a national-chain restaurant (let alone a mom-and-pop diner) and get service without expecting to be delayed, demeaned, insulted, angered, or even asked to leave. Never mind that they had fought for and won the right to be served at public accommodations in the 1960s and should have had such rights more than two hundred years earlier. The juxtaposition of the two articles seemed to me to drive home an important lesson—the role of social tensions in affecting performance. It seems clear that for many or most African Americans, virtually all social transactions with the white majority involve an extra burden of distrust, risk, and social tension that most white Americans don't face with such consistency. Such tensions must affect people's willingness and ability to focus and give their best in demanding social situations, including school and IQ tests, whether the result is played out at the conscious or the subconscious level. Why should members of a discriminated minority feel comfortable or confident taking such tests? We know, after all, that anger and anxiety affect human performance at all kinds of tasks, including intellectual ones.

It seems likely, too, that even very young minority children might learn to feel such tensions just by observing their parents, even if they don't comprehend the exact meaning of specific social encounters. Herrnstein and Murray point out that the IQ gains of black children in foster care with white families are temporary—that their IQ scores (which are elevated by foster care) tend to fall as the children grow older. This suggests, they say, that intelligence is really genetic and that changing the environment can't make a permanent difference. My idea, which has a much better basis in human experience, using real, known factors instead of postulated genes, is based on the fact that young children are cute. I suspect that young black children fostered in white families for a time escape the hatred and discrimination they might otherwise experience. As they get older, the wrath of the society comes full force against them, negatively affecting the kind of focus and motivation I am discussing here. So their performance declines. Families, after all, are only a small part of the total environment.

The problems of testing and performance may be particularly intractable when minorities within a more powerful culture are involved. A minority culture fighting for survival may also actively teach people *not* to focus on the things that are important to the mainstream culture, as a matter of defining identity, separateness, pride, and group coherence. I suspect that much of the "failure" of some minorities at some simple real tasks, both in school and on the job, has to do with different style and focus and different sets of practiced skills—but also with real resistance at the conscious or unconscious level.

We would do well to consider cultural differences as they affect performance and our evaluation of it. But we must also consider anger and resentment among American minority groups and their accurate perception that they have less to gain through excellence in school performance than those in the white mainstream. Many African Americans, Native Americans, and Hispanics are in some ways like the colonized North African populations described by Albert Memmi. They feel the same pressures and almost certainly develop some of the same resentments and reactions.

Whatever its historic roots, "Black English" is not simply bad English; it is one or more distinct dialects or languages with different vocabulary, different grammar rules, different idiomatic uses of words, different accompanying gestures and body language, and so forth. Similarly, separate African American cultures are not simply failed middle-class American culture; they are separate cultures with their own rules. The cultures, of course, have been kept separate by patterns of discrimination and by the resistance that discrimination has fostered. So, many African Americans, although born and raised in the United States, to some degree learn standard English as a foreign language and middle-class American culture as a foreign culture. Such individuals may eventually become fully bilingual and bicultural, but they grow up practicing different mental and physical skills. Some anthropologists and linguists have argued for a long time that Black English is a separate language. However, the recent debate about "Ebonics" notwithstanding, the question of whether Black English is a complete, distinct language or merely slang or a dialect in the minds of linguists is completely irrelevant. The only important question is whether a child born in a world where Ebonics (or any other dialect) predominates can completely understand the words, slang, nuance, idiom, and accompanying gestures and body language of mainstream English and whether such a child can switch fully and successfully into standard English whenever he or she chooses. A child who, to varying degrees, cannot do those things is at a severe disadvantage, whether or not what he or she speaks is officially a separate language.

But, cynics ask, why don't African Americans or Hispanic Americans—who have been in the United States for generations—do as well on IQ tests or other school performance tasks as Jews or Asians (or even recent Hispanic immigrants) with shorter histories of residence, whose native cultures may be more dissimilar from mainstream American culture? The answer is not completely clear. But biological inferiority should be near the bottom of any list of likely explanations, given what we know about the biases of testing and schooling, the complexities of the human mind, motivation, and behavior, and the extreme improbability that group differences reflect systematic differences in genetic mental ability. (A genetic explanation is particularly unlikely if we remember that Mexican immigrants who do comparatively well and the Hispanic natives of California and the Southwest, who do poorly, are genetically similar—unless, of course, we assume that the innate, relatively high genetically determined intelligence of pure-bred Hispanics has been watered down in the United States by generations of intermarriage with Anglo-Americans!) There are too many other, more obvious explanations to make natural endowment a likely choice, unless the whole point is to find not an explanation of performance but a justification for racism.

One possible explanation is to remind ourselves of the real meaning of culture. Those who are cynical about a possible cultural explanation of poor performance are basing their judgment on a very superficial sense of what culture is. There is little question that black Americans share more of the trappings of culture (clothing styles, music, media, sports) with mainstream Americans than do recent immigrants from other countries and may have greater use of a common language and greater familiarity with American rules. But these similarities are misleading. I think that the cultural gulf that divides poor blacks and whites in this country *is* greater than that between whites and other ethnic groups. Other groups may appear more distinct in the superficial forms we usually measure, yet are more like the white mainstream in a number of subtler but more important cultural ways such as goals and values, beliefs about family and community, a sense of how the world or a human society works, understanding of commercial success and how it is achieved, the sense of their own potential, the will to get ahead, and a host of others.

I think that poor black Americans clearly face more racism than any other group despite their greater imagined cultural similarity to white Americans. I think that it is visible in our actions; I also think that it is to be expected from our history. Colonizing powers are forced to develop racist stereotypes of their conquered subjects, and both groups respond accordingly. Other minorities can be received as relative equals because they are less threatening, and demand less self-justification on the part of the mainstream. And the minorities respond in kind to the way they are treated.

Perhaps a more compelling answer to the question has been proposed by John Ogbu, an anthropologist at the University of California, Berkeley, and has been elaborated and tested by Ogbu and other educational anthropologists. Ogbu argues that a "culture of resistance" develops among minorities that, like African Americans and Hispanics, have been included in the society involuntarily (by slavery and conquest). *Voluntary* immigrants such as many recently arrived Asians and, earlier, Ashkenazi Jews, although leaving oppression behind, come in search of opportunity, with positive motivation, so they focus especially hard, learn the system well, and often use schooling to get ahead. In contrast, involuntary or captive minorities, incorporated by conquest or enslavement and exposed to subordination and discrimination for decades, see little hope of getting ahead through education and resist the mainstream culture. They maintain a necessary and protective sense of themselves by being purposefully different and unresponsive to the pressures of the mainstream society—and often by mocking or discouraging friends who attempt to emulate the larger culture. Members of some African American communities who excel at "white" activities have to fear the wrath not only of whites but of blacks as well. In short, many of the cultural rules of involuntary minorities directly oppose mastering the cultural subtleties that IQ tests measure and that school and job performance demand. This should not be a surprise. Not only does success divide their own communities, but successful African Americans, Hispanics, and Native Americans have long been punished for their achievement and are still occasionally punished physically in some parts of the country. Sometimes they bring punishment on their communities as well.

All this suggests that even if IQ tests were not culture-bound there would be many cultural reasons—conflicting values, tension, focus, resistance, and so forth—to explain why some groups might do poorly. Given the large number of factors with obvious influence on test outcomes, jumping immediately to an unsupported assumption of genetic inferiority to explain them is absurd if not willfully destructive.

The fact that the tests successfully predict school success (to a limited degree) and career success (to a much smaller degree) doesn't prove that they are valid indicators of intelligence. It supports only four points: (1) success on the tests opens doors for people in a kind of self-fulfilling prophecy; (2) the tests are designed to measure and facilitate certain kinds of tasks that are useful in American schools; (3) the tests have become so pervasive that they actually shape the tasks they are designed to measure—i.e., they influence the ways we teach and perhaps even the ways we work and think; and (4) tests, schools, and careers all have the same cultural biases in content, presentation, and organization, and, to some extent, bring on the same built-in performance problems, moods, and anxieties.

Individuals clearly are differentially endowed in various physical and chemical ways, like height or blood type, to adapt to specific aspects of the contemporary (or historical) environments. And different human populations clearly have different frequencies of these endowments. This means that individuals also probably differ slightly in various specific mental capacities, and it is possible that populations differ statistically in such mental capacities, too.

However, we have no reason to think that intelligence is *one* mental capacity, rather than an array of skills that are differently distributed; and, given what we know about other well-mixed patterns of human variation, the idea of unitary intelligence is inherently improbable. Furthermore, we have no idea to what degree intelligence (or, more likely, each of its component parts) is the result of genes or how genes and environmental variables interact to produce the capacity for intelligent behavior. We can see that cultural, motivational, and emotional factors have an enormous influence on performance, far outweighing intelligence, anyway. Most important, we have no reason to think that we are capable of measuring that intelligence objectively. Cultural differences pose enormous (I believe insurmountable) difficulties in trying to assess innate mental capabilities. The tests are culture-biased to their very core, not just in their superficial details; and the test-taking situation poses more barriers to success for members of some groups than others.

Moreover, the nature and focus of the tests are highly arbitrary. We insist on testing people working alone and ranking them by number. We use timed, paper-and-pencil multiple-choice tests, focusing on the English language and analytical skills that are chosen and shaped by American culture, while ignoring other qualities such as aesthetic, manual, linguistic, and social skills and thoughtful analysis of complex problems. We use questions that consistently embody unconscious cultural assumptions in structure as well as content. In short, the tests create a far narrower and more arbitrary hoop for people to jump through than do real-life challenges, which can usually be solved by *groups* of people, and can be solved or avoided in many ways, allowing different skills to come into play. We limit people's freedom to solve real problems by unnecessary cultural assumptions, by discrimination, and by outright force, and we further discriminate or justify existing discrimination by adding the very arbitrary hurdle of the tests. But in excluding "others," we also lose their creative range, which might help solve problems in different ways. In addition, we artificially channel the creativity of those who are successful by narrowing the entrance requirement that they, too, have to pass.

IQ tests, in fact, probably primarily test participation in upper-middle-class mainstream American culture, reinforce certain values of that culture, and force people to become more standardized in their thinking. Schools serve much the same goals. Perhaps that is valuable, or was valuable under certain historical circumstances; but it undoubtedly inhibits much creativity that might otherwise be beneficial. (After all, having the largest variety of choices is often the way to select the best alternative, as any business person knows. Limiting variety, although it makes us more predictable, also inhibits invention. So the problem for any culture is to find the right compromise.) But even if we decide that the benefits of standardized testing (and schooling, and other forms of cultural homogenization) are worth the costs (and I doubt it), we shouldn't make the mistake of assuming that what they measure is "real" or that poor performance reflects "natural" inferiority. We can recognize that some demands are arbitrary, even as we make them in the name of necessary conformity. There are better ways to address poor performance than branding people with numerical labels and arguing that poor performance is in their genes. There are important values besides excelling at the tiny, specific, arbitrarily defined tasks on the tests.

Until we have an alternative to "intelligence" testing, we should recognize that the tests contain significant biases, and we should make appropriate adjustments, by making places available to individuals from groups the tests themselves discriminate against, as some affirmative action programs have done.

Why not make an allowance for group differences based on discrimination and unfamiliarity with mainstream culture and adjust the scores of discriminated, captive minorities accordingly so that differences in scores based on culture and discrimination are factored out? Similar adjustments are already made routinely, as, for example, in attempts to make male and female scores comparable, and they would have to be made to compare Americans and Japanese. When the tests are "standardized," scoring patterns on different tests or between the sexes or populations are adjusted to meet certain assumptions or theoretical expectations, so there is precedent for such adjustment.

Why not assume that white male scores will tend to be high because of the nature of the tests and "correct" their scores downward accordingly? This isn't giving "preference" to others; it is removing a preference that is built into the tests. It is just leveling the playing field. Realistically, because of cultural advantages, the scores of whites and blacks are not equal measures of ability; a white person or a rich one who gets the same score as a black person or a poor one probably isn't as capable as the poor or the black. Or, instead of trying to factor all of this into the scores themselves, why not do what colleges routinely did before the recent round of lawsuits and recognize that exam scores aren't the final measure of a person's worth or desirability as a candidate for admission or employment (a practice that I certainly hope will continue)?

Such candidates still won't get in the door unless employers are educated about the real meaning of tests and quality and the depth of cultural diversity, and about their responsibility to help correct a major social problem. If such prodding for voluntary action doesn't work, then it is necessary to think in terms of more structured policies.

School and Job Performance

Herrnstein and Murray, reflecting the common American theme that our society is a meritocracy open to all, suggest that success on the job and even access to good jobs are functions of inherent ability or IQ. The lower class is poor and unemployed, the authors say, largely because they lack genetically determined cognitive ability.

Yet my anthropological colleagues who do ethnographic research with the poor or with illiterate, nonwhite, or non-American populations often express amazement at how clever and resourceful such people are at solving problems that are important to them, in the contexts in which they live, with the tools available to them, and in ways deemed appropriate in their cultures. At the same time, they appear helpless in mainstream American culture, as we, in turn, are in theirs. Most white Americans couldn't survive in the world of the ghetto or solve the problems that would confront them there.

Critics of *The Bell Curve* have pointed out that IQ predicts some job success and access to various professions but doesn't have much to do with doing a job well. Too many other skills—too many other kinds of practical intelligence and experience—are involved. The critics point out that the correlations Herrnstein and Murray report between test scores and performance aren't actually very strong and (like other correlations) do not indicate a cause-and-effect relationship. Two things can be correlated because they are both related to a third thing, by coincidence, or as a result of a causal relationship that is different from or even the reverse of the one postulated. Once we get away from the assumption that IQ is a single entity, inherited through genes, it is fairly easy to see that poverty and racial discrimination are likely to be the causes of poor performance in school or on the job, just as they are the causes of low IQ test scores.

Problems stemming from subtle cultural rules and tensions and overt bias extend not just to tests but to the classroom itself and to behavior in social contexts and on the job. Of course, there are individual differences in job performance at specific tasks and in talents in specific areas. But group differences in performance almost certainly reflect different standards, pressures, training, and experience, not inherent inferiority or superiority. Cultural idioms, speech styles, postures, patterns of physical movement, ways of categorizing, styles of reasoning, ways of recognizing what is culturally important, ways of solving problems, ways of interacting with peers, teachers, and employers all are critical to school and job performance (narrowly construed as we usually define performance), as well as to IQ tests. But they are not necessarily important for the reasons we think. That is, they do not involve objectively measured natural superiority or inferiority. Teachers, employers, and colleagues tend to have arbitrary definitions of correct behavior, just as standardized tests impose very narrow definitions of intelligence. Certain cultural rules seem so obvious to some people that there appears to be no reason to spell out the rules; yet they may not be obvious to members of another cultural group. I have seen white farmers in Africa berate their nonwhite employees for being "too stupid" to use a piece of equipment, apparently oblivious to the fact that using the equipment requires prior exposure and experience, not just with the specific machine but with the larger world of mechanical devices. I have seen white employers in the United States berate domestic employees as being "too dumb" to load a dishwasher properly, although to some degree this is an acquired skill requiring a bit of trial-and-error learning—and although even people familiar with a particular dishwasher may have different definitions of "proper" loading and may have difficulty loading someone else's machine to that person's satisfaction. A failure to perform well in some jobs may be related to different experiences in those roles. Some employees may have had no prior practice because there are few dishwashers or similar appliances in their homes.

Tasks required in school or on the job may involve various subtle cultural skills that we don't consciously perceive. Children practice complex and subtle tasks as part of their maturation and play, and adults continue to develop their repertoires of skills, not just by practicing each specific task, but by gaining experience in similar situations, using similar patterns of thought and movement. Adult success at adult tasks almost always depends on the degree to which the new task builds on a practiced skill or some aspect of that skill. For example, adult physical abilities may be related to the degree to which a certain required movement was practiced in childhood, albeit as part of a very different play activity. A particularly skillful move on a basketball court does not have to be practiced in its entirety, but it is composed of pieces practiced and perfected at an earlier time and reassembled as needed. When I did archaeological field work in Kenya, some African workmen, who were perfectly well-coordinated but had never done archaeology before, were very awkward with the shovels and trowels that Americans prefer. They had no practice in the muscle movements involved. Given hoes and machetes, whose use built on muscle movements in their own cultural repertoire, they became superb excavators. Allowing them to do the job in their own style, using their own practiced skills, rather than attacking their incompetence in my style, resulted in excellent work.

Similarly, specific adult intellectual abilities may be related to the degree to which adult cognitive problems can be handled using aspects of mental skills practiced in childhood. In a crude sense, adults solve both physical and intellectual problems the same way great basketball players improvise or build their best moves—by recombining practiced skills, making analogies with their previous experiences, and using those experiences to summon the behavior needed to solve the new problem. My physically skilled African workmen had great difficulty loading a truck because the problem of fitting things tightly into a confined, rectangular space had no counterpart in their experience. Practice has to be part of one's upbringing, of one's culture.

The same applies to more strictly cognitive ("higher") functions. If parents train children to enjoy puns and word games, they are also, even if unintentionally, providing practice in a certain kind of mental gymnastics which has other applications in later life. If they present their children with number puzzles, they are honing mathematical skills. If they discuss current events, they help their children practice social perception and judgment. The children recombine those skills with other practiced skills as needed to solve new problems, much as an athlete improvises "moves." It is difficult, if not impossible, to think of any intellectual or physical task that is not performed more successfully if an individual has some helpful basis or templates in previous experience. But different cultures provide different experience, different patterns of practice, reinforcing different skills. American school and job expectations and evaluations tend to measure the kinds of mental activities that are built into the childhood experience of mainstream Americans. But these differ from those of other cultures. A person who is perfectly competent in his or her own culture may be at a disadvantage answering our questions or doing things "correctly" because he or she has practiced different models of reasoning or worked on different kinds of problems.

Moreover, the same problem in adult life may have equal but *different* analogues in previous experiences in two cultures (i.e., may call forth different practiced skills or mental "analogies") so that different people approach the same task in unlike ways. But we equate success with using *our* skills and doing the job *our* way. It is as if I had demeaned or fired my Kenyan excavators for being clumsy with the tools that I considered appropriate without waiting to see how well they could do the job with tools of their own choosing.

There is one additional category of skills and childhood practice that we have to consider in this context: the skill of "reading" social situations and people to know what is required and to judge whether one is succeeding without being told. That is a skill that some parents practice with their children. But even the most attentive parents can't teach their children the social skills they might need in another culture as effectively as they can teach their own. So minority children come to school and later to the job with less practice in reading the culturally defined modes of unspoken communication in the mainstream. Their poor "performance" often results from the fact that they don't "read" their employers as successfully or give off the social signals that mainstream employers or teachers expect.

An additional problem is that we are quick to pick up on the tasks and responses that have overtones in our own cultural experience and to which we are sensitive. It is these responses by which we evaluate job performance, and it is these that promote our sense of "superiority." But we are oblivious to areas in which our own culture may limit our ability because these areas are the ones outside our blinders. For example, as I pointed out earlier, Americans don't count foreign language acquisition as a measure of intelligence because we don't consider it necessary, and Americans tend to be inept at foreign languages. Some people we write off as lacking in mental ability speak many languages and expect that any adult with even minimal intelligence will speak more than one. But we don't give them credit for this.

Objective measures of job performance are generally very hard to define, especially in a complex society or organization—partly, of course, because most jobs, unlike school and tests, involve teamwork. Identifying the contribution each individual makes and measuring it objectively are extremely difficult tasks, and the attempt to evaluate is inevitably colored by the supervisor's previous perception of the individual. As a result, we see "success" partly when we see people doing things we expect and doing them in the way we expect them to. But that definition of success is too narrow in terms of both fairness and efficiency. Many tasks can be solved in more than one way, based on different sets of prior experience, and a variety of approaches helps get the job done. In short, by establishing arbitrary standards of success, we don't allow people of other cultures to solve problems in the ways they would normally pursue, and that in turn prevents the enterprise in question from benefiting from their competence.

This doesn't deny that some standardization is important on the job. We have to insist on certain common standards for the sake of coherence in the workplace, just as we have to insist on some cultural and legal standards for the country as a whole for the sake of safety, predictability, and efficiency. But on the job, as in the larger culture, we have to separate necessary standardization from arbitrary and often unconscious cultural style. In all our spheres of activity, performance could be improved (and lives enriched, of majority and minority alike) by greater tolerance of cultural differences in style of response. The key to improved performance is real acceptance of others so that some of the individual and cultural barriers come down. And that, in turn, means that we need to look carefully at whether our various cultural assumptions are necessary or destructive.

CHAPTER SEVEN

Affirmative Action and Curriculum Inclusion

LIKE MANY OF OUR CONTEMPORARY political debates, the debate about affirmative action in employment and university admissions is distorted by Americans' imperfect perception of ourselves and our society. It is affected by the narrow and arbitrary nature of our assumptions and the definitions we place on such things as equality, efficiency, justice, and merit. It is affected by our strange sense of what society is for and what our social policies ought to accomplish. It is also distorted by the limits that our blinders place on the range of options that we are willing to consider.

Like any cultural category, the definition of "affirmative action" depends on where we draw arbitrary lines. Moreover, what things we see or fail to see, and what things appear problematic or not, largely depend on what our culture trains us to notice or ignore. For example, we ignore an enormous range of affirmative action-like behaviors that already permeate our society. Critics tend to find affirmative action reprehensible only if the government mandates it and even then only if it benefits women or minority groups.

Affirmative action is designed to provide real equality of opportunity because, in light of some of the issues I discussed in chapters 5 and 6, the legal proclamation of equality has not been sufficient to create or even promote real equality. Affirmative action is designed to permit and encourage greater participation in the work force and the mainstream economy by people who have previously been denied access to career opportunities and membership in the middle class.

Proponents of affirmative action argue that American society will be better for everyone, not just the beneficiaries of the affirmative action themselves, if more members of society are permitted and encouraged to participate in its various activities. At present we endure a legacy of waste, unnecessary social costs, crime, and tension which sap our collective strength and wealth so that even white males suffer. Moreover, we are subject to the artificially limited range of thought and creativity that a narrowly defined work force creates.

Affirmative action recognizes that, for reasons described in the previous chapter, psychological and cultural factors make it very difficult for members of minority groups to become "integrated" in society even when legally permitted to do so. It also recognizes, again for reasons discussed earlier, that cultural expectations make it very difficult to judge quality or merit accurately or objectively when it comes in unusual forms from people who are "different." Affirmative action recognizes that merely removing legal barriers to participation is not sufficient to alter the behavior of the privileged majority or of the excluded minorities themselves because the habits and attitudes fomented by centuries of discrimination are not easily altered, even among people of good will. It argues that de facto changes in habits in which people begin to deal with one another on a face-to-face basis has to occur in order for age-old attitudes to be reshaped. Although it is rarely stated or even recognized, affirmative action also helps break down arbitrary, unnecessary, and even damaging cultural assumptions about the qualities actually needed for good job performance (as it has in medicine, law, and education, not to mention sports).

In short, affirmative action is about taking cultural blinders off and enriching our lives. It is about recognizing that there is more than one kind of "efficiency" and that allowing women and minorities to participate will enormously increase our country's capacity to meet its human needs and responsibilities. Affirmative action, I think, is even about long-term improvements in economic and corporate efficiency in the narrow sense because new players will expand the range of options available to solve problems and accomplish tasks. (It is certainly about improved corporate efficiency if we assume that corporations, along with the rest of us, bear some responsibility for the present condition of society and must be taxed in part to cover the costs of talents not being put to use and lives that are now being wasted.)

Despite loud claims to the contrary by many of its critics, affirmative action policies do not "reverse the cognitive advantages of birth." But they do recognize that wealth, sex, and color have always bestowed great advantages on some people at birth and that, conversely, discrimination creates severe disadvantages which are far deeper and more lasting than most people realize. Affirmative action attempts to offset some of those advantages and disadvantages. It recognizes that the playing field is sharply tilted in favor of some by its very nature, and that a laissez-faire attitude on the part of government will not level the playing field because laissez-faire always favors those who already have power.

When women and minorities were permitted by law and custom to knock on the door of education and employment, the competition for jobs and education seemed about to be extended. But the mere option of hiring women and minorities could be—and was—ignored, regardless of the quality of the applicants, so neither competition nor quality increased. In order to get the full benefit of the new competition, the United States has had to force the white male monopoly to give the new players serious consideration through affirmative action rules. Without such rules, even superior women and minorities were never viewed as quite as good as the white male competition. Margaret Mead apparently had to scramble for promotion at the American Museum of Natural History, despite the fact that her accomplishments exceeded those of the men passing judgment on her. Every field has such examples.

Reasonably applied, affirmative action does not violate American values of justice, merit, or freedom. It demands only that people who seek jobs, schooling, or other opportunities be granted access which has otherwise been withheld on the basis of irrelevant criteria. It does not assert that "only group membership rather than individual merit" counts; rather, it attempts to reverse a longstanding pattern of favoritism denying individual merit by giving preference to wealthy or white males as a group. It recognizes that favoritism toward white males has always been with us and that modern problems have been shaped by the history of such preference.

To a large extent, all that is being demanded is equal affirmative action. Modern affirmative action programs aren't about privilege;

they are about balancing the privileges afforded to others. Affluent white males themselves have always received the most affirmative action, some by law, some by custom and practice, and some by factors so subtle and so deeply ingrained in our cultural training that we generally don't consciously recognize them. Their families, communities, employers, and even their government have provided them—and still provide them—with a number of powerful forms of privileged access to education and employment. The success of white males, as a group, depends very heavily on those privileges, and it is those privileges which must be balanced. Moreover, these other types of discrimination or "affirmative action" *against* minorities and women have generally been far more exclusionary than those now being proposed as countermeasures. The old rules demanded complete or nearly complete exclusion of women and minorities. Contemporary affirmative action demands only outreach efforts and serious consideration of all candidates or perhaps, if necessary, the setting aside of some *fraction* of opportunities for groups that have previously been excluded.

One often hears it said—usually with derision—that affirmative action is designed as atonement or punishment of the majority for ancient sins of discrimination or even for slavery. "Why should we be forced to suffer now for things that our ancestors did?" "My family never owned slaves; they hadn't even come to the United States yet." "Just because some black or woman failed to get a job in 1948, why should that affect hiring decisions now?"

In one limited sense, affirmative action is about past sins, but not in the sense of exacting retribution or assuaging guilt. Rather, the point is one of recognizing that past (and continuing) discrimination has left a legacy which continues to distort contemporary practices. Affirmative action is necessary because American society and American cultural assumptions have created the attitudes and patterns of behavior that cause the problems; culture and society cause the patterns that people like Herrnstein and Murray now measure and describe as inherent genetic inferiority or superiority. The sins of the past have left a legacy of separateness, depression, rage, withdrawal, indifference, learned helplessness, and resistance to mainstream culture that is common to colonized peoples and makes it impossible for people once discriminated against to compete on a level playing field simply because some legal barriers have now been removed. People discriminated against for generations do not all remain crowded up against the fence, waiting to rush forward into the land of opportunity, like the people in the Oklahoma land rush, the minute the whistle blows signaling the end of restraint. As Albert Memmi described, the psychological costs of remaining ever-hopeful just outside the fence are far too high. Instead, people facing discrimination find other ways to survive, involving psychological, social, and cultural adjustments. They may be slow to come forward when legal discrimination finally ends because those psychological and cultural structures restrain them. People have to refocus their attention and expectations gradually. And because people inherit such attitudes from their parents, the adjustment to new opportunities may take a generation or more and may have to result from the actual experience of opportunity that can be trusted, not merely the promise. Affirmative action isn't about helping people who are inferior; but it is about helping people whose social circumstances may push them toward inferior performance or who may merely be perceived as inferior because they don't look right or fail to do things in a culturally correct manner.

Moreover, the experience of slavery and discrimination, handed down, has left a pattern of perceived superiority on the part of white males which impedes efforts to offer fair evaluation of others. In addition, the legacy of past discrimination powerfully assists all of us who are white and male whether or not our families ever owned slaves and whether or not we can remember discriminating personally. The discrimination of the past has suppressed our competition and contributed to the elevated platform of culture, family experience, and wealth from which many of us began our individual job search. These patterns have to be broken and new patterns *experienced* before people can break their old ways of thinking. Changes in attitude have to follow changes in the reality of people's lives.

However, affirmative action is not primarily about past sins but about ongoing discrimination. Despite recent civil rights laws that have legally and officially removed constraints and opened opportunities for women and for people who are not white, real barriers of wealth, class, and prejudice clearly remain. Official segregation may have ended in the 1960s, and strides toward the inclusion of women and minorities have unquestionably been made. But, anyone who thinks that the playing field is now level and that no more help needs to be given to minorities need only read about the "glass ceiling" of passive resistance, indifference, and outright hostility that bars the advancement of women and minority individuals in corporate structures. Or one can read about incidents at Denny's restaurants reported in 1993-94 (to which I have already referred) or about deliberations at Texaco where in 1996 officials were recorded contemplating illegally blocking a discrimination suit and referring to nonwhite employees by a variety of racial epithets, gleefully noting that the employees were "stuck to the bottom" and suggesting very clearly that, at Texaco, at least, the playing field is hardly level. Or one can listen to the conversations of one's own fellow employees, wherever one works.

Anyone who thinks that the playing field is level also hasn't considered a host of subtle ways in which the field is tilted, ways that are not recognized or categorized as "affirmative action," or ways that are invisible because they seem natural or normal owing to the fact that they are outside our culturally defined patterns of perception.

One common complaint is that affirmative action undermines the quality of job performance by restraining the freedom of employers to select and hire the best qualified applicants. Economics students are taught that protective tariffs and other special protections have a tendency to weaken the quality and competitive ability of the products and industries they were designed to protect. Some critics of affirmative action draw the analogy that, by protecting women and minorities, affirmative action policies are undermining not only the quality of the work force and the competitive ability of American industry but the abilities of women and minorities themselves.

But economists surely know that protective tariffs have also played a role in stimulating the growth of fledgling industries until they are developed enough to compete on their own, at which point the emergence of those industries presumably repays the earlier investment in their protection. The goal of such tariffs presumably is not just the health of the industries themselves but the good of the country, whose long-term strength may depend on maintaining industries that are not immediately able to compete. Despite our professed ideal of "free" markets, tariffs have been used repeatedly in this manner in American history, and American industry has not been loath to ask for protection or even for aggressive help from government in surviving or establishing itself in new markets. So the principle of special protection provided by government is hardly revolutionary, nor does it violate our cultural values or our economic practices. We have given special protection to all kinds of interests for all kinds of purposes. Why is it only protection for minorities and women that is so disturbing? Why are we so intent on making this kind of affirmative action a matter for resolution by the courts when it is only one item in a large category of similar behaviors addressed toward various segments of society? Why do we not recognize that, in the long run, the interests of the country as a whole are served by affirmative action as much or more than by tariffs?

In 1996, Congress passed a law permitting the northeastern states to set up their own protective tariff *within* the United States in order to protect the region's dairy farmers, who claimed that they couldn't survive in open national or international competition. Such a tariff is likely to raise milk prices for consumers, lower "efficiency," and perhaps even lower milk quality; but apparently it is important to protect this group of dairy farmers, rather than letting the free market destroy them, even though some competing milk producers in other regions may be forced out of business. Early in 1997 the U.S. government imposed a tariff against Mexican tomatoes in order to protect our own tomato growers. Because Mexican tomatoes, unlike the American competition, are vine ripened, consumers would get tomatoes that are more nutritious as well as cheaper if there were no tariff.

American sugar production is routinely protected from external competition even though the tariff makes sugar prices artificially high. Sugar is hardly in short supply, and sugar production pollutes the environment (particularly in the vicinity of the Florida Everglades). The cultivation of American tobacco is protected and subsidized even though the product is now known to be addictive, to have major negative health consequences, to add a heavy burden to the health care system, and to generate enormous excess costs to consumers and employers. The export of arms is both promoted and subsidized by the government, so even arms dealers apparently merit affirmative action. Every industry that gets a subsidy, a tariff, or government intervention, including the arms, sugar, and tobacco industries, is getting affirmative action—that is, special government help in succeeding in the "free" market. Subsidizing foreign advertising (even for companies like McDonald's, which hardly need any help) is affirmative action. So is buying surplus produce, subsidizing exports, or permitting ranchers and miners to lease land at artificially cheap rates. It is affirmative action if governments provide research and marketing assistance and absorb costs and risks for corporations and then turn over the profits. These forms of affirmative action harm the rest of us in many ways—through increased threats to our security, through the waste of our tax dollars, through artificially high prices, and often through real costs to our health, as increased production of tobacco or sugar or the export of arms are hardly desirable for the rest of us. So there is clear precedent for specific government protection which ebbs and flows according to the group involved and the politics of the moment, not according to obvious principles of justice, not according to logical principles written in stone or logical consistency, and not even according to the Constitution. Reality mocks our efforts to obtain weighty legal opinions about whether affirmative action for women and minorities is constitutional rather than about whether it is just. The choices are political, and the legal uncertainties are where political forces choose to look for them—or not to look for them—rather than in hallowed legal pronouncements. Where we choose to look is a matter of arbitrary political stimuli and cultural definitions, not truth or logic.

One of the things that affirmative action for women and minorities should do is to work in precisely the same way as a tariff—as a temporary protection for fledgling groups building themselves up to market strength. This application of the protection principle seems far more legitimate than the others just mentioned because it serves the needs of people, not just of corporate interests. Affirmative action, like any legitimate protection for a needy group, should be permitted despite the fact that those who are not in the temporarily assisted groups have to absorb some relatively minor secondary costs. All protective laws demand some sacrifice from others. The laws are adopted and the sacrifice demanded and accepted in the belief that the good of the society as a whole is being served by the temporary protection of a particular group.

In the 1960s, people who recognized that granting civil rights was not sufficient to enable oppressed groups to rise out of poverty and cultural exclusion used to talk about affirmative action as "priming the pump." They meant that, just as with an old-fashioned water pump, you had to put something in, without immediate benefit, before you could get anything out of it; but you would then profit many times over, justifying the initial investment. Affirmative action, like any well-conceived tariff, may involve some initial cost to the public. It may take a generation or more to bear its best fruit because of the cultural and psychological complexities I have outlined. The long-term profit to our society as a whole comes from a more varied and more productive work force and from reduced social costs in support of poverty. It also comes from a more peaceful, less crime- and tension-ridden, and culturally richer society. Such an investment will be rewarded many times over; but much of it will be repaid in public rather than private profit and some will be paid in ways not measurable in dollars.

We still have to deal with other unspoken but powerful cultural assumptions that mold our perceptions about the definition of *quality* and *profit*. For one thing, we have to remind ourselves that corporate efficiency, productivity, and the pursuit of profit—important as they are—are not the only human values or the only American values. By considering the needs of our fellow citizens and our wish for a peaceful, just, and harmonious society, affirmative action improves various social efficiencies whether or not it improves corporate profits (although in the long run I think it will). Our society tends to let corporations pursue their profits without a social conscience, and we then complain because the human and environmental costs are too high and involve too much taxation—as if the corporate behavior played no part in creating those costs and as if the profits and the costs were entirely unrelated to the tax burden the rest of us face. We might reasonably say instead that some contribution to solving various social problems—including the employment and social participation of all people (in addition to the job security of established employees)—is part of the cost of doing business, part of the price of a license to make the profit.

Who Benefits from Affirmative Action Now?

The most important kinds of ongoing "affirmative action" in our society are undoubtedly those given to wealthy people. Individually, they benefit from wealth itself and family and friends, and they benefit from the fact that universities and corporations may be eager to curry the favor of their families. The best predictor of one's social class is not one's IQ or supposedly objectively measured ability; it is the social class of one's parents. Wealth guarantees access to college and career for anyone of even modest ability. Very few captains of industry or heads of government reached their exalted positions without the support of wealthy families and/or personal ties to other people of wealth and influence. How did John Kennedy and George Bush become President? What qualifies Steve Forbes to run? Their superior IQs? Whether or not they are wealthy, moreover, people who rise through the ranks do so at least as frequently because they are the personal protegés of those already in power as because they have inherent merit. How often does one read that an executive or politician was "groomed" or hand-picked for the job by another? Cronyism in corporate or political appointments and promotions is "affirmative action" for the powerful. How did Lyndon Johnson become President?

Does anyone really think that our traditional system of selecting leaders works so well—that our leaders are the most intelligent among us and that that is their primary qualification for office? Robert McNamara, former secretary of defense and head of Ford Motor Company, recently admitted that all the great brains of Washington were much less perceptive and less logical about the Vietnam War than were millions of scruffy protesters. President after President has turned out to be terribly flawed. The CIA (in the wake of the Aldrich Ames scandal and other even more recent scandals) and the FBI (in the wake of J. Edgar Hoover, i.e., through most of its history) are by most accounts disastrously corrupt and incompetent—at least for the tasks of law enforcement and international security that they are supposed to be performing. Merit in both agencies seems to be measured primarily by willingness to carry out the secret and often illegal personal agendas of one's superiors. This itself forms a kind of affirmative action for those without scruples. One memoir or exposé after another describing public life reveals that various parts of the government were and are corrupt or strikingly incompetent. In fact, a careful reading of American history suggests that our present circumstances were molded as much by the incompetence, corruption, and greed of past officials as by the greatness of our heroes.

A similar pattern can be found in the private sector. The American automobile industry lost its huge early lead in the world market through disastrous errors in its selection of what to produce and market. Chrysler had to be saved with the kind of welfare payments we want to deny the poor. The heads of the great tobacco companies are extraordinarily blind to any values other than their own profits. IBM passed over the chance to own the technologies that were the foundation of both Xerox and Microsoft. And it is not clear that the white male monopoly at any other level has done any better. All of these institutions would be better served if their pool of prospective employees was more open to competition from more diverse individuals and outsiders.

The wealthiest classes also get a great deal of "affirmative action" as a group. Not only does wealth open doors that should be opened only by merit, it is also rewarded by any number of government policies. Tax deductions and loopholes are heavily slanted toward the rich, and tax collection is heavily slanted toward the working class—a pattern newly confirmed in 1996 by disclosure of tax favors to corporate executives, and exacerbated by the 1997 budget agreement between the President and Congress.

Allowing corporations and the wealthy special access to government officials and special ability to direct the content of legislation—or to write it themselves, as was widely reported to be the case in the 104th Congress—is "affirmative action." Cutting the entitlements only of the poor, not of the rich, in times of budget limits is "affirmative action." Government decisions favoring its corporate patrons is "affirmative action." Promoting or breaking ground for businesses abroad is "affirmative action." So is government intervention in strikes on behalf of employers or allowing individuals to slip back and forth between businesses and the government agencies that regulate those businesses. The awarding of government contracts embodied "affirmative action" for the powerful and for special friends of politicians long before set-asides for minorities were in place; but that favoritism was less forthright than affirmative action and produced fewer social benefits. Setting lesser criminal penalties for the rich than the poor is "affirmative action." Using government force first and foremost to protect property, not people, is "affirmative action." Slanting government services toward the rich and cutting those primarily for the poor is "affirmative action."

It is also "affirmative action" for the wealthy if we base financial policy (manipulating interest rates, inflation, the strength of the dollar, trade agreements, and so forth) on the needs of corporations and the wealthy without paying equal attention to how those policies affect the poor. In fact, despite all the defamation of the unemployed that we hear, government policy intentionally *maintains* a degree of unemployment in its zest to control inflation on the theory that it is good for "the economy" as a whole. We have recently discovered that there aren't enough jobs available when we throw people off welfare, so they enter into a fruitless competition with the working poor. If we control inflation in a manner that necessitates high unemployment, don't we have some responsibility for the poverty that results? Whose interests come first? Is there such a thing as "natural" unemployment—many other societies do not suffer such a pattern—or does unemployment exist only in relation to our economic policies and assumptions and our cultural definitions, which all provide affirmative action for the wealthy? Shouldn't part of the wealth that these policies help to generate go to provide jobs for those forced out of work?

The whole ideology of freedom and independence and individual responsibility is "affirmative action" for those born with wealth and power (especially if the government also protects property and preexisting privilege). It is "affirmative action" if we draft the poor and the nonwhite to fight wars in the interests of the wealthy (or even if we have a "volunteer" army whose attraction is largely to poor people, who have no other way to earn a living). It is "affirmative action" for the wealthy if we use tax dollars to support corporate enterprise, extend its interests, or bail it out of trouble, but we refuse to spend on the poor.

Many other factors also provide affirmative action for privileged groups. For example, local funding of various public services but particularly of public hospitals and schools acts as affirmative action for the wealthy by perpetuating inequality in the environments in which children grow and the education they receive. Children whose school systems (or parents) can't afford to provide access to computers or other needs have significant limits on their ability to compete in the job market. Allowing schools in poor districts to decay, as we have always done but are now doing even more aggressively, is affirmative action for the middle class. Not only does it save "our" tax money; it assures that middle-class children, even those who are not very diligent scholars, will receive a better education than the poor and therefore gain a leg up in the job market. Thirty years ago I taught in the Upward Bound program, which was designed to help impoverished high school students who had real potential but marginal accomplishments get through college. A common complaint from the (middle-class) public then was that "those" Upward Bound kids were taking up seats in college that belonged to "our" kids. At some level we are very well aware that our access to opportunities is based on holding others back. The recent movement in favor of using tax money to provide school vouchers and school "choice" programs rather than simply improving public schools also provides affirmative action for the wealthy. It perpetuates or even extends their educational advantage by letting them concentrate themselves and exclude the students who are poor or nonwhite or of another religion (unless, of course, the vouchers are combined with open enrollment so that the poor, the nonwhite, or the non-Catholic or Protestant are afforded the same choices).

New York State is now moving aggressively to take public higher education away from those who can't afford the high cost of private education. That, too, is affirmative action for the affluent because it guarantees that only they will apply for professional positions. Doing away with *official* affirmative action while simultaneously reducing funding for public colleges and schools (except in affluent neighborhoods, which can take care of their own funding) further reduces competition and doubly damages the prospects of minorities and the poor.

But those without individual wealth also use their own private systems of affirmative action to protect what privilege they have. In the world of labor and commerce, preference is constantly given to members of the religion, "race," ethnic group, or sex of people already in the door, their friends and family, people from the same hometown, and so forth. It is commonplace for certain professions and unions to recruit preferentially if not exclusively from the ethnic group or even the specific families of their existing membership. Historically, why were so many Boston police officers Irish or longshoremen Italian—because the Irish or Italians routinely got the highest scores on placement exams? And it is common for members of a particular ethnic group or family, or just white men, to experience more camaraderie and gain more help on the job than women or members of minority groups who are lucky enough to gain admission. Women and minorities have had no peers already established to help pull them up into the ranks of employment. There has been no one to speak for them from the inside, no one to recognize their different but real capabilities. Working-class white males get help from the government, too. Anthropologist Karen Sacks has pointed out that even the GI Bill, the apparently egalitarian measure provided by the government to advance the careers of veterans after World War II, which enabled many of them and subsequent generations of their families to enter the middle class, was heavily slanted in its application to favor white males. Black GIs were systematically denied similar benefits.

If, historically, any working-class or middle-class group has received affirmative action it has been white males with their de facto monopoly of jobs and education. In their world, competition has clearly been limited and quality has suffered as a result. Every white male in the country has benefited from "affirmative action," and American quality and productivity already suffer. White men, myself included, have benefited from the fact that women and minorities could not compete on equal footing for a job. We didn't get our jobs in a "free" market. I know that I got some jobs through the kinds of unspoken prejudice and shared understanding that lead white males to prefer to hire "one of our kind," just as I now may be losing some opportunities due to fair hiring laws and affirmative action practices that bring to the forefront qualified candidates who would otherwise have been overlooked. I don't like not getting those jobs. But I can see the justice in the new practices.

Racism, sexism, discrimination, sexual harassment, segregation, and prejudice have always provided "affirmative action" for white males—and that is a large part of their purpose—to eliminate or reduce potential competition. Throughout American history, the fear that Chinese or Irish or Eastern European immigrants or African Americans or women would take "our" jobs has been one of the major causes of intolerance and a major reason for the promulgation of laws and informal practices to exclude and denigrate those "others."

Traditional training for girls which directs them to put their energies into noncompetitive, noneconomic pursuits (like homemaking) or to rely on being cute and helpless rather than being smart and able is also "affirmative action" for males. The image of women as pretty but unproductive, even dim-witted housewives that American culture once cultivated (the *I Love Lucy* image), does not reflect on the nature of women even if our media present it as "naturally feminine" behavior. (Perhaps the media have stopped presenting women in this light; but this too may take a generation or more before it ceases to be part of our thinking. And *Lucy* still airs regularly.) Any comparison of our gender roles to those in other cultures shows how bizarre a cultural (not biological) assumption this stereotype is. It shields white males from competition in the work force as well as protecting male power and privilege at home. It works

to be strong, commanding, authoritative, or even funny. So if they do not come across as powerful and dominant they are downgraded as professors. But if they adopt a stronger, more assertive (more "masculine") style, they are considered unfeminine and are downgraded as people and as professors as well. This occurs despite the fact that their culturally dictated "feminine" qualities involving patience and interaction, rather than confrontation and authoritative lecturing, enhance their teaching. Female professors have also found that they are evaluated on many measures that are largely irrelevant to their job performance and that male professors don't have to face. For example, they are graded, at least unconsciously, on their clothing and makeup and on their "looks"—in short all of the cultural baggage that Americans attach to their definition of the female role. Another hurdle such women face is outright hostility imposed by some of their male colleagues or by some male students, some of whom clearly think that simply being a man ranks them above female professors. After all, many have never had the experience of working with a woman who is in charge or in a position of respect or power.

In short, being a strong, commanding, and authoritative figure in the classroom doesn't have much to do with real teaching, but being a good teacher isn't sufficient to garner approval if you don't do it in the expected way. The approved styles are based on cultural definitions of proper male and female behavior—and that, too, acts as affirmative action for the in-group. This is exactly the situation that ethnic minorities face all the time. They are supposed to succeed, but the unspoken criteria of success include factors that are more a matter of adopting (white male) style than of getting results. But if members of a minority are seen as acting "too white," they are likely to be demeaned and insulted by members of their own group and the mainstream population as well.

Even the way we perceive and teach our own history acts as affirmative action for white males because it constantly reinforces the idea that white males have contributed all of the great advances in human history. In short, our misperception of ourselves and our ideals, our very perception of our history and the way we teach history in schools, have become affirmative action for the group that is traditionally favored.

And, of course, IQ and other standardized tests, which are supposed to make evaluations "objective," act as affirmative action for those in the mainstream culture who do things in the mainstream style. What is worse, the tests, which measure mainstream knowledge and style, if anything, proclaim that they are measuring innate intelligence. They thereby reinforce the negative images (including self-images) that exist as a result of the history of racism and discrimination. The tests reinforce the stereotypes. As Herrnstein and Murray point out, IQ and other standardized tests do act as important means of affirmative action for poor and powerless but "smart" (or at least culturally literate, white) individuals. They have helped to displace wealth and family as the only bases of recruitment. But because of the tests' cultural biases and for the reasons I outlined in chapter 6, they don't open the door to people from various minority groups to the extent that they should. In fact, they tend to bar the door to such people.

For all of these reasons, affirmative action has to be more than outreach or special efforts to find qualified female or minority candidates. Such candidates still won't get in the door unless employers have experience with female or minority workers and are educated about the real meaning of tests and quality and the depth of cultural diversity, and about their responsibility to help correct a major social problem. If such prodding for voluntary action doesn't work (as too often it does not), then it is necessary to think in terms of quotas or set-asides that operate like any tariff.

The idea that removing recent affirmative action programs in universities, corporations, or federal and state governments without correcting the rest of the biases or removing the other protective barriers will restore equality of opportunity, level the playing field, or make us a color-blind society again is laughable. When were we ever color-blind? Laissez-faire does not produce equal opportunity if some people start at a disadvantage and if society presents other, cultural and social barriers to equal opportunity. If those other barriers to equal opportunity were removed we would not need affirmative action programs to balance them. But there is little indication that that ideal state will be reached anytime soon.

Our cultural myth that (at least without government affirmative-action programs) our system is open and based primarily on merit deserves far greater scrutiny than it receives. With our cultural blinders on, we are so inured to these other kinds of affirmative action for the privileged that we consider them the normal operation of our "merit" system, if we think about them at all.

Affirmative Action and the Dilution of Quality

Even if we give preference to the narrowest economic values in measuring costs, benefits, and efficiency, we have to ask whether the new patterns of affirmative action actually threaten the quality of school or job performance any more than existing preferences or set-asides do. Principles of special protection (which I also consider "affirmative action") are already consciously and unconsciously applied to many groups of people. We favor those with union seniority, or faculty tenure. We provide enormous "affirmative action" for incumbent politicians. We favor veterans, athletes, beautiful people, cronies, people who "look right," local people, and many other groups. All of these preferences presumably undermine the quality of performance.

Colleges have never relied on simple test score rankings in their admissions policies. If test scores or class rank are all that should count (as those who protest affirmative action appear to assert), college admissions have always been unfair and should have been subject to lawsuits long ago. Colleges have long given favored treatment to student athletes. They give preference in admission to the children of their own alumni or of their wealthy benefactors ("legacies"). They have long favored regional diversity and regional balance in their student populations, so that Eastern schools give "affirmative action" to students from the West and vice versa, and both favor students from small communities or foreign countries not represented in their student population. So students who have better test scores but who come from a part of the country heavily represented by applicants may lose out to people with lower scores from obscure places or to athletes or to legacies. All of that favoritism presumably lowers the quality of the institution.

Colleges also give "affirmative action" (as they should) to people with unusual skills or interests whose test scores may not be competitive. They give "affirmative action" to students whose other qualities appear more important than their test scores or to students whose real abilities appear to belie their scores on particular tests. In short, college admissions policies have always been based on a range of criteria, many of which are logically and morally identical (or inferior) to the preferences for "race" and sex recently enacted which are now often being repealed under pressure. If regional diversity is important for colleges and is a permissible basis for choice (as I believe it should be), why not ethnic and gender diversity, which are far more important categories in terms of the "diversity" they provide the college? Yet those other discriminatory practices continue, largely ignored or approved of, even as affirmative action for minorities and women is being challenged. There was no uproar until these groups became the focus of policies, and even now as preferences for women and minorities are being challenged in the courts, the old favoritism remains comfortably in place. Affirmative action's vulnerability to lawsuits doesn't reflect logic or justice. It reflects the ease with which women and minorities can always be targeted as scapegoats.

If we repeal affirmative action rules, colleges won't turn to simple test-based ranking for admission; they will revert to the complex system of admissions that prevailed before—or at least I hope they will, because as a college educator I have found that the most interesting, most creative, and most motivated students aren't necessarily those with the best test scores, those who are white, or even those who initially appear most "educated." Taking other factors into account in admissions improves the student body, if it increases variety.

The example of college admissions makes an important point. Colleges have long been saying that a simple linear ranking by test scores is not a sufficient basis for judgment. Quality (like intelligence or health) is not a unitary thing that can be measured by a simple test and ranked on a linear scale. Determining who is most qualified is always a complex, multifaceted judgment. Moreover, colleges are saying that diversity, more than high test scores, enriches everyone's experience and contributes to the quality of the institution in valuable ways. The ability of an applicant to add diversity to the campus *does* improve that person's qualifications for admission. Those principles ought to apply to women and minorities as well as to the other favored groups.

There is no reason to think that affirmative action will reduce the quality of school or job performance by inhibiting competition. On the contrary, it should open competition, broaden our awareness of the ways in which tasks can be done, heighten the competitive awareness of men who got their positions in an artificially limited market, eliminate the fraction of white males who have always been mediocre or worse but survived for lack of competition—in short, improve job performance overall.

Sometimes the new players themselves dramatically improve the quality of performance. It isn't hard to find examples of situations in which affirmative action was necessary to unleash qualities which, in retrospect, turned out to be superior to what was replaced with the result that the product itself got better. Perhaps the most famous and embarrassing example (although hardly the most important) occurred in 1947 when it took acts of "affirmative action" to integrate major league baseball. Black and Latin American players, who were once excluded and who everybody "knew" weren't good enough to play in the major leagues, now set most of the standards of excellence. The overall quality of play in the leagues has certainly improved.

Affirmative action given to a small pioneering group of women in medical schools has resulted in an enormous influx of women and an increase in competition for admissions. More important, those women have had a significant (and, I believe, positive) impact on the way that medicine is taught and practiced. They have reinforced the need for humanity and personal interaction in medical practice and helped lower the pedestal on which doctors were placed, changes which should provide significant health benefits for reasons described in earlier chapters. Affirmative action for a few women entering the practice of law has also produced a large influx of women in the field and some shift in the practice of law. Some observers think that lawyers have become more interested in compromise and negotiation and less determined to have litigation as a result of the influx.

Once such results have been achieved, in baseball, medicine, or law (or in specific departments of any business or university), affirmative action ceases to be necessary and it is dropped.

I can provide a smaller example, but one more in keeping with experience most of us have on the job. On the campus where I teach there are five senior women who have been awarded the rank of distinguished teaching or service professor. They are indeed among our most productive scholars, teachers, and organizational players. But they clearly would not have squeaked past their male competition to be hired in the first place without the assistance of a strong affirmative action push in the 1970s. Some of these women were told that they were being hired only as a matter of affirmative action and were stigmatized by being introduced to the campus and to campus assemblies as the product of affirmative action.

The number of women promoted to distinguished professorships on the campus is far greater than one would expect from the number of women on the campus in their fields. The chances that five men hired in their places would have had such distinguished careers is extremely small, judging by the proportional success of their male peers. Clearly, without affirmative action, the selection process would not have recognized the superior capabilities of these women at the time of their initial job interviews.

These women and other female faculty members (many hired without such fanfare based on the example set by the earlier group) enriched our campus not just because they were good but because they brought new sets of skills, values, and perceptions that some of their male counterparts didn't have. The debate on campus is far livelier than it used to be, the range of opinions expressed is far wider, the scope of issues addressed is far greater. Even the style of communication and committee work and internal deliberation has changed for the better.

In a university, affirmative action hiring and diversity may be especially important to increase the quality of the institution. College ought to be a place where students forge their own thoughts, their own model of the world, by selectively combining elements from the smorgasbord of ideas and perceptions offered by professors. The wider the range of offerings, the better these students' chances to be thoughtful, well-informed people. Colleges thrive on diversity of opinion. But colleges also thrive on providing diverse role models for students. Female and minority students want and need professors whom they can not just relate to but be like. Otherwise, like Erikson's black child who wanted to be Red Ryder in a society that repeatedly tells blacks they can't cross that line, female and minority students may not be able to see themselves as participants in the work and perhaps not even as members of the profession. So it may well be as important for a professor to be different from the others as to have a unique academic specialty or intellectual perspective. Minority students and women aren't the only ones who would gain. White male students would gain a broader range of experience and insight and would benefit from personal exposure to different kinds of people in unaccustomed roles. Enforcing narrow standards for academic employment is likely to limit everyone's knowledge and creativity.

But perhaps the most important point is that affirmative action is valuable because it creates situations in which different kinds of people can get to know one another, much as the first women or minority individuals successfully hired opened the door for others. I have heard it said more than once that government officials and other individuals who are most sensitive to the needs of African Americans are people who have lived and worked as peers with people of color in situations in which they had to cooperate and were able to put forth their best efforts together. Athletes on sports teams are just one example. Having black and female friends and colleagues enormously broadens one's horizons as well as generating greater understanding and warm ties. Exposure in a positive context breeds understanding. The ultimate goal is to make affirmative action unnecessary by defusing people's fears and biases.

If Affirmative Action Hiring Results in a Poor Selection

Suppose that an individual affirmative action search fails, after all, to hire the best candidate. So what? We have been failing all along to hire the best candidates at least on some occasions because search and hiring procedures are imperfect (and because we have been excluding so many potential candidates). How many job searches of every kind fail to find the "best" candidate? With or without affirmative action, poor selections are sometimes made.

Mediocre job performance didn't begin with affirmative action, but any failure or incompetence in affirmative action searches and the resulting candidates draws special attention. Everybody notices. When a white man fails at his job, that is his individual fault and he personally was a bad choice. When a woman or a member of a minority fails, it is thought to reflect on his or her sex or "race" and on the affirmative action process.

The same principle applies in day-to-day interaction on the job. We hear a lot about the incompetencies of minority and female colleagues. Everybody has some shortcomings. But in the case of minorities and women we too often slip into talking about incompetence of a general sort, and because the individual is isolated, he or she has no defenders. Too often we ignore, explain away, or even cover for the failings of our regular coworkers (generally other white males) while focusing on the failings of those "others" as a way to prove our preconceptions. Besides, we confuse competence with doing things in our style and criticize people whose styles are just different from ours. It is too easy, whenever there is a real but potentially healthy difference of opinion among colleagues, to find the isolated female or minority individual at fault rather than exploring the difference—unless, of course, those individuals have had a chance to earn respect.

The "Shame" of Being an Affirmative Action Employee

One corollary of all of this is that there is no shame in being helped by affirmative action. It doesn't mean that one got a job despite inferior qualifications or inferior intelligence or ability. (It may sometimes mean getting a job despite getting lower scores on standardized tests, but, as we have seen, the tests are biased the other way—and lots of people get jobs or college placements without having the highest test scores.) It means mostly that one got help to negotiate the existing biases, and all the other powerful "affirmative action" that always helps wealthy people or people in the mainstream. It makes me cringe to hear members of minority groups or women who have "made it" say that affirmative action should be eliminated because it demeans minority successes. If that is true, then almost all white males and their accomplishments are demeaned because they got where they are without minority or female competition but with the help of their sex and their skin color and perhaps with powerful and wealthy family ties, like John Kennedy or George Bush—or George Washington, who achieved fame with a strong boost from his family's wealth. It makes me weep particularly when the individuals making the pronouncements ignore the role that affirmative action played in their own lives, as Justice Clarence Thomas has done, or ignore the affirmative action role of wealth in their own lives, like George Bush. Why should minority individuals and women be the only ones that don't get affirmative action?

In recent years, a number of people, including black conservatives, have argued that offering affirmative action will weaken the black community and that individuals instead should be encouraged to make it on their own merits by pulling themselves up by their own efforts.

This perspective, I believe, involves two serious errors. It argues from within the blinders of the American mainstream and uncritically accepts the piece of American cultural mythology that individuals succeed or fail on their own. In fact, with rare exceptions, *no one* in our society, from George Bush and Steve Forbes to the individual who gets a helping hand from a cousin into a union, makes it without help and support at least from friends and communities—their financial backing, their connections, and their accumulated know-how. People are helped by family ties and by family connections to the outside. If nothing else they are helped by family wisdom and experience. If your community lacks some of these things, you are at a severe disadvantage. (We consider Abraham Lincoln perhaps the quintessential self-made man, born in a log cabin and rising to the White House by his own efforts, and his record is unquestionably impressive. But as a young man he was rather a failure at business and often in debt. He had a number of wealthier, better connected patrons along the way who helped him and who knew how to work the system. He would not have had these patrons if his neighbors had not included people of greater sophistication and economic substance than himself and if he had not been an accepted member of their communities.) In short, what we think of as individual initiative almost always exists in a context of social institutions. Even contemporary Asian immigrants who often "pass" blacks along the road of upward mobility, benefit from family connections, traditions of learning, family funds scraped together, traditions of small-scale enterprise, an awareness that mobility is possible, a practiced, successful way of defining choices, and a sense of how to make the mainstream system work. Why should we expect the residents of a ghetto, deprived of some of these things, to do what no one else can do?

Second, the bootstrap argument invokes a very shallow sense of what culture is and what it contributes to any individual. As I pointed out in earlier chapters, a viable culture consists not just of visible trappings but of patterns of thinking, including a sense of how things work, goals and values, motivation, a sense of how one succeeds, a sense that success is within reach, a structure of supportive ties and institutions, established patterns of positive interaction, and so forth. One cannot succeed without such a structure any more than one can speak without a language, because culture provides the "grammar" of one's thoughts and actions. People's "merits" must be derived, at least in part, from that structure and their "bootstraps" are inevitably grounded in it because culture provides the "program" with which an individual thinks. Viable cultures provide workable frameworks, as any number of cultures, in Africa as elsewhere, have done for millennia. But, the effect (and part of the purpose) of slavery and discrimination in the United States has been to deprive poor black Americans of the necessary structures or to distort them to the point where the structures are not fully functional in the mainstream society. Colonizers *must* do this to make colonization work. Poor blacks are being asked to make it in the mainstream without cultural and institutional supports that others routinely get. They may need to be assisted temporarily not because of "racial" inferiority but because of the systematic stripping of their access to mainstream culture.

Poor blacks have systematically and deliberately been denied knowledge of—and social ties to—the system in which we now ask them to compete. Telling them to help themselves is a bit like cynically giving former colonies their independence when their resources are owned by outsiders, their institutions are directed toward outsiders, and people have been deprived, through conquest, of some of their sense of how to manage their own affairs.

The Fate of White Males

We hear a lot about how white males are frustrated by recent government affirmative-action initiatives. Perhaps they are. Their position has declined from one of relatively privileged access to one of slightly less privileged or—at worst—equal access. But where does it say that their frustration is more important than the decades or centuries of frustration on the part of all the other groups? (except, of course, in our unspoken cultural assumptions that white males are somehow more real and more important than other groups of people).

The nation's attempts to define and enforce affirmative action have generated complaints, some legitimate, some less legitimate. But any system, no matter how well designed, generates arbitrary judgments as well as complaints. For the most part we live with the risk of imperfect applications or abuse of any particular system if the system as a whole accomplishes an important purpose. Affirmative action is working, though it needs to be extended and improved, but we are denying it the same forbearance which we give other systems of law, custom, or policy—from the uneven enforcement of speed laws to the unequal burdens imposed by zoning laws, the necessary imperfection of any method of hiring or college admissions, or even the triage system of hospital emergency rooms. All of these leave some individuals feeling that they have received less than their due and all have required adjustment. The fact that in the case of affirmative action, as in the case of welfare cheats, we are so willing to focus on the occasional errors and abuses at the edge rather than the goals and accomplishments of the system says more about our lack of commitment to equal opportunity than it does about the failings of the affirmative action system.

One proposed correction to affirmative action policy has been to suggest that it be targeted more at the poor, regardless of "race" or sex, thus eliminating what some people view as unfair favoring of specific groups. Affirmative action for poor people, regardless of sex or "race," is an excellent idea, but it should supplement, not replace, affirmative action for minorities and women—especially the involuntary minorities. These groups face other barriers in their attempt to enter the job market in addition to poverty. Besides, once the poor actually begin to get affirmative action, they will face exactly the same backlash and exactly the same anger from middle-class white males about who gets preference and who doesn't that minorities and women now face—as long as the pie stays small. In order to put such a program in place under our present assumptions, we will have to make the same kinds of definitions and distinctions we make now. We will have to draw lines somewhere, and if employers do not respond, rapidly and voluntarily, we will have to set quotas for the employment of the poor at some level. Some people will still feel that they ought to be in the protected group or that the system is harming them. The joints of the system will still creak. The only solution is to teach people what affirmative action is for—and of course provide enough opportunities so that individuals desiring access to jobs or education aren't left out entirely.

Many complaints concerning affirmative action result from the fact that it has functioned repeatedly as a scapegoat for other ills. Individually, many men use affirmative action as a rationale to justify their failure, unable to admit that they just might have been less qualified than a competitor, especially if the competitor is female or a person of color. I suspect, too, that a good deal of white male resentment of affirmative action results from the fact that it is a convenient excuse for employers to use when turning down a job applicant, whether or not the excuse is true. Employers may not take recourse to affirmative action as a scapegoat quite so explicitly, but rejected candidates can easily come to this conclusion from the common reference to "the large pool of qualified applicants." (There is, of course, a more insidious form of such scapegoating, when the candidates rejected in this manner are themselves women or minorities and when—unbeknownst to the applicants—there are a limited number of affirmative action slots to fill so these candidates are led to think that they are losing out to competition with one another when in fact all are up against a quota system.)

Assigning Responsibility

Despite all I have said, many complaints of white males are well founded. The real problem is that those complaints are directed at the wrong targets. This is one piece that is almost always left out of the discussion of affirmative action. In part the problems result from natural competition. But, through American history, employers repeatedly have made use of newly arrived ethnic groups as a threat to strikers or pitted group against group to bargain wages down, fomenting hatred in the process. Part of the stress generated by the contemporary affirmative action programs reflects that history. But much of it reflects the fact that our affirmative action programs themselves, as currently designed and implemented, are yet another instance of unnecessary pitting of poor and working-class people, white and black, against one another. The programs almost appear designed to generate tensions. But the tensions need not be an inherent part of the process.

Why do we assume that positions for affirmative action candidates must be taken from the ranks of other (typically working-class white male) workers? Those other workers or their ancestors are often the people least responsible for the problems, as they protest. Why not insist that salaries and benefits for affirmative action positions come out of the profits of the company, or out of extremely high executive salaries? Or they could come out of other areas of growth or inflated company expenses (such as the advertising budget or the budget for lavish entertainment and offices, the budget for legal representation or lobbyists) rather than coming at the expense of the jobs of people well down the pay scale. At many corporations, the money to pay for one inflated executive package of compensation might fund the salaries of several hundred or more minority workers, without any layoffs. To get a sense of the power of corporate wealth to help solve the tensions in affirmative action without hurting working-class white males, consider the following example. In late

1996, the Walt Disney Company paid its second-in-command $90 million to *go away* after only a brief tenure. Invested at a modest 6 percent, that money could fund between two hundred and six hundred entry-level jobs indefinitely. A fraction of the profit margin of most corporations could support untold additional workers. Those who profit and those who receive very high compensation have at least as much responsibility for implementing affirmative action as those who labor for modest wages. The former would experience only slight reductions in their very high quality of life; the latter may not get jobs or incomes at all. Besides, corporations and executives now undermine affirmative action by behaving as if this is not a problem they share or one that those with wealth and power should care about. We should demand that they take it very seriously indeed.

The Real Problem: Assumptions About the Distribution of Wealth

The most important sense in which affirmative action is a scapegoat is much more vicious, because it is a major cause of misplaced racism. The backlash against affirmative action has occurred at a time of a hardship for workers resulting not from an economic downturn but from a period of prosperity combined with enormous profits, very high management salaries, and increasing wealth for the richest few percent of the American people. The problem results from unspoken and seemingly immovable cultural assumptions about the distribution and purpose of wealth. Various groups of workers are told that the reason they may be unemployed is "those other people getting the affirmative action" so that they won't question the basic economic redistribution that favors the wealthy. (The "other people" getting their jobs are more often workers overseas who labor for a pittance, increasing the profit margin of the corporations.) The powerful are creating the impression (and, for the workers, the reality) of "limited good"—an image that pits workers against one another, even though there is no such immediate limit to the wealth that could be available for general distribution. Not only are the real economic factors hidden but mutual intolerance and hatred are fomented, diverting people's attention (perhaps intentionally) from the real source of their economic problems. This point addresses what is perhaps the major single flaw in the structure of American cultural and economic assumptions. It is not the "inexorable" functioning of the market nor the "inevitable" competition between workers that pushes workers out. The solution is not to abandon affirmative action that guarantees opportunities for all. Instead, we must actively teach cultural values—or, if necessary, make laws—that provide some checks on the profit motive and force us to balance economic profits against other values. That is a cultural choice. The market is inexorable only if we allow it to be. Many wealthy women have stopped wearing fur coats because wearing fur no longer receives the approval of their peers, and peer approval is more important than the coat. Other predilections can be shaped in the same manner.

One final point: it is now common to hear that affirmative action should be abandoned because it adds to tensions between white and nonwhite. But we cannot say we have achieved social peace if there is continued deprivation of some groups, and we cannot buy peace at the expense of so many members of our population. Moreover, it is not consistent with American values and history to preserve domestic tranquility at the cost of justice. If we had done so in the past, African Americans would have neither emancipation nor civil rights; women would not have the vote; countless ethnic groups would not be part of mainstream American culture; and even white males would not receive a living wage. It took tensions and much more to achieve these goals. It may require some tensions to secure equal access to jobs and education for all Americans. But the tension can be minimized by good leadership and common sense on all sides. The pain, however, will be all the more acute if our leaders reinforce social ambivalence or antagonism toward those goals, if we do not educate people about the need and purpose of affirmative action, and if we do not share the costs of affirmative action equally among all classes of people in the mainstream culture.

Curriculum Inclusion and Multicultural Education

Another current topic of public discussion involves the role of affirmative action in the marketplace of ideas—that is, the movement advocating multicultural education and the reaction against it.

The struggle between supporters of multicultural education, on the one hand, and the proponents of traditional classical Western education, on the other, is not primarily a struggle about "quality" in education, as it is usually portrayed. If multicultural education confines itself to celebrating ethnic clothing, food, song, and dance and provides uncritical promotion of the greatness of certain other cultures, as it sometimes does, then it does little to improve the quality of education. But, if mainstream teaching of Euro-American culture and history focuses shallowly and uncritically on our own greatness, as it often does, it is no better. Without question there are some people who teach multicultural subjects badly and who deserve our scorn; and as every student knows there have always been many people who teach the classics badly, even at some of our best universities. Bad teaching did not begin, or even accelerate, with curriculum inclusion.

The subject matter is not the issue where quality is concerned. Quality in education comes from the way students are encouraged to engage the subject matter, the way they think about significant problems and how to solve them, and the way they speak and write their thoughts. I can teach Shakespeare and make studying his works a matter of meaningless rote memorization, as some of my teachers did, or I can teach *Jack and the Beanstalk* and generate meaningful thought and discussion among students, as the heroic young teacher portrayed in the film *Blackboard Jungle* did. My colleagues and I have found that some of our best teaching has involved subjects like Bigfoot, ESP, the Lake Champlain monster, and the book *Chariots of the Gods* (about prehistoric space invaders), which we consider silly subjects from a scientific point of view but which are on students' minds. Properly taught, these subjects stimulate student thought about serious subjects and generate excellent discussions. They make students practice principles of scientific reasoning and review their knowledge, and the students emerge much more thoughtful about science and much more skeptical of pseudo-science than they would be if we had simply lectured them about science or "the truth."

Even young schoolchildren can have serious discussions of ideas and issues, if they are asked meaningful questions, and can hone their skills for later inquiry. I have had such discussions many times in both primary and secondary classrooms. Teaching young children to discuss ideas thoughtfully would provide an enormous boost to their growing minds. Teaching American history or science as untouchable myth or cultural icon, as is usual, dulls students' interest and their motivation to do well. It may even dull their faculties. But we also have to judge our audience well. Even good teaching will have no real value, whatever the subject, unless our students (at any age or of any group) are ready to deal with the language, issues, and dilemmas involved. Too often we teach subjects uncritically and without regard for their meaning to the audience. Students cannot appreciate Shakespeare if they are not ready to deal with the feelings and dilemmas he describes. It has been observed repeatedly that a study of white male heroes marching steadily forward through history has little meaning to groups trampled or pushed aside in the process.

As educational conservatives insist, there must be a core of shared knowledge that permeates our culture and must permeate our education if we are to attain real coherence as a nation. I do not dispute that premise in the least. There must be such a core even if our goal for the country is not a melting pot but a union of diverse groups. There must be a basis for communication and shared understanding. But, students need to share not just (or even primarily) a core of known facts. Facts are the least important part of the educational process, even if they usually dominate it. The value of facts is to stir thoughts, create patterns, or help us to evaluate hypotheses. Dates are meaningless except insofar as they help us to correlate events or put them in sequence, the better to understand their meaning. (And facts themselves are much more easily learned once they have been placed in context.)

Students need to share a core of intellectual skills and a common awareness of problems and issues. They need to share a core of knowledge about how things work and why things are important so that they can exercise good judgment and communicate with one another. They need to be aware of and to debate (but not necessarily to share) a common core of important ideas. And the things we teach must be important; they can't be part of the core just because they always have been, as is all too often the case. Students have to be in a position to think about the importance of things, not just memorize a list.

Alternative perspectives such as those of women, minorities, and other cultures must be included, not because they are "right" and traditional white male perspectives are "wrong," and not even just because they exist. These alternative perspectives, if honed in the scholarly marketplace, as all ideas should be, have to be included because they are different and can thereby stimulate thought, and because they are as likely to be partly right as traditional ideas. They force students (and the rest of us) to reevaluate rather than merely memorize the traditional ideas. In the process they enrich our understanding and allow students to make thoughtful choices. Additional perspectives improve training and judgment and increase freedom of thought. They should even help students have a greater appreciation of the traditional ideas themselves.

The shared body of knowledge also has to grow and adjust as our knowledge of the world changes. Shared American knowledge clearly must now include some knowledge of automobiles, airplanes, electricity, computers, global warming, the movement of continents, radioactivity, the process of evolution, and a host of other things that were not part of core education fifty or one hundred years ago. And shared American knowledge must now, more than ever, also include knowledge of other people, other classes, sexes, and "races," other cultures, other nations, and other countries or states which, like recent inventions or scientific discoveries, play an increasingly important role in our lives. To the extent that the curriculum is standardized it must be standardized on a broad vision of the contemporary world in cultural as well a scientific terms, not on old-fashioned knowledge or perception.

The core of shared knowledge should not be the total curriculum, however, at any level of education. The richness of our cultural tradition is based in part on the degree to which our knowledge and perceptions also *differ* from one another. This should characterize our educational system as well. What would be the point of talking if we all knew the same things? The common core of knowledge has to be balanced by diversity in education. We don't all need to read the same Shakespeare plays in order to discuss Shakespeare—in fact, the discussion may be richer if we have read different plays. We don't all need to study a historical event from the same perspective. The discussion will be richer if we bring our individual points of view.

In the past few years Americans have debated whether a relatively "minor" American historical figure such as the African American feminist reformer Sojourner Truth deserves as much attention in textbooks as, say, Thomas Edison. Edison, most Americans would agree (with their typical American focus on technology and progress rather than on moral or spiritual issues), undoubtedly had a greater impact on our lives. But history is not only about who is more "important" or whose name and dates and accomplishments students should memorize (the approach most teachers take with Edison). Teaching history should involve studying people whose lives and ideas raise important issues for students to think and talk about (the approach more often taken with Truth). If classes discussed the social, economic, and political context in which Edison's accomplishments were possible and valuable, the way he worked, and the real impact of his inventions (often hidden or delayed) on our society and values, he would merit as much attention as Sojourner Truth. But we just list Edison's discoveries and call him a genius. So by the standard of challenging students to think and feel, Sojourner Truth wins easily. Students could also learn to think critically about how history is taught by debating who was more important and why, after finding out something about Truth and Edison.

In the same vein, Ken Burns's 1989 special on public television entitled *The Civil War* was dramatic and beautiful. But I hope that no more than a small sample is used in classrooms. Many serious historians marveled that it was possible, in the late 1980s, to treat the Civil War once again as if it were nothing but battles between great armies over union and slavery. Where was discussion of the subtleties of the causes of the war? Where were the real people; the slaves themselves; the real lives of northerners and southerners, free black and white, before, during, and after the war? Where were the questions about the draft; the economic tensions between North and South other than slavery itself; the effects of the war on industrialization and finance; the role of industry and industrial spokesmen; the profiteers; the growth of great fortunes; patterns of employment; class and ethnic divisions among whites and among African Americans; the role of immigrants; urbanization; rural life and farm production; the roles of women; the structure of families, the ways in which the aftermath of the war had unexpected consequences for the country?

Wars aren't simply about armies or noble ideals. They are also about people, societies, and cultures. Students need to think about processes in history and the significance of historical events in people's lives. We desperately need to teach them that wars are not just about the advance and retreat of military campaigns over a depersonalized map. If we did, people might stop thinking that war is glorious and we would have fewer wars, or at least be more thoughtful about whether and when war is necessary—and less surprised that in contemporary conflicts our soldiers can be maimed or die and families ripped apart. We need more varied perspectives in our reading and teaching to make these events meaningful. The shallowness of traditional education as much as its narrowness has provoked the call for multicultural education.

I do not question the importance of teaching American history and values. But I question the worth and even the honesty of teaching them without context, and without the point of view of other peoples. Most important, I question the value of teaching American history and values as if they had no imperfections and therefore no potential to be discussed and evaluated, and the values perhaps modified, which is how they are too often taught. Yes, George Washington must be part of our core education—but not the George Washington of traditional fantasy. We have to teach the real, multifaceted George Washington, warts and all, as a means of understanding the issues of his time (and ours).

Moreover, multicultural education has to be part of the core because it is the key to understanding the idiosyncrasies of any one culture and the power of any culture to mold people's thoughts in both obvious and unseen ways. It is the key to understanding "human nature" and variations in human biology that are essential to our health now and in the future; and it is the key to searching for a morality that surpasses the morality of any one cultural system.

The struggle between the two visions of education is actually a struggle about cultural blinders—about whether Western culture, narrowly perceived, is uniquely correct or valuable and therefore should be taught by memorization without being questioned or argued or even put in context. I submit that such an image of ourselves can only be held or taught with powerful blinders. The struggle over multicultural education is also a struggle about whether we can ignore the contributions and perspectives of other people and other cultures, or whether we need to consider them in order to widen our horizons in the search for understanding. It is a struggle about whether we need to use the knowledge and perspectives of other people to enrich our understanding of ourselves and of the Western cultural tradition. It is a struggle about whether our judgments about the quality of our own values and our own classics are reviewed, questioned, modified, and renewed in each generation from a variety of perspectives, or whether they are simply recited. If we don't question and review we are in danger of perpetuating American myths as truth. The very idea of a "canon" (a term which proponents of classical education like to use to describe the essential core of American education) refers to church dogma, to information that is to be learned by rote and obeyed blindly rather than material which is to provide the basis for thought. The issue therefore is whether education is about thought or only about rote patriotism. I think that multicultural teaching will lead to better, more thoughtful patriotism, as well as better education.

The movement to return to a classical education is a yearning for a former, simpler world whose values were supposedly clearer (but only because of our blinders), a world that, in any case, does not exist. In fact, that simpler world never did exist because those "other" people have always been there and have figured more prominently in our lives, our history, and our accomplishments than proponents of an insular view of world and American history recognize. The opposition to multiculturalism is a bit like a horse asking to have its blinders put back in place because it is afraid of all the things it can see. (Or perhaps it is the lower classes that are the horse and the upper class that is the driver who doesn't want the horse to see anything more but who pretends to be speaking for the horse.)

What curriculum inclusion really threatens is the monopoly of ideas that Western (white, male) culture has long enjoyed in our education, the blinders that have limited our debate. And it threatens the idea that that monopoly simply reflects the natural superiority of those traditional ideas. If free-market competition is good for business and for getting the best people for the job, why isn't it good in the realm of ideas, where we have the most to gain and the least to lose in human terms from free competition? We have an enormous amount to gain in ideas, values, and perception by opening the market.

We shouldn't continue to teach the classics just because previous generations found them great; in a free market of ideas they ought to be able to reaffirm their own greatness to new students and new scholars who have a wide enough exposure to world literature, music, philosophy, and values to make an independent judgment. Shakespeare and Mozart will probably survive, but some lesser "classics" that remain only because real competition has been minimized may not. Of course, judgments about what is good literature are themselves inevitably grounded in cultural assumptions that will necessarily vary from group to group. Has Shakespeare been translated into so many languages because the plays are great or culturally universal? I strongly doubt the latter. In "Shakespeare in the Bush," Laura Bohannan has written an excellent account of her efforts to discuss Shakespearean dilemmas with an African tribal group—a group that has its own rich repertoire of stories that convey social morals. The group translated the elements of the Shakespearean plot into their own cultural idiom, restructuring the dilemmas we find so poignant to fit their own values, role definitions, and assumptions. The meaning they found in the story wasn't a meaning that most Western readers share. That Shakespeare's dramas are couched in terms specific to our own cultural experience is not a criticism; they could hardly have been otherwise. Within our culture they have a universality that makes them great. Similarly, his beautiful use of words exists within the sound and nuance of English grammar and vocabulary that cannot be translated. I strongly suspect that Shakespeare's widespread appeal outside English culture (notwithstanding the quality of the work) has more to do with European political and cultural hegemony than with literary standards. There is also the "emperor's new clothes" effect; no learned person, in any language or culture, dares to say that Shakespeare is only so-so.

In the debate over curriculum inclusion, we are really talking about cultural patriotism and cultural chauvinism: whether Americans can afford to let our children and our students explore alternatives or whether we wish to use literature and history only as a kind of flag proclaiming the superiority of American and European heritage and of upper-class standards. The classics are an upper-class possession, and we are saying that to be allowed to play you must accept them as the standard of what is good.

In his reactionary attack on multicultural education and the decline of traditional educational focus on the greatness of Western civilization (*The Closing of the American Mind*, 1987), Allan Bloom wrote: "America tells one story: the unbroken, ineluctable progress of freedom and equality. From its first settlers and its political foundings on there has been no dispute that freedom and equality are the essence of justice for us" (p. 55). He also states: "The United States is one of the highest and most extreme achievements of the rational quest for the good life according to nature. The regime established here promised untrammeled freedom to reason" (p. 39).

Bloom actually proves my case, not his own, by these statements that clearly stem more from irrational patriotism than from historical knowledge, clear perception, or thoughtful analysis. These statements represent ignorance of the lives and perspectives of the lower and middle classes, Native Americans, African Americans, women, and immigrants, and to some degree even the ruling class—in short, the great majority of people in the United States, not to mention the rest of the world. With his extraordinarily powerful blinders, Bloom ignores those other lives and dismisses the possibility of other perspectives. But his statements also represent ignorance of many indisputable facts of American history concerning the treatment of those groups. They ignore the well-documented actions of presidents, Congress, the Supreme Court, and others. It even ignores well-documented but unflattering facts about people like George Washington and Benjamin Franklin. This is the kind of arrogant ignorance that easily leads to complacency and racism. Without alternative points of view, Bloom's cherished rationality is an empty exercise in circular reasoning and tautology in which we endlessly re-"prove" what we already know without ever questioning whether its underlying axioms are correct or whether they accurately measure the real world. We can't achieve Bloom's goals for education without exposing students to a broader range of ideas.

But if the market of ideas is to be "open," why should there have to be rules about curriculum inclusion in colleges? Part of the answer is that students will not naturally choose all the things that educators think necessary, and faculty will not independently chose to teach all those things, either, often for reasons quite unrelated to issues of quality or "academic freedom." Many English professors don't want to teach freshman composition courses, for example, for reasons that are hardly related to educational quality or issues of political coercion. It is hard, often frustrating work that most people don't want to do unless required. Adding new perspectives to courses is hard work, too, and many faculty members don't want to bother. So there need to be rules for the same reasons that major disciplines have lists of required courses and colleges have general education programs and English writing requirements. Colleges make lots of rules and set lots of standards about what must be taken, what must be taught, and what must be covered. Arguing that a rule about multicultural inclusion is an intolerable infringement of freedom ignores the reality of what goes on in colleges all the time. Such an argument involves a large degree of selective perception.

But, an additional reason for the curriculum inclusion rules is that, as any business person or economist knows, sometimes "free" markets have to be forced open before free competition can exist. The arena of curriculum design is one such market. We have spent more than two hundred years forcing other markets open around the world in the name of free enterprise, usually with military force or the threat of force—so the idea is hardly foreign or un-American. But in the case of curriculum inclusion the force that is being applied is merely the force of younger, broader scholarly opinion and peer pressure, the kind of force on which change ought to be based, rather than physical force or government edict.

The real manipulators in the curriculum struggle are not those who are arguing, sometimes loudly, that the market of ideas has to be forced open to include teaching about others or to allow work by women and minorities to compete. The real manipulators are those who quietly protect the monopoly of traditional cultural assumptions and traditional power groups while pretending to say nothing—or who argue that they have the "academic freedom" to ignore other people and works by or about women and minorities. Because curriculum inclusion operates as a kind of affirmative action for ideas, it is necessary for all the same reasons that affirmative action for people is necessary. Most of us cannot make "quality" judgments independent of our cultural blinders or the blinders of "race" or sex or class—at least not without being exposed to alternatives. The existing array of course offerings is heavily biased and needs to be expanded before we can make such judgments.

The whole point of the rules of liberal arts education, "general education," or "core curriculum" in any college is and always has been to *broaden* student exposure to the world and to ideas beyond what they study in more specialized courses and majors, or even in the elective courses they choose themselves. The theory is that students need to be good citizens with rich lives, not just trained employees, and they can't make good choices if they don't know what is out there.

In the modern world, "broadening student exposure" has to mean requiring students to have some awareness of the vast array of "others" who often do not figure in their thinking and have not traditionally figured in much of American education. It also means requiring students to become familiar with the fact that there are alternatives to our/their cultural assumptions. Do we want to "prepare" them for the real world without such knowledge? Is it even possible to do so?

Teaching general education without attention to other people and other cultures is like teaching the multiplication tables without mentioning the numbers 3 through 9. We can not teach the subject without including them, nor can we permit colleagues to do so. Omitting those numbers is not a matter of "academic freedom." The other people and other cultures I have referred to are undeniably part of the human "multiplication table." Now, more than ever, they are factors in our "equations" despite our previous tendency to ignore them. Those "others" have an undeniable stake not only in "our" politics, sociology, and economics but even in the reflections we see in art and literature; and we have an undeniable stake in understanding them.

Who is being political about education? Perhaps I should say, who is being politically correct? "Political correctness" has become a pejorative phrase, a put-down used to imply that unwarranted political pressure is being placed on a marketplace that would supposedly have no politics if left alone. The phrase is also used to imply that it is women and minorities and those on the left who have recently introduced political coercion into the "free" marketplace of ideas. But political manipulation of ideas and "political correctness" have long dominated our lives and pervaded our thinking in powerful ways. The only question has been whose political correctness would be tolerated. If traditional depictions of George Washington as a patriotic saint or descriptions of the United States as interested only in peace, justice, and freedom are not political, and politically correct in this larger sense, nothing is.

It is not political or politically correct to insist on teaching the entire multiplication table or all of the aspects of any issue. What is undeniably political is to insist on one's right to omit whatever portion of the table or whichever facets of the issue one cares to omit. It is also political to continue to omit a portion, in the face of undeniable new knowledge, just because one always has. Moreover, this issue does not become political just because it has now been put squarely on the table or brought to our collective consciousness. It has been political by omission and unspoken coercion for decades. It has, in fact, been all the more political because it was allowed to go unrecognized and unchallenged for so long while distorting our knowledge and teaching about American history, the world, and the human condition.

If women and minorities seem strident (or, in the favored pejorative word, "shrill") in their pressure for curriculum inclusion, we ought to remember an old principle from the theater: if you command center stage you can speak softly and be heard, but if you are forced to deliver your lines from the wings, you have to shout. It doesn't matter how reasoned your arguments or how accurate your facts if no one hears or is willing to listen. White males with traditional ideas still control the central stage of our discourse, and others have to shout to be heard at all—even though it may make them seem less dignified—not because of who they are but because of where they are forced to stand.

Teaching about other people and other cultures is one of the most important tasks our educational system can undertake (even as it teaches what mainstream American assumptions are). It should be among the first things on the educational list, not the last (or omitted altogether, if conservatives have their way). We say we want students to learn to think; but they can't do so if they are taught only established "truth" or even established, inviolate standards of greatness. What is worse, they cannot be taught as established "truth" what their own instincts and intelligence tell them is arbitrary convention, much of which violates common sense and real-life experience. How seriously can any thinking person take a George Washington who never lies, is always noble, and never acts like any real person? Even young white children can't relate to that role model.

CHAPTER EIGHT

Transforming the Culture of Intolerance

IT HAS BECOME COMMONPLACE for some politicians and even some scholars to express concern that the United States is heading toward a future of extreme social stratification. They foresee increasing class distinctions involving a growing economic, social, and political gap between the rich and the poor and more poverty and hardship for those at the bottom of the social ladder, inevitably accompanied by increasing tension between groups and between "races." But much of that stratification has already occurred. As I have pointed out, the wealthiest Americans already enjoy property and incomes that are thousands of times larger than even those with moderate salaries can earn or amass and millions of times what the poor can earn or save. This disparity is a major factor in contemporary social strains. In particular, tensions between the lower and middle classes result from the fact that they are fighting for shares of a very small portion of the economic pie.

More important, these gloomy predictions of the future misstate the causes of the trend toward increasing stratification. In *The Bell Curve*, Richard J. Herrnstein and Charles Murray suggest that it will happen because natural, genetic superiority (primarily within the European "race" and the Asian "race") will rise inexorably to the top now that we have supposedly removed the barriers to the recognition of natural merit. More liberal scenarios bemoan the discrimination that still exists, the effects of growing up in poverty, and the weaknesses in our educational system, including the lack of high-tech education for American workers—all of which are real enough.

But both explanations miss the point badly. *The trend will occur— has occurred—because our arbitrary and very narrow system of economic, social, and political assumptions makes it inevitable.* It will happen also because too many people are happy to have others excluded from the pursuit of success. It will happen because, despite professed ideals, there is too little commitment to equal opportunity and racial justice and the well-being of all of our residents. Too few people are willing to sacrifice even a little personal freedom and privilege to help bring about change for the better. The reality and the ideal in American culture are very far apart.

It will happen because society does not demand that wealth be shared or used for collective purposes, even though society itself generates, protects, and preserves that wealth. No private individual, no matter how "intelligent," could generate or preserve such wealth without society's massive assistance. The prediction will come true also because society, led by the wealthy and the money managers, has decided that only an extremely narrow range of human skills, those producing immediate profits in dollars in private hands, are worthy of reward. It will come true as a result of all the contemporary cost cutting and downsizing, outsourcing, contracting in, contracting out to people who will work for less and without benefits or job security—all to increase "efficiency" in the midst of large profits and enormous salaries for top executives. We are rapidly and purposely building the lower class. It will happen as a result of "getting government off our backs"—reducing government services, eliminating funding for the arts, schools, and social services, and so forth, all of which employ real people in addition to enriching our lives. Eliminating those services not only reduces the quality of life for all, it eliminates middle-level skilled jobs. It forces people who have chosen to serve human needs other than profit into menial jobs or unemployment. Other socially productive career choices become impossible. There is a great deal of talk about merit and meritocracy without the realization that ever narrower, increasingly arbitrary limits are being set on the kinds of merit that are rewarded (not to mention that most of us have only limited ability to judge actual merit as opposed to a candidate's preexisting ties or membership in a favored group). At the moment, the definition of rewardable merit leaves out an enormous number of skills and ignores an enormous number of tasks that need to be done in order to improve the quality of our lives—tasks that involve caring for and educating people, generating knowledge, promoting beauty, caring for the environment, ensuring the health and welfare of others, and improving the state of our communities. Many of those tasks are not being carried out now, and increasingly they will not be carried out in the future. But it will not be because "they can't be done" or because "there is no money for that," but because the society, despite its wealth, chooses not to see the needs, pay the costs, or reward the skills.

"It can't be done" in modern parlance usually means that no private company will undertake it because it provides no immediate, private, dollar profit. Or it means that no politician can see an angle of personal advantage, as if those things were synonymous with real need and real potential. "There is no money for that" usually means that there is no money in a particular narrow and arbitrarily defined budget category. Health, education, human needs, and the environment must compete for funds, but for the most part military spending does not (even "defense" spending grotesquely in excess of any conceivable need). Projections for the future suggest that the balance between the military and nonmilitary budgets will get worse.

To say that there is no money for a project also carries with it the unspoken assumption that it is not possible to reevaluate our tax strategy to tap the enormous private wealth—more than the rest of us have put together—that is in the hands of a relative few. Our society has great natural and capital resources; it has a near-infinite range of human and environmental needs, and it has a huge number of people who are capable of addressing at least some of those needs. Jobs that need doing have people waiting in vain to do them. If the society can't use its wealth to employ people to take care of those needs, something is wrong with our assumptions, not our capabilities. Societies with far fewer resources (societies that we dismiss as "primitive") have managed to provide meaningful roles and economic support for all their people and managed to keep them housed and reasonably well-nourished without destroying the environment. If they can, why can't we?

If members of minority groups are left behind, now and in the future, it will not be because they lack capabilities or intelligence; it will be because too many people with wealth and power are determined to leave them out. It will be because their very real skills (except in narrow channels like sports or music) are not recognized or cultivated and they are not provided with genuinely equal access to education, training, and employment or allowed to live in circumstances that encourage participation rather than withdrawal. At the moment minorities are being left behind as a matter of fairly deliberate policy, not inferiority. They are being left behind as a matter of age-old hatreds but also as a matter of ongoing affirmative action for white male Americans who fear that others will take their jobs. White males fear that they will be left out of what they perceive to be an ever decreasing economic pie unless they maintain their social advantage. It is assumed that any gain minorities make must come from fragile gains of lower-class and lower-middle-class white men and that any assistance given to minorities must come from those who are their most immediate competition.

The whites are right to fear that they, too, may soon be left out, and they are right to resent the assumption that benefits for minorities must come primarily at the expense of their jobs. But the minorities are not their enemies, and the danger of being left out is not because of minority competition. Nor is the pie really shrinking—the only thing that is shrinking is the portion of the pie shared by the bottom 90 percent of the population. Blacks do not need to be pitted against whites, and welfare recipients need not be pitted against the working poor, unless we assume that there must be very narrow artificial limits on opportunities and the wealth available to all.

If the gap between our society and the Third World continues to widen, it will not be because the people in those areas are naturally inferior or because their cultural systems are inferior or natural resources are in short supply. To a large extent it will reflect those countries' own political and economic inequalities that divert wealth from human needs. But, too often, it will be because of a colonial legacy and a postcolonial structure that continue to siphon off wealth while demanding the repayment of debts—incurred largely to remake those countries in the image demanded by the colonizers. When the colonial powers gave those areas back their "independence," they too often gave them back their social problems, exacerbated rather than solved by economic distortions and other problems resulting from colonialism; but they forgot to return their natural resources or sources of productive wealth, or they left such a burden of debt or permitted the wealth to be concentrated in so few hands (while proclaiming democracy) that the wealth cannot be used for social purposes. Too often independence was given to small cadres of people willing to play along with colonial desires in order to enhance their own wealth rather than finding solutions to their country's problems. Such willingness to accede to the West, far more than any theoretical commitment to freedom or democracy, is the reason for the American government's continuing approval and support of some regimes rather than others.

Sources of Intolerance

People of different cultures face somewhat different problems and, having their own values, they sometimes find different solutions to common problems. No culture has a monopoly on good solutions. The cultures of the world exhibit enormous behavioral variation, which has the capacity to enrich our lives, protect our common future, and increase the range of possible solutions to the vast array of human problems. In the long run, cultural variation, like genetic variation, is a major guarantee of the future success of the species. We should celebrate it and reinforce it, not denigrate it.

Intolerance and racism don't result from the genetic inadequacy of some people or even from biological differences between groups of people, except that the few visible differences provide an easy target for human tensions. Nor do they stem from other people's cultural inadequacy. They do, however, stem in large part from the nature of cultural systems and the cultural filters through which human beings view the world and one another. Much of the tension we see between populations attempting to live together results from misunderstanding of cultural differences and misinterpretation of their significance. People seem unable to comprehend other peoples' behavior—or even to perceive and measure it accurately when it violates the standard categories and expectations of their own culture. We fail to recognize that most problems can be approached in more than one way. People on all sides are unable to recognize what is arbitrary and conventional in their own behaviors and beliefs. Cultures not only blind their members to alternatives but also actively foster chauvinism and intolerance as a way of reinforcing group identity. In the ancient world, in which each group was economically independent and relatively homogeneous—when societies and cultures had the same boundaries, faced only a limited number of neighbors, and had only limited weapons—such chauvinism may have been valuable. In the modern world of multicultural states, interdependence, rapid transportation, international communication, and weapons of mass destruction, such chauvinism is extremely dangerous.

American culture (like most) makes it difficult to recognize the value of others. There is a "natural" but irrational tendency to assume that our own culture is superior, not just in particular areas or for particular purposes where it may actually, if temporarily, excel, but in any and all ways. Intolerance is reinforced by a lack of positive exposure to, or education about, other people and their cultures, a lack that in turn reflects the very narrow limits of our system of education. "World" and American history are too often taught without regard for the successes and contributions of others, including minorities, and with a blinding disregard for the errors and shortcomings among our own very real successes.

Intolerance also results from the fact that many Americans, like members of other cultures, have a dangerous and anachronistic need to distinguish themselves from others as the chosen people with a manifest destiny. Our intolerance results from failure to perceive that there are alternative ways of doing things, alternative valid sets of beliefs and goals, and from the assumption that our culture is naturally superior to all others.

Intolerance results from the strong need felt by people subject to discrimination to define themselves as different and to defend themselves against the loss of identity that threatens all colonized peoples. Many of the distinctive behaviors of American minorities, particularly those that are "captives" or involuntary minorities, represent reactions to intolerance and hatred. Similarly, the nativist cultural revitalization movements—revolutions against modernization and Westernization which are often explicitly anti-American—occurring in recent years in many countries, including Iran and Turkey, are in part a reaction to American intolerance vis-à-vis other world cultures. These movements reject the idea that people must become Westernized or even Americanized in order to share the fruits of the modern world—or even if they don't care to share them. They resent the fact that so much of the space and wealth of their own countries is structured to serve Western needs. The movements also reflect the realization of a significant portion of the populations of those countries that no matter how "Western" they become, Western powers are not going to allow them full and equal access to the world's riches or even to world citizenship. The policy of the United States—to counter such resistance with coercion—confuses cause and effect and makes the problems worse. Reducing intolerance and permitting people the freedom to enjoy their own culture along with real access to the benefits of the world system will reduce the resistance.

Of course, intolerance and resistance are reciprocal. To some extent minorities would be more accepted into the mainstream if they expressed less hostility or were less determined to be separate and different. Similarly, it would be easier for many Americans to tolerate and appreciate Third World populations if these peoples expressed less hostility toward the United States. Resistance, hostility, and intolerance feed each other. But we can't reasonably expect the poor of the world who possess the least and have the greatest cause for fear and anger to initiate better relations; those in power have to start the trend. They have to "prime the pump"—and allow a reasonable period of time, perhaps several *generations*, for the priming to produce results.

Intolerance grows out of the need to find scapegoats. No cognitive system, no system of values, including our own, produces all the gratification everyone might wish. But culture demands that we not lose faith in the rules or the system itself. So we find reasons why the rules didn't work in a particular case, places to put the blame—on luck or witches, or, often, on other people, women or blacks or homosexuals or Jews, or, more recently, on Iraqis or Iranians. Scapegoats are safety valves for the cultural system against the pressure of disappointment. And, of course, leaders who have a particular stake in maintaining the status quo and avoiding an explosion of discontent have a particular interest in deflecting blame, so they encourage the pursuit of scapegoats or identify scapegoats to justify their own initiatives. Going to war helps relieve social tensions at home. (We have reached the stage in the United States where radio and television commentators can discuss—in matter-of-fact-tones—the possibility or even probability that a certain war was started at least in part to get a particular president reelected, to boost his popularity, or to prop up his administration.)

Intolerance increases because our leaders exploit narrow self-interests to play groups off against each other rather than taking the lead in promoting mutual understanding. In the United States leaders have played off whites against Native Americans, African Americans, Chinese, Japanese, Irish, Jews, and Hispanics; north versus south; rural versus urban. They have played off immigrants against those already here; men against women; the middle class against the lower class; and, most recently, the working poor against the welfare poor. They have even discouraged these groups' efforts to coexist and work out their differences.

Racism and the resistance of minorities in the United States stems from the fact that our culture and law set arbitrary, legalistic definitions of correct conduct and make interpretations of the law that are often skewed to benefit the powerful, as a substitute for common sense, human decency, good judgment, and good will. The government then enforces the laws unevenly in a manner heavily slanted to serve upper-class interests. The resistance and occasional lawlessness of minorities stems in large part from their accurate perception that the laws do not serve them.

Intolerance also grows out of setting arbitrarily narrow hurdles to full participation in society such as IQ tests and white, male styles of performance and referring to them, very unscientifically, as tests of innate ability and as measures of inherent quality. At the same time, the conduct of white males too often is permitted to fall far below the stated standards and far below what the standards would be if there were open competition for jobs. Members of minority groups accurately perceive the distinction between stated rules and standards and the application of those standards, and, not surprisingly, they resent it.

Intolerance comes from employment practices that favor the in-group, the rich, and the powerful, creating the inequality in performance which is then measured to justify the status quo. Intolerance thrives because it acts as affirmative action for the group in power, limiting competition and promoting the educational and career chances of people in the mainstream. The need for government-sanctioned affirmative action results not primarily from the legacy of slavery or past discrimination, but from the narrow monopoly of opportunity that these conditions created and still maintain.

Intolerance also grows out of guilt, as Albert Memmi has said. If one believes that enslaving other human beings or treating them unfairly is intolerable, but slaves or poor people are needed to work plantations or menial jobs, one finds people who can be defined as not quite human to be enslaved or demeaned—and then one proceeds to make them appear (and even become) as inhuman as possible. If one is a European (or any other) colonizer in Africa or elsewhere and has absorbed democratic principles from a European education or any other, how does one explain one's automatic privilege as a European in the colony except by defining the natives as inherently inferior or even subhuman? And if one is a white American man whose success has been built on such exploitation (or merely on the exclusion of women and minorities), how does one justify one's privilege except by racism, sexism, and the results of IQ tests, which appear to prove what people "know in their hearts" must be true—that other people really are inferior?

Intolerance results from the fact that every "interracial" encounter in American society carries with it the fear and tension of previous encounters, real and imagined. It's hard to find a member of the "other" group ready to meet you as an individual and potential friend, so the problem is self-perpetuating. Part of the solution is to put people in positions where they can get to know each other as people.

All societies, and particularly all civilizations—very large, complex organizations of heterogeneous groups of people, divided into social classes and held together by power—generate or have generated many of these same tensions. But certain American cultural beliefs compound the problem. Intolerance resides not just in individuals or political pressures but in the fabric of American culture, that structure that is instilled in us so early in our lives. Intolerance results from adhering to an arbitrary cultural code we are unwilling even to think about, much less to question. We live in a society whose conventional cultural rules actively create intolerance. Conventional racial beliefs are obviously part of the problem, but I am specifically referring to cultural ways of thinking that lie at the very core of our society—which few people associate with "race." For example, we insist that things and people must be ranked in a linear order. There has to be a top and a bottom, a winner and a loser, even though most human processes do not have such zero-sum outcomes. We have to act and be measured as individuals, although that is not really the way most human processes operate, either. We insist that it is our manifest destiny to race ahead toward some goal which no one can define. Intolerance results from the fashionable emphasis on being "number one" without regard for others or the community. We want to be number one, even if often it is not clear what being number one means. We want to "grow" economically, although it is not clear what growth accomplishes, either. We want to identify "losers" and dominate them.

Most Americans are taught arbitrary and often extreme values and rules about things like freedom and property and the profit motive which get in the way of finding solutions to human problems. These rules produce economic pressures that undermine job security and wage scales for large segments of the population, leading to intolerance and racism. These values and rules often are presented as if they are beyond examination, reevaluation, or adjustment.

And, there is the principle of limited good, which says that there is a fixed and limited supply of good things in the world, whether land, water, wealth, success, health, or even happiness. So, if you get more, I have to get less. I have to resent your success for fear that you are somehow getting what should be mine. This way of thinking characterizes many Americans' outlooks, despite the realities of economic growth, just as it does "primitive" peasants', and it contributes to our intolerance. The idea that affirmative action for minorities and women must take jobs from white males is a good example of the image of limited good in action. So are the resentments toward blacks or Irish or Chinese immigrants who appeared to be taking "our" jobs—a pattern as old as American history.

But, particularly in the context of economic growth, the good doesn't have to be limited (at least in the relatively short period that concerns us), and educated people are supposed to have advanced beyond that point in their thinking. The whole point of economic growth, presumably, is so that there are more goods to go around. And our wealth is growing rapidly, yet the division of the spoils makes "limited good" a reality for most of our population even as we are bombarded with images of affluence and consumerism. But, of course, it is intolerance of one another which keeps those who are not rich from pursuing our common goals through unity in democratic processes, such as voting for changes in the economic rules that affect us. And therein lies much of the latent power of our intolerance—it is a major weapon in defense of the excessive privilege of the upper class.

Finally, problems are generated or maintained by our limited perceptions and narrow assumptions as citizens. As in any culture, it is hard to contemplate or even recognize solutions that fall outside the closed circle of preexisting thought. Part of the problem is that portions of the American public seem unable or at least unwilling to think about issues of any complexity, to explore new ideas, or to move out of areas of thought that are comfortably familiar. Supporters of intelligence testing would undoubtedly say that this proves that those people are of inherently inferior intelligence. I don't think so. It is true that many people don't learn as children to deal with the subtleties and complexities of issues in the mainstream culture or to explore new ideas. They don't learn to deal with such issues at least partly because their parents never did. It's a matter of learning where and how to focus one's intelligence and a matter of practicing, beginning in childhood. Ignorance and insensitivity perpetuate themselves in families, but not primarily (if at all) for genetic reasons. (This is one of the ways in which affirmative action for parents would help improve the skills of their children, producing benefits in the next generation.)

But the ideas that the mainstream culture offers to families tend to make the problems worse, not better. The media bombard people with messages about being number one, as if nothing else mattered. The popular media—movies, television, advertising, music, magazines—teach us that violence is the path to glamour and success. They teach that money, profit, and material goods are all that matter: basketball shoes, not the ideas in people's heads, the cultural or natural beauty around them, not even the other people in their lives. And it teaches them that the ways to get ahead are magical or simpleminded, or associated with the use of a particular product; or they teach that getting ahead involves the one-in-a-million shot of the lottery or stardom, not the far more common pathway of productive diligence.

Our culture also teaches children that school is a waste of time. Over and over, in movies and television shows and popular music, school is portrayed as a distraction from real life in which fools purvey ritual knowledge that no one needs to know. The idea that school provides practice in mental skills that can be recombined for later use is completely lost. But that message is also conveyed more widely through the disdain with which many Americans collectively hold teachers and schools. Our system of allocating resources tells students that the wisdom we learn through schooling is not valued by the society. From the condition of school buildings, it is clear that what goes on there is not as important as selling stocks and bonds or even selling shoes or cosmetics. And the message is conveyed by allowing so much of the curriculum to be taught so poorly. If the size of the classroom makes no difference, if one teacher can teach (or baby-sit) any number of students, that is a clear signal that what happens in the classroom doesn't count. The fact that the unionized

seniority rights or "academic freedom" of teachers appear to out-
weigh issues of competence or concern for students sends a similar
message.

Many Americans have also learned disdain for scholarly inquiry.
Conveying the real value of scholarship and knowledge itself also
requires some education of the citizenry. The public, and politicians,
too, need patience and imagination to appreciate the potential value
of research and scholarship. Scholarship is like the antennae of a
society, always needing to extend in all directions beyond the main
body of the society for exploration and protection, even if not every
scholar is reporting essential information at any given moment. But,
scholars, in turn, have to be far more willing than they often are to
relate their studies to human needs and to communicate their significance clearly.

The people also learn their ignorance directly from the media,
which actually undermine intelligent thought. They hear celebrities,
politicians, and even some scholars using words that are meaningless,
illogical, and obviously inaccurate (in a large sense, not in the sense
of minor grammatical errors) in the context in which they are used.
They hear words deliberately misused or stretched beyond their
meaning in order to mislead. They hear their leaders constantly making statements in "sound bites" designed to activate emotional "hot
buttons" in an audience rather than to stimulate thought. They hear
politicians debate ethics in such a partisan manner that ethical principles are entirely lost in a sea of political chatter. It is hard not to
come away with the impression that "unethical" means "whatever
the other guys do." The news comes in short clips that lack intellectual content; they are often rote recitals that are both patriotic and
chauvinistic instead of being critical, thoughtful, or insightful. Television fails to stretch the minds of even the least thoughtful viewers
and teaches such a simplified version of human experience that it
dulls perception and sensitivity. Viewers learn an oversimplified,
self-centered morality and an idea of logic and of human issues that
are utterly lacking in depth or subtlety. They then become impatient
with real-life problems that don't have quick and simple solutions.

Improving the System from Within

It does not have to take a revolution to change our cultural assumptions and our sociocultural system. Mindlessly defying or rejecting

the old system, as many protesters have done in recent decades, isn't the way to improve it. Revolutions are rarely very selective or accurate in identifying what to fix. The point is not that other lifestyles are "good" and ours is "bad." We can continue to revere our existing values—in fact, most of what I have written here is in defense of American values that need more of our honest attention. We need only to look more carefully at the balance among these values and to put more effort into some, like justice, equality, and even some important measures of real freedom that are getting only lip service now. We need to undertake thoughtful, selective reexamination of the ways we apply some of those values. We do not have to abandon belief in the right to individual initiative, profit, or private property. We don't have to live in a society so egalitarian that there is no incentive for people to be clever or creative. We don't have to embrace communism, although we ought to be able to examine it or any other social theory honestly to see what valuable lessons we might learn. We don't have to abandon the advantages of capitalism. We simply have to recognize the enormous debt capitalism owes to the social order in which it operates. We can soften capitalism by seeking a wiser, gentler form that pays attention to the needs of the community as it seeks its profits. We can allow profits but still limit or tax them to meet social needs. Capitalism has thrived in other times and places while providing more fully for the needs of the populace and without creating such a gap between rich and poor and such indifference to the poor. In fact, no other country in the industrial, capitalist world (including some with economies which have done as well as or better than ours in recent decades) has as great a gulf between rich and poor as we have come to consider natural and necessary. We certainly don't have to abandon our pride or our patriotism. What better way to be "number one" than to take world leadership as a society that is truly just and at peace and has a true balance of individual freedoms with community needs?

But if we ask those without wealth and power to be patient, thoughtful, and selective in their demands for change, we must first ask those with the wealth and power to be forthcoming in their offers of real reform. When one percent of the population controls nearly 40 percent of the wealth, there is enormous potential to bring wealth to bear on society's problems without forcing people into unemployment and poverty, without exploiting the Third World, without advancing the poor on the backs of the lower middle class, and without "soaking" the rich very severely. On the other hand, pretending that such wealth doesn't exist when discussing our social and financial problems simply generates cynicism and rage, as it should.

We can achieve a society with more freedom, equality of opportunity, and justice without cultural separation and also without cultural homogenization. We can be more varied, more multicultural, *and* more united, more efficient, and better educated if we comprehend the arbitrary nature of many of our cultural assumptions and if we tolerate the self-determination of others (within the limits of conformity and order that are truly necessary, not just conventions). We can learn to appreciate and perhaps adopt each other's wisdom as we have learned to appreciate and perhaps adopt each other's food. We also need to provide genuine (not just legalistic) fairness of opportunity, making equal participation possible.

Ideally, individual choices about how and where to contribute to the society and earn a living would be based on skills and inclination. Given free choice, people could choose their employment. Ethnic differences in patterns of participation might or might not emerge. We may find that members of certain groups gravitate toward certain professions, as Mohawk Indians in New York once gravitated toward high-rise construction, because those professions match experiences in their own culture and upbringing or reinforce their values. But individuals would be free not to follow the trend, and the patterns that emerge would reflect genuine choice, not options limited and funneled by lack of education or social pressures. They would emerge with less resentment and inhibition (perhaps none).

If the mainstream became more varied and more multicultural, people would be free to choose a style or to alternate between being mainstream Americans and enjoying their own ethnic patterns as well as those of other people. Many of us, particularly men who are white but with ethnic backgrounds, have become comfortable in the mainstream. We feel that the mainstream includes not only us but some of our heritage and some of the features of our ethnic cultures. We feel free either to practice or to ignore the traditions of our individual heritage and to share portions of that heritage with family and with friends (including friends who have different roots but who enjoy learning about ours).

We also feel free to express our ethnic heritage on the job. Our colleagues are familiar enough with each other's heritage that we can do this without endangering communication or team work. Our colleagues enjoy and benefit from our distinctive perceptions on the job. But they don't force us to play ethnic roles that we do not wish to adopt or to be ethnic at times we chose to focus on the common culture. We contribute to the quality of job performance and to the cultural and economic mainstream in our various individual ways, often enriched by our varied cultural heritage but without being constrained by it, and, most important, without being required by others to play the part. If we can maintain such tolerance (which is once again being threatened) and extend it to people who aren't "white" or who are female or gay, we will have a society in which everyone is more productive. Far more important, everyone can be assured of respect, dignity, and greater comfort.

Skin color and sex are, of course, more visible distinctions than ethnic heritage. However, many whites, myself included, have names that are almost as immediate a basis for stereotyping as color or sex and our names must be presented to others almost as immediately as our color; but, for the moment at least, we don't suffer the constant effects of stereotypes. The point is not that differences should be invisible or that people should be anonymous—quite the contrary; the point is to have friends and neighbors, members of one's community and one's nation, willing to accept one as a person even though they can see from your skin or your name that your roots are different from theirs. The same freedom that many white male "ethnics" now share should be extended to female, gay, and non-white individuals, people with disabilities—in fact, to all. But I know that we aren't there yet. People in other countries—and their traditional systems of values and behavior—should also be extended the same respect and the same basic rights and freedoms we extend ourselves. But I know we aren't there yet, either. It will require taking a good hard look at our values; and some of us, mostly those who have by far the most, will have to give up a little.

Greater tolerance and fairness have to come through learning and education. We can use our ability to understand the meaning of culture and society to tease apart the complex interrelationships among their various facets. We can separate the essential qualities and functions of our institutions from their cultural trimmings and from the myths and assumptions that surround them. We can learn how the pieces of a sociocultural system are related to one another and anticipate what will change or will have to be changed if we change one thing. In short, we no longer need to be blindly bound by the complex interrelationships among facets of culture that resist change or produce unanticipated results. We can begin to separate benefits from costs.

In a democracy, we count on an educated electorate to direct the views and actions of their elected representatives. We have to organize as voters to demand that politicians address the needs of the citizens and residents of the country as their first priority before the needs of special interests or their own wealth and reelection. We have to demand the reform of policies like lobbying laws that give enormous advantage to the rich. Each of us has to be willing to vote for something beyond his or her own individual immediate self-interest, recognizing common goals as well as the legitimate needs of others.

The solution to the problems is not merely to change the laws or government policies or the behavior of corporations—even if some of that is obviously necessary. We must also change how we look at and react to one another. Citizens, not just governments, have to change some of their ways. So education is a key—but not just formal education and certainly not just higher education. The education has to come through all our schools, textbooks, families, media, leaders, celebrities, each other.

To begin with, Americans have to stop *teaching* prejudice and hatred. Whatever "natural" or even cultural tendency people may have to prefer their own kind and fear "others" can clearly be redirected by formal and especially informal education. We do it all the time. Hated "others" become friends and allies when they are traded to our basketball team, move to our school, play different roles, become known as individuals, or become allies in fighting a particular battle or war. So the notion that our particular patterns of hatred are "natural" is just absurd, as well as being dangerous.

We have to construct situations in which people will be exposed to one another under conditions that make positive interaction possible and permit them to build mutual respect. We have to teach all Americans about other people's humanity, their successes, their real and potential contributions, and their rights and needs. We have to teach about the impact of poverty and racism on the human spirit. We have to celebrate real biological and cultural diversity to the full depth and meaning of "culture." And we have to be willing to think and teach about the imperfections of the mainstream culture, as well as about its great strengths and contributions. We have to be willing to teach the realities, not just the glories, of American history. We have to remember why it is important that we teach about people, their needs, their artistic creations, their environment, their history, and the working of their societies—not just about jobs—so we can remember the other purposes and pleasures in our lives and understand the larger consequence of our actions.

Americans have to teach one another to be committed to our society and all our neighbors, not just to our flag. We have to teach ourselves that community is as important a value as freedom is. We have to remind ourselves of the wide range of things societies must do and of the fact that the profit motive is not sufficient to get some of them done. We have to remind ourselves that there are other values besides profit; that people of other colors in other places have made substantial contributions to our contemporary success; that commitment to excellence not the privilege of our white, male American skins (or IQs) will get us ahead.

We have to teach the rich and powerful to recognize that luck, affirmative action, and enormous contributions from the society that nurtured them (often, but not always, accompanied by hard work and ability) got them where they are. We have to teach them that they have an obligation to society, an obligation that, like the wealth and the services society renders them, is greater than that of poorer people. And we have to demand, by law, that they honor that obligation far more than they do. It is the discrepancy between rich and poor, not the number of out-of-wedlock births, that is our biggest social problem. The assertion that possessing property entails no obligations to community (and the failure of the community to demand what it is owed) are the most dangerous kinds of extremism that we now face. We have to use our power as consumers, investors, and voters to direct the market in favor of corporations that meet standards of social responsibility. Capitalism can be driven by socially conscious consumers, the power of opinion, the investment choices people make, and the social and political education of investors. By boycotting Nestle, consumers managed at least temporarily to put a halt to the harmful dissemination of infant formula in the Third World. (But that experience suggests that vigilance has to be maintained.)

Education is a primary road to resolving many of these problems, and that education has to extend beyond the elite. If only the elite understand how things work, our solutions will always continue to serve their narrow interests. The current movement to devalue or eliminate public higher education will have exactly that result, whether or not it is part of the intended purpose of the movement.

But education is a more complex and difficult process than most people seem to understand. One cannot educate by throwing facts or even ideas in the general direction of lecture halls of six hundred people or television audiences or even captive groups of twenty-five of any age who are permitted to receive but not to react. "Efficiency" in money saved by forcing students to learn in ever larger groups is not efficiency in education.

Education is not about providing "truth," particularly since we cannot agree what truth is. Education involves students reacting to real problems and real options (appropriate to their age) and learning how to get along in groups. Students must see that most problems are not solved in a simple way (as they are on IQ tests), that knowledge usually comes in graded shades of "truth" that must be evaluated, not memorized, and that real-life problems have complicated solutions that take time to work out, require balancing many things, and demand wisdom and judgment. This is one reason why multicultural education is necessary: it supplies the context for discussing the kind of problems that can help shape productive, thinking citizens, not cheerleaders for Western civilization and the American way.

Education also means students realizing that they must be actors in determining solutions and truths. As I emphasized at the outset, it also means encouraging students constantly to probe "knowledge" for unspoken and perhaps unwarranted assumptions—which is what really makes people free. All of this demands interaction between teachers and students and among students, in small classes, with teachers who themselves are able to think about complex issues and who will tolerate their students' explorations. Technology can facilitate these processes if it is subservient to teaching and learning; but high-tech teaching designed to serve ever larger, passive audiences without creating challenging problems and interactive paths to solutions isn't education at all. Simply putting a lecture on tape or disk or television and letting a student push an "on" button at his or her leisure isn't education. It fosters convenience, not thought.

But the schools can't do the job alone. Proper education also requires a home and a nation that will invest in learning not only with their financial resources but with their expectations. Parents and citizens should demand genuine education from teachers but also prepare students to accept their responsibilities. Most students don't know what they are supposed to contribute to the process, and we don't tell them until they are sitting in a college classroom, if ever.

We also need to communicate a sense of mutual interdependence and community responsibility in our homes, our churches, our political events, and our media. Our politicians and our media could be helping parents and teachers to raise standards of thought and tolerance. We can teach better values through television and radio by molding the choice and content of programming. We can use the power of advertising to suggest that high-quality teachers, clean streets, decent housing, health and nutrition, beautiful parks, dedicated care for children and the elderly, and many other values are as important and as worthy a "purchase" as the latest basketball shoes. But we seem unwilling to invest in the quality of our lives, because it doesn't provide any "profit" in the narrow sense— or perhaps because our leaders fear the power of an educated, thinking electorate.

A massive effort has to be made to feed, clothe, educate, and provide medical care for the poor. The effort will involve a commitment by government, which is the only institution that can undertake it on the scale and for the length of time (perhaps two generations) that is needed. The solution may well mean revising welfare "as we know it," but the revision cannot be one that begins and ends with a desire to "cut costs" and take even more money away, that denies social responsibility, or that sneers at the recipients of its own assistance. The costs do not have to be borne by the middle class. They can be paid by levying a reasonable tax on the very wealthy individuals who control the great bulk of our resources. We might begin simply by rescinding the Reagan tax breaks to the rich and more recent tax breaks.

The most important thing about a democratic society or state is that it represents the interests of its people, rather than the government having an agenda of its own which is at odds with their welfare. (The latter has been the norm throughout most of human history, as I pointed out in chapter 3.) We have to insist that "growth" and "efficiency" be used to serve people. The purpose of money is to lubricate social and economic interactions among people, to buffer them against shortage, and to enable them to lead decent lives. We have lost track of this goal to the point where our notion of economic efficiency is directly opposed to preserving the quality of American lives. When are Americans going to realize that the people who lose their jobs as companies are downsized to produce tiny increments of efficiency and savings are their friends, relatives, neighbors, the people they depend on, and ultimately themselves. When are they going to realize that those people who look a little different are biologically as similar to them as they are to one another and—more important—could be their friends and allies?

By various estimates one-fifth to one-quarter of all American children are born into poverty, while a tiny fraction of the population controls the vast majority of the wealth; racism and hatred of other people are rampant; more Americans proportionally are in jail than are people in any other Western industrial country; more wealth is devoted to militarism than in any other Western country; schools are decaying, colleges and hospitals closing, while prisons are being built. Is our system, then, so perfect (or so brittle?) that it does not dare to examine its conventional assumptions? The slogan does not have to be "America—love it or leave it," as bumper stickers sneered a few years ago. The slogan can be instead: "America—love it and improve it." We have to help our country live up to its own high ideals.

Suggested Reading

The following bibliography is not intended to be exhaustive. Rather, it lists works that express, explain, or summarize certain aspects of my arguments particularly well or contain cited material. Most have been chosen also because they are readily comprehensible to a lay reader.

Bodley, John. 1990. *Victims of Progress*. Mountain View, Calif.: Mayfield.

Bohannan, Laura. 1966. "Shakespeare in the Bush." *Natural History* (August–September).

Brown, Donald. 1991. *Human Universals*. Philadelphia: Temple University Press.

Cavalli-Sforza, Luigi, and Francesco Cavalli-Sforza. 1995. *The Great Human Diasporas: The History of Diversity and Evolution*. Reading, Mass.: Addison-Wesley.

Chomsky, Noam. 1985. *Turning the Tide*. Boston: South End Press.

———. 1991. *Deterring Democracy*. London: Verso.

Cohen, Mark. 1989. *Health and the Rise of Civilization*. New Haven: Yale University Press.

Cole, Michael, John Gay, Joseph A. Glick, and Donald W. Sharp. 1971. *The Cultural Context of Learning and Thinking*. New York: Basic Books.

Cole, Michael, and Sylvia Scribner. 1974. *Culture and Thought*. New York: Wiley.

Dawkins, Richard. 1976. *The Selfish Gene*. Oxford: Oxford University Press.

DeMott, Benjamin. 1995. *The Trouble with Friendship*. New York: Atlantic Monthly Press.

Desowitz, Robert. 1981. *New Guinea Tapeworms and Jewish Grandmothers*. New York: Norton.

Dettwyler, Katherine. 1994. *Dancing Skeletons*. Prospect Heights, Ill.: Waveland Press.

Ember, Carol, and Melvin Ember. 1995. *Cultural Anthropology*. 8th ed. Englewood Cliffs, N.J.: Prentice-Hall.

Erikson, Erik. 1963. *Childhood and Society*. New York: Norton.

Fanon, Frantz. 1963. *Wretched of the Earth.* New York: Grove.

Foner, Eric. 1988. *Reconstruction: America's Unfinished Revolution.* New York: Harper and Row.

Fraser, Steven (ed.). 1995. *The Bell Curve Wars.* New York: Basic Books.

Frisancho, A. R. 1993. *Human Adaptation and Accommodation.* Ann Arbor: University of Michigan Press.

Gentry, Curt. 1991. *J. Edgar Hoover: The Man and His Secrets.* New York: Plume.

George, Susan. 1977. *How the Other Half Dies: The Real Reason for World Hunger.* Montclair, N.J.: Allenheld, Osmun.

Gordon, Daniel. 1991. "Female Circumcision and Genital Operations in Egypt and the Sudan: A Dilemma for Medical Anthropology." *Medical Anthropology Quarterly* 5:3–28.

Gould, Stephen Jay. 1993. *The Mismeasure of Man.* 2d ed. New York: Norton.

Hardin, Garrett. 1968. "The Tragedy of the Commons." *Science* 162:1243–1248.

Harris, Marvin. 1997. *Culture, People, Nature.* 7th ed. White Plains, N.Y.: Longman.

Heath, Shirley Brice. 1983. *Ways with Words.* Cambridge: Cambridge University Press.

Jacoby, Russell, and Naomi Glauberman (eds.). 1995. *The Bell Curve Debate.* New York: Times Books.

Kappler, Victor, Mark Blumberg, and Gary Potter. 1996. *The Mythology of Crime and Criminal Justice.* 2nd ed. Prospect Heights, Ill.: Waveland Press.

Kerbo, H. R. 1996. *Social Stratification and Inequality.* 3d ed. New York: McGraw-Hill.

Lee, R. B. 1969. "Eating Christmas in the Kalahari." *Natural History* 78:10.

Loewen, James W. 1995. *Lies My Teacher Told Me.* New York: The New Press.

Marks, Jonathan. 1995. *Human Biodiversity: Genes, Race, and History.* New York. Aldine de Gruyter.

Memmi, Albert. 1991 (1965). *The Colonizer and the Colonized.* Boston: Beacon.

Mitford, Jessica. 1993. *The American Way of Birth.* New York: Plume.

Morison, S. Eliot. 1965. *The Oxford History of the American People.* New York: Oxford University Press.

Moyers, Bill. 1987. *The Secret Government.* WNET Public Affairs Television.

National Geographic. 1920–present. (Scattered miscellaneous portraits of indigenous people from around the world.)

Ogbu, John. 1991. "Immigrant and Involuntary Minorities in Comparative Perspective." In *Minority Status and Schooling: A Comparative Study of Immigrants and Involuntary Minorities,* ed. Margaret A. Gibson and John U. Ogbu, 3–33. New York: Garland.

Relethford, John. 1996. *The Human Species.* 3d ed. Mountain View, Calif.: Mayfield.

Rich, Bruce. 1994. *Mortgaging the Earth.* Boston: Beacon.

Robbins, Richard H. 1993. *Cultural Anthropology: A Problem-Oriented Approach.* Itaska, Ill.: Peacock.

Sacks, Karen. 1994. "How Did Jews Become White Folks." In *Race,* ed. Roger Sanjek and Steven Gregory, pp. 78–102. New Brunswick, N.J.: Rutgers University Press.

Sharpe, Lauriston. 1952. "Steel Axes for Stone Age Australians." In *Human Problems in Technological Change*, ed. E. H. Spicer. New York: Russell Sage.

Turner, Victor. 1967. "A Ndembu Doctor in Practice." In *Forest of Symbols.* Ithaca: Cornell University Press.

U.S. Commerce Department. (Annual). *Statistical Abstract of the United States.* Washington D.C.: Bureau of the Census.

Weiss, Kenneth M. 1993. *Genetic Diversity and Human Disease.* New York: Cambridge University Press.

Zinn, Howard. 1995. *A People's History of the United States.* 2d. ed. New York: Harper Perennial.

Index

Aboriginals, Australian, 78, 82, 97–98, 103, 225

Abortion, 120, 124, 201

Adaptation, human biological, to environmental variation, 31–37

Affirmative action, 207, 246, 252–81, 290, 296, 300, 303; and efficiency, 253; and laissez-faire, 254, 269; equality of, 254–55; and past sins, 255–56; and ongoing discrimination, 256–57; compared to tariffs, 257–60; affects quality of performance, 257–60, 270–73; for the wealthy, 260–64; and selection of leaders, 260–61; improves performance in occupations, 271–73; in education, 263–64, 267–69; for middle-class white males, 264–67, 277–78; history/racism/sexism/ IQ tests act as de facto, 265–69; and college admissions, 270–71; and African-American poor, 275–77; as scapegoat, 278–79; as responsibility of wealthy, 279–81; for ideas, 281

African Americans: history and politics, 2, 12, 50–51, 84, 85–86, 95, 145, 155–56, 187, 190, 284–85, 299–300; biology and health, 22–23, 38–39, 45; and IQ, 217, 232–33, 238–43, 246; affirmative action and, 254, 262–65, 270–71, 275–77

Africans: biology of, 18, 23, 32–33, 44–48; cultural variety of, 72, 75, 77, 85; sociopolitical affairs, 178–80; work styles, 248–49

AIDS, 15, 28, 93, 107, 151, 177

American aggression, 126, 144–46, 158, 170–71, 178–79, 182, 185–89, 296–97

American culture, 1–8 passim, 54–55, 60–78 passim, 82–87, 97–130 passim; arbitrary nature of, 134–37; medicine in, 137–42; and public health, 141–42; and freedom, 142–59; and property, 159–65; and taxes, 165–68; and profit, 168–72; and efficiency, 172–74; and growth, 175–76; and progress, 175–80; and colonies, 178–80; and manifest destiny, 182–88; and militarism, 188–89; and equality, 189–92, 204; and justice, 192–203; and law, 193–203; and cognition, 215; cognitive patterns affect IQ tests, 212–38; affect performance, 238–46; on the job, 247–51; and affirmative action, 252–81; and curriculum inclusion, 281–92; and intolerance, 297–303; and the future, 304–10

American education, 64–65, 67, 80–81, 86, 102, 107–8, 131, 143, 151, 182–83, 281–92, 303, 309–10

American flag symbolism, 104–5

American health, 22–23, 32–41, 137–42, 176–78

American history: in nineteenth century, 3–4, 64–65, 155–56, 158, 176–78, 182–83, 189–90, 284–85; in twentieth century, 3–4, 104–5, 133, 158, 171–72, 176–77, 256, 261, 263–64, 284–85, 299–301; precolonial, 47,

American history (continued)
60–61, 64–65, 78, 176, 182–83, 190;
colonial history, 183–88, 190
American social classes, 1, 3, 145, 156, 165–
67, 189–92, 204, 216, 238–43, 278–79, 280–
81, 298–312 passim
American tragedy, 1–10
American Way of Birth, 140
Analogies: between culture and language, 67–
74; and thinking, 96–97; problems based
on, 226–29, 233–34; and skills, 248–50
Anthropology, 11, 44, 46, 62–77 passim, 86,
88, 99, 101, 109–110, 111–27 passim, 134,
191, 241–46 passim, 264–65
Asians, 210, 242–43
Assumptions: American, 1, 7–8, 62, 85–86,
134–203, 217–37, 294; nature of, 1–8; and
education, 6, 73–74, 287–88; of culture, 7,
73–74, 88, 95–96, 107, 118–19; about race,
41; of limited good, 99; about efficiency,
172–74; about intelligence, 204–37; in IQ
tests, 217–37; and job performance, 247–
51; and affirmative action, 252–81; about
wealth, 160–72, 278–81; and curriculum
inclusion, 281–92; about quality, 287–88;
as obstacles to solving problems, 294

Behavior: and sociobiology, 51–56
Bell Curve, The, 3–4, 98, 204–10, 226, 232–
34, 239–40, 247, 293
Binet, Alfred, 216
Blinders: cultural, 8, 48–49, 50–51, 109, 111,
145, 165–66
Bloom, Allan, 4, 111, 186–87, 288
Body language, 80, 250
Brain: genetic and environmental factors in
development, 56–59, 204–13
Breast-feeding: in third world, 19, 139; and
fertility, 19, 139; and health, 39, 139–40;
cultural barriers to, in U.S., 101, 139–40;
and IQ, 139, 209–10
Breast fetish, 140
Burns, Ken, 285
Bush, George, 142, 261, 275

Cancer, 15, 22, 28, 33–35, 39, 92, 94, 139,
151, 177
Capitalism, 146, 147, 154–55, 159–75, 178–
81, 293–97, 304–12 passim
Captive minorities, 243–44
Categories: as basis for logic, 95–97, 226–29
Chase Manhattan Bank, 158

Chauvinism, 3–4, 85, 104, 136–37, 182, 205–
6, 287–90, 297
Chief: as leadership style, 71, 76, 168
Childhood and Society, 187
Children: genetics and development, 16–20,
23–25, 27–28, 30–31, 36, 39, 51, 53; and
IQ, 56–59, 206–12, 216, 221–44;
socialization of, 68–70, 84–85, 86, 96–97,
107–8, 115, 131, 151, 169, 172, 184–85,
187, 200, 236–44, 248–50, 287, 291, 303,
310–11; circumcision, 119–23; infancy,
139, 141; deaths in orphanages, 178
Chosen People myth, 103, 182, 298. *See also*
Manifest destiny
Christianity: right-wing, 2
CIA, 158, 261
Circumcision: male, 120; female, 120–23; as
test of relativism, 120–23
Civilization: and natural selection, 28; and
disease, 28, 92–93, 176–78; and quality of
life, 28, 92–93, 113, 178, 181; evolution of,
61, 183; as organization, 63, 149, 195–97;
demand on resources, 126; and freedom,
149–50; obligations of, 180–81
Civil rights, 156–57, 259
Civil War, 158, 190, 285
Civil War, The, 285
Class: pitted against, 3, 166–67, 190–91, 295–
96; justified, 3, 204–8; building the lower,
4, 170–71, 293–96; and health, 18, 176–78;
maintained, 107–9; denied, 144, 189–90;
and taxes, 165–68; and U.S. history, 184–
92; benefits of, 191–92; versus justice,
power, and law, 192–203; and IQ, 207–46
Classics, 66, 83, 136, 182, 228, 281–88
Classification: racial, 11–13, 19, 41–51, 212;
cognitive, 95–97, 226–29, 232–34
Closing of the American Mind, The, 4, 288
Cognition: defined, 90–91, 95–96; imperfect,
95, 206; and world view, 97–99;
socialization for, 102, 249–50; and latent
functions, 105–9; expanding American,
136–47; cross-cultural misunderstanding,
77–86, 90–97, 145–46, 233–34; and g, 214–
15, 233–34; "deficits" and advantages in,
233–34, 246, 253
College admissions: and affirmative action,
270–73
Colonialism: impact of, 55, 62, 63, 72, 116–
17, 124, 144, 179–80, 296–97, 298, 300;
defined, 183–84; in America, 183–88;
effects on participants, 186–87, 277

Colonizer and the Colonized, 186
Communication: barriers to, 61, 92;
    conventional nature of, 63, 67–70,
    71–72, 80–81, 131, 250–51; drawings
    and IQ tests, 81, 221–23, 230; art as,
    81–82; socialization in, 102, 131, 208,
    249
Communism: family, 115; primitive, 115;
    in the U.S., 144, 153; in Cuba, 144
Community: as environment for individual,
    4, 276; vis-à-vis the state, 86, 102; change
    and dislocation of, 116–26; balanced
    against freedom, 148–55; balanced against
    wealth and profit, 163–72, 192, 309; and
    law, 193–203; disadvantaged, 241–43, 275–
    77; and affirmative action, 252–81;
    freedom and responsibility within, 306–12;
    need to teach, 306–12
Confidence: and health, 94–95; of investors,
    158; and test performance, 234–35, 237
Conformity, 103, 130–33, 135, 143, 245
Congress (U.S.), 105–6, 152, 171, 258, 261
Conservatives, 11, 150, 156–57, 198, 204–5,
    275, 281–85
Constitution (U.S.), 104, 129, 130, 147, 152,
    184, 190, 193, 200, 202, 258
Consumers, 89, 157, 168–70, 258, 309
Core curriculum, 283–86
Corporations: and profit motive, 2; as future
    rulers, 4; multinational as a society of
    their own, 63; served by war, 105;
    bargaining with false representatives of a
    society, 116–17; lobbyists manipulate
    market, 146; aided by laissez-faire, 147;
    and free speech, 154–55; aided by
    government, 158, 257–59; loyalty to
    workers, 164–65, 169–70; fostering
    competition between workers, 278–79;
    Nestle boycott, 309
Cost of living: increase estimated, 167–68
Costs to society: of development, 118–19; of
    departing corporations, 164–65; of
    corporate greed, 170–71; of "efficiency,"
    172–74; to health by "progress," 176–78;
    of colonialism, 178–81; of welfare fraud,
    200; of loss of creativity, 245; of excessive
    standardization, 250–51; of poverty, 253;
    of tariffs, 258–59; of narrow job
    descriptions, 271–73
Covert action by the United States, 158
Creation: and human variation, 44;
    described by other cultures, 97–98

Creationism: and free speech, 153–54
Crime, 120, 174, 198–200, 204, 207, 260, 262
Cuba, 144
Cuisine: ethnic, 136; as social boundary, 75–
    76
Cultural assumptions, 4–8
Cultural blinders, 8, 44, 109–10, 111, 144–
    45, 165–66
Cultural relativism: 111–33; defined, 111–12;
    success of other cultures, 113–15; and
    health, 114; and styles of exchange, 115;
    recognizing latent purpose, 116–17;
    unexpected effects of change, 118–19;
    purposeful change, 119–26; morality, 126–
    30, 132–33; conformity, 130–33; and
    golden rule, 131–32
Culture, 7–8, 60–110; confused with
    biology, 1, 15–23, 51–59, 60; defined, 5, 7–
    8, 63–74; American, 6, 7, 8, 34–35, 54, 61,
    64–65, 134–203; assumptions of, 7–8, 54–
    55; of intolerance, 11–12, 19, 293–312;
    and sex roles, 51–52; and intelligence, 56–
    59; transmission, 58, 102, 211–12, 239–40;
    as system, 60–74; as barrier to
    understanding, 61, 292, 298, 301–12;
    constraints imposed by, 62, 66, 73–74;
    boundaries created by, 65–66; compared
    to language, 67–74; universals, 74–110;
    biological needs and, 74–75; dissected, 74–
    110; ownership and exchange, 76–78;
    decision making, 78–80; communication,
    80–83; translation, difficulties in, 71–74,
    78–79, 80–82, 84–85, 91–92; artistic
    expression, 83; supernatural, 83; roles and
    statuses, 83–87; deviance, 86–87; goals and
    values, 87–88; means, 88–89; perception,
    89–90; cognition, 90–97; structure of
    categories and analogies, 89–90, 95–97;
    health care, 92–95, 106–7; philosophy
    created, 97–99; creation stories, 97–98;
    controlling emotion, 99–101; regulating
    sex, 101–2; socialization in, 102, 281–92;
    loyalty demanded, 103–5; latent functions
    of, 105–6; and law, 192–203; of IQ tests,
    206–37; and test performance, 233–51;
    and job performance, 247–51; and
    affirmative action, 252–81
Culture of resistance, 243–44
Curriculum inclusion, 281–92; and
    educational quality, 281–83; and "core
    education," 283–89; and educational
    richness, 284–91; and cultural patriotism,

Curriculum inclusion (continued)
286–89; and thought, 286–89; opening the market, 289–92

Dancing Skeletons, 123
Dawkins, Richard, 52
Debt: of third world countries, 178–80, 296–97
Declaration of Independence, 190
Democracy, 203, 308; of small-scale societies, 78
DeMott, Benjamin, 147
Denny's restaurants, 257
Denying the Holocaust, 153
Desowitz, Robert, 118
Dettwyler, Katherine, 123
Development, economic, 119, 150, 176–81, 183
Developmental disabilities, 24, 39, 307
Discrimination: as energy drain, 62; disorientation caused, 103–4; and *The Bell Curve*, 204–6; effects on IQ test performance, 238–44; and affirmative action, 255–77, 260–69, 276; reaction to, 239
Diversity: as element of quality, 64–65, 130–33, 267–73, 282–84, 306–7
Domestic tranquillity: and affirmative action, 281
Downsizing, 294
Drawing conventions: and IQ tests, 224–26

Ebonics, 241
Economics: predictions, 1–4, 293–94; of small societies, fertility as asset in, 19, 123–25; social rules constraining, 74–78, 85, 116–19, 160–65; modern, as closed system, 91, 110; communism of families, 115; communism of small societies, 115; demand principle, 125–26; "free market," 146–47; government assistance, 158–59, 258–59, 262–63; profit, 161–71; obligations to society, 161–72; estimating cost of living adjustment, 167–68; "efficiency" in, 172–75; growth and progress, 175–79; and social class, 189–92; welfare fraud, 200; and affirmative action, 252–57, 262, 278–81
Edison, Thomas, 284–85
Education: multicultural, 66–67, 281–92, 308–10; in small societies, 97–98, 102–3, 196–97; latent functions of, 107–8; as an industry, 108; language, 131; and free speech, 153–54; and chauvinism, 182–88, 281–92; family, 237–39; discrimination in, 263–65; access to, 270–71; affirmative action in, 270–73; classical, 281–92; as part of the problem, 302–3; and curriculum inclusion, 281–92
Efficiency: analyzed, 172–74
Egalitarianism: in small-scale societies, 76, 78, 87–88, 160–63; American myth of, 189–92, 263
Electorate: power of, 309
Emotion: and health, 17, 86, 92–94; as defined by culture, 73, 82–83, 85, 86, 92–93, 99–101, 103–4, 124, 132, 135, 201; and test performance, 234, 237–43
Endorphins: and behavior, 51–52, 88
Environment: and disease, 15–23, 28–29, 38–41, 176–78, 181; and human variation, 15–23, 31–38, 46–50; and intelligence, 21, 56–59, 204–17, 237–44; and human evolution, 23–29; protection of, 97–98, 114, 147, 169, 173, 258, 295
Erikson, Erik, 187, 273
Ethnic cleansing, 112
Ethnocentrism, 60–61, 104, 136; *See also* chauvinism
Europeans: culture patterns, 19, 77–78, 79, 101; genetics, 33–39, 45–51; political dominion, 61, 78, 79; history, 78, 79, 82, 91, 98, 124, 176–87, 189–90, 209
Evolution: biological processes, 23–31, 42–44
Extremism, 135, 309

Family, 17, 19, 22–25, 29–30, 39, 53; of all humanity, 42–44; and intelligence, 56–59, 96–97, 204, 207–8, 211–12, 237–40; as social unit, 72, 77, 86–88, 101–2, 108, 115–25, 128–29, 137, 149, 159, 169; and success, 255, 260–61, 264, 265, 275, 285, 302–3
Fashion: limiting freedom, 1–4, 65, 104, 139–40, 143, 204
FBI, 199, 261
Fertility: biology of, 19; third world, 19, 124–25; nursing and, 139–40
Fetal development, 39–40, 140–41; aborted, 66, 119; and brain, 56–59; of twins, 211
Fitness: biological, 25–29, 32–37
Focus: affects IQ, 223, 232, 237–44
Foner, Eric, 156

Forbes, Steve, 261, 275
Force: defined by culture, 61–62, 72, 89; defines civilization, 62–64, 78; use by U.S., 156, 157–59, 170–71, 184–85, 188–89
Freedom: culture as limiting, 6–8, 11–12, 72–77, 84, 96, 111, 130–33, 142–59, 171–72, 245–56; as American fetish, 127, 142–43, 148–50, 301–2; legal, 130–33, 146–47; freedom from versus freedom to, 150–52; government as source of, 147–48; reciprocal nature of, 150; selective application of, 155–59; academic, 287–91, 303–4
Free market, 146–47
Free speech, 7–8, 152–55

Gates, Bill, 161–63, 167
Gays, 86–87, 95, 107, 231, 307
Gender: and sociobiology, 52, 55, 73; cultural definitions, 84–85, 100–101, 117–25, 143–44, 239; and infanticide, 119–20; and circumcision, 120–23; and math anxiety, 239; and affirmative action, 252–81; as valuable variety, 267–68, 271–73, 306–7
General education, 281–92
Genes: function, 15; interact with environment, 15–25; and behavior, 51–59; and intelligence, 56–59, 209–11; of brain, 56–59, 209–12
Germ theory, 93–94, 141, 229
Germ warfare, 112
GI Bill, 148, 264
Glass ceiling, 256
Golden Rule, 131–32
Gould, S. J., 212–16
Government: trend toward elimination, 1–2; defined, 63, 78–79; and freedoms, 130, 142–59; and wealth and profit, 163–72; law and justice administered, 192–203; and affirmative action, 252–81; and affirmative action for the wealthy, 260–63
Grammar: of language, 58, 72–73; of culture, 73–110, 132, 135–36; of IQ tests, 220–37

Hakim, Albert, 171
Hayes, Rutherford B., 156
Health: biological factors in, 18–23, 33–41; as used for cultural purposes, 76, 79, 92–95, 118–19, 128; American, 137–42; affected by progress, 113, 176–78, 181
Health and the Rise of Civilization, 176

Health care, 38–41, 91–95, 105; in other cultures, 76, 91–95, 118–19; American, 93–95, 107, 118–19, 139–42, 181, 214–15, 258, 272, 294–95
Health insurance, 142, 147–48
Heritability: measurement, 20–23; of disease, 22–23; of intelligence, 208–14
Herrnstein, Richard, 3–4, 204–11, 217, 234, 269, 293
Hispanic, 186, 190, 242–43, 299
Human family tree, 42–45
Human genome project, 14
Humoral system (hot/cold), 228–29
Husband role, 83–85, 122–23, 155
Hygiene, 137–38

Ideals: American, 2, 142–75, 85–88, 192, 203, 283, 304–12; as defined by culture, 73, 87–88
Immigrants, 65–65, 69, 70–71, 86, 119, 147, 189–90, 210, 216, 236, 242–43, 276, 283, 284, 299
Incarceration, 4, 145, 174, 312
Independence: American, 183–88; of others, 186, 296
Inequality, 1–2, 11–12, 163–68, 189–92, 260–64, 312
Infanticide, 112, 119–20, 124, 128
Infant mortality, 106, 142, 144, 178
Inheritance: genetic, 15–43, 56–57, 207–12, 247; cultural, 57, 74–110, 169, 185, 207–12, 237–44, 255–56, 281, 291; of property, 163–66
Integration, 85–86, 133
Intelligence, 204–51; genes and, 17, 20–22, 56–59, 207–12, 240; environmental effects on, 56–59, 207–12, 238–44; unitary or multiple, 212–15; on the job, 246–51; twin studies, 210–12
Intelligence tests: 3, 204–46, 301; bias in test item content, 217–20; bias in test "grammar," 220–37; bias in "reaction time" tests, 234–35; translation and cross-cultural comparisons, 233–34; factors in individual performance, 237–44; factors in minority performance, 240–44
Interpersonal skills: affect job performance, 250
Intolerance: and media, 2–3, 152; and relativism, 111–13; history of, 182–91; and GI Bill, 264; serves the upper class, 279, 302; causes, 295–303

Iran, 79, 101, 146, 158, 182, 298
Iran-Contra affair, 171
Islam, 64, 79, 85, 91, 120–21, 128, 182–83

Jensen, Arthur, 234
Jobs: and affirmative action, 252–81; and
   IQ, 207, 247; performance, 247–51
Justice: and absolute morality, 126–27;
   versus profit, 169–72; colonial, 186;
   American value, 192–203, 304–12; and
   affirmative action, 252–81

Kamin, Leon, 234
Kennedy, John F., 261, 275
Kenya, 63, 97, 248–49
Kerbo, H. R., 167, 191
Kinship: biological, 42; in society, 76–77, 83–
   84, 89, 115

Laissez-faire, 146, 156, 254, 269
Language: structure dissected, vocabulary,
   67–70; grammar, 72–73
Latent functions: defined, 105–10
Law: in small societies, 76–79, 194–95;
   defining approved means, 88–89; and
   freedom, 146–47, 152–59; and wealth, 163–
   72; and justice, 192–203; and affirmative
   action, 252–81
Lee, Richard, 88
Libertarians, 149–52, 156–57, 193
Life expectancy: historic, 176–78, 181;
   American, 106, 141, 142, 181
Limited good, 99, 280–81, 302
Lipstadt, Deborah, 153
Logic: based on cultural categories, 95–97;
   on IQ tests, 226–29

Manifest destiny, 103, 182–83, 298, 301
Market: as mode of exchange, 76; "free,"
   125, 146–47
Marriage: purposes, 85, 120–23, 129, 132
Maya, 126, 179
MacNeil-Lehrer NewsHour, 142
Means: culturally permitted, 88–89
Media, 2, 142, 145, 148, 299
Melanin, 33–35, 45–46, 48
"Melting pot," 64–65, 86, 110, 147, 186, 241–
   44, 283
Memmi, Albert, 186, 277, 300
Merit: as falsely perceived, 110, 190, 204–5;
   as narrowly measured, 245, 252–54, 294;

and affirmative action, 259–61, 267–68,
   271–74; rewards for, 167
Metaphor: in expression, 81; culturally
   defined, 81; in other cultures, 92;
   confounds understanding, 219–20, 247
Mexico, 158, 182, 188, 242
Minuit, Peter, 78, 184
Mismeasure of Man, 213, 216
Mitford, Jessica, 140
Money: as medium of exchange and storage,
   76–77, 125, 162–64, 179–80
Monopoly: and evolution-creation debate,
   153; in international economics, 180; of
   white male employees, 253–55, 264–68; of
   intellectual marketplace, 286–88
Morality: as culturally defined, 73, 88–89, 97;
   and cultural relativism, 111, 115, 119–20,
   123, 126–33; absolute, 126–28, 129; of
   U.S., 135, 162, 199, 284–85
Moyers, Bill, 158
Multiculturalism, 60, 67, 143, 281–90, 306
Murray, Charles, 3–4, 204–10, 217, 233, 269

Nation, 64–66, 103, 115, 190, 192, 197
Nation-state, 64
Native Americans: biology, 22–23; blood
   types, 30–31; colors, 33; history, 64, 78,
   104, 186–90, 241, 299; land ownership, 78
New Guinea Tapeworms and Jewish
   Grandmothers, 118–19
Newshour with Jim Lehrer, 145, 148
Newton, Isaac, 183, 229
New York Times, 115, 205, 239–40
Nuance: effects on cross-cultural
   understanding, 68, 80, 219–20, 230, 233,
   241, 288
Nutrition: and obesity, 17–18; and the
   brain, 58; and disease, 17–18, 93; latent
   functions of, 117, 136; culture limits
   choices, 136, 139; American assumptions
   about, 141; in history, 176–78; third
   world, 176, 180; of the poor, 176, 311

Obesity, 17–18, 141
Ogbu, John, 243–44
Oppression: effects on culture, 62; of
   American minorities, 132–33; by
   corporations, 2, 4, 147; colonial, 186–90;
   and IQ tests, 216–17, 239–44; and the
   workplace, 256–57
Oral literature, 83

Order: social, in all cultures, 78–80; competes with justice, 195–97
Orphanage, 178

Paradigms: cultural, 86, 90–97, 111
Patriotism: as cultural necessity, 65, 103–5, 135; reinforced, 97, 202, 205–6, 286–89; and ethnocentrism, 104; affects choices of behavior, 106; as blinders, 109–10, 169–72, 182–83, 188–89
Peace, 64, 127, 130, 148, 188, 260, 281, 292
People's History of the United States, 190
Perception: misdirected, 4–5, 8, 62, 79–80, 89–90, 99, 110, 115, 134–35, 169–72, 182–83, 188, 197, 205–6, 249–50; directed by culture, 8, 73, 102; American, 110, 115, 121–22, 134, 142, 169–72, 182–93, 188, 197, 204–8, 212–37, 249–51, 301–4; enriched by exposure, 133, 136–37, 281–89; and test performance, 212–37; and affirmative action, 252–81
Political correctness, 291
Politics: of the American tragedy, 1–8, 11–12, 25, 144–45, 166–68, 258–59, 275–77, 288–89, 293–312; world, 61–63, 99, 113–14; and health, 79, 93, 140
Polygamy, 109–10, 128–30
Poverty: in U.S., 1–3, 108–9, 120, 150, 190, 262–65, 275–77, 293–94; third world, 120, 124–25; resulting from "progress," 176–80; and IQ, 204–7, 239–44, 247; and affirmative action, 275–77; deprivation by, 275–77, 308
Power: as a social principle competing with justice, 195–97
Prestige: as economic commodity, 76, 122, 162
Privilege: American, 1–3, 153–54, 165–67, 171–72, 178–79, 184–85, 192, 275; and perception of history, 175; colonial, 184–87, 301; and affirmative action, 252, 258–64, 270, 275, 278–81
Profit: motive, 76, 88–89, 106, 137, 168–74, 185, 187, 301–2, 311–12; in "development," 119, 126, 136, 139–40; in human terms, 115, 260; multinationals, 147; American, 156, 163–64, 258–60, 280, 285, 293–95
Progress: lack of, in biological evolution, 23–29; questioned, in human history, 28, 38, 110, 114, 119, 150, 168, 172–81, 195;

American vision of, 91, 119, 172–81, 188, 284; real, 141
Property: cultural definitions of, American, 76, 137, 156, 159–68, 179, 184–85, 193, 199, 202, 293–94, 298, 304, 309; in other cultures, 76–78, 123, 137, 179–80
Public health, 38–41, 140–42
Public television, 142, 148, 285

"Race:" as cultural perception, 11–12, 38, 50; as scapegoat, 11–12, 104; not a biological reality, 11–59; and behavior, 51–56; and "intelligence," 56–59, 204–7; stereotyping, 84; and law enforcement, 197–98; and job performance, 247–51, 264–65, 275–76
Racism: causes, 1–8, 60, 104, 186–87, 200, 279, 288–89, 297–302, 308; effects of, 147, 186–87, 242–52, 265, 269; history, 184–85; as justification for mistreatment, 204–7, 239–45, 301
Ranking: in evolution, 23–29; in language, 67; as a world view, 98; American preoccupation, 98, 214–15; in school, 107–8, 212, 244–45, 271
Reaction time tests, 234–35
Reagan, Ronald, 167, 171
Reconstruction, 156
Reconstruction: America's Unfinished Revolution, 156
Religion, 2, 57, 71, 126–33 passim
Resistance: to disease, 14–15, 25–27, 39, 58–59, 92–95; to political pressure, 62, 131, 238–43, 255–56, 299; culture of, 243
Revitalization, 299
Riddles: as related to test questions, 221–24
Right to eat, 127, 162, 202
Role: defined, 83–87, 92, 265–68, 288, 294, 306–8; conflict, 84–87, 92, 118, 122–23, 239–43; models, 238–39, 272–73, 292

Sacks, Karen, 264–65
Scapegoats, 11, 95, 203, 204–5, 279–81, 299
Secret Government, The, 158
Seeds in greenhouse: as parable of heritability, 20–22
Segregation, 2, 55–56, 265
Selfish Gene, The, 52
Selfishness: American, 1–4; as outcome of evolution, 53–54, 56, 66, 88, 168
Sex: biologically defined, 23–24, 30–31, 42, 73, 101, 120–23; as redefined by culture,

Sex (continued)
    55, 73, 85, 100–102, 107, 121–23, 140, 149,
    157, 228, 239
Shakespeare, William, 66, 282, 288
Shakespeare in the Bush, 288
Sharpe, Lauriston, 116
Sickle-cell anemia, 14–15, 18, 28, 32, 39, 41,
    45, 47
Skin color: biology of, 11–12, 33–35, 48–50,
    209; social interpretation of, 12, 187, 306–
    8
Slavery, 112, 155, 190, 202, 243, 255–56, 276–
    77, 284–85, 300
Social contract, 150–52, 159, 165–66, 193–94
Social control, 78–80, 192–93; supernatural,
    79, 196
Social Security, 108–9, 167–68
Social Stratification and Inequality, 190–91
Society: 62–62, 128; American, 1–8, 134–
    205, 239–44, 293–312 passim; defined, 62–
    63; description of, 63–117; as contributor
    to individual success, 160–65; and private
    property, 160–65; colonial, 178–81, 183–
    90; and IQ, 204–46; affirmative action,
    252–81; and curriculum inclusion, 282–92
Sociobiology, 51–59
State, as mode of organization, 63–64, 197–
    98
Status: defined, 83–87; low, 194, 197–98;
    high, 171–72, 197–98; markers of, 67–68,
    100, 116, 120–21, 124, 143; access to, 110,
    124–25, 204–6; limits to freedom defined
    by, 148–49, 171–72
Steel Axes for Stone Age Australians, 116
Stereotypes: racial, 11–13, 19, 31, 41–42, 48–
    51, 204–6, 269; and visual perception, 48–
    51; of behavior, 54; of sex roles, 55, 265–
    66; sources of, 84, 195, 243; versus
    individual friendships, 306–7
Sugar, politics of, 126, 144, 258
Supernatural: as part of culture, 83, 88; as
    social control, 79; in healing, 92–93
Supreme Court, 152, 200–203, 289
Symbols: value of, 94, 119, 128; patriotic,
    104–5, 148, 171, 189; as latent functions,
    117; of circumcision, 120–23; respect for
    other people's, 128–32; misuses of, 129–
    31, 135, 148; of wealth, 162–63; on IQ
    tests, 224–26; of marital status, 231

Tariffs: as analogue for affirmative action,
    257–59

Taxes: expenditures from, 2, 146, 148, 174,
    253–54, 260, 261, 263; base, 7, 109, 144,
    145, 164–68, 190, 262, 295, 305, 312; local,
    166; colonial, 179; tariffs, 257–59
Technology, 61, 75–76, 106, 117, 140–41,
    172–74; American focus on, 140–41, 284
Terra nullius, 78
Texaco, 257
Textbooks: and free speech, 144, 154; and
    chauvinism, 182–83, 188; and curriculum
    inclusion, 284–85; role in finding
    solutions, 308
Third world, 100, 114–26, 173, 176, 179–81,
    296–97, 309
Thought: defined by culture, 63, 73–74, 90–
    99, 111–12, 249–50; limits of American,
    103, 134–203, 204–51, 301–2; broadened,
    133, 271–74, 282, 286–88; and IQ, 204–37
Tobacco: halting production, 123;
    subsidized, 126, 258; affirmative action
    for, 258; executives, 261
Tolerated theft, 77
Trade: and disease, 28, 176–77; and third
    world/ indigenous populations, 55, 75,
    116, 144, 179–81; and government, 105–6,
    144, 157–58, 163–64, 257–59, 262–63
Tragedy: defined, 4–5; American, 1–8
Transportation, 63, 75, 174, 176–77
Trouble with Friendship, The, 147
Truth, Sojourner, 284–85
Twins, 22, 210–12; studies of, 210–12

Values: American, 1–5, 87–88, 106–7, 134–
    203, 260, 301–2, 303–12; functions in
    culture, 73, 87–88, 104, 106, 109–10;
    training in, 97–98, 103–4; relativism and,
    126–33
Variation: human biological, 11–59; as
    scapegoat, 11; and race, 11–12, 41–51;
    complexity of, 11–16; gene-environment
    interactions in, 11–23; hidden, 13–15;
    and health, 18–19, 22–23, 31–41; in
    fertility, 19–20, 124–25; heritability
    of, 19–23; evolutionary processes and,
    23–31; proof of adaptive value, 31–37;
    specific variations, 31–48; gradual nature
    of, 46–47; mixed nature of, 47–50;
    and behavior, 51–56; and intelligence,
    56–59
Vietnam War, 65, 158, 189
Vocabulary: of language, 67–70, 241, 288; of
    culture, 73

Voters, 145, 154–55, 165–66, 279–81, 308, 311–12

Walt Disney Company, 279–80
War, in American history, 157–58, 184, 188
Washington, George, 102–4, 185, 275, 289, 291
Ways of learning, 230
Ways with Words, 80–81
Wealth: power of, 1–2, 125–26, 145, 146, 147, 155, 190, 308; in small societies, 76–78, 85, 87–88, 124–26; right to, 87–88, 125–26, 156, 159, 160–64, 305; and limited good, 99; and "development," 119, 124–26, 180–81; obligations of, 142, 144, 159–60, 164–67, 168, 178, 180, 293–296, 300, 305, 309, 311–12; and freedom, 150, 155, 168–72, 190–92, 295–96; maintained by government, 155, 156–57, 163–64, 190, 195, 202; and affirmative action, 257–64, 278–81
Welfare: corporate, 163–64, 300; for the poor, 167, 170–71, 179, 200, 296, 311
Wife: role defined, 85, 128–29, 238

Women: womb environment, 17–18, 36, 39–40, 58, 211; fertility, 19, 124, 139–40; rickets in, 33–34; breast cancer, 39; nursing, 39, 139–40; "nature of," 54–55, 84–85, 100; abortion, 119–20, 124, 201; status, 119–24, 252–81, 194, 202; circumcision of, 119–23; breast fetish, 140; birthing, 140; in history, 185–86, 190, 202; affirmative action and, 194, 252–81; and math, 239; curriculum inclusion and, 281–92
Work: women's, and nursing, 140; efficiency, 172–74; IQ and individual job performance, 247–52; and affirmative action, 252–81; value of variety and, 272–73, 306
Working class: losing out, 4, 109, 164, 166, 170, 174, 293–94; life expectancy (historical), 178; taxes on, 165, 166, 167–68, 190–91
World Bank, 119
"World system," 183–91
World view, 97–99

Zapatistas, 158
Zinn, Howard, 190, 199